British General Elections Since 1964

Diversity, Dealignment, and Disillusion

Second Edition

DAVID DENVER AND MARK GARNETT

OXFORD

UNIVERSITY PRESS

OXFORD
UNIVERSITY PRESS

Great Clarendon Street, Oxford, OX2 6DP,
United Kingdom

Oxford University Press is a department of the University of Oxford.
It furthers the University's objective of excellence in research, scholarship,
and education by publishing worldwide. Oxford is a registered trade mark of
Oxford University Press in the UK and in certain other countries

First Edition published in 2014
Second Edition published in 2021

Impression: 1

Published in the United States of America by Oxford University Press
198 Madison Avenue, New York, NY 10016, United States of America

British Library Cataloguing in Publication Data
Data available

Library of Congress Control Number: 2020952667

ISBN 978-0-19-884495-2 (hbk.)
ISBN 978-0-19-884496-9 (pbk.)

DOI: 10.1093/oso/9780198844952.001.0001

Printed and bound by
CPI Group (UK) Ltd, Croydon, CR0 4YY

Preface

Anyone wishing to pursue an interest in post-war British general elections would almost inevitably turn first to the 'Nuffield studies'. These volumes began with the 1945 election and from the outset the aim was 'to give a reasonably clear and balanced picture of the events, issues, and personalities of the election' (McCallum and Redman, 1947: vii). Although electoral analysis has made huge advances since 1945, that has remained the basic function (and strength) of the series. The eponymous college of Oxford University supported the original project and has continued to be associated with the series, not least in the person of Sir David Butler, the *doyen* of electoral analysis in Britain, who provided 'valuable work on the statistics of the election' for the 1945 study (xiv), was the named author of an Appendix providing an analysis of the 1950 results (Nicholas, 1951) and, thereafter, authored or co-authored every volume until stepping down in 2010. For this book, we have made extensive use of the relevant volumes in the Nuffield series and are glad to acknowledge our debt to Sir David and the various other authors.

Although they retain their well-deserved prestige, the Nuffield accounts of individual elections no longer monopolize the attention of academics and interested others. Over the course of the post-war period several other election series have appeared, with contributions written from a variety of perspectives. *Britain At The Polls* first appeared in 1974 (Penniman, 1975) and was originally one of a series of studies of national elections across a selection of democracies by the American Enterprise Institute (AEI). Although the AEI ended its involvement after 1983—when there was a hiatus—publication resumed under the leadership of Anthony King for the 1992 election and has continued to date (see Penniman, 1981; Ranney, 1985; King, 1993, 1998, 2002; Bartle and King, 2006; Allen and Bartle, 2011, 2018). These edited volumes include chapters by leading experts in the field and aim, according to King, to complement the Nuffield studies by 'offering a series of interpretations of the election and its outcome' (King, 1993: vii).

Another set of books on British elections, the *Political Communications* series, focusing particularly on opinion polls, the mass media and the campaign and communication strategies of the parties, began with the 1979 contest and has continued since then (Worcester and Harrop, 1982; Crewe and Harrop, 1986, 1989; Crewe and Gosschalk, 1995; Crewe et al., 1998; Bartle et al., 2002; Wring et al., 2007, 2011, 2017, 2019). These collections are notable for the fact that they include contributions from polling and media professionals, and people involved at a high level in planning and implementing the campaigns of the major parties as well as academics.

Two other series were late into the field and eventually merged. A special issue of the journal *Parliamentary Affairs* covered the 1992 election (volume 45, number 4, October 1992) and the venture was repeated at the next three elections. In 1997, 2001, and 2005 the journal articles also appeared in separately published books with the title *Britain Votes* (Norris and Gavin, 1997; Norris, 2001; Norris and Wlezien, 2005). From 1997 Andrew Geddes and Jonathan Tonge began to edit a series of general election books, aimed mainly at undergraduates and A-level students. In 2010, however, this venture entered a coalition with *Britain Votes* and books with that title have appeared after each election since then (Geddes and Tonge, 2010, 2015; Tonge et al., 2018, 2020).

One final short series is rather different from the others. Since 1997, Robert Worcester, founder and former chairman of the polling company originally known as MORI and now Ipsos MORI, and Roger Mortimore, director of political analysis for the company, have been lead authors of five election volumes (Worcester and Mortimore, 1999, 2001; Worcester et al., 2005, 2011, 2016). As might be expected, these are packed with opinion poll data, as well as being highly readable accounts of the public's reactions to parties, leaders, policies and events.

Added to the continuing Nuffield series, these publications provide ample coverage for anyone who wants to immerse himself or herself in individual British general elections. Another major resource is the British Election Study (BES)—which David Butler was also influential in establishing in the 1960s. We discuss the BES and the major reports on British electoral behaviour arising from it in Chapter 1 and also at various points throughout this work. It is not just the published material that is vital for understanding elections in Britain since the 1960s, however; all of the survey data collected by the BES over fifty years are freely available for analysis by researchers and we have made frequent use of this facility.

Invaluable as they are, all of the publications mentioned are inevitably limited by their focus on a single election; invariably they discuss key developments over the period between elections, but it is not their primary concern to provide a long-term perspective on changes in British parties or the electorate which makes the fateful choice on polling day. This book is an attempt to supplement the existing literature on specific elections, by reviewing a series of contests over a more protracted period. As well as being interesting in historical terms, this approach, in our view, is helpful in explaining the contemporary dilemmas facing strategists within the main political parties. While we hope that the book will be useful to undergraduate students of British politics, our intention has been to write an account of elections since 1964 which will enlighten anyone seeking to understand the contemporary party battle as well as how elections have changed over the past sixty years or so—whether they are enrolled on courses on British politics at school, college or university, or are pursuing a private passion for this fascinating subject.

We should like to thank the anonymous referees of our original book proposal and Dominic Byatt of Oxford University Press for his encouragement, patience, and assistance with this project, especially during the preparation of this second edition when life (never mind work) was difficult for everyone due to the coronavirus pandemic. Thanks also to our respective families for listening (even if not entirely willingly or always attentively) to endless talk about British elections.

David Denver
Mark Garnett

Lancaster, October 2020

Contents

List of Tables and Figures

Tables

Figures

1

Introduction

Although it is now a long time ago, 1945 remains a key historical reference point for many students of modern British politics. This is not just because the end of the Second World War provides a convenient dividing line, reflected in the ubiquitous term 'post-war'. The policies pursued by the Labour government that took office in 1945 were far-reaching and long-lasting in their effects, so that in many policy areas governments of the twenty-first century are still wrestling with the legacy of Prime Minister Clement Attlee and his colleagues.

For students of UK elections in particular, 1945 is again an obviously interesting and important date. The result of the general election of that year was a genuine sensation—a landslide victory for Labour, heralding the first-ever majority Labour government and ousting a hugely popular wartime leader, Winston Churchill—which left the Conservative MP and diarist 'Chips' Channon 'stunned and shocked by the country's treachery' (Channon, 1993: 409). The election also demonstrated the potential value of the fledgling business of opinion polling, although this was little noticed at the time. On the day before electors were due to cast their votes, the *News Chronicle* reported on its front page the results of a Gallup poll of 'the civilian electorate'. Had observers paid more attention to this, the outcome of the election would have been less of a surprise, since the poll showed Labour having a clear lead over the Conservatives. Gallup's director in Britain, Henry Durant, commented later: 'Nobody believed us, including all the *News Chronicle* people' (Worcester, 1991: 5–8).

Despite its importance, it remains the case that students of *contemporary* British elections have little to learn from 1945, even as a point of comparison. It was, after all, a very unusual election: the intervention of war had prevented a national contest for ten years and the country was, indeed, still at war with Japan, with millions of voters serving overseas. Although party conflict had not disappeared completely, 'normal' hostilities had been suspended during most of the war in Europe and, in a departure which was unprecedented and never repeated, serving members of the armed forces had been provided with lectures on current political issues. In short, this election was unusual even when compared with the contests of 1950 and 1951. Yet it can be argued that those later contests are barely more relevant than 1945 to an understanding of contemporary British elections. The country was still in what might be called the 'immediate post-war' period. Austerity had not ended and food rationing still existed; house-building

British General Elections Since 1964: Diversity, Dealignment, and Disillusion. Second Edition. David Denver and Mark Garnett, Oxford University Press. © David Denver and Mark Garnett 2021. DOI: 10.1093/oso/9780198844952.003.0001

programmes had only just started; television broadcasting was in its infancy and very few people owned what was then known as a 'receiver'. Politically, the great majority of voters belonged to one or other of two 'tribes', which almost always backed either Labour or the Conservatives regardless of their party's performance, while political campaigning was closer to the practice of the 1930s than the pattern that had developed by the 1960s. During the 1950 campaign, for example, the Prime Minister undertook a tour of Britain in his pre-war family saloon car. He was driven by his wife and accompanied by a single detective. If the party was ahead of schedule they would stop by the roadside, where Mrs Attlee would catch up with her knitting while her husband relaxed with a crossword and his pipe (Nicholas, 1951: 93–4). Such travel arrangements for party leaders would have been inconceivable by the 1960s—even if the politicians concerned had been as self-effacing as Mr Attlee.

Other reviews of modern British elections have taken 1945 as their starting point (Butler, 1989; Norris, 1997). Here, however, we begin our account with a 'transitional' election—that of 1964—in which elements of the old 'aligned' electorate of the 1950s were still clearly discernible but unmistakable symptoms of a new era were also evident.

In 1963, Gabriel Almond and Sydney Verba published their classic comparative study of political attitudes underpinning democracy, *The Civic Culture*. These (American) political scientists held British political culture in high regard as representing the closest match to the ideal attitudinal underpinnings for a thriving democracy. While the involvement and participation of citizens in politics were approved and encouraged, the democratic tide was held in check by widespread deference towards political leaders. Unfortunately for Almond and Verba, by the time their painstaking study was published British deference had taken some significant knocks. 'The establishment' in general had become a target for satirical comment rather than quiet acceptance; and political developments, notably the Profumo affair of 1963, had provided much ammunition for the critics. In 1965, Anthony Sampson published the second edition of his *Anatomy of Britain*. Although this was only three years after the first edition, he commented that in the interim 'the changes seem spectacular . . . Reverence and stuffiness are out of fashion, and nearly everyone, from the head of the BBC to the Lord Chancellor, likes to think of himself as being "anti-Establishment"' (Sampson, 1965: 668). A decline in deference towards political institutions and politicians in particular was also identified by the British academic Bernard Crick, just a year after the publication of *The Civic Culture*, when he reflected on 'the undoubted public scepticism about Parliament and the growing antipathy towards the whole profession of politics' (Crick, 1964: 13).

Television was the perfect medium to convey the new spirit of rebellion. Having been a rarity in 1950, almost three-quarters of British households owned a television by the end of the decade. It was not until 1962, however, that the BBC—previously a prime example of establishment attitudes—offered the public a weekly programme which openly poked fun at politicians, in *That Was The Week That Was*.

Despite the immediate success of TV satire, not everyone in Britain watched it; and older people, in particular, still tended to regard established institutions and leading public figures with respect. However, the contrasting attitudes towards politics which were in evidence by the time of the 1964 general election serve to make that contest more convincing as the 'transitional' starting point for this work. Coincidentally, the early 1960s also saw the first major national survey study of voting in a British general election. Studies of voters based on surveys had begun in Britain during the 1950s, but these were restricted to individual towns or constituencies (see, for example, Benney et al., 1956; Milne and MacKenzie, 1958). In 1963, however, a national survey of the British electorate, unprecedented in the scope of its questions as well as the number of respondents, was undertaken under the direction of David Butler of Nuffield College, Oxford, and Donald Stokes, an American expert on voting behaviour. This was followed by a similar exercise at the time of the 1964 election—the first of what came to be known as the British Election Study (BES) series, which surveyed the electorate at every subsequent general election.

The 1964 election resulted in a change in the governing party for only the second time since 1945. Entering the campaign, the Labour Party had been out of office for thirteen years, having lost the three preceding elections. It had only recently (February 1963) chosen a new leader, Harold Wilson, who quickly established a reputation as a 'modernizer'—famously proclaiming at the 1963 Labour party conference that the future of the country would be 'forged in the white heat of this (scientific) revolution'. The Conservative government also had a new leader. Following the resignation on health grounds of the once popular Harold Macmillan (known as 'Supermac' in his heyday) in October 1963, Sir Alec Douglas-Home 'emerged' as Prime Minister. A Scottish laird and member of the House of Lords (who was quickly found a seat in the Commons) he lacked the charisma of his predecessor and did not greatly impress the voters, having previously admitted in a newspaper interview that he did not expect to become Prime Minister as he had to use matchsticks to do calculations. This made for a sharp contrast with Wilson who had previously been a statistician.

Figure 1.1 summarizes trends in party support since that election, showing the shares of votes gained by the Conservatives, Labour, Liberals/Liberal Democrats and 'others' across the UK in general elections from 1964 to 2019. In 1964 the major parties dominated. Labour took 44.1 per cent of votes and the Conservatives 43.4 per cent while the Liberals (as they then were) trailed with 11.2 per cent, leaving just 1.3 per cent for all other parties and candidates combined. In the next

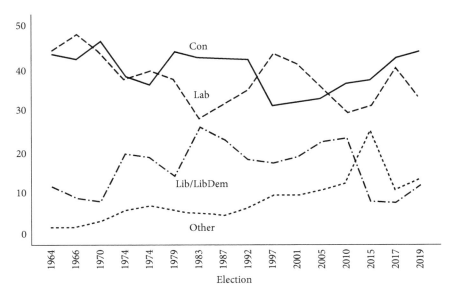

Figure 1.1 Party shares of votes (UK), 1964–2019

Note: Here and in Figure 1.2 the votes and seats won by the Ulster Unionists are treated as
Conservative up to 1970 and as 'other' from February 1974.

two elections (1966, 1970) the votes for the two leading contenders seesawed a
little but there was no threat to their dominance.

In February 1974, however, the long-heralded Liberal 'revival' finally took off
(after a number of false starts) and it went a stage further in 1983, when the party
fought in alliance with the newly founded Social Democratic Party (SDP), which
was a breakaway from Labour. As a consequence, support for the Conservatives
and Labour declined. Although the former easily outpolled the latter from 1979
to 1992, they won smaller vote shares in those elections than in 1970. From 1997
to 2005, Labour was in the driving seat but commanded significantly less support
than it had attracted back in 1966 as the Liberal Democrats and 'others' increased
in popularity. By 2010, the two major parties had lost much of their old appeal.
The Conservatives led with 36.1 per cent while Labour mustered only 29.0 per
cent. The Liberal Democrats were not that far behind on 23.0 per cent while 'the
rest' reached 11.9 per cent—their largest share to that point.

Figure 1.1 shows clearly how support for 'others' rose steadily over the period
to 2010 (although there was something of a hiatus in the 1980s). In part, of course,
this is explained simply by the greater availability of 'other' candidates to vote for;
but it also reflects rising support for the Scottish National Party (SNP) in Scotland
and Plaid Cymru in Wales as well as increasing disaffection from mainstream
parties elsewhere. In 2015, however, the share of votes won by the 'others' shot up.
Although the Conservatives led with 36.8 per cent of votes in that election,
Labour managed less than a third (30.4 per cent) and, following their less than

enjoyable experience in government, the Liberal Democrats tumbled to just 7.9 per cent. The main stories of the election, however, were the advances of the SNP to take 50 per cent of the votes in Scotland (and become the second-largest party in the House of Commons) and of the UK Independence Party (UKIP), which jumped to third place with 12.6 per cent of the UK vote (although this brought them just one seat). The Green party also improved its position and, overall, 'others' rose to 24.9 per cent of votes. In electoral terms, the two-party system characteristic of the 1960s seemed a distant memory.

In the 'snap' election unexpectedly called by Prime Minister Theresa May in 2017, however, the trends established over many years went abruptly into reverse and there appeared to be something of a return to what could be seen as 'normality'. Support for UKIP plummeted to just 1.8 per cent and the two major parties together mustered 82.3 per cent of votes—the largest proportion since 1970. In one respect, however, the result was not 'normal' in that, despite having a clear lead in votes over their main rivals, the Conservatives lost their majority in the House of Commons and were forced to rely on the support of the Democratic Unionist Party (DUP) from Northern Ireland to remain in government. Just two years later, the 2019 election saw Labour fall back significantly while the emergence of another new party (the Brexit party) and improved performances by the Greens and the SNP put the 'others' once again on an upward track.

Changes in the party system over the years from 1964 were particularly significant in the peripheral nations of the UK. In Scotland in 1964, the SNP contested just fifteen of the seventy-one seats and was rewarded with only 2.4 per cent of the votes. In 2015, as noted above, the party routed its opponents, winning 50 per cent of the votes and fifty-six of the fifty-nine seats at stake. This was no temporary fluke. In 2019, forty-eight seats were taken on 45.0 per cent of the Scottish vote. The SNP had also done well in elections to the devolved Scottish Parliament and formed the Scottish government in Edinburgh continuously from 2007 to date (albeit as a minority between 2007 and 2011 and after 2016). In Wales, the story for the nationalist Plaid Cymru is less spectacular but still one of significant change The party contested twenty-three constituencies, winning only 4.8 per cent of votes (and no seats), in 1964; in 2019, four seats were won with 9.9 per cent of the votes. In Northern Ireland, on the other hand, change has been dramatic. In 1964, the Ulster Unionist Party (UUP)—then aligned with the Conservatives— dominated, taking all twelve seats on 63.0 per cent of the vote. By 2019, the UUP had only 11.7 per cent of votes and no seats. The party system had fragmented with the DUP, which had broken away from the UUP in 1971, now taking most seats (eight) followed by Sinn Fein (seven), the Social Democratic and Labour Party (two) and the non-sectarian Alliance (one).

In translating votes into seats in the House of Commons, the operation of the first-past-the-post electoral system ensured that the fragmentation in party support among the electorate after 1964 was dampened somewhat (Figure 1.2). The Conservatives and Labour together commanded more than 90 per cent of seats

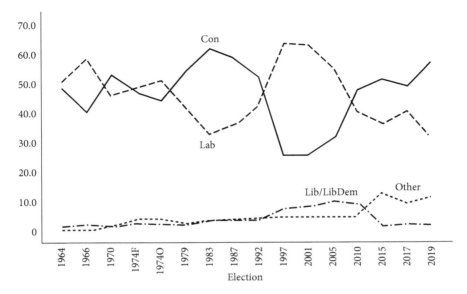

Figure 1.2 Party shares of seats in the House of Commons, 1964–2019

until the 1997 election. Even so, the slightly increased representation of Liberals and nationalists in the late 1970s required the Labour government to reach an agreement with the former ('the Lib–Lab pact') in order to ensure a working majority in the House. Later, it became more and more difficult for one of the major parties to achieve an overall majority. Even in 1997, although most commentators expected Labour to win decisively, Tony Blair engaged in negotiations with the Liberal Democrats to ensure that they would support him if his party fell short of an overall majority. After the 2010 election, no party had a majority of seats and the Conservatives were forced to form a coalition government with the Liberal Democrats. To most observers, the surprise was not the absence of a majority but the willingness of the Liberal Democrats to go into coalition with the Conservatives. In 2015, against expectations, David Cameron led his party to an overall majority of ten seats but in 2017, as noted above, when almost everyone expected this to be increased, the Conservatives were once again reduced to a minority and forced into an agreement with the DUP (which involved promising increased government spending in Northern Ireland). Two years later, however, under Boris Johnson, the party emerged with a handsome overall majority of 80—enough, in all probability, to ensure that the next election would be some years away.

Parties are not passive recipients of votes. They campaign for them, both nationally and locally in the constituencies, and this is another aspect of elections which has changed markedly over the years. Superficially, the national campaigns of the parties in 1964 and the second decade of the twenty-first century look similar. In both cases, the major parties commissioned surveys and used PR professionals to plan their campaigns, design posters, and suggest slogans. In both, the main focus was on the party leaders, who undertook nationwide tours; and the parties attempted to communicate their messages via press advertising, posters on hoardings, and election broadcasts on television and radio. Nonetheless, things had changed considerably in the intervening years. Whereas the party leaders in 1964 used trains and (occasionally) scheduled flights to travel across the country, almost always delivering set-piece speeches to large audiences when they reached their destinations, today private jets and carefully controlled 'walkabouts' or visits to locations such as hospitals, schools, or factories are the order of the day. Any large meetings addressed are ticket-only affairs confined to cheering supporters. Heckling by members of the audience has long since disappeared. Party election broadcasts on television in 1964 went out simultaneously on both the channels then available and mostly involved party personalities speaking directly to the camera. There was no escape for viewers. By contrast, in the modern multi-channel environment, the remote control furnished numerous options for those seeking relief from politics while the broadcasts themselves were more like commercial adverts.

Perhaps most significantly of all in terms of media coverage, however, 2010 saw the first-ever televised debates between the party leaders. In 1964, the Labour leader, Harold Wilson, challenged the incumbent Prime Minister, Sir Alec Douglas-Home, to a televised debate (Butler and King, 1965: 112), but, as on many subsequent occasions, this came to nothing. There was a significant innovation in 1964, however, which again marks it out as a transitional election. On three consecutive evenings at the start of the campaign, the major party leaders appeared separately on a programme called *Election Forum*, which was broadcast simultaneously on BBC television and radio, to answer questions sent in by voters. To many this seemed a first step towards direct televised exchanges between leaders, but it was not until 2010 that the parties were finally persuaded to take that particular plunge. In that election, three leaders' campaign debates were aired on three consecutive Thursdays. They were accompanied by enormous media ballyhoo and came to define the campaign. As the Nuffield study of the 2010 election comments: 'They effectively became the national campaign, sucking the life out of many of the more traditional aspects of campaigning' (Kavanagh and Cowley, 2010: 158).[1] Moreover, the electorate appeared to be paying attention as the first debate had a dramatic (positive) effect on the popularity of Nick Clegg, the Liberal Democrat leader, and of his party. In 2015, however, the parties and the broadcasters found it difficult to agree on the timing and format of debates. In the end, there was only one in which the Liberal Democrat and Conservative leaders participated and that was something of a farce as it involved the leaders of no fewer than seven parties. Things went from bad to worse in this respect in 2017 when the Prime Minister declined to take part at all. Debates nonetheless went ahead with the representatives of seven parties again involved. The voters appeared to be becoming less enamoured with this form of campaigning, however, as in both 2015 and 2017 audiences were well down on the figures recorded in 2010 and the broadcasts appeared to have no discernible effect on trends in party support. The 2019 experience was somewhat different in that there were two 'head to head' debates labelled 'Prime Ministerial' between the Conservative and Labour leaders, which attracted larger audiences than those in the two previous elections, as well as others involving the leaders of the other parties.

Another significant and even more recent development is what party professionals now refer to 'e-campaigning'—texting, emailing, using websites, Facebook, Twitter, and so on—all of which were unheard of even in the 1980s, never mind the 1960s. Although previous expectations that digital campaigning would come to dominate elections had never quite come to fruition, by 2015, as the authors of the Nuffield study noted, there was 'a clear qualitative change in the use of digital campaign tools from any previous British election' with all parties using Facebook very heavily (Cowley and Kavanagh, 2016: 150). The Conservatives claimed to be reaching seventeen million people per week during the campaign by this method while Labour raised over £3 million in online donations. In 2017 e-campaigning was even more important. For the first time, the *Britain Votes* series devoted a chapter to the digital campaign (Dommett and Temple, 2018). Facebook was again the dominant focus of the parties' efforts but there were also 'satellite campaigns' by non-party (but often partisan) organizations and groups. Many attributed Labour's unexpectedly good performance to its superior digital campaign which appeared to be particularly successful in attracting younger voters. This success was not repeated in 2019 although, once again, all parties expended much time, expertise and money in e-campaigning.

The prominence of television and social media in recent election campaigns does not mean that the press was eclipsed. Voters who took a serious interest in the leaders' TV debates would nonetheless be keen to sample the views of pundits in print; and, as usual, almost all the national newspapers were ready to offer advice to their readers about which party to support. However, compared with 1964, the ranks of those readers had diminished considerably (Table 1.1). The bestselling daily in that year, the *Daily Mirror*, sold just over five million copies and had an estimated readership of more than fourteen million. In 2017, the paper with the largest circulation was the *Metro* (1.4 million) which is distributed free on trains and buses, at railway stations and airports, and so on. *The Mirror* itself was down to about half a million in sales and while *The Sun* had the largest number of paying customers (1.2 million) this was well down on its peak figure of almost four million achieved in 1987. The fall from grace of the *Daily Express*— ranked second behind *The Mirror* in 1964 with a circulation of 4.19 million and over eleven million readers—was even more spectacular; in 2019 its circulation

Table 1.1 Circulation of national daily newspapers, 1965 and 2019

	1965	2019
Mirror/Record	5,019	561
Express	3,087	298
Mail	2,484	1,133
Sun	1,274	1,217
Sketch	844	–
Star	–	289
Metro	–	1,421
I	–	220
Telegraph	1,337	309
Times	254	365
Guardian	270	129
Financial Times	152	163
Total	*14,721*	*6,105*

Notes: Figures shown are in thousands. The *Sketch* disappeared in 1971 while the *Star* first appeared in 1978, the bewilderingly named *I* in 2010 and the (free) *Metro* in 1999.

Sources: These are Audit Bureau of Circulation figures. Those for 2019 are from the Press Gazette (http://www.pressgazette.co.uk) while those for 1965 are from Seymour-Ure (1966: 150).

was down to less than 300,000 copies. The performance of the 'quality' press was more mixed. While the circulation of the *Telegraph* slumped by over a million and that of *The Guardian* fell by more than half, sales of *The Times* improved and the (highly specialized) *Financial Times* more than held its own.

A number of factors lie behind the steep overall decline in the circulations of newspapers in print. Changing technology (along with Mrs Thatcher's trade union reforms) had released most national newspapers from cramped conditions in the City of London (and from endemic restrictive work practices enforced by the print unions) from the 1980s. Far from ensuring a more profitable future for the press, however, the developments which had allowed it to flee Fleet Street also enabled potential purchasers to browse online without payment. As well as reading (some) newspapers online for free rather than buying printed copies, enthusiasts for politics could also follow freelance internet bloggers, who were at liberty to express their irreverent personal views without having to pay attention to any editorial line. By the 2010s, even factual reporters were struggling against the input of first-hand witnesses using social media such as Facebook and Twitter.

These changes were bound to have some effect on more traditional modes of political coverage. Back in 1962, Anthony Sampson had deplored the impact of television, with its 'hectic aggressiveness', on media commentary (Sampson, 1962: 129). In hindsight his strictures might seem misplaced, since most journalists of the time continued to show a degree of deference towards senior politicians, and the intrusion of a more combative style could be seen as a healthy development in a mature liberal democracy. However, Sampson had detected a trend which, over time, created a new and equally unhealthy imbalance between politicians and journalists. By the 1990s, most politicians felt obliged to treat journalists (not to mention newspaper proprietors) with the exaggerated respect which television interviewers had formerly shown towards senior ministers. The depths to which the media and politicians had dragged each other were partially exposed and explained by the so-called Leveson Inquiry (being chaired by Lord Leveson, a senior judge), which had been initiated by the government to report on the culture, practices, and ethics of the press in the wake of assorted phone hacking scandals and which reported in 2012. If the Internet had not existed, the Leveson Report might have had a salutary effect; as it was, the difficulty of extending a tougher regime of regulation to the 'virtual' world made it seem like an enquiry into the abuses of horse-drawn transport after the invention of the steam engine.

Despite these momentous changes in the national context, there has been some continuity in the methods of campaigning at local level. As in 1964, volunteers still deliver leaflets, knock on doors (or press intercom buttons), and speak to residents in order to identify supporters, then try to ensure that the latter turn out to vote on polling day; while candidates accost members of the electorate (and their non-voting offspring) in convenient public places such as shopping centres. Election addresses are produced, featuring photographs of the candidates (and, if applicable, their families) for postal distribution. Public election meetings addressed by candidates are much rarer now than in 1964, however. After the latter election, Gallup found that 8 per cent of respondents claimed to have attended an indoor public meeting (Butler and King, 1965: 222). Butler and King also contrasted the large number of meetings held in rural areas with towns, where 'candidates more usually contented themselves with one meeting a night, or less, during the last ten days' (221). A case study of one constituency (Finchley) reported that the Conservative candidate, Margaret Thatcher—described as 'an attractive mother of twins' (244)—held ten meetings with a total audience of 1,300, while her Liberal opponent (John Pardoe) addressed eight, which attracted less than 500 people. In contrast, in their accounts of constituency campaigning, the 2010, 2015, and 2017 Nuffield studies don't even mention local public meetings. More specialized research on local campaigning found that in 2005 across all three main parties the average number of public election meetings addressed by candidates was less than one.[2] Other changes in constituency campaigning include a shift in emphasis from canvassing voters on the doorstep to telephone contact from national and regional call centres and the use of specialized computer software for targeting voters and recording data. Overall, there is also much greater involvement on the part of party headquarters (especially in target seats). Finally, as at national level, there has been a growth in e-campaigning at constituency level. In 2017, overall, more than two-thirds of candidates had Twitter accounts (Ward and Wring, 2018: 212).

Whatever the merits or otherwise of modern campaigning, new techniques have not prevented a marked decline in electoral turnout over recent decades. The proportion of the eligible electorate that turned out to vote in 1964 was 77.1 per cent; in 2001, a post-war low of 59.4 per cent was recorded. Figure 1.3 charts UK turnout at all general elections from 1964. Between 1964 and 1997, there is no real trend but a series of ups and downs. Turnout fell in 1966 and again in 1970, when the campaign took place in hot and sunny weather and 18–20 year olds were eligible to vote for the first time. In February 1974, however, on a fresh electoral register, turnout zoomed up to 78.8 per cent, only to fall back in October of the same year. A rise in 1979 was followed by a slight drop in 1983; but turnout improved in both 1987 and 1992. The decline between 1992 and 1997 was steep, but turnout in the latter election, at 71.4 per cent, was still not markedly out of line with levels to that date. In 2001, however, as noted above, turnout plummeted. In the four subsequent general elections there was a steady, if unspectacular, improvement but in 2019 (when the election took place in the depths of winter) the figure fell back slightly (to 67.6 per cent). Clearly, then, participation levels in the twenty-first century have been significantly lower than the norm of the previous 30 years.

This development has provoked a good deal of comment, research, and even political action to remove the few remaining inconveniences facing would-be voters. Even before the sharp fall in turnout in 2001, Labour ministers introduced postal voting 'on demand' under the Representation of the People Act 2000. This was partly in response to declining turnout, but also (although this was, of course,

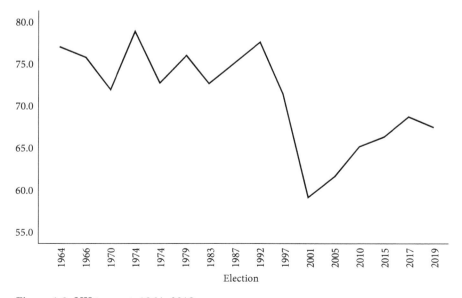

Figure 1.3 UK turnout, 1964–2019

unstated) partly because Labour expected to derive some electoral benefit from such a change. Previously, postal vote applicants had to provide an approved reason for the request—such as old age, illness, or absence because of work commitments—and the relevant application form had to be countersigned by a responsible person (such as a doctor). Now, electors could claim a postal vote simply by ticking a box on the annual electoral registration form, and would not be removed from the postal voters' list at future elections unless this was specifically requested. This particular piece of 'modernization' in election administration had unforeseen consequences, however. It led to some well-publicized instances of corruption, undermined public confidence in the electoral system and required further legislation to try to deal with the problems created. Ironically, it also appears to have backfired on Labour by, if anything, benefitting the Conservatives (Denver, 2011). Nonetheless, it makes for another contrast between 1964 and more recent elections—in the very manner of voting. In 1964, just over 700,000 postal votes were included in the count (2.6 per cent of the total); in 2019, the respective figures were 6.7 million and 20.9 per cent.

It is possible that the proportion of the electorate claiming postal votes will continue to increase, albeit more slowly than hitherto. However, the fact that so many can vote at their leisure rather than making a trip to a polling station on the appointed day between specified hours is already impacting on election campaigns. In many cases, party appeals—such as the final election broadcasts in the last week of the campaign—and candidate calls will be made *after* people have voted. What 'on demand' postal voting has *not* achieved is a restoration of turn-out levels to the pre-2001 norm. Indeed, while voting by post appears less troublesome than going to a polling station, elections in the UK have seen significantly lower turnouts since it was made an easily available option.

There is one respect, however, in which participation in elections has sharply *increased*. As Figure 1.4 illustrates, many more candidates are now put forward (or put themselves forward) than used to be the case. In 1964 there was a total of 1,757 candidates, representing an average of 2.8 per constituency. The number then rose steadily, topping 2,000 in February 1974 and 3,000 in 1997 before peaking at 4,150 (an average of 6.4 per constituency) in 2010. There was a slight decline in 2015 and a sharper fall in 2017—largely because that election was unexpectedly called at short notice, leaving minor parties and others little time to get candidacies organized. In 2019, the third election in just under five years again presented difficulties for 'others' but, even so, at 3,320 the number of candidates was still almost double that for 1964.

The steady increase in candidates contesting elections during the 1970s was driven largely by the increased involvement of the nationalist parties in Scotland and Wales (as noted previously) and the ability of the Liberals to fight elections on a much broader front than previously. The Liberals contested 365 seats in 1964

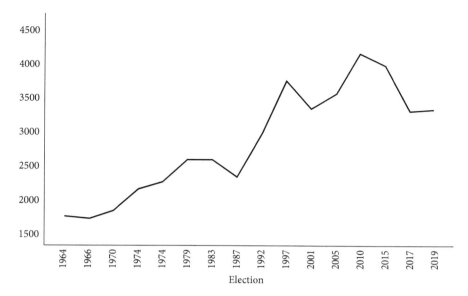

Figure 1.4 Total number of candidates in UK general elections, 1964–2019

(and even fewer in 1966 and 1970), but had 577 candidates in 1979. In the 1990s and after, it was the increased presence of minor parties that mainly accounted for the upsurge in candidate numbers. In 2010, for example, there were 558 candidates representing the UK Independence Party (UKIP); 338 for the British National Party (BNP); 335 for the Green Party, and 107 English Democrats, as well as many other concerned, aggrieved, or eccentric groups and individuals. One reason for the expansion of candidate numbers may be that the financial cost of failure has become distinctly less onerous. In 1964, candidates had to pay a deposit of £150 (a figure that had been unchanged since 1918 and was the equivalent of about £500 by the later date), which was forfeited if he or she obtained less than 12.5 per cent of the votes cast. From 1987, the deposit was raised to £500, but by way of compensation the threshold for saving it was cut to 5 per cent of votes. Had the deposit increased in line with inflation since 1987, by 2019 it would have been about £1,400. Given that every candidate receives a free postal communication to every elector, and that any party with fifty or more candidates is granted a free election broadcast on television, £500 for a frivolous or futile candidacy looks like an increasingly good bargain.

The consequences of increased numbers of candidates for the form of party competition in the constituencies have been marked. In 1964, almost a third of constituencies in Britain (192) saw a straight fight between Conservative and Labour. Fifteen years later, in the 1979 election, there were just three such cases and there have been none at all since then. In 1964 more than half of constituencies (317) had three-way contests involving the two major parties and the Liberals. There was only one of these in 2010 and none in 2015. The number rose to twenty-one in 2017, however, when, as previously explained, minor parties and others were rather caught on the hop by the unexpected calling of the election, and was seventeen in 2019.

Partly for the same sorts of reasons, by-elections have also attracted increasing numbers of candidates. From 1964 to October 1974, the mean number of candidates in eighty-two by-elections in mainland Britain was 3.8; between 2001 and 2010, twenty by-elections were contested by 11.1 people on average (including twenty-six in Haltemprice and Howden in July 2008); from 2010 to 2019 the average was 9.5 in thirty-three cases. It is now something of a tradition that by-elections will be contested by assorted oddballs, publicity-seekers, and people with a bee in their bonnet, as well as minor parties and serious single issue campaigners (see Norris, 1990: 178–81).

In 1964, as in recent elections, the progress of the election campaign was charted by public opinion polls which attracted much interest and comment. Figure 1.5 shows how the number of such polls has changed over the years. In 1964 there were only twenty-three national campaign polls carried out by just four companies—Gallup (ten), NOP (seven), *Daily Express* (four), and Research Services (two)—and the figure remained below thirty until 1983. In that election and the next, the emergence of the SDP and the Alliance gave added interest, which may account for the increase in polling, while in 1992 a close result was

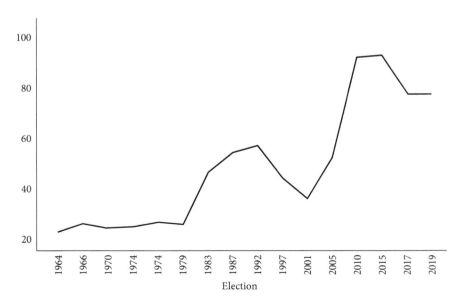

Figure 1.5 Number of national opinion polls during campaigns, 1964–2019

anticipated. In 1997 and 2001, however, there was a falling-off in the number of polls undertaken. This was probably a product of the fact that in advance of these elections the outcomes were not thought to be in serious doubt. In addition, some people's faith in the polls had been shaken by their relatively poor performance in predicting the result of the 1992 election. In 2005, however, there was a resurgence in polling—at least partly because it was considered unlikely that Labour would win as easily as it had done in 1997 and 2001—while in 2010 the number of campaign polls soared to ninety-one. These were produced by twelve different polling firms and included ten separate polls published on the eve of the election (or, in one case, on election day itself) alone. This surge in polling activity came partly in response to expectations of a very close contest but also thanks to a sharp reduction in the costs involved. The latter was a consequence of the advent of online polling, pioneered by YouGov, which by this time was producing a poll virtually every day. In addition, the leaders' debates greatly increased the demand for polls, as the media wanted to know and report which of the three participants had 'won' at the earliest opportunity—even as the debate in question was still in progress. Although the televised debates declined in significance subsequently, polling activity remained frenetic in 2015—'the most polled in the history of British elections' according to Cowley and Kavanagh (2016: 232). In the next two elections the number of national polls declined a little (to seventy-seven) but, even so, along with those in Scotland and Wales there were enough to keep the most avid poll-watcher satisfied. In addition, during the 2010s, there was a sharp increase in the number of surveys undertaken in individual constituencies during election campaigns and there were around thirty-two such polls in 2019.

It goes without saying that the political parties pay close attention to public opinion polls. In addition, however, they commission private polls—and have been doing so since the 1960s—to help them plan and implement their campaign strategies. Face-to-face and telephone polls are costly, but they are only one element in central party spending on elections, which has grown rapidly over the years. Another is the cost of employing campaign consultants—often from abroad—a practice which was unheard of in the 1960s.

In the run-up to the 1964 election, Labour spent just over £300,000 on national campaigning (mainly on press advertisements), while the Conservatives spent almost £1 million and the Liberals virtually nothing (Butler and King, 1965: 372–4). By 1997, campaign expenditure in the twelve months preceding the election had reached around £28 million for the Conservatives, £26 million for Labour and £3.5 million for the Liberal Democrats (Fisher, 2001). Under the Political Parties, Elections and Referendums Act passed in 2000, however, an attempt was made to restrain the spiralling costs of campaigning. For the first time, national campaign expenditure was capped. In 2017, the permitted expenditure over the preceding year for a party contesting all seats across Great Britain was close to £19 million. In the event, the Conservatives spent £18.6 million, Labour about £11.0 million, and the Liberal Democrats £6.8 million, giving a total of £36.4 million for the three major parties alone (Electoral Commission, 2018). These may appear to be very large figures, but they pale in comparison with campaign spending elsewhere. In the United States in 2012, for example, candidates for just one seat in the Senate (for Massachusetts) spent more than $77 million (equivalent to more than £50 million).[3] It is salutary to note that the total expenditure of the leading British parties in 2019 fell far short of what top-flight Premier League football teams are prepared to shell out nowadays for just one star player. Even so, the parties have much more difficulty than football clubs in raising the necessary cash.

Election expenditure at constituency level has been limited by law since the late nineteenth century. In Great Britain in 1964, the average amount spent by Conservative candidates was £792, by Labour £760, and by Liberals £583, with respective overall totals of about £490,000, £470,000, and £211,000 (based on Butler and King, 1965: 228). In 2019, the average expenditure figures for Conservatives was £8,775, for Labour £7,551 and for Liberal Democrats £4,450, with totals of £5.4 million, £4.7 million, and £2.6 million, respectively (Electoral Commission, 2020a). The bulk of this was spent on printing and purchasing leaflets and election addresses for distribution to the electorate. The authors of the Nuffield studies in the 1960s (and later) tended to dismiss any notion that the amount spent by a party in a constituency (or, indeed, the local campaign effort more generally) made any difference to election outcomes. More recently, that view has been seriously undermined. Despite the media obsession with the national campaign, the level of constituency spending (to be understood as an indicator of campaign effectiveness) has been shown repeatedly to have an impact on party performances in recent elections—the more they spend, the better they do (see, for example, Pattie et al., 1995, 2017).

That is but one example of how the academic study of elections and voting has developed over the years since 1964. As noted above, Butler and Stokes initiated the BES in 1964 and they also oversaw the studies for the 1966 and 1970 contests. A team from the University of Essex led by Ivor Crewe and Bo Sarlvik took over for both of the elections in 1974 and that of 1979. From 1983 until 1997 Anthony Heath, Roger Jowell, and John Curtice were the principal investigators, while from 2001 to 2010 the baton passed to David Sanders and Paul Whiteley at Essex, together with two election specialists from the United States (Harold Clarke and Marianne Stewart). From 2015 to 2019 the BES was based mainly at the University of Manchester and was the responsibility of a team of five principal investigators (the 'scientific leadership') supported by two research fellows, a consultant professor (John Curtice), an Advisory Board and an 'Impact Stakeholder group'!

The BES surveys have resulted in a number of major works on voting in Britain and hundreds, possibly even thousands, of book chapters, scholarly articles, and papers. The major reports on the elections from 1964 to 2005 are by Butler and Stokes (1969, 1974), Sarlvik and Crewe (1983), Heath et al. (1985, 1991, 1994, 2001), Evans and Norris (1999), and Clarke et al. (2004, 2009). For the most recent elections, however, the team has concentrated on disseminating survey data to interested parties and providing a series of online reports (see http://www. britishelectionstudy.com).

One basic element of the BES has remained unchanged over the decades in order to provide continuity: a post-election, face-to-face survey of a representative sample of British voters, aimed not only at recording but also at explaining how, why, or whether they voted. Over time, however, the scale and complexity (not to mention cost) of the studies have increased considerably. The 1964 study was based on two survey rounds involving 2,009 respondents in mid-1963 and 1,830 follow-up interviews in the two months after polling day. In addition to the traditional face-to-face survey, the 2017 version included panel surveys comprising thirteen waves of data collection dating back to 2014 and involving some 30,000 respondents. As the public's interest in elections has declined, it appears that scholarly effort and attention has moved in the opposite direction.

Unsurprisingly, the explanations of party choice offered by BES authors have evolved over the years. The approach of Butler and Stokes in the 1960s is summarized (in a simplified form) in Figure 1.6. This is the 'classic' explanation of party choice which has provided the starting point for almost all subsequent British voting research. In brief, it was argued that the voter's choice of party was largely based on class and party identification (the sense of being a party supporter), both of which were to a considerable extent inherited through the family (although also a product of interactions in the wider community). Most working-class people voted Labour and most middle-class people voted Conservative. This basic class 'alignment' was supplemented by the fact that most people also thought

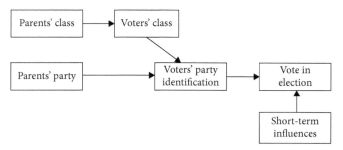

Figure 1.6 The Butler–Stokes model of party choice

of themselves as supporters of one party or another (with upwards of 40 per cent of the electorate describing themselves as *very strong* party supporters), and thus developed an enduring loyalty to a party which, in most cases, would be maintained through thick and thin. Somewhat paradoxically, given that the book produced by Butler and Stokes was entitled *Political Change in Britain*, the emphasis in this explanation is on stability—class and party identity didn't change much and so most people always voted for the same party—rather than change. Short-term influences, such as the popularity of party leaders or party policies on specific issues, had only a marginal influence. From this perspective, electoral change would inevitably be slow and gradual (if not glacial); the chances of any third force breaking the Labour/Conservative duopoly looked remote.

By the 2010 election a different approach to explaining voting behaviour—known as the 'valence politics' model—had been advanced and almost universally accepted among academic election specialists (Clarke et al., 2004, 2009). Figure 1.7 is an attempt to represent this graphically (again in a much simplified form). The starting point in this explanation is so-called 'valence' issues. These are topics of public concern on which nearly everyone is agreed about the goal to be pursued—for example, reduced crime, a thriving economy, or a well-run health service. It is argued that these sorts of issues, rather than 'position' issues—that is, those on which the desired outcomes are contested (such as whether the railways should be publicly or privately owned)—now dominate voters' concerns and hence elections. The question for voters is not which party has the ideological or policy positions that they approve of but which is likely to be most competent at achieving widely shared goals. Making judgements like this is not straightforward, however, and so many voters rely on a convenient short-cut, using their assessments of the party leaders—whom we see and hear about often enough—as

Figure 1.7 The 'valence politics' model of party choice

the basis for their choice of party. Nonetheless, party identification has remained a statistically significant influence on voting. As traditionally conceived, however, identity has little to do with judgements or evaluations, reflecting, rather, the sort of tribal loyalty more often associated with supporting a football team. Valence theorists surmount this difficulty by seeing party identification as more *dynamic* (i.e. subject to change), in that it is continually updated in the voter's mind as he or she acquires new information, reacts to events, and makes ongoing judgements about the competence of parties, governments, and leaders. In this conception, it is not so much an inherited emotional attachment that endures but more of a general *inclination* towards (or against) a party, based on how the different parties and leaders seem to be faring currently.

From 2010, then, explanations of party choice focused on voters' views about how well parties performed (or might perform) in office and how they rated the different party leaders. Unlike voting based on class and party identification as formerly conceived, evaluations of government performance and of leaders can be subject to violent short-term fluctuations. As a result, voters are much more volatile in their party preference than they used to be, and swings in opinion are much larger. For example, in September 2007, according to Ipsos MORI, 44 per cent of the public were satisfied with the performance of the then Prime Minister, Gordon Brown, and 26 per cent were dissatisfied. Less than a year later, in July 2008, 21 per cent were satisfied and 72 per cent were dissatisfied. Over the same ten months, monthly poll averages showed Labour falling from 40 per cent to 26 per cent of voting intentions, while the Conservatives went from 33 per cent to 45 per cent. An even more spectacular turnaround in opinion occurred during the 2017 election campaign. In April of that year Theresa May's net satisfaction rating was +19 while Jeremy Corbyn stood at −35; just five weeks later the respective figures were −7 and −11 and Labour had risen from 27 to 37 per cent in voting intentions.

The changes in how most voters decide which party to support transformed the aligned and stable electorate of the 1960s into dealigned and fickle voters in the twenty-first century; they gave rise to a gradual movement from a situation in which party leaders scarcely mattered for electoral success to one where they are seen as central to a party's prospects. These developments underpin our account of elections over this period.

Notes

1. After each election since 1945 a volume has been published (entitled *The British General Election of . . .*) providing an account of the election campaign and analysis of the results. The series is known as the 'Nuffield studies' because of its connection with

Nuffield College, Oxford. From 1951 to 2005 every volume was authored or co-authored by David Butler.

2. This figure comes from data collected via a national survey of election agents under-taken by one of the authors and other colleagues.

3. See http://www.opensecrets.org/overview/topraces.php?cycle=2012&display=cur rcandsout.

2

The Way Things Were

Elections, 1964–70

In July 1957, the Conservative Prime Minister Harold Macmillan introduced one of the best-known British political catchphrases when he told a party rally that 'most of our people have never had it so good'. Often misunderstood as an expression of complacency, it was actually delivered as part of a warning that excessive pay rises (and the price inflation that was thought to follow) were endangering the country's prosperity. By the time of the 1959 general election, however, Conservative publicists were happy to paraphrase their leader and overlook the original context of his remarks. 'You're having it good. Have it better' featured prominently among the campaign slogans of that year (Ramsden, 1996: 56). Another expressed the same sunny mood: 'Life's Better with the Conservatives— Don't let Labour Ruin it'. Macmillan's government was duly returned with an overall majority of 100. It was the third successive victory for the Conservatives, achieved under three different leaders (following Churchill in 1951 and Eden in 1955) and by growing margins.

This was thoroughly demoralizing for the Labour Opposition, whose fortunes continued to decline after the election (Figure 2.1). The outlook was not brightened by survey evidence which suggested that Labour's association with the working class was becoming a liability, rather than the recipe for electoral dominance which it had once appeared to be (Abrams and Rose, 1960). The party leader, Hugh Gaitskell, was convinced that Labour's electoral appeal had been damaged by Clause IV of its constitution, which committed it to 'the common ownership of the means of production, distribution and exchange'—in other words, nationalization. However, his proposals for reform met strenuous union opposition and, far from scrapping the Clause, his unrepentant party decided in 1960 that it should be printed on membership cards. In the same year, Labour's annual conference narrowly voted to adopt a policy of unilateral nuclear disarmament, forcing Gaitskell to vow that he and his allies would 'fight and fight and fight again to save the party we love'. Shortly afterwards, he comfortably defeated a leadership challenge from Harold Wilson; and at the 1961 conference the unilateralist policy was overturned by an overwhelming majority.

Although Gaitskell had shored up his personal position, voters had good reasons to regard Labour as a divided party. As a result, the Opposition failed to reap the full benefit as the Conservatives drifted downwards in popularity during

British General Elections Since 1964: Diversity, Dealignment, and Disillusion. Second Edition. David Denver and Mark Garnett, Oxford University Press. © David Denver and Mark Garnett 2021. DOI: 10.1093/oso/9780198844952.003.0002

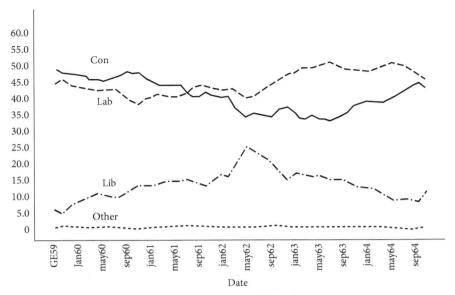

Figure 2.1 Monthly voting intentions, 1959–64 (Gallup)

Notes: The 1959 and 1964 election results in Great Britain form the starting and finishing points. The data have been smoothed by plotting the three-monthly moving average in each case.

1961. In another (over-)familiar Macmillan quotation, the Prime Minister confessed that his worst fear was 'events'. He would have been more accurate, though less memorable, if he had alluded to 'adverse economic trends'. In response to an increasingly difficult economic situation, in July 1961 the government raised taxes, cut public expenditure plans, and introduced a much-resented 'pay pause'. Sensing that the country was being outperformed by members of the European Economic Community (EEC), Macmillan reversed what had been British policy since the Schuman Plan of 1950 and applied for membership. However, the negotiations proved difficult and were still dragging on in July 1962, when Macmillan summarily sacked seven Cabinet ministers. This so-called 'Night of the Long Knives' did little to revive the government's sense of purpose and nothing for its popularity (Figure 2.1).

With Labour still nursing its self-inflicted bruises, the main beneficiaries of government unpopularity were the Liberals, under the widely respected Jo Grimond (leader since 1956). Starting from a low base in 1959, the third party steadily increased its share of voting intentions in the Gallup poll for more than two years and also performed impressively in local elections and parliamentary by-elections. This trend culminated in a sensational by-election win at Orpington in Kent in March 1962, where the Liberals surged from third place, more than 15,000 votes behind the Tories, to win the seat by almost 8,000. The attendant publicity helped to produce a major boost for the Liberals in the polls—indeed, one NOP survey after Orpington placed them ahead of their two rivals—but the fillip proved short-lived. Before the end of 1962, the party's rating had fallen back to below 20 per cent, and its support declined steadily up to the 1964 election. Nevertheless, after a long period in the electoral doldrums Orpington became symbolic of the Liberals' ability to pose a significant threat to the major parties in mid-term, and held out the possibility of a more substantial 'revival' in the long run.

Hugh Gaitskell died unexpectedly in early 1963—just four days after President de Gaulle announced France's veto of Britain's bid for EEC membership—and was replaced as Labour leader by his unsuccessful challenger of 1960, Harold Wilson. Despite an earlier association with the left, Wilson sought to portray himself as a down-to-earth modernizer, and this appears to have gone down well with the public. In Gaitskell's final months, Labour had finally established a strong lead in voting intentions over the Conservatives and this was consolidated under Wilson as the government continued to flounder in the wake of de Gaulle's veto. The scandal involving the Secretary of War, John Profumo, which ended with the minister resigning in June 1963 after admitting that he had lied to the House of Commons over his relationship with a prostitute, seriously undermined confidence in the government. Although he had pledged to battle on as Prime Minister, Macmillan resigned on health grounds in October. Despite his (temporary) indisposition, Macmillan was able to manipulate the informal procedures of his party in the ensuing leadership 'race', so that his chosen successor, the previously unconsidered dark horse, the Earl of Home, emerged to canter to victory (Gilmour and Garnett, 1997: 186–201).

Sir Alec Douglas-Home, MP (as he quickly became, thanks to the newly introduced ability of peers to renounce hereditary titles and a conveniently arranged by-election in Kinross and West Perthshire) appeared an unlikely candidate as a party leader for the 1960s. A tweedy aristocrat, he epitomized the archaic and class-bound Britain that Harold Wilson sought to sweep away. The choice of Douglas-Home as leader would have made more sense if he had demonstrated previous ministerial expertise in some area of domestic policy; yet he freely confessed to ignorance of economics, and it was difficult for an erstwhile enthusiastic supporter of Neville Chamberlain's policy of appeasing Nazi Germany in the 1930s to impress the public as a master of foreign affairs. Not blessed with a voter-friendly physical appearance, the new Prime Minister was a reluctant media performer. Even so, under Douglas-Home the Tories narrowed the gap with Labour. Although that may have happened whoever was in charge, Douglas-Home is the only post-war Prime Minister to date who has left office with better personal ratings in the polls than when he came in (Denver and Garnett, 2012). Nonetheless, these ratings lagged far behind those of Harold Wilson. Despite well-founded arguments in favour of going to the country in the spring of 1964, Douglas-Home decided to hang on until the autumn. In September, he asked the Queen to dissolve Parliament for an election on Thursday, 15 October.

The 1964 Campaign

Labour's 1964 campaign slogan was 'Let's Go With Labour', accompanied by a thumbs-up sign. These visual enticements were the creation of public relations specialists, who had been shunned by senior Labour strategists in previous campaigns. The snappy Conservative slogans of 1959 had clearly made an impression on Labour, whether or not they had swayed the voters. A second development was a sharper focus on the party leader. Mr Wilson 'dominated his party's campaign to an unprecedented degree', according to Butler and King (1965: 150). He determined the strategy, made twenty set-piece speeches to large audiences across the country, and also regularly chaired the party's morning press conferences in London. This dynamic display gave rise to Conservative claims that Labour was a one-man band. However, Wilson led one of the most talented of shadow cabinets; indeed, his desire to dominate was partly inspired by a fear of conspiracy amongst his colleagues. Whatever the causes, his style of leadership combined with simultaneous developments within the mass media led to speculation about a new 'presidential' form of politics, departing from Britain's long-established tradition of parliamentary rule. It seemed telling that, in a book published in 1963, one of Wilson's front-bench colleagues, the spokesman on education Richard Crossman, had written persuasively about an increase in prime ministerial power (Crossman, 1963).

If Wilson was a new kind of 'presidential' party leader, semi-consciously inviting comparisons with the recently assassinated John F. Kennedy, his opponent in 1964 preferred to act as though the Great Reform Act of 1832 had never happened. On the day that the election was called, Douglas-Home agreed to appear in an ITV broadcast. True to form, when he was told before the recording began that he would be asked to discuss some key issues, he replied, 'Oh, I'm not doing anything like that, I'm not going to talk politics' (Howard and West, 1965: 153). The Prime Minister toured the country in a sort of 'meet the people' exercise, which might have invigorated Conservative constituency parties but also reintroduced the leader to the kind of robust exchanges on the hustings which he had been spared since inheriting his peerage in 1951. While Douglas-Home concentrated on this traditional form of campaigning, younger, 'meritocratic' colleagues were entrusted with the more modern means of engaging the voters. Press conferences were chaired by Reginald Maudling (Chancellor of the Exchequer since 'Supermac' had wielded his knife), while Edward Heath (the unavailing but highly regarded negotiator of EEC membership) fronted most election broadcasts. Maudling and Heath had graduated from Oxford, but both won this privilege by competing for scholarships. An unwanted distraction for the Conservatives was provided by Quintin Hogg (Eton, Oxford), who until 1963 had traded under his hereditary title of Viscount Hailsham. Responding to a shout of 'Profumo!' at one of his public meetings, Hogg insinuated that there were adulterers on the Opposition front bench. Since this was October 1964, if Philip Larkin was right, Hogg's hint might have been susceptible to proof; but as a seasoned lawyer he should have backed his accusation with evidence or kept silent. Later, Hogg enlivened proceedings by suggesting at a press conference that anyone who contemplated voting Labour must be 'stark, staring bonkers' (Butler and King, 1965: 124).

This was the first election at which the vast majority of the electorate owned a television (90 per cent of homes compared with 70 per cent in 1959), and there was an unprecedented level of political programming as broadcasters began to slip free of the legal shackles that had previously been thought to bind them. In addition to party election broadcasts, there were several special election programmes on radio and television, and extensive coverage during news bulletins. The televised party election broadcasts were shown simultaneously on both BBC and ITV at 9.30 p.m.; they lasted fifteen minutes and had an average audience of 12.7 million (Harrison, 1965: 182 fn.). Such figures could not reveal how many viewers and listeners actually paid attention to the broadcasts, as opposed to keeping the television on while waiting for another programme to start. The broadcasts were allocated in the ratio 5:5:3 between the major parties and the Liberals (in rough proportion to the number of candidates that each put forward). The final broadcasts of all three parties featured the leader speaking straight to camera. As noted in Chapter 1, the campaign also featured the innovative *Election Forum* broadcasts. The separate television programmes, featuring each of the party leaders in turn, also attracted large numbers of viewers—5.3 million for Grimond, 7.8 million for Douglas-Home, and 8.1 million for Wilson (Harrison, 1965: 161–2). Forced away from his comfort zone of defence and foreign affairs by viewers who sent in questions on domestic issues such as pensions and housing, the Prime Minister's reputation as a well-meaning bumbler seemed to be confirmed. Wilson, on the other hand, dealt confidently with viewers' questions over a range of issues, and the engaging Grimond also impressed those who watched his programme (Wyndham Goldie, 1977).

Almost three decades after the event, Wilson's biographer Ben Pimlott characterized the 1964 contest as 'exciting' (Pimlott, 1992: 311). However, the contemporary verdict of David Butler and Anthony King was that the campaign failed to arouse much enthusiasm among the voters, and even some of the candidates found it dull. Among the exceptions, however, was the tiny handful of analysts for whom this was 'the most absorbing [election] since 1945' (Butler and King, 1965: 155). The most sensible way to reconcile these contrasting views is to conclude that although the 1964 general election did have many 'exciting' features, it was held in circumstances which overcame the initial enthusiasm of many participants and observers. By the time Douglas-Home called the election, the parties had been campaigning and rehearsing their arguments for a considerable time, in the expectation of an earlier poll. Even voters who were watching their first televised election campaign would have found it difficult to sustain their original levels of interest over such a protracted period. The growth of television coverage—the nature of which demanded a steady flow of spectacular 'events', rather than the relentless analysis of 'trends'—might also have demonstrated to a larger number of voters that, in terms of ideology and practical policies, there was little to choose between the main parties. Finally, the incident which stands out in hindsight— Douglas-Home's humiliating encounter with hecklers at the Birmingham Bull Ring on 8 October, when the audible section of his speech began and ended with an unwise claim that 'it's no good trying to drown me down' (Howard and West, 1965: 194)—was the kind of thing which had occurred many times before, and thus could not strike contemporaries as especially worthy of notice. The audiences of 1964 were not in a position to know that, in response to the advent of television coverage, party strategists would do their best to ensure that such incidents would recur only through unfortunate accidents.

The misleading impression of a dull campaign can be reinforced by selective analysis of the opinion polls. Support for the Conservatives and Labour shifted very slightly over the course of the 1964 campaign (see Appendix, Figure 2.A1). Although Labour held the lead for the most part, the closeness of the race between the two main parties meant that there were several individual polls suggesting that the government might hang on to office. Three polls in the week that the election date was announced produced average voting intentions of 44.7 per cent for the Conservatives and 46.6 per cent for Labour. In the last week of the campaign, five polls averaged 44.3 per cent and 45.5 per cent, respectively. However, these overall figures conceal individual fluctuations, such as an NOP survey published in the *Daily Mail* on 30 September, which put the Conservatives ahead by three points (Howard and West, 1965: 174). Support for the Liberals in the opinion polls increased slowly over the course of the campaign, from 8.3 per cent to 9.7 per cent. Many observers attributed this slight upward trend to the party's more viewer-friendly, relaxed (and cheap to produce) television election broadcasts; but the figures were a dismal disappointment compared with the heady prospects suggested in the aftermath of Orpington. Meanwhile, in the constituencies, Butler and King (1965: 215–16) thought that the Conservative effort was better organized and more efficient than those of the other parties, although all concentrated to a greater extent than before on marginal seats. In line with an already established position, however, the Nuffield authors remained sceptical about the electoral efficacy of local campaigning by the major parties (Butler and King, 1965: 352).

The 1964 Results

In the event, the polls underestimated Liberal support but were otherwise reasonably accurate (for Great Britain). The outcome of the 1964 election over the UK is shown in Table 2.1.

Turnout in 1964 declined by 1.6 percentage points from 1959 and was below the post-war average. In some ways this is surprising, as the election was clearly going to be close and a change of government was in the offing. With hindsight, however, the very high turnouts in the 1950 and 1951 elections—in excess of 80 per cent in both cases—were exceptional, and the 1964 figure was close to normal at that time. There was, of course, considerable variation around the overall turnout figure across constituencies—ranging from 51.3 per cent in Stepney to 87.1 per cent in Wellingborough. Commentators had always had a fair idea about the sources of turnout variation. It was already well known, for example, that mining seats had unusually high turnouts; that inner-city seats tended towards the lower end; and that levels of participation were generally higher in marginal than in safe seats. In 1964, the much-increased television coverage of the campaign did nothing to alter these long-established patterns.

Electoral analysis took a major step forward when census results (from the 1966 sample census) were made available at constituency level for the first time. These made it possible to calculate precise measures of the strength of the association between a variety of social indicators, on the one hand, and turnout or levels of party support, on the other. The statistics most commonly used for this purpose are correlation coefficients. These can range from −1 through 0 to +1. A positive sign indicates a positive relationship—that is, as one variable increases in size then so does the other. Where the sign is negative an increase in one is associated with a decrease in the other and the closer to zero the coefficient, the weaker the relationship.

Table 2.2 shows how the level of constituency turnout across Britain was correlated with a variety of factors in 1964. We will not be repeating this analysis for

Table 2.1 Election results (UK), 1964–70

	1964		1966		1970	
	Votes	Seats	Votes	Seats	Votes	Seats
Con	43.4	304	41.9	253	46.4	330
Labour	44.1	317	48.0	364	43.1	288
Liberal	11.2	9	8.5	12	7.5	6
Others	1.3	0	1.6	1	3.0	6
Turnout	*77.2*		*76.0*		*72.2*	

Note: Figures for Votes are percentages.

every election in our survey because—with minor variations and additions—the basic pattern found in 1964 was repeated and eventually intensified in subsequent elections. In general, turnout was consistently higher in more middle-class constituencies with high levels of owner occupation and also in more rural areas; it was consistently lower in less affluent, more working-class, and more densely populated areas with high levels of private renting and people then known as 'New Commonwealth' immigrants. Overlaying these aspects of social make-up, the previous marginality of constituencies was clearly related to turnout—the more marginal the seat, the higher the turnout. It is important to emphasize that the coefficients in Table 2.2 tell us nothing about the behaviour of individuals, only about constituencies. Thus, for example, we cannot infer from the strong positive correlation between the percentage of owner-occupiers in a constituency and turnout that larger proportions of owner-occupiers turned out than those with other housing arrangements. This *may* be true; but from constituency-level data we can only draw conclusions about constituencies and not about the individuals who comprise them. To do the latter we require survey data, which are considered later in the chapter.

In terms of party support, Labour improved on its 1959 performance by a modest 0.3 points while the Conservatives slumped by six points (giving an overall Conservative to Labour swing of 3.2 per cent).[1] Strikingly, although their excellent by-election performances were now a fading memory, the Liberals almost doubled their vote share from 5.9 to 11.2 per cent. This was partly due to an increased number of candidates (216 to 365), but even in the 196 seats fought in both 1959 and 1964 their share increased by more than three points. Among their nine victorious candidates was Eric Lubbock, the shock winner at Orpington in the 1962 by-election.

The swing from Conservative to Labour was repeated all around the country, with only twenty-eight constituencies moving in the opposite direction (including, notoriously, Smethwick, where the Conservative candidate ran an overtly anti-immigrant campaign and was returned on a 7.7 per cent swing from Labour). Nonetheless, there was a portent of things to come in the fact that the swing to Labour was noticeably higher in Scotland (4.9 per cent) and the North of England

Table 2.2 Correlations between turnout and constituency characteristics, 1964

% Professional & managerial	0.28	% Manual workers	−0.16
% In agriculture	0.20	Electors per hectare	−0.73
% Owner occupiers	0.57	% Council tenants	−0.02*
% Retired	0.18	% Private renters	−0.69
		% With no car	−0.57
Constit. marginality 1959	0.24	% Ethnic minority	−0.59

Notes: All coefficients are statistically significant except the one asterisked. N=618. Marginality is defined as 100 minus the difference in percentage share of votes between the top two parties.

Table 2.3 Correlations between party shares of vote and constituency
characteristics, 1964

	Conservative	Labour	Liberal
% Professional & managerial	0.66	−0.81	0.25
% Manual workers	−0.64	0.72	−0.05*
% Owner occupiers	0.36	−0.51	0.24
% Council tenants	−0.38	0.50	−0.22
% Private renters	−0.05*	0.15	−0.21
% Retired	0.09	−0.28	0.40
% In agriculture	0.16	−0.43	0.54
Electors per hectare	−0.10	0.26	−0.33
% With no car	−0.45	0.65	−0.28
% Ethnic minority	0.06*	0.03*	−0.25

Notes: All coefficients are statistically significant except those asterisked. N=618 for
Conservative and Labour, and 363 for the Liberals.

(4.1 per cent) than in the Midlands (2.0 per cent) or the South outside London
(3.1 per cent).

As with turnout, when constituency census data became available analysts
could be more precise about the factors which were associated with varying levels
of party support across constituencies. Table 2.3 shows the relationships found for
1964. As would be expected, the figures show the Conservatives doing better in
more middle-class and also more rural areas, while the pattern for Labour is a
mirror image of that for the Conservatives. In terms of class and class-related
variables, the pattern of Liberal support is a paler reflection of that for the
Conservatives. However, the more rural a constituency the better the Liberals did
(coefficient for per cent in agriculture), while they had poorer results in more
densely populated areas (electors per hectare) and those with larger ethnic minority populations. In contrast, these last three factors were not strongly associated
with variations in Conservative support. In later chapters we will investigate the
extent to which the aggregate patterns of party support have changed over time.

Labour returned to power in 1964 with an overall majority of only four seats,
thus ending, as a Labour campaign slogan claimed, 'thirteen wasted years' of
Conservative rule. On the face of it, the result confounded commentators who
had argued that Labour's proudest achievement in government—the improvements
in welfare provision which had subdued if not slain William Beveridge's 'Five
Giants' of squalor, ignorance, want, idleness, and disease—had helped to foster an
'Age of Affluence' in which the party would be condemned to permanent opposition.
On the other hand, given Macmillan's misadventures and the unimpressive
performance of Douglas-Home before and during the election campaign, a more
convincing victory might have been expected. Only a second, and more decisive,
election victory could make Labour look like a party of government again.

1964–6: A Pre-Election Parliament

Given Labour's slender margin of victory in 1964, even a less calculating Prime Minister than Harold Wilson would have been forgiven for watching the polls very closely in the hope of finding the best opportunity to improve his party's parliamentary position. The popularity of the parties during the short parliament of October 1964 to March 1966 is shown in Figure 2.2. After a brief honeymoon with the electorate, Labour's standing declined steadily (and that of the Conservatives rose) until the autumn of 1965. The polling evidence was verified by a significant swing to the Conservatives in the local elections of May 1965. From the autumn the roles were reversed, as was dramatically illustrated in the Hull North by-election in January 1966. Labour had won the seat from the Conservatives in 1964 with a majority of just over 2,000 votes. In the subsequent by-election, the party achieved a swing of 4.5 per cent and won a majority of more than 5,000. This was enough evidence for Wilson to start preparing for an early election.

Although the trend in government popularity in this period followed an already familiar (if on this occasion not very pronounced) pattern of decline and recovery, the 1966 Nuffield study describes Labour's upswing from late 1965 as

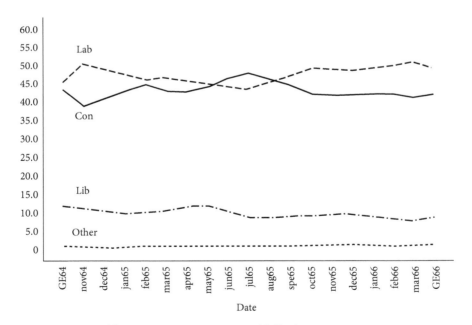

Figure 2.2 Monthly voting intentions, 1964–6 (Gallup)

Notes: The 1964 and 1966 election results in Great Britain form the starting and finishing points. The data have been smoothed by plotting the three-monthly moving average in each case.

'something of a mystery' (Butler and King, 1966: 16). The government had inherited serious economic problems—especially a large negative balance of payments between imports and exports and the weakness of sterling—which resulted in some unpopular decisions. Increases in income tax, petrol duty, and national insurance contributions were announced in November 1964, followed by hikes in alcohol and tobacco duties and also car taxes in the April 1965 Budget. In July, public expenditure cuts and a credit squeeze were implemented. However, the worst seemed to be over by the end of 1965. Much of the government's and Mr Wilson's energies were devoted to dealing with the crisis in Rhodesia, where the all-white government unilaterally declared the country independent. Fortunately for Labour's prospects, this was an issue that aroused considerable and conflicting Conservative passions. Although Wilson had taken stances which could have proved equally divisive—notably the government's declared intention to limit pay increases and its moral support for the USA in the Vietnam War—the feeling that the government should be given a fair chance to win a workable majority in a re-run of the 1964 contest was strong enough to restrain most potential parliamentary dissidents on the Labour side.

For the Conservative Party, the most important development during these months was the choice of a new leader. Following an adverse public reaction to the secretive process which had allowed Douglas-Home to succeed Macmillan, MPs were given the right to elect future leaders. In response to growing criticism within the party, Sir Alec resigned in July 1965, and Edward Heath became the first Conservative leader to be chosen by a ballot of his parliamentary colleagues. Even before the 1964 general election, officials in the Conservative Research Department had sensed that the party was losing touch with the electorate, and worried that Labour had seized the initiative by conducting intensive surveys into changing social trends and attitudes. Conservative work in this field began in earnest after the 1964 defeat, while Home appointed Heath as coordinator of a wide-ranging policy review. The surveys played a crucial role in shaping Conservative strategy for the next election; more than five million 'target voters' were identified, and the party's campaign focused sharply on the issues which seemed most likely to affect them (Butler and King, 1966: 59–69, 90–3). Unfortunately for the Conservatives, the surveys also confirmed that they had acquired a negative image during the 1959–64 parliament; and although Heath's personal ratings were initially high his lustre wore off when Wilson began to take his measure in parliamentary exchanges. After August 1965, Heath and his party trailed Labour badly in the national polls. Having been granted the chance of a direct vote in the choice of leader, when their exaggerated expectations of Heath were not realized some Conservative MPs began to wonder aloud if they should be given a second opportunity before Wilson called the election (Campbell, 1993).

For the Liberals too, this was a disappointing period. If neither of the major parties had secured an overall victory in 1964 and the Liberals had held the balance of power (even with only nine MPs), Jo Grimond would have been able to concentrate the minds of his colleagues on a momentous choice of alliance. As it was, Labour's victory was slender enough to tempt Grimond into tentative offers of parliamentary support, and to make Wilson consider the possibility of a deal which could include the replacement of the first-past-the-post method of electing MPs with the Alternative Vote (AV) system. However, the by-election losses which would have forced Wilson to talk seriously with Grimond never materialized. In March 1965, David Steel comfortably took Roxburgh, Selkirk, and Peebles from the Conservatives in a by-election, thus helping to hasten the retirement of Douglas-Home, who was obviously something less than an electoral talisman even in his native Scottish borders. However, support for the Liberals drifted slowly downwards as the party debated its attitude to the two major parties in a fashion which only emphasized divisions within its puny contingent of MPs. It performed poorly in the last three by-elections of the 1964–6 parliament, and in January 1966 it was widely (and correctly) rumoured that Grimond was contemplating standing down as party leader (McManus, 2001, 243).

The 1966 Campaign

Like Home in 1964, Wilson found it difficult to choose between a spring or autumn election; even after his party's victory at Hull North his public remarks gave conflicting signals. His decision to opt for the spring was announced on 28 February, shortly after his return from a state visit to Moscow. The poll was to be held on 31 March, but Parliament would sit until 10 March. Thus MPs would continue to act as legislators despite the distraction of an imminent election campaign; indeed, the last few days of the parliament included the momentous announcement by the Chancellor, James Callaghan, that the UK would convert from shillings and pence to decimal currency within five years. However, MPs could not have been unduly disconcerted by the gap between Wilson's announcement and the dissolution, since they had been operating under the shadow of the ballot box ever since the October 1964 election.

While two years earlier Home had hung on in the hope that something better might turn up, Wilson had wavered because he feared that the situation being reported by the polls might prove too good to be true. Entering the 1966 campaign, Labour was clearly ahead of the Conservatives in voting intentions (by 51 per cent to 42 per cent on average) and, unsurprisingly, the bookmakers had Labour as heavy odds-on favourites to win. As the campaign progressed, there were fewer fluctuations in individual polls than in 1964. Of the twenty-four campaign polls, only four placed Labour at (marginally) less than 50 per cent. The Conservatives, meanwhile, slipped slightly to just under 40 per cent on average in the last week's polls. Although they once again improved slightly during the campaign, there was no sign of a breakthrough for the Liberals (see Appendix, Figure 2.A2).

All parties followed broadly the same pattern of activity. Each held a morning press conference in London, after which the leaders dispersed to make major speeches in provincial centres. Campaigning on a slogan echoing the party manifesto—'Action Not Words'—Heath attended the Conservative daily press conferences before travelling (by helicopter as well as in cars) to ticket-only meetings across the country. He encountered some heckling, but like Wilson he proved capable of turning such interventions to his advantage; indeed, some suspected that 'hostile' questioners at his meetings were really Conservatives who had been recruited to give him the chance to match Wilson's quick-witted repartee. Labour's campaign slogan was 'You Know Labour Government Works', and Wilson spread this message by addressing at least one meeting every night from 11 March through to polling day. The inclusion of Birmingham's Bull Ring in Wilson's campaign itinerary was clearly inspired by the Prime Minister's confidence that he would fare better in that venue than Douglas-Home in 1964. Even when he was hit in the eye by a stink bomb in Slough on 22 March, Wilson recovered quickly to deliver a humorous response—'with an aim like that the boy ought to be in the England eleven' (Butler and King, 1966: 100).

The trend of electors following the campaign mainly via television was now firmly established, and in 1966 around 90 per cent of households owned a television. Special television news teams were attached to each of the major party leaders to record their speeches and send back excerpts for broadcasting on news programmes. In what was already becoming a hollow ritual, the main opposition leader challenged the Prime Minister to a televised debate. On this occasion, Wilson (who was more concerned about the remote possibility of a disaster than confident of making gains) retorted with the suggestion that Grimond should also be included, at which point Heath lost his initial enthusiasm (Butler and King, 1966: 99–100). As far as party election broadcasts were concerned, there was the same number (thirteen) as in 1964 for the major parties, but the total time allocated was reduced by forty minutes. In addition, however, the Communist Party (which was contesting fifty-seven seats) was given a five-minute broadcast, while the SNP and Plaid Cymru were also allocated five minutes in their respective countries. The Liberals' broadcasts were anchored by Ludovic Kennedy, a well-known television commentator; but Jo Grimond was unable to appear in any because of the suicide of his son during the campaign. Edward Heath had previously failed to impress on television, but he appeared in the first and last Tory broadcasts and made a reasonable showing, especially in the latter. Wilson, appearing appropriately Prime Ministerial, also starred in the first and last of his party's broadcasts— during which he made forty-two mentions of 'Britain', thirty-nine of 'government', and none at all of 'Labour' (or, less surprisingly, 'socialism') (Butler and King, 1966: 136). The pose paid off. During the campaign, Gallup found that much larger proportions of voters thought that Wilson had a strong personality, and was sincere, warm, and trustworthy than thought the same of Heath (Butler and King, 1966: 266).

At this time, the parties were relatively well supplied with full-time constituency agents—499 in the case of the Conservatives, 202 Labour, and sixty Liberals—and under their leadership local campaigning continued along its well-worn groove. The Nuffield study authors asked 100 candidates whether there had been any new features in their campaigns, and almost all had nothing to report. Even the few innovations mentioned were, in Butler and King's words, 'hardly radical' (1966: 192)—a portable music apparatus on the candidate's car, a motorcade, hats and balloons adorned with the candidate's name, and so on.

Rather quaintly, Butler and King (1966: 100) described the 1966 campaign as 'void of sensational events'. As in 1964—but with more justification this time—many media commentators complained that it was 'boring'; and, as had rapidly become an inevitable chorus accompanying elections, the public moaned about there being too much politics on television. Although there is evidence to the contrary—for example, viewing figures for the party election broadcasts were the largest ever, and children pressed against school railings to cheer as Wilson was driven past—these reactions probably reflect the fact that the parties had actually been in electioneering mode for much of the time since the beginning of 1964. The short campaign of 1966 represented a change of gear rather than a fresh start. Yet if these factors were not in themselves sufficient to drain the contest of excitement, this was an election in which professional advisers of various kinds were being recruited—and heeded by the major parties—in greater numbers than ever before. For such individuals, a cardinal rule of the democratic process is that candidates should only 'meet the people' if such encounters preclude the possibility of negative publicity. If their impact was a token of things to come, then dull elections were likely to be the rule rather than the exceptions. Risky engagements, such as Wilson's venture into the Birmingham Bull Ring, would be eschewed unless they were dictated by imperative tactical considerations. Based on the experience of 1966, it was obvious that broadcasters would be faced with a considerable challenge if they wanted to keep their audiences interested throughout the weeks of campaigning.

The 1966 Results

As widely anticipated, Labour duly won a handsome victory in the election—although it was not as handsome as the campaign polls had suggested—achieving an overall majority of almost 100 (see Table 2.1). The 1964–6 swing from Conservative to Labour was a relatively modest 2.7 per cent, but was very similar across the country. Only twenty-two seats in Britain swung to the Conservatives (and in eight of these the Liberals had been in first or second place in 1964). Notably, however, the swing to Labour in large cities was greater than elsewhere. As with regional variations in 1964, this was a harbinger of greater geographical polarization in support for the major parties.

The Liberals' vote share dropped by 2.7 points, although they won three more seats than in 1964. The first 'other' elected in our period was Gerry Fitt, representing Republican Labour in Belfast West. Despite correctly predicting the winner, there was an early warning of future dilemmas for pollsters, in that every organization over-estimated Labour's lead in their final published surveys. This disparity offered the Conservatives one stale crumb in what was otherwise a comfortless contest.

Turnout in the election (excluding the Speaker's seat) ranged from 50.8 per cent in Liverpool Exchange to 87.5 per cent in Cornwall North. Overall, however, it fell to 75.8 per cent—the lowest figure since the war. The pattern of variation across constituencies remained very similar to that in 1964. Correlating constituency turnouts in 1964 and 1966 gives a coefficient of 0.93, which indicates very considerable continuity.

1966–70: The Election Cycle Par Excellence

In electoral terms, it could reasonably be claimed that the 1966–70 inter-election period was the most dramatic in British politics to that date. It witnessed the governing party reaching uncharted depths of unpopularity and the emergence of the SNP and Plaid Cymru as significant players in the electoral politics of their respective countries.

The 1966–70 Labour government introduced (or ensured the passage of) numerous pieces of legislation which (according to taste) either reshaped British society or merely recognized developments which had already occurred. Abortion was legalized, divorce made easier, homosexual activity decriminalized, Sunday observance laws relaxed, theatre censorship abolished, the breathalyser introduced, and capital punishment finally abandoned. In addition, the voting age was reduced to 18, the move to comprehensive schooling began, the first Race Relations Act was passed, and the British armed forces were withdrawn from bases 'east of Suez'. For good or ill, all of these clearly marked very significant developments in British society. Despite these—often contentious—changes, however, the popularity of the government was almost entirely dependent on its handling of the economy.

As usual, things started well; but Wilson's second honeymoon turned out to be no more protracted than his first (see Figure 2.2). Just four months after the election, pressure on sterling forced the government to introduce a deflationary package, including expenditure cuts and increased taxes on alcohol and petrol as well as a statutory wage freeze. This was just the beginning of what was perceived as continuous crisis for the next three years, which included a devaluation of the pound (in November 1967). The latter was a personal and political disaster for the Prime Minister, who had staked his reputation on preservation of the existing parity. It also appeared to confirm long-held views among the electorate that Labour was incapable of managing the economy competently (the Labour government of 1945–50 having also been forced into a devaluation). To compound his difficulties, in a televised address on the issue Wilson notoriously reassured viewers that 'the pound in your pocket' had not been devalued (which it obviously had, since imported goods would now take more money out of people's pockets). Unsurprisingly, Labour's share of voting intentions in the December 1967 Gallup poll was only 32 per cent, while the Conservatives reached almost 50 per cent. Even worse was to follow, however. The March 1968 Budget introduced large tax increases, which resulted in massive losses in May's local elections and huge anti-Labour swings in by-elections. Having already lost Hamilton—previously a very safe seat—to the SNP (in the person of Winnie Ewing) in November 1967, Labour lost a further six seats to the Conservatives in the thirteen by-elections in England from March 1968 to March 1969. All of the latter had double-digit swings against the government, averaging 15.6 per cent. In the Gallup poll in May 1968, at the nadir of the government's fortunes, Labour registered 28 per cent of voting intentions against 56 per cent for the Conservatives.

There was little respite during the rest of 1968—the country was plagued by industrial disputes, and another deflationary Budget was introduced in November in order to sustain the new and reduced value of sterling. At the start of 1969, the outlook for the government was still bleak, as it engaged in a brief but bitter struggle with its own supporters in the trade unions over plans to reform industrial relations. From the summer of 1969, however, there was at last some indication that all the pain would pay off, as the balance of payments figures showed a marked improvement, and Labour subsequently began to creep back up in the polls (Figure 2.3).

Labour's revival reflected the fact that the Conservatives had problems of their own in this period. Disagreement between the main parties concerned detail rather than fundamental principle, so the Opposition could do little more than plead that they would manage very similar policies more competently than Labour. The problem was that Edward Heath continued to underwhelm the voters—despite the travails of the government, he only rarely achieved net positive personal ratings from Gallup respondents. Moreover, there were bitter divisions within the Conservative Party over the legacy of empire—reflected particularly in attitudes to Rhodesia and the related issue of race. In April 1968, Enoch Powell, the Wolverhampton MP, delivered his famous 'rivers of blood' speech in which he warned of dire consequences flowing from unrestricted

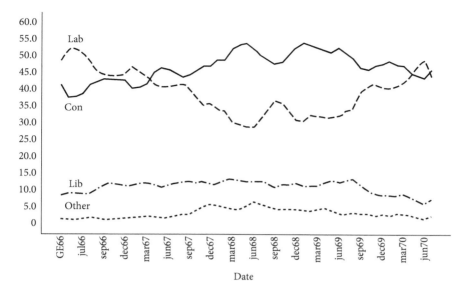

Figure 2.3 Monthly voting intentions, 1966–70 (Gallup)

Notes: The 1966 and 1970 election results in Great Britain form the starting and finishing points. The data have been smoothed by plotting the three-monthly moving average in each case.

immigration. The next day, Heath sacked him from the shadow cabinet. Powell had considerable support among grassroots party members (as well as London dockworkers, who marched to Parliament to demonstrate in his favour), and his intervention exacerbated Tory divisions on the Race Relations bill that was then going through the House of Commons.

The performance of the Liberals throughout the 1966–70 parliament was oddly flat. Despite an unpopular government and not very popular Opposition, they simply failed to make an impact. They did clinch one by-election success in Birmingham Ladywood in June 1969, but this was mainly down to local factors as their candidate, Wallace Lawlor, was a popular local councillor. The most significant event for Liberals was the resignation of Jo Grimond as leader in January 1967. His replacement, Jeremy Thorpe, was a flamboyant parliamentary performer and an ebullient campaigner; but the 1970 Nuffield study credited him with 'wit rather than weight' (Butler and Pinto-Duschinsky, 1971: 114) and his party subsequently had grave reasons to regret his elevation.

In contrast to the unexciting performance of the Liberals, 'others' made a significant appearance in the inter-election polls for the first time ever. In November and December 1967, they rose to an unprecedented 6.0 and 6.5 per cent of voting intentions, and hit a new height of 7 per cent in July 1968 before gradually fading.

The 'others' concerned were, almost exclusively, the SNP and Plaid Cymru, and the increase in their support both underlay and was boosted by sensational by-election results. In Wales, the Plaid breakthrough came in Carmarthen in July 1966, where the party, in the person of Gwynfor Evans, its long-standing President, leapt from third place to seize the seat from Labour with an 18 per cent swing. Although no more seats were gained, Plaid came a good second in two very safe Labour constituencies (Rhondda West and Caerphilly) in later by-elections. In Scotland, the SNP contested the Glasgow Pollok by-election in March 1967, finishing a creditable third with 28 per cent of the votes. As already noted, in November of the same year Winnie Ewing sensationally took the previously very safe Labour seat of Hamilton with 46 per cent of votes, despite there having been no SNP candidate in that constituency in either 1964 or 1966. This triumph instigated an upsurge in SNP support in Scotland. In the local elections of May 1968, the party took just over 30 per cent of the votes, winning more than 100 council seats. Although it was not clear to all observers at the time, the nationalist parties in both Scotland and Wales were henceforth significant players in the electoral game in their respective countries. Their new electoral prominence clearly owed much to deep-rooted local factors; but it also arose from a more general sense of dissatisfaction, which was beginning to undermine the traditional dominance of the main UK parties.

Responding to symptoms of strain within the UK, Wilson established a Royal Commission on the Constitution in April 1969. A typical Wilsonian attempt to kick a topical and ticklish issue into the long grass, the Commission did not report until 1973. By September 1969 there was evidence that his main concern, the economy, had turned the corner; the balance of payments had moved into surplus. The effect was a sharp closing of the gap between Labour and the Conservatives in the polls. Although there was a slight reversal in January–March 1970, the Budget in the latter month was well received (although it was by no means over-generous), and in April the Conservative lead was only 4.5 points. This was merely the prelude to a dramatic turn-around; in two polls in May, Gallup reported significant Labour leads of around seven points. The temptation was too much for Wilson to resist, and in mid-May he announced that an election would be held on 18 June.

Observers and participants had long been aware that there tended to be a regular pattern in party support between elections. At least since the 1950s, governing parties generally became more unpopular between elections and the main opposition benefitted—leading in the opinion polls, making gains in local elections, and winning seats in parliamentary by-elections. As the next general election approached, however, support usually flowed back to the governing party. 'Mid-term blues' were forgotten, and the big opposition leads previously recorded were whittled away. Although there were occasional 'random shocks' (such as the election of a new party leader), producing sudden changes in the parties' fortunes, the effect of these was usually short-lived, and the basic pattern was quickly re-established. Many commentators have attributed this cycle in government popularity to the effects of a parallel economic cycle. After a government was elected (or re-elected), harsh deflationary measures were often implemented; but as the next election approached the economy would begin to improve, and governments would take more voter-friendly decisions. The 'misery index', combining inflation and unemployment levels, was found to be a good predictor of government popularity (Goodhart and Bhansali, 1970). Whatever explains it, the 1966–70 parliament provides a particularly clear example of the electoral cycle. The popularity of the governing party fell steeply to the lowest level ever measured, yet Labour recovered sufficiently to enter the 1970 campaign as hot favourites to win.

Labour's chances were unaffected by an incident which would have caused a sensation in more recent times. A fortnight before announcing the election date, Wilson physically assaulted a young BBC reporter, John Simpson, on Platform 7 of London's Euston station. The inexperienced Simpson had been audacious enough to approach the Prime Minister in the quest for a quote about election rumours. Wilson's violent response was observed by several representatives of the media (including photographers); but the story was not publicized during the campaign or, indeed, during Wilson's lifetime. Far from speculating that Wilson's conduct might cost his party the forthcoming election—or that the Prime Minister might make history by appearing before a magistrate—those who witnessed the fracas thought that it would cost Simpson his job (Simpson, 1999: 92–4). Clearly, the rules of engagement between politicians and the media were heavily tilted towards the former, even at the end of a decade which had been notable for a decline in deference.

The 1970 Campaign

The 1970 campaign was conducted in blazing sunshine throughout. After a quiet first week, in which the only issue to arouse much interest was the question of whether the impending tour by the South African cricket team should be cancelled (it was, following a request by the Home Secretary), the parties got down to what could by now be described as the rituals of national campaigning—press conferences, leaders' tours, and broadcasts. There was one difference, however, in that the Prime Minister now preferred 'walkabouts' to formal meetings. The Conservative leader, Heath, initially planned to address mostly ticket-only meetings as in 1966, but his schedule was soon amended to include additional walkabouts.

Despite the facts that one of Labour's posters was entitled 'Labour's Winning Team' and a flattering collective profile of senior Conservatives was published just before the election, the campaigns of both parties focused more than ever on their leaders (Stacey and St Oswald, 1970). The press largely portrayed the contest as one of Wilson versus Heath. Towards the end of the campaign, however, a strike by printers meant that no national papers appeared from 10 to 13 June. The most reported figure after the two main party leaders was Enoch Powell. His election address called for an end to immigration, and provoked an intemperate response from Anthony Wedgwood Benn (as he then was), implicitly comparing Powell and his supporters to Nazis. As a consequence, Powell received more coverage in both the press and television news than all Liberal politicians combined.

Partly because of the fine weather (and partly also because there was competition from the football World Cup), viewing figures for television programmes on the election, and party election broadcasts specifically, were down on 1966. Even so, some 8.5 million people watched the *least* viewed election broadcast. While Labour and Liberal broadcasts followed a familiar pattern, those by the Conservatives were innovative and effective. All five were introduced jointly by two politicians with professional television experience, Chris Chataway and Geoffrey Johnson-Smith, who mimicked a pair of quick-fire news presenters. Much use was made of 'vox pops' and there were even mini 'adverts', such as a pound note being cut in half to represent the 'ten bob pound' that was claimed to be the result of Labour's policies. As in 1966, Heath appeared in the last broadcast and was generally thought to have done a competent job, especially in contrast to Wilson, who for understandable reasons concentrated on exposing the perceived inadequacies of the Opposition. Overall, Martin Harrison described the Conservative broadcasts as 'the most striking attempt yet seen in a series of party broadcasts to reach the television audience through the verbal and visual idiom to which it has become accustomed', and having 'a professional polish never previously achieved in party election broadcasts' (Harrison, 1971: 220, 224).

In the constituencies, there were signs that Labour's 'mid-term blues' had inflicted lasting damage; the battering that the party had taken in local elections in 1968 and 1969 severely dented morale and weakened organization. In addition, divisions over some of the government's policies had contributed to an outflow of members and activists. Conversely, the Conservatives had been boosted, so that in terms of organizational strength the gap between them and Labour was wider than ever. By the time of the election, for example, the number of Labour full-time agents had declined to 141, while the Conservatives employed almost 400. Before and during the campaign, the Conservatives concentrated more intensively than ever on 'critical' seats—providing extra resources from the centre to the key constituency battlegrounds.

Underlying the whole campaign, however, was the steady drumbeat of the opinion polls, which dominated newspaper and television reportage as never before, partly because the newspapers which commissioned them had dropped their rights to exclusive publication since 1966. The relentless story told by the polls was that Labour was going to be re-elected (see Appendix, Figure 2.A3). Using the averages of published polls, Labour led by 3.4 points in the first week of the campaign, and by the fourth week this advantage had widened to 6.5 points. Things tightened again in the final week, as Labour's reported advantage was reduced to 3.1 points. Even so, four of the five final polls forecast a Labour victory (by between two and nine points), while only one (ORC) gave the Conservatives the edge, by 46.5 to 45.5 per cent of the vote. The message of the polls was absorbed by the public. Marplan found in mid-June that 67 per cent of voters thought that Labour would win the election, with only 14 per cent predicting a Conservative victory. Ladbrokes, at one point, offered odds of 20-1 *on* Labour winning. Among commentators a Labour victory was universally anticipated. However, Edward Heath apparently remained steadfastly optimistic, and, although their views might have been affected by hindsight, many Conservative candidates subsequently reported that their canvassing experiences were much more positive than the message of the published polls.

In the last week of the campaign, however, two events occurred which may have altered the atmosphere in which votes were cast. First, on the Sunday before polling, the England team was knocked out of the football World Cup. At the time, political commentators tended to compartmentalize current events, assuming that the public regarded elections as entirely separate from what was going on in sport. However, even Anthony Wedgwood Benn recorded in his diary that the defeat was likely to affect the public mood in the last days of the campaign—and Benn did not add the morale-sapping details that the team had allowed a 2-0 lead to slip away, resulting in a quarter-final defeat to West Germany, of all countries (Benn, 1989: 292).

On the day after England's World Cup defeat, the balance of payments figures for May were published, revealing a deficit of £31 million. This was a serious embarrassment to Labour campaigners, who had been making much of previous, more encouraging, figures as evidence of the party's success in restoring the health of the economy. Apart from those who spoke for the party in the national campaign, more than three-quarters of Labour candidates had claimed in their election address that the balance of payments was strong (Butler and Pinto-Duschinsky, 1971: 437). Benn had thought on the previous day that 'we are going to win quite comfortably', but he quickly realized the significance of the figures and urged Wilson to make a robust defence. The Prime Minister, however, told him not to worry (Benn, 1989: 292). While Benn continued to fret on the eve of polling that Labour's campaign had been too complacent, his colleague Richard Crossman was explaining in his own diary why Wilson had got it right. In his view, Labour was about to register an effortless triumph, emulating the 1959 victory of Harold Macmillan's Conservatives (Crossman, 1977). Crossman, a former Oxford University Fellow, had failed to appreciate that the electorate in 1970 was already more volatile than it had been in Macmillan's day.

The 1970 Results

Whether the bad sporting and economic news at the last gasp made the difference or not, the election outcome stunned almost everyone and was a major blow for the polling companies. With a swing of 4.7 per cent in their favour, the Conservatives won an overall majority of thirty seats. Among the Labour losers was George Brown, the party's deputy leader, who had stumped the country as in 1964 and 1966, addressing ninety-eight meetings in two weeks. This was aptly described as 'the last of the old style campaigns' (Butler and Pinto-Duschinsky, 1971: 147), mounted by a politician whose spectacular lapses into insobriety made him unsuitable for the demands of the new-style media. The Liberals saw their parliamentary tally halved to six—so that once again the entire Parliamentary Liberal Party could be accommodated inside a single taxi. Although the SNP lost Hamilton, it took Western Isles (the party's first-ever win in a general election) to keep a toehold in the House. The five 'others' elected comprised four from Northern Ireland and the 83-year-old S. O. Davies, triumphantly returned as an Independent after being denied re-nomination by the local Labour Party in Merthyr Tydfil. Only twelve seats across the country recorded a Conservative to Labour swing, and most of these are easily explicable by local circumstances. Nonetheless, the trend towards geographical polarization of party support continued, with Labour holding up better in Scotland and big cities than elsewhere.

Turnout in the 1970 election, at 72.0 per cent, was the lowest since 1935. It peaked at 85.3 per cent in Cornwall North but was less than 50 per cent in nine seats (all in inner London). Variations across the country were much as before, although there was a big decline in the Potteries where the election coincided with local holidays. Although the ill-founded expectation of a third successive Labour victory might have played a part, the low turnout was more likely to be explained by the recent extension of the franchise to 18–21-year-olds. Then, as now, young people were very poor at turning out to vote. Another change introduced in 1970—extending the hours of polling from 9 p.m. to 10 p.m.—obviously made no difference (other than to delay the counting of votes and announcement of the results). Although unrelated to turnout, it is also worth noting that this was the first election at which candidates were allowed to provide a description—a party label in almost all cases—beside their name on the ballot paper. It was a telling change, reflecting the overwhelming importance of the party allegiance of candidates. It could no longer be assumed—if it had ever been true—that the local electorate would be familiar with the names (let alone the personal qualities) of rival candidates.

The consensus in explaining the inaccuracy of most opinion polls was that there had been a late swing to the Conservatives among the voters, which was not detected by most polling companies because they stopped interviewing respondents too soon. ORC had avoided this pitfall, and alone predicted a Conservative lead in votes. Other firms would not forget this lesson. The World Cup explanation of sudden defections from Labour is somewhat deflated (though not entirely punctured) by the fact that in Scotland and Wales there were also swings to the Conservatives, albeit smaller in Scotland than in England. In these parts of the UK, England's footballing misfortunes are unlikely to have been greeted with widespread disappointment. The balance of payments announcement and Mr Heath's impressive last broadcast appeal are more likely to have pricked Labour's bubble.

The swing in 1970 was greater than at any previous post-war election; and yet Labour's recovery in the polls from the spring of 1968 to 1970 had also been unprecedented. Together, these facts strongly suggested that there was now greater volatility among an electorate that had previously been regarded as eminently stable in its support for one party or another. During the next decade, however, electoral volatility increased further, to heights undreamed of in the 1960s.

Explaining Voting Behaviour: 1964–70

The first edition of David Butler and Donald Stokes's *Political Change in Britain*, subtitled *Forces Shaping Electoral Choice*, was published in 1969. A second edition, incorporating material on the 1970 election, appeared in 1974. This hugely influential book[2] reported the results of the first ever national academic surveys of voting behaviour, previous work having been confined to individual constituencies or towns.

Butler and Stokes paid scant attention to turnout. They noted that people may vote to influence the outcome of the election (instrumental motive), to express support for their party (expressive), or because they feel it is their duty to do so (normative). They also included differential turnout from one election to the next as a factor affecting electoral change but provided no data or sustained discussion on who votes, who doesn't, and why.

The broad explanatory framework advanced by Butler and Stokes to account for party choice has already been introduced (Chapter 1). As explained there, class voting and party identification were the twin pillars, as it were, sustaining a system in which party support was generally stable. By and large, working-class people voted for (and identified with) Labour; the middle class voted for (and identified with) the Conservatives. Summarizing in terms of a crude non-manual/ manual workers distinction, over the three elections from 1964, on average, the former voted 62 per cent Conservative, 25 per cent Labour, and 12 per cent Liberal. The division of support among manual workers was 29 per cent Conservative, 64 per cent Labour, and 7 per cent Liberal. The differences between solidly middle-class professional and managerial groups and unskilled manual workers in terms of their support for the Conservatives and Labour were even more marked. As Butler and Stokes commented (1969: 76):

> Our findings on the strength of links between class and partisanship in Britain echo broadly those of every other opinion poll or voting study . . . there were strong enough cross-currents in each class for partisanship not to have been determined entirely by class. Yet its pre-eminent role can hardly be questioned.

The same point had been made more memorably two years previously by Peter Pulzer, who asserted that 'Class is the basis of British party politics; all else is embellishment and detail' (1967: 98). This is not to deny that there was much of interest in the 'embellishment and detail'. There were, for example, significant differences in voting patterns relating to sex, age, religion, and region. Regardless of class, women were consistently more Conservative than men, older voters more than younger voters, Anglicans more than Nonconformists, Catholics, or those with no religious affiliation; and those who lived in the South more than those in the North, Wales, and Scotland. The important (and obvious) question of why about a third of the working class continued to support the Conservatives also received a good deal of attention, including two significant books on the subject (Nordlinger, 1967; McKenzie and Silver, 1968). Probably the most convincing explanation of this phenomenon was offered by Butler and Stokes themselves, who argued that working-class Conservative support was at least partly a product of Labour's relatively late arrival as a major party. Loyalties to other parties had already been established and passed down through families, so that it required major disruptions to socialization patterns—such as those caused by both the First and the Second World War—for Labour to make electoral breakthroughs. It is no accident that the party first became more than part of the political fringe in elections of the 1920s, and that it was the 1945 election that saw it form a majority government for the first time.

   As far as party identification is concerned, over the 1964, 1966, and 1970 elections Butler and Stokes found that on average 90 per cent of survey respondents identified with a specific party (81 per cent with Conservative or Labour), and 40 per cent described themselves as 'very strong' Conservative or Labour identifiers. Party identification is conceptually distinct from voting for a party. It is something that is *ongoing* while voting is *episodic*; it is *psychological*—existing in people's heads—while voting is *behavioural* and can, in principle at least, be directly observed. Identification also *varies in intensity*—some people support a party strongly while others are more lukewarm—whereas a vote cast enthusiastically counts the same as one arising from a temporary whim. According to Butler and Stokes, most individuals developed a party identification through socialization in the family and community more generally and, once acquired, this usually remained stable. On election day, the party identifier did not really have a decision to make: he or she would vote (and the stronger the party identification the greater the likelihood of turning out) to support the party that he or she had always supported.

Notably absent from this discussion is any mention of voters' opinions on issues or party leaders; but these were, in fact, investigated quite thoroughly by Butler and Stokes. In order for an issue to affect someone's vote, they argued, three conditions must be fulfilled. First, the voter must have some awareness of the issue concerned. Second, he or she must have some attitude towards or opinion about the issue. Third, the voter must perceive different parties as having distinctive policies on the issue. To qualify as an 'issue voter', the individual must then vote for the party perceived to be closest to his or her own position.

On reviewing the evidence, Butler and Stokes found that large numbers of voters fell at each of these hurdles. In relation to awareness, for example, 40 per cent of respondents to the 1964 BES survey were unable to name two important questions facing the country, and fully 80 per cent had minimal (or no) recognition of the meaning of the terms 'left' and 'right' in a political context. Politics and political issues were simply peripheral to most people's concerns. In addition, even when they were aware of an issue, many voters did not really have 'genuine' attitudes towards the issues concerned. Over four interviews, for example, less than half (43 per cent) of BES respondents were consistent in either supporting or opposing further nationalization—an issue that had been at the centre of political controversy in Britain for a long time and on which the parties took clearly different stances. Perception of differences between the parties on specific issues (the third condition for issue voting) varied considerably, depending upon the nature of the issue. On 'big' or broad issues, such as welfare spending or nationalization, most voters were able to perceive a difference between the Conservatives and Labour; but on a series of more precise or detailed policy questions (and also on immigration) this was not the case. In addition, 1960s voters were notably unable to assign policy stances of any kind to the Liberals. Finally, even voters who passed the first three issue-voting tests frequently flunked the last one. Despite having an opinion which they knew was contrary to a party's policy, some would nevertheless go ahead and vote for that party. In sum, then, voting in the era of partisan and class alignment can fairly be described as virtually 'issueless'. Voters were as likely to change their policy preferences to fit their party as they were to change their party to fit their policy position.

A similar conclusion was reached regarding the influence of party leaders on party choice. As would be expected, Butler and Stokes found that the Prime Minister and Leader of the Opposition were highly visible figures about whom most voters had opinions. But these opinions were themselves largely produced by a voter's pre-existing party identification. When assessments of the leaders and the parties were in conflict, it was the latter which proved more influential. As if to prove the point, Harold Wilson was preferred as Prime Minister over Edward Heath in 1970; yet it was the Conservatives who won the election.

The Butler and Stokes model portrayed an electorate that was largely stable in its party choice. Somewhat ironically, a book entitled *Political Change* largely explained why the British electoral process exhibited such remarkable *stability* in the early post-war period. Nonetheless, even in the first edition of their book, Butler and Stokes noted a potential weakening of the class alignment—a key source of stability. By the second edition they had more solid evidence, and also noted that the electorate was displaying greater volatility in party choice. In recognition of this, the second edition was subtitled *The Evolution of Electoral Choice*. Nonetheless, evolution is a slow process, and Butler and Stokes still expected future electoral change to be slow and incremental. As the next chapter shows, however, this expectation soon proved to be misplaced.

Appendix: Campaign Polls

Here and in subsequent chapters we show the mean weekly results of all published campaign polls of voting intentions. For this purpose we have made extensive use of the invaluable collection of poll results made available by Mark Pack (see https://www.markpack.org.uk/opinion-polls/). We define 'campaign' polls as those for which data collection ended after the announcement of the election date. The 'result' shown in Figures 2.A1–2.A3 relates to Great Britain, as Northern Ireland is not included in national opinion polls.

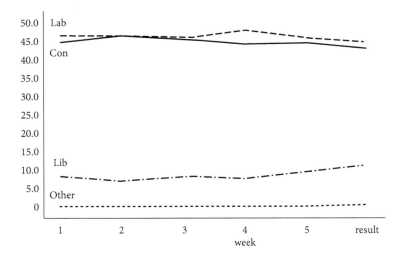

Figure 2.A1 Campaign polls, 1964

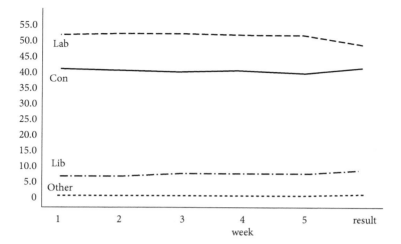

Figure 2.A2 Campaign polls, 1966

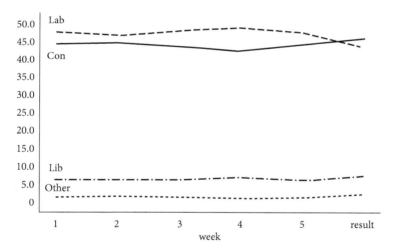

Figure 2.A3 Campaign polls, 1970

Notes

1. 'Swing' is a measure of net electoral change involving two parties. It is defined as follows:

$$\frac{(C2 - C1) + (L1 - L2)}{2}$$

C1 is the percentage share of the total vote obtained by the Conservatives at the first election and C2 the percentage at the second; L1 is Labour's share at the first election and L2 Labour's percentage at the second. A positive score indicates a swing to the

Conservatives; if the score is negative the swing is to Labour. This formula relates to 'Butler' or 'total vote' swing—which we use throughout the book. A variant known as 'Steed' or 'two-party' swing ignores votes for all other parties so that the two major parties' vote shares always total 100 per cent.

2. In 2010, it was voted the best British book in political science published over the previous fifty years by members of the Political Studies Association (PSA). David Butler was able to accept the award in person.

3

'Decade of Dealignment'

Elections, 1974–9

The Conservative government that took office under Edward Heath in 1970 suffered remarkably bad luck, not all of its own making. It was beset by industrial unrest at home and the shock of a steep rise in the price of key imported commodities (notably oil) in 1973. Although negotiating Britain's entry into what was then known as the European Economic Community (EEC) was then (and remained, of course) a subject of fierce controversy within and between parties, Heath at least succeeded in this respect where Macmillan and Wilson had failed. Attempts were made to reform the policy-making process (by creating the Central Policy Review Staff, for example) and amalgamate government departments. A major—and, given that some historic boundaries were altered, inevitably controversial—overhaul of the structure of local government was undertaken. However, the abiding image of this government is of a series of policy reversals and an inability to control either the trade unions or rampant price inflation. Alan Clark, the Conservative diarist and historian who entered the House in February 1974, later summed up the experience of the Heath government as 'the most frustrating and melancholy of all interludes in the Conservative Party's twentieth century history' (Clark, 1999: 411).

An early indication that the Heath government would not be the favourite of fortune came within a month of the 1970 election, when the new Chancellor of the Exchequer, Iain Macleod (no economist, but a shrewd tactician and a brilliant orator) died suddenly at the age of 56. Thereafter, it was economic and industrial policy which proved the government's undoing, forcing it to change course more than once in what were derided by sections of the press as a series of 'U-turns'. Initially the focus was on the battle against inflation, but that priority was superseded in a 'dash for growth' from July 1971, followed by renewed concerns about inflation after the summer of 1973. In the end, the counter-inflation strategy made little difference, as British consumers were forced to adjust to a world of inexorable increases in prices.

At first, the Conservatives seemed to be advocating a return to the operation of the free market as a remedy for economic problems which had arisen under the interventionist Labour governments of 1964–70. Harold Wilson knowingly exaggerated the extent to which Heath and his colleagues wished to depart from the general post-war approach—most crudely, by depicting a fairly inconclusive

British General Elections Since 1964: Diversity, Dealignment, and Disillusion. Second Edition. David Denver and Mark Garnett, Oxford University Press. © David Denver and Mark Garnett 2021. DOI: 10.1093/oso/9780198844952.003.0003

meeting of Heath and his shadow cabinet at the Selsdon Park Hotel in Surrey as an attempt to revive a prehistoric brand of cut-throat capitalism (Garnett, 2005: 211–14). Failing firms ('lame ducks') would not be bailed out by the government, and the levels of prices and incomes would be determined by the market. But for all their tough talk at the outset, senior ministers were petrified by the prospect of mass unemployment and its possible political consequences. This fear prompted the government to nationalize a major firm (Rolls-Royce) as early as February 1971; intervene to restructure Upper Clyde Shipbuilders; and introduce a statutory prices and incomes policy (with a Pay Board and a Prices Commission to administer it) in 1972.

Throughout these years, industrial relations proved a consistent source of difficulty. An Industrial Relations Act was passed (1971) which, among other things, required unions to register with an official body in order to obtain various legal immunities. This served only to sour the atmosphere between unions and the government. Union protests against the Act were loud and long, and the Trades Union Congress (TUC) instructed its members not to register. Meanwhile, strikes by workers were frequent and bitter. Those involving key groups of workers—in electricity supply, the docks, railways, and, especially, coal mines—were extremely disruptive. Unions saw themselves as defending their members' standard of living in inflationary times, while the government argued that inflationary wage awards simply made things worse. The fact is, however, that industrial militancy appeared to pay off in the short term and the government was unable to do anything about it. Commentators feared that over-mighty unions, able to 'hold the country to ransom', were on course to make the United Kingdom ungovernable (King, 1975). The latter impression was reinforced by the re-emergence of political violence on the mainland, as the Irish Republican Army (IRA) sought to advance its argument for a united Ireland with bombs and bullets.

Given the difficulties encountered by the government, it was no surprise that the popularity of the Conservatives declined swiftly after they assumed office (Figure 3.1). There was a mini-recovery in the second half of 1971, followed by a further decline which was gentle until the spring of 1973 and then fairly sharp. Labour, meanwhile, peaked in the summer of 1971 and then drifted downwards right through to the general election. The big surprise in the trends in party support during these years was the sudden upsurge in Liberal support, which began in late 1972. Doubtless reflecting widespread dissatisfaction with the two major parties, it involved and was spurred on by some spectacular victories in by-elections—Rochdale and Sutton and Cheam in 1972 and Isle of Ely, Ripon, and Berwick-upon-Tweed in 1973. In addition, in the latter year, the Liberals made dramatic advances in English local elections. Although Liberal support declined from its peak in late 1973, the party nonetheless entered the first of two 1974 elections in a stronger position than had been seen in the post-war period.

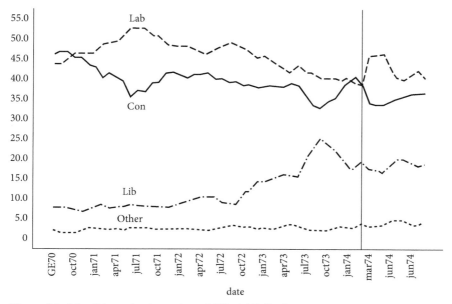

Figure 3.1 Monthly voting intentions, 1970–4 (Gallup)

Notes: The 1970 and October 1974 election results in Great Britain form the starting and finishing points. The February 1974 election is indicated by a vertical line. The data have been smoothed by plotting the three-monthly moving average in each case.

The coming of the election in February 1974 is itself a dramatic story. In late 1973, the National Union of Mineworkers (NUM) sought to exploit the oil crisis by putting in for wage increases which would clearly breach the norms set by the prices and incomes policy and, in support of this claim, called an overtime ban. In response, the government declared a state of emergency which placed restrictions on electricity supply. This involved, among other things, stopping television programmes at 10.30 p.m. As negotiations with the miners' representatives got nowhere and the situation was exacerbated by a work-to-rule by train drivers, the government announced in mid-December that a three-day working week would be introduced on 1 January in order to save electricity. Later in January, the NUM decided to hold a strike ballot, and the result, announced on 4 February, was a large majority in favour. Over the previous few weeks there had been intense speculation about whether an election would be called. Opinion polls had given the government some encouragement—as Figure 3.1 shows, the gap between the major parties disappeared in the last months of 1973. On 7 February Mr Heath announced the date of the general election (28 February). As the Nuffield study comments, 'it was unprecedented for an outside challenge to government policy to force a dissolution' (Butler and Kavanagh, 1975: 44), but the Prime Minister was caught between the prospect of a damaging strike, on the one hand, and the resistance of the Conservative Party to anything that smacked of surrender, on the other. Characteristically, Heath refused to exploit the crisis for electoral gain when the sense of panic was at its height. By the time he was persuaded to call the election, the power cuts and other restrictions were becoming a source of public irritation rather than a reason to rally behind the government.

The February 1974 Campaign

The campaign in February 1974 was short and—against expectations—relatively tranquil. Not unexpectedly, the miners' strike, which began on 10 February, dominated the first full week of campaigning. This suited the Conservatives, who wanted the election to be about the need to uphold government authority, the importance of the prices and incomes policy, and the menace of union militancy. Labour, for its part, wanted price rises—especially rises in the cost of food—to be at the top of the electorate's agenda. Initially, as the Conservative agenda dominated, the government established a clear lead over the Opposition in the polls and appeared to be heading for victory (see Appendix, Figure 3.A1). Given the government's need to secure a decisive public vote of confidence, however, its lead over Labour was never very impressive; and over the course of the campaign a series of events undermined the Conservative position. First, the government itself announced that the miners' pay claim would be referred to the Pay Board, and that it would accept the Board's decision on any increase. This raised questions about Heath's decision to call a crisis election in the first place. Later, on 21 February, the Pay Board revealed new statistics which suggested that miners' pay, instead of being relatively high for manual workers in manufacturing, was actually below average. This finding was strongly disputed but it received wide publicity, and seemed to vindicate the miners' case in the dispute rather than that of the government.

The Pay Board's intervention was not the only statistical problem for the Conservative campaign. On 15 February, the retail price index showed a record level of monthly price inflation, while publication of the balance of trade figures revealed the largest ever monthly deficit—twelve times the level that had caused Labour such discomfiture in June 1970. These data, of course, were gleefully seized on by Wilson and his colleagues to support their argument that the government was hopelessly incompetent. Finally, in the last week of the campaign, Enoch Powell, who had announced his decision to stand down as an MP at the start of the campaign, urged voters to make Europe their key concern, and revealed that he himself had already voted Labour (by post). Given that he was not even a candidate, it is remarkable that Powell attracted front-page coverage in the national press on five days during the short campaign.

These distractions prevented the Conservatives from keeping the electorate's attention focused on the problem of industrial relations. Over four campaign polls, Gallup reported that the percentage nominating strikes as the most urgent problem facing the country fell from 34 per cent at the outset to 23 per cent in the last week. Meanwhile, the proportion nominating prices rose from 35 per cent to 49 per cent. However, the Conservative decline was not entirely to Labour's benefit. Although the gap between Labour and the Conservatives narrowed somewhat, it was still at 3.3 points in the last week of the campaign. Harold Wilson was not dispirited, however, thinking that 'the Liberals will help us' by taking votes from the Conservatives (Donoughue, 2005: 33). Certainly, the Liberals were advancing steadily. It seems unlikely that this had much to do with the Liberal campaign per se, since the party's programme and tactics had barely changed compared with recent elections and had not previously resulted in conspicuous success. In this case, however, recent advances in local government provided the Liberals with more solid electoral bases and enabled them to capitalize on the mood of disillusion with the major parties. The governing performance of both parties since 1964 could hardly inspire confidence, and the Liberals benefitted from the fact that they had no recent record in office to defend.

In terms of the parties' campaigning activities, February 1974 provided few innovations. One oddity, however, was that the Liberal leader, Jeremy Thorpe, directed affairs from his North Devon constituency (where he was defending a majority of only 362 votes), being interviewed on television and appearing at press conferences via a specially installed visual link. His enforced absence from London probably helped him appear to be above the 'yah-boo' party squabbling, which fitted well with the general Liberal line. It is also worth noting that for the first time Labour undertook daily polling, with Robert Worcester of MORI reporting every morning to the campaign committee. MORI's findings did little to minimize the scale of the challenge facing Labour; as late as the Saturday before election day, the private polling suggested that the party was trailing by seven points (Donoughue, 2005: 33).

As was normal by now, the election was covered comprehensively by the broadcast media, with television providing 'a fuller and more varied service than ever before' according to Martin Harrison (1974: 152). The BBC broadcast an hour-long, mid-evening news programme on television every weekday, while ITN extended *News at Ten* to forty-seven minutes. There were various attempts to involve ordinary voters in election programmes, and in this respect the BBC's *Election Call* was regarded a major success. It was broadcast daily on Radio 4 at 9 a.m., and featured members of the public putting questions to the politicians by phone. The programme regularly attracted an audience of more than a million and, although the approach had been prefigured in 1964 by *Election Forum*, Harrison (1974: 158) suggested that 'a new campaign tradition had been born' in that the participating politicians now had to engage directly, live on air, with callers.

The February 1974 Results

Despite their difficulties during the campaign, the Conservatives retained their lead over Labour to the last; all of the six polls published on polling day showed a Conservative lead ranging from two to five points. In this context, the results of the February election brought a surprising end to what was in any case a remarkable interlude in British politics (Table 3.1). First, while the Conservatives did indeed win most votes—although only just—Labour won most seats (301). This was not enough for an overall majority, but the outcome was certainly a defeat for Heath and the Conservatives. Second, the Liberal surge in the opinion polls had not been misleading; the party's vote share in Britain increased by almost 14 percentage points as compared with 1970. We have already suggested that the reasons for this did not indicate a wave of warmth towards the Liberal Party itself. Even so, the result marked a step change in the nature of the British party system—at least in terms of support among the electorate. Third, the nationalist parties made significant progress. In Scotland, the SNP's vote share almost doubled, from 11.4 per cent in 1970 to 21.9 per cent, which yielded the party seven seats. As well as profiting from general disillusion with the major parties, the SNP were bolstered by the recent discovery of significant oil deposits in the North Sea, which apparently undermined arguments that Scotland was too poor to go it alone. The party duly campaigned on the rather selfish-sounding slogan 'It's Scotland's Oil'. In Wales, although Plaid Cymru's share of votes declined a little, to 10.8 per cent, the party nonetheless won its first-ever seats (two) at a general election.

   Across the UK there was a swing of 1.4 per cent from the Conservatives to Labour, but the corresponding figure for Great Britain was only 0.8 per cent (the unusually large difference between the two figures being explained by the fact that the Ulster Unionists were now fighting as a separate party, having broken their historic link with the Conservatives in protest at the 1973 power-sharing Sunningdale Agreement). Scotland and Wales both countered the national trend by producing swings from Labour to Conservative (of 1.4 per cent and 1.5 per cent,

Table 3.1 Election results (UK), 1974–9

	February 1974		October 1974		1979	
	Votes	Seats	Votes	Seats	Votes	Seats
Conservative	37.9	297	35.8	277	43.9	339
Labour	37.2	301	39.3	319	36.9	269
Liberal	19.3	14	18.3	13	13.8	11
Others	5.6	23	6.6	26	5.4	16
Turnout	*78.9*		*72.9*		*76.3*	

Note: Figures for Votes are percentages.

respectively), while the results in England showed a more solid 2.4 per cent swing from Conservative to Labour. Analysis at constituency level is complicated by the fact that February 1974 saw the implementation of the first review of constituency boundaries since 1955. In almost 60 per cent of constituencies the boundaries were altered to a greater or lesser degree, with major changes being especially common in the big cities. It is worth noting, however, that there were unusually large swings to Labour in Enoch Powell's former seat of Wolverhampton South West (16.6 per cent) and in the other Wolverhampton seats (10.6 per cent in North East, 7.7 per cent in South East), as well as in some other neighbouring constituencies, such as Staffordshire South West (11.4 per cent), Dudley East (11.4 per cent), and Warley East (10.2 per cent). Even those who doubt that the 'Powell factor' played a key role in the Tory victory of 1970 would be hard pressed to deny the electoral significance of his interventions in February 1974.

Despite wet weather over most of the country, turnout in the election, at 78.8 per cent, was at its highest level for more than twenty years. This is partly explained by the fact that the electoral register was unusually fresh, but the atmosphere of crisis in which the election had been called no doubt also heightened interest. In addition, the Liberals contested many more constituencies (517) than in previous elections. While the anticipation of a close result was obviously a factor, the same had been true in 1964 and 1970. This time, however, the pre-election speculation had been briefer than in 1964; and whereas Labour supporters might have abstained though misplaced complacency in 1970, in February 1974 both of the dominant parties (as well as the minor ones) had good reasons to scramble for every vote.

The Aftermath

When an incumbent party loses a general election in Britain, the transfer of power to the winner is usually swift. Furniture vans rumble into Downing Street on the day after polling to remove the effects of the outgoing Prime Minister; the winning party leader visits the monarch that afternoon, and by the evening is photographed entering 10 Downing Street to start the business of forming a new government. In February 1974, however, the situation was not normal. For the first time since 1929 an election had failed to deliver a majority for a single party. Edward Heath was not obliged to resign and took time to consider his options. He contacted the Liberal leader, Jeremy Thorpe, to explore the possibility of forming a coalition between the two parties (although, even combined, they could not command a majority in the House of Commons). At a formal meeting between the two on the Saturday, Heath broached the possibility of reform of the electoral system as an incentive to the Liberals. A meeting of Liberal MPs on the following Monday rejected the offer, however, and Heath resigned. Harold Wilson duly became Prime Minister of a minority Labour government, which had received a smaller share of votes than the Conservatives—indeed, by far the smallest share Labour had received in any post-war election to that date. Labour's numerical support had been equally dismal; it attracted fewer votes than in 1959, when the defeat of Gaitskell's party had provoked pessimistic analyses of its long-term prospects. In the intervening years, the electorate had increased by more than four million.

The Shortest Parliament

The gap between the February and October elections in 1974 (224 days) was the shortest in modern times. Given the balance of party strength in the House of Commons, it was inevitable that a new election would be called sooner rather than later. Although the opposition parties were well aware that the public would not reward them for forcing another election quickly, it was equally clear that Labour could not embark on an ambitious programme of legislation; rather, the party would use its tenuous hold on power to prepare for an election and to do what it could to ensure an outright victory when it came. Thus the miners' strike was swiftly, if expensively, ended and, in a Budget at the end of March, the pugnacious Chancellor Denis Healey announced substantial rises in old-age pensions, a freeze on rent increases, and a programme of subsidies on the cost of food. These popular measures were balanced, however, by increased income tax. In a second Budget in July, VAT was cut from 10 per cent to 8 per cent. Overall, these policies clearly paid off for the government, as Labour enjoyed a comfortable lead over the Conservatives in opinion polls for the duration of the parliament (Figure 3.1).

As well as having to contend with a government able to announce electorally appealing changes, the Conservatives had troubles of their own. After its narrow defeat in 1964, the party had tried to renew itself by embarking on a policy review and electing a new leader. However, Sir Alec Douglas-Home had been replaced by Ted Heath only once it had become clear that Labour would not be seeking a more substantial mandate during 1965. A similar period of respite was never likely to follow February 1974. Indeed, many observers considered June to be a more plausible option for the next election than October. Even Heath's numerous detractors within the Conservative Party could appreciate the argument for leaving the incumbent leader in place until Wilson called a second election at the most propitious time for Labour. It would not be sensible to have a new leader start off with (what now looked like) an inevitable defeat on his or her first electoral outing. Heath himself was determined to hold on to the Conservative leadership, apparently unaware that this was likely to reduce rather than enhance his chances (already minimal) of a long-term political renaissance. His diminishing authority was illustrated by his inability to prevent his former cabinet colleague Sir Keith

Joseph from delivering speeches which implied that Heath (and all previous post-war party leaders) had surrendered to 'socialism' rather than preaching the pure free-market message which Joseph and his allies identified with the Conservative tradition (Denham and Garnett, 2001: 226–76).

Worryingly for both major parties, it seemed that the February surge in Liberal support was not a temporary phenomenon, despite the fact that the Liberals spent much of the time between the two 1974 general elections brooding over their narrow brush with coalition government in February. Polls suggested that large swathes of the electorate would seriously consider voting for the Liberals if they stood a realistic chance of winning outright. Perhaps emboldened by such data (even though answers to hypothetical polling questions are notoriously unreliable and *this* hypothetical scenario was particularly far-fetched), in June the party's National Executive ruled out any coalition deal offered by either Labour or the Conservatives (Butler and Kavanagh, 1975: 49). It was never clarified whether this indicated a preference for a 'grand coalition' (in which Liberals would serve alongside representatives of both major parties) or a refusal to join in any kind of governing arrangement.

In the early part of September, there was the usual intense media speculation about the likely date of the election. That was put to an end on 18 September when the Prime Minister announced that polling would be on 10 October.

The October 1974 Campaign

The public could have been forgiven for thinking that the October election of 1974 was a case of 'here we go again'. For the fourth time in a row, Mr Wilson and Mr Heath led their respective parties into battle, and their appeals on this occasion were always likely to resemble their previous pitches. The relevant Nuffield study dubbed this 'the quiet campaign', and reported that even some of those involved thought it 'a tedious and unrewarding ritual' (Butler and Kavanagh, 1975: 273). This time—as in the comparable circumstances of 1966—such a dispiriting judgement was difficult to challenge. The likely winner (Wilson) could hardly claim that only the absence of a workable parliamentary majority prevented him being a resounding success as Prime Minister. To compound the dampening effect of well-worn issues and shop-soiled leaders, the weather was miserable. Media coverage of the campaign—both on television and in the press—was considerably reduced in quantity as compared with February. This was only partly because of a strike by ITN journalists. The time devoted to the campaign by the main BBC TV evening news was halved compared with February. This did not prevent a record proportion of poll respondents (40 per cent compared with the previous high of 31 per cent in February) saying that there was far too much coverage of the election on television (Harrison, 1975: 162).

The debate between the major parties centred once again on inflation and wages. Labour's answer to the obvious problems facing the country was the 'social contract'—an agreement between trade unions (or, more correctly, trade union *leaders*) and government, whereby wage claims would be moderated in return for government action on a range of issues including prices and pensions. For his part, Edward Heath was anxious to appear conciliatory and moderate rather than abrasive and confrontational. Encouraged by the party's pollsters, he floated the idea of a government of national unity to deal with the economic problems facing the UK. Plausible enough in the abstract as a tactical response to the February result, the idea was deeply flawed in practice. Since Labour was unlikely to participate in a coalition led by Conservatives, a true government of 'national unity' was never on the cards. In addition, the gambit asked a lot of Conservative candidates and activists, since it would require them to campaign as hard as ever for a government which might include members of other parties. There was also the question of whether Heath, who was still widely regarded as a divisive figure, should express his willingness to stand down as leader if the electorate endorsed his own party's appeal for unity. In the event, it was not surprising that the Conservative presentation of the 'unity' theme failed to generate much-needed public excitement.

An IRA bomb exploded in Guildford (killing five off-duty soldiers) on the last Saturday of the campaign, but the major parties responded in the well-rehearsed bipartisan spirit, and no other major incident occurred to disturb the soporific progress towards polling day.

The unexciting nature of the campaign was reflected (and reinforced) by the results of the opinion polls, which barely changed over the four-week period (see Appendix, Figure 3.A2). Labour held a secure advantage throughout and, although the final polls somewhat overestimated the size of the lead, it was never seriously in doubt that the government would be able to continue in office with, at worst, a slim overall majority. There was also nothing to suggest further progress for the Liberals, as the party's support consistently hovered at just under 20 per cent. In Scotland, however, things were different, as it was not at all certain how the SNP would fare in relation to Labour. Indeed, the final poll by System Three (a polling firm which provided Scottish voting intention data on a monthly basis for Glasgow's *The Herald*), had the SNP leading Labour by 36 per cent to 33 per cent.

The October 1974 Results

The October 1974 election was contested by a record number of candidates (2,252 compared with 2,135 in February), but the increased choice that this represented did not prevent a decline of 6 percentage points in overall turnout across the UK compared with February (Table 3.1). Outside Northern Ireland, turnout fell in all but three seats. In Northern Ireland, turnout increased by 6.6 points in Down South (where Enoch Powell resurfaced as an Ulster Unionist) and, more modestly, in three other constituencies. To an extent, the decline in turnout represented a less accurate electoral register—the same register was still in use but more people would have died or moved since February—but there was clearly a significant real decline in participation. As before, turnout across constituencies was positively related to marginality in the previous election. The more marginal the seat, the higher was the turnout; the safer the seat, the lower the turnout. The original analysts of this relationship attributed it to the fact that the intensity of party campaigning varied with the perceived marginality or safeness of constituencies (Denver and Hands, 1974, 1985). In this election the association between marginality and turnout was stronger than ever before (correlation coefficient 0.48).

The overall swing from Conservative to Labour in October 1974 was small (2.1 per cent) and—outside Scotland—fairly consistent across Britain. Only twenty-one of the 623 mainland constituencies showed a net movement to the Conservatives, and in almost three-quarters seats in England and Wales the swing to Labour was between 1 and 4 per cent. Despite an increased number of candidates, the Liberals' vote share fell back after February's notable advance. Although they decreased overall by only 1 percentage point, in constituencies which they fought in both February and October (518) their share fell from 23.6 per cent to 20.2 per cent, leaving the party with just thirteen seats in the House of Commons. In Scotland the election outcome differed significantly from that in the rest of Britain. While Labour support remained virtually unchanged, the Conservatives' plummeted from 32.9 per cent to 24.7 per cent of votes, and the Conservative to Labour swing was 3.9 per cent. More strikingly, the SNP advanced to 30.4 per cent, winning a remarkable eleven seats as a result. In Wales, in contrast, Plaid's vote share was static.

Across the country, although Labour recorded a handy lead of 3.5 points over the Conservatives, this translated into an overall majority of just three seats (Table 3.1). In fact, Labour failed to win as many seats as would have been predicted on the basis of a uniform swing of around 2 per cent. The reason for this was that the Conservatives, while receiving their smallest vote share of the twentieth century thus far, had better results than average in marginal seats that they were defending—probably on account of superior local campaigning. So the October election was hardly the decisive victory that Labour had hoped for, and the party's next period in office looked sure to be difficult.

'Tumult': October 1974–9

If the October 1974 election was quiet, the next five years proved to be tumultuous ones in British politics. Among other developments, new leaders emerged in all three major parties (although in very different circumstances); the government was forced to negotiate a loan from the International Monetary Fund (IMF) on disadvantageous terms; and the period ended with a wave of industrial unrest in the public sector which led to renewed questions about Britain's 'governability'. All of this did nothing to enhance public confidence in political leaders or the democratic process.

Four issue areas preoccupied the government: the Common Market (as the EU was then known); Rhodesia; devolution to Scotland and Wales; and the economy in its broadest sense, including inflation, unemployment, the weakness of the pound, and industrial relations. The first of these was dealt with swiftly and, in terms of party management, successfully. The government (at least formally) fulfilled its pledge to renegotiate the terms for British accession to the Market, and in June 1975 put the issue to the people in a referendum—the first-ever national poll of its kind in British history. Although the government recommended a 'Yes' vote, individual members of the cabinet and the Labour Party as a whole were divided on the merits of entry. The Prime Minister—an instinctive 'Little Englander' whose preference for membership arose entirely from practical considerations—suspended collective cabinet responsibility to allow seven ministers to campaign on the 'No' side, although the great majority of mainstream politicians took a break from bickering and lined up for a 'Yes' vote. Public understanding of the EEC and all that membership entailed was barely affected by the campaign, but the referendum produced what was accepted even by the losing side as a decisive result. Two-thirds of those who voted supported the UK's continued membership of the Market (see Butler and Kitzinger, 1976).

The Rhodesian issue was less amenable to Wilson's tactical genius. The government maintained previous policy by refusing to countenance independence for the country while it continued to be ruled by the white minority. Throughout the period 1974–9, while virtual civil war raged in Rhodesia, there were various attempts at a settlement; but none was successful. Beyond Westminster, however, this issue excited little interest among the British population. It does not feature at all, for example, in Gallup's monthly reports on the electorate's views about the most urgent problems facing Britain during these years.

Devolution was an issue with more serious electoral ramifications. The success of the SNP in both the 1974 elections convinced the government that something had to be done to stem the nationalist tide, despite deep divisions in Labour ranks over the issue. In November 1976, a Scotland and Wales Bill, proposing elected assemblies in both countries, was brought forward. In February 1977, however, a guillotine motion introduced to try to speed up progress on the Bill was defeated—partly because of defections and abstentions among Labour MPs. This meant, effectively, that the legislation was lost and separate new Bills for Scotland and Wales had to be introduced in November 1977, providing for referendums on the proposals in the two countries. These, thanks to Liberal support for the government, finally passed in the summer of 1978.

There was to be a sting in the tail, however, as the results of the referendums were crucial in precipitating Labour's downfall.

Despite everything else going on, the economy and related issues remained crucial to the popularity or otherwise of the government. Here the news in this period was consistently bad. Unemployment rose steadily, the pound was under almost continuous pressure, and price inflation continued at record levels. Between February 1974 and the end of 1978, prices rose by more than 100 per cent. The government's responses included a voluntary (for the unions) pay policy (which developed in a series of phases), tax rises, and cuts in public expenditure—not a promising recipe for electoral success. In late 1976, as sterling plunged in value, the government was forced to apply to the IMF for a loan, which was granted on condition that the public sector borrowing requirement would be reduced by a combination of yet more public spending cuts and tax rises. The effect of these events was a slump in Labour popularity, and a significant lead for the Conservatives in voting intentions from the autumn of 1976 (Figure 3.2).

In March 1976, to general surprise, Harold Wilson announced his resignation from the premiership. The Yorkshire-born Oxford intellectual, with the Gannex raincoat and pipe-smoking affectations, had led Labour in five general elections and lost only one. But his memory was not as clear as it had been at its astonishing peak and the gravity of Britain's difficulties had sapped his appetite for office-holding. He was succeeded by James Callaghan. Labour MPs, who at this point elected the party leader, saw the genial 64-year-old Callaghan as a safe pair of hands, and he easily defeated the former left-wing firebrand Michael Foot in the final ballot.

On the Conservative side there was also a new leader. In February 1975, the former Education Secretary, Margaret Thatcher, challenged Edward Heath in a leadership election, and in the first ballot beat him into second place by 130 votes to 119. Heath—who had responded bluntly 'if you must' to Mrs Thatcher's telling him of her intention to oppose him (Thatcher, 1995: 267)—resigned immediately. In the second ballot, Thatcher was rewarded for her courage in standing against Heath by defeating four (male) rivals to become the first-ever woman to lead a major British party. Although her rhetoric was certainly more stridently right-wing than Heath's had been and her most significant ally, Sir Keith Joseph, loudly extolled the virtues of free-market capitalism, at this stage Mrs Thatcher was fairly moderate and cautious in practice.

There were two other sources of problems for the government. The first was the Labour Party itself. The National Executive Committee (NEC) and the party conference had become increasingly dominated by the left. Both of these bodies (encouraged in particular by Tony Benn—as Anthony Wedgewood Benn now styled himself) engaged in constant sniping against the government for being insufficiently 'socialist'. At the 1976 conference, for example, while Chancellor Denis Healey was negotiating the IMF loan and after the Prime Minister had made plain the need for restraint, resolutions were passed demanding massive increases in public expenditure. In a section of his conference speech written by his monetarist-influenced economist son-in-law, Peter Jay, Callaghan told the conference that although 'We used to think that you could spend your way out of a recession', this approach had simply succeeded in making inflation worse and, consequently, increased unemployment. In any case, owing to the post-war decline in Britain's relative economic position it was no longer realistic to pursue the idea (Morgan, 1997: 535). This death sentence for the 'electoral Keynesianism' practised by successive governments since 1945 was rewarded with muted applause—and duly ignored by Callaghan's party. Instead, the NEC's 'Labour's Programme 1976' proposed a wide range of new and improved welfare benefits, as well as endorsing the nationalization of banks and insurance companies.

The second problem was the government's lack of an adequate majority in the House of Commons. Although there were few issues on which the various opposition parties were likely to unite to defeat the government, by the end of 1976 the loss of three seats in by-elections had deprived Labour of its overall majority. One of these was Walsall North, formerly held by John Stonehouse, a government minister who had mysteriously disappeared after faking suicide in late 1974. He eventually turned up in Australia with his mistress but returned to face trial on various charges, including fraud. Stonehouse was imprisoned and resigned his seat. Labour lost the by-election to the Conservatives in November 1976 on a swing of 22.6 per cent. Two more seats were taken by the Conservatives in the spring of 1977, one of these being the mining seat of Ashfield in Nottinghamshire, where once again there was a swing of over 20 per cent against Labour. In response to by-election losses, Callaghan opened negotiations with David Steel, who had taken over as Liberal leader after Jeremy Thorpe had been mentioned in connection with serious criminal allegations. The talks between Steel and Callaghan produced the 'Lib–Lab pact', under which the Liberals would back the government on any matters of confidence in return for being consulted on major policy initiatives. The pact lasted until the summer of 1978.

The Liberals welcomed this arrangement because they themselves were languishing in opinion polls (Figure 3.2) and did not want to see a government led by Mrs Thatcher. With public attention focused on the battle between the two main parties, support for the Liberals declined fairly quickly after the October 1974 election. As noted above, the previous party leader had become embroiled in a scandal. Thorpe was accused of conspiracy to murder a male model who claimed to have had a homosexual affair with the Liberal leader—and supplied the press with alleged salacious details. Perhaps even worse, the plot went awry and the target's dog (Rinka) was shot (see Freeman and Penrose, 1996). Although Thorpe was later acquitted, the associated publicity did nothing to improve his party's fortunes; in stark contrast to previous inter-election periods, the Liberal vote share declined in all but two of the thirty by-elections held between October

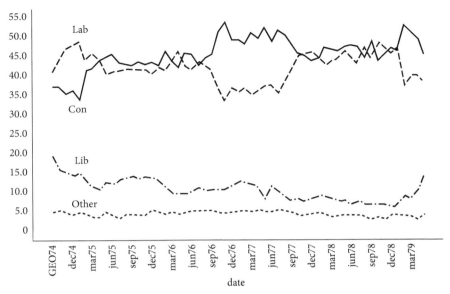

Figure 3.2 Monthly voting intentions October, 1974–9 (all polls)

Notes: The October 1974 and 1979 election results in Great Britain form the starting and finishing points. The data shown are the monthly means for all published polls.

1974 and the 1979 election. Ironically, the very last by-election of the parliament, held in March 1979 on the day after the government lost a vote of confidence in the House of Commons, resulted in a spectacular gain from Labour in Liverpool Edge Hill. Given the vicissitudes that it encountered between 1974 and 1979, the fact that Britain's third party was able to survive at all is testimony both to the devotion of its activists and the yearning of the country's voters for a viable alternative to Labour and the Conservatives.

From late 1977, however, the outlook for the government got better. The mind-boggling rate of inflation declined, the pound strengthened, the balance of payments improved, and (during 1978) unemployment began to fall. These developments were reflected in increased economic optimism among the electorate and in voting intention figures, with Labour and the Conservatives now running virtually neck and neck. It was widely expected that Labour would seize its chance and call an election in the autumn of 1978. However, Callaghan decided against. There were good enough reasons for this decision—Labour's prospects of a more comfortable parliamentary majority were very uncertain—but as things turned out it proved disastrous.

Labour's supposed trump card in appealing to the electorate was that it could deal with the unions, thus ensuring industrial peace and moderate wage settlements. Yet this strategy began to crumble when the 1978 Labour conference rejected the government's pay policy. Phase IV of the policy involved limiting wage increases to no more than 5 per cent. This ceiling was quickly exceeded following strikes at the Ford Motor Company and the BBC. In December and January, there was an outburst of industrial action by lorry drivers, ambulance drivers, local government manual workers (including some gravediggers on Merseyside), and other groups, all demanding increases well in excess of 5 per cent. With well-publicized examples of militant picketing, rubbish piling up in the streets, the sick being turned away from hospitals, and the dead left unburied, the so-called 'Winter of Discontent' was not misnamed in terms of its effects, even if media coverage tended to pay little attention to the plight of the low-paid workers who were taking action. With trade union leaders clearly unable to control their members, Labour's 'special relationship' with the unions had become a serious liability rather than an electoral asset. Although the public continued to doubt the Conservative leader's credentials, Mrs Thatcher's argument that tough measures were needed to deal with the union problem found a ready audience. In January 1979 the two parties were almost level in voting intentions; in February, the Conservative lead was sixteen points and in March, eleven points.

To compound the government's woes, its general unpopularity helped to ensure that the referendum on the devolution proposals in Scotland on 1 March produced just about the worst possible result. The division of the vote was 51.6 per cent 'Yes' to 48.4 per cent 'No'; but the Yes vote was well short of the 40 per cent of the electorate required to allow devolution to proceed (as specified by a successful amendment to the Scotland Act proposed by a (Scottish) Labour backbencher). The government had no option but to drop its plans for devolution. This outraged the SNP, whose representatives claimed that the '40 per cent rule' was unfair and that the (slim) referendum majority for devolution provided an adequate basis to implement the policy. SNP MPs tabled a motion of no confidence in the government, and the Conservatives followed suit. The parliamentary debate took place on 28 March, and ended dramatically with the government losing by one vote; had the Prime Minister insisted on the attendance of Sir Alfred Broughton, a Labour MP who was days from death, Labour would have won on the Speaker's casting vote. The next day, Callaghan announced that Parliament would be dissolved and the next general election held on 3 May.

The 1979 Campaign

The 1979 campaign was unusually protracted—partly because it encompassed Easter but also because Callaghan believed that, with Labour lagging behind the Conservatives, a lengthy campaign would give the government an opportunity to close the gap by exploiting the relative unpopularity of Mrs Thatcher. The Prime Minister's private view two weeks into the campaign was that the polls gave his party reasons for optimism, 'unless there has been one of those sea changes in public opinion towards Thatcher. If people have really decided they want a change of government, there is nothing you can do' (Donoughue, 2008: 483). Although Callaghan's remark is sometimes cited as proof that a 'sea-change' (rather than a typical swing of the electoral pendulum) had taken place, the gap did indeed gradually close (see Appendix, Figure 3.A3). Contrary to a persistent myth, it is unlikely that many voters in 1979 hoped (or feared) that the election would bring a period of 'consensus' politics to an end. On the last weekend of the campaign, an NOP poll caused jitters in the Conservative camp when it reported a small Labour lead. This proved to be a flash in the pan, however, as other polls continued to show the Conservatives clearly ahead. Meanwhile, the Liberals began to advance in the last two weeks of the campaign—benefitting, no doubt, from the unpopularity contest between the major parties.

The Conservative campaign strategy in respect of advertising, media relations, and broadcasting was masterminded by the PR firm Saatchi & Saatchi, which had taken on the job in 1978 and had produced a poster—'Labour isn't working'— which purportedly featured a long queue of unemployed people. Despite its dubious message and content—senior Conservatives knew at the time that their policies would cause much *greater* unemployment, at least in the short term, and the supposedly desperate individuals depicted were actually Young Conservatives from north London—the poster was widely admired in the advertising industry. During the campaign further posters appeared, but the main effort was on improving the leader's television image by making her seem more caring. A series of 'media events' was staged, involving Mrs Thatcher cuddling a calf, having a cup of tea with pensioners, and engaging in other such 'image-softening' activities. There was criticism from opponents that the campaign amounted to the 'selling' of Mrs Thatcher, who had been taking professional advice about her speaking style long before she became leader and had also been guided in her choice of outfits. Recognizing the importance of personal presentation, she was sensitive to the needs of the camera crews following her, asking if they needed retakes or additional material. Callaghan, on the other hand, appeared to find cameramen and journalists an irritant. Both parties, however, were anxious to avoid a personal slanging match—which was known to be unpopular with the voters—and, together with the absence of major gaffes or sensational events, this produced a relatively low-key campaign despite the apparently epoch-making outcome.

There were two significant deaths during the campaign. Just a day after the election was called—and while Parliament was still sitting—Airey Neave MP, a close confidant and supporter of Mrs Thatcher, was murdered by Irish Republicans as he drove out of the Commons' underground car park. As a consequence, security surrounding leading politicians was intense throughout the campaign. Meetings addressed by the leaders were all-ticket affairs and their travel plans were not released in advance. On 23 April, the teacher and left-wing activist Blair Peach was killed by a member of the Metropolitan Police's Special Patrol Group, during a protest against the far-right National Front in Southall. All involved in the election joined to condemn violence, however, and any impact that these events might have had was minimized.

There were four unusual features of the campaign. First, the general tone involved an odd reversal of the usual proclivities of the parties. The Conservatives were projected as the party of radical change (including having a woman and self-described 'conviction politician' as potential Prime Minister), while Labour was seen as the custodian of the status quo, with its leader pushing the message 'steady as she goes'. Second, although the Conservatives consistently led Labour in voting intentions, Jim Callaghan was clearly preferred to Margaret Thatcher as the best person to be Prime Minister. While it is likely that, although his party lost, Harold Wilson would have led Edward Heath as the favoured Prime Minister if the polls had asked such a question in 1970, 1979 was the first election for which relevant polling data are available in which there was a clear disjunction in preferences for leaders and parties—and that situation has never recurred. Third, mainly because of Callaghan's relative popularity, there was a reversal of roles on the perennial question of televised debates between the party leaders. On this occasion, the call was supported (albeit with serious misgivings) by the governing party. Mrs Thatcher herself was willing, but (to Callaghan's private relief) her senior colleagues advised against the experiment. Finally, 1979 saw the first use of telephone polling. As the Nuffield study presciently remarked, 'More will undoubtedly be heard of political telephone surveys in Britain' (Butler and Kavanagh, 1980: 269).

The 1979 Results

The Conservatives won a clear-cut (but far from crushing) victory in 1979, with a seven-point lead over Labour in the popular vote and an overall majority of forty-three seats in the House of Commons (Table 3.1). Labour's share of votes was its smallest since 1931. The overall swing, at 5.3 per cent, was the largest since the war. However, across constituencies there was greater variation in changes in party support than usual, with particularly clear evidence of a North–South divide. In Scotland, there was a swing of less than 1 per cent to the Conservatives—hardly heartening for the latter after their poor results in 1974—and in the three most northerly English regions the figure was 4.3 per cent. In the rest of Britain the swing was 5.9 per cent. The Liberals did not do as badly as their supporters had feared at the start of the campaign but still experienced a significant drop in popularity, to less than 14 per cent of the vote. Jeremy Thorpe, who had insisted on defending his North Devon seat despite his troubles, lost by more than 8,000 votes.

When the SNP precipitated the vote of confidence that led to the government's defeat and the general election, Mr Callaghan had jeered that this was an example of 'turkeys voting for Christmas', and the outcome showed that there was a lot of truth in the jibe. In Scotland, the SNP share of votes plunged from 30.4 to 17.3 per cent and the party lost nine of its eleven seats. There had also been a referendum on devolution in Wales in March 1979, and the vote was a decisive 'No' by a margin of four to one. As part of the fallout from the referendum result, the popularity of Plaid Cymru sagged. In the election, the party's share of the Welsh vote fell from 10.8 to 8.1 per cent, and it was reduced from three to two seats. Overall, the distribution of votes and seats among the parties in 1979 appears to suggest something of a return to normal two-party dominance after the excitements of 1974. In fact, however, despite the Thorpe factor and the demise of devolution, the Liberals and nationalist parties were still in markedly stronger positions than they had been in the 1960s.

Turnout in the election increased to 76.0 per cent across the UK. The first general election to feature a woman as a major party leader—especially since the woman in question was already a controversial figure—was bound to attract more interest than usual, but the rise in turnout is largely attributable to the electoral register being more up to date than in October 1974. As usual, there was an enormous range in turnout across constituencies. Of the lowest twenty seats, sixteen were in inner London, with Stepney and Poplar bottom of the pile at 53.3 per cent. At the other end of the spectrum, Kingswood, near Bristol, recorded a turnout of 86.2 per cent.

Voting Behaviour in the 1970s

For the three elections considered in this chapter, responsibility for the British Election Study had passed to a team at the University of Essex led by Ivor Crewe and Bo Sarlvik. Their major work on the elections (Sarlvik and Crewe, 1983) is considered below. First we look at two specific topics—non-voting and support for the Liberals—on which their research was particularly original and enlightening.

Voting and Non-Voting

We noted above that in their pioneering studies Butler and Stokes had virtually nothing to say about non-voters. They made no attempt to describe or explain who voted, who didn't, and why. Part of the problem was that surveys tended to produce very few respondents who admitted to not voting; much larger propor-tions of respondents claimed to have voted than actually did so in the relevant election. In part, this is because people who are willing to answer survey ques-tions about politics are also more likely to have voted because they are more interested in politics. In addition, some people on the electoral register will have eluded the reach of any survey, either by moving house or dying. Finally, voting is a culturally valued activity—the good citizen goes to the polls—and it appears that some people are unwilling, or perhaps ashamed, to admit that they failed to vote.

Crewe and his colleagues sought to overcome the problem of small numbers of non-voters by using the combined results of BES surveys at the four general elections between 1966 and October 1974 to provide the first substantial individual-level study of non-voting in Britain (Crewe, Fox, and Alt, 1977). They found, first of all, that in this period very few people were consistent non-voters. Only 1 per cent of their respondents who were eligible abstained in all four elections. Someone who did not vote in one election was quite likely to vote in the one after, or the one after that. This phenomenon was linked to the reasons people gave for failing to vote, which were overwhelmingly 'accidental' or 'apathetic'. People said that they were away on polling day, or ill, or simply forgot. Hardly any were *deliberate* abstainers in the sense of refusing to vote on principle.

The second major conclusion of the study was more surprising. Crewe, Fox, and Alt investigated the effects of a series of social variables on propensity to vote and found that, contrary to common assumptions, most seemed to have little effect. Working-class people were as likely to vote as the middle classes, women as likely as men, the poorly educated as likely as the highly educated, for example. Only four interconnected social characteristics were associated with poor turnout: being young (the most important), being unmarried, living in privately rented accommodation, and being residentially mobile. Crewe and his colleagues explained higher levels of non-voting among these groups in terms of isolation from personal and community networks. Such networks are characteristic of stable communities and encourage conformity with the norm of voting. Finally, and much less surprisingly, a clear relationship was confirmed between the strength of respondents' party identification and their likelihood of voting. Whereas 84 per cent of 'very strong' party supporters voted in all four elections from 1966 to 1974, this was true of only 54 per cent of 'not very strong' supporters.

Liberal Support: 'Angels in Plastic'

As the preceding pages have shown, a remarkable rise in support for the Liberal Party (albeit somewhat reduced in 1979) was a marked feature of the elections of the 1970s. This afforded the BES team an opportunity to examine voting for the Liberals in detail (Alt et al., 1977). They found that Liberal support was much more volatile than that for the major parties. People tended to move in and out of voting Liberal rather than sticking with the party. Thus, over the three elections from 1966 to October 1974 only 4 per cent of the electorate voted Liberal on each occasion. This, together with the fact that Liberal voters also had only a very weak sense of party identification, led Alt et al. to describe them as 'Angels in Plastic'—a pointed contrast to the conception of Conservative working men as 'angels in marble', attributed to Disraeli by *The Times* in 1883.

The 'core' Liberal vote—those voting for the party more than once—was heavily middle class. In contrast, 'occasional' Liberal voters (comprising 21 per cent of the electorate) were broadly representative of the public in social terms. The 'core' was also fairly distinctive in terms of attitudes—having generally radical views about participation and racial and sexual equality, for example—but this was less true of the 'occasionals'. The images that both groups had of the party tended to lack policy content, however. Rather, it was seen in diffuse terms such as 'moderate' or 'in the middle'. Although there were some positive aspects to voting Liberal—especially in relation to the party's leadership—its support was largely based on negative views about its main rivals. This dissatisfaction was the main driver of Liberal voting, but clearly it constituted a shaky basis of support for the party. Alt et al. concluded (368): 'There is no doubt that [the Liberals] owed some of their attractiveness to widespread dissatisfaction with the main parties, and this may continue to benefit them in the near future. On the other hand, were the Liberal Party to become part of a future coalition government, it might well lose the ability to draw on this support of the dissatisfied.' In view of the fate of the Liberal Democrats when they joined the Conservatives in a coalition government after the 2010 election, this seems a remarkably prophetic comment.

Dealignment and Issue Voting

The Essex BES team published another article in 1977, for which the over-used adjective 'seminal' is entirely appropriate, not least because it introduced the concept of 'dealignment' into British electoral analysis (Crewe, Sarlvik, and Alt, 1977). The arguments introduced in the article were taken up and expanded in the book *Decade of Dealignment* (Sarlvik and Crewe, 1983), the main BES report on electoral behaviour in the 1970s.

As previously discussed, the electorate portrayed by Butler and Stokes was, broadly, 'aligned' in two ways. First, there was a clear alignment between class and party. To a considerable extent, the class to which a person belonged (or, more strongly, *thought of* himself or herself as belonging to) determined which party he or she would vote for. Second, the great majority of the electorate aligned themselves *psychologically* with a party by thinking of themselves as party supporters—in other words, by adopting a party identification. In the late 1960s, however, both of these alignments began to weaken, and this process continued through the 1970s.

There are a number of measures of the extent of class voting. Two of the simplest and most common are the Alford index (Alford, 1964) and the level of (so-called) 'absolute' class voting. The first is normally calculated by subtracting Labour's percentage share of the vote among non-manual workers from its share among manual workers (although it could also be applied, in reverse, to voting for the Conservatives). The index score can vary between 0 (equal percentages vote Labour in each class and there is, therefore, no class voting) and 100 (all manual workers vote Labour, no non-manual workers do so). The second measure, 'absolute' class voting, is defined as the proportion of voters supporting what would be presumed to be their 'natural' class party. In other words, it is the number of non-manual workers voting Conservative plus the number of manual workers voting Labour, as a percentage of all voters.

Table 3.2 shows scores on these measures for elections from 1964 to 1979. Both indicate a significant decline over the period. By 1979, the Alford index scores indicate that although class voting was still in evidence, it was at a much lower level than in elections of the 1960s. There was also a decline in absolute class voting, so that by 1979 only just over half of voters opted for their 'natural' class party. Other analysts, using rather more sophisticated statistical techniques, reached much the same conclusion (see Franklin, 1985: ch. 4; Rose and McAllister, 1986: ch. 3).

A similar story of decline applies to party identification. Table 3.3 shows that the great majority of electors continued to identify with a party, and, even by 1979, three-quarters still thought of themselves as basically Conservative or Labour supporters. However, the strength of their attachment to parties had diminished to a remarkable extent, with a particularly steep decline in the 1970s. In just ten years the proportions describing themselves as 'very strong' supporters of a party, or of the Conservatives and Labour in particular, had halved.

This 'partisan dealignment' was potentially even more important than class dealignment for elections and electoral behaviour. Stronger party identifiers were (and are) more likely to vote than others; more likely to vote for their party consistently; more likely to make their minds up about their voting decision well in advance of the election; more likely to be positive about their party's leader; and less likely to be swayed by campaign activities or party propaganda. As they declined in number, a fall in turnout would be expected. Moreover, the expanding segment with weak or non-existent attachments to a party would be likely to become more changeable in terms of party choice, more likely to be swayed by

Table 3.2 Measures of class voting, 1964–79

	1964	1966	1970	Feb. 1974	Oct. 1974	1979
Alford index	42	43	32	35	32	27
Absolute class voting	63	66	60	55	54	55

Source: BES surveys.

Table 3.3 Party identification, 1964–79

	1964	1966	1970	Feb. 1974	Oct. 1974	1979
Identify with a party	92	90	89	88	88	85
Very strong identifiers	43	43	41	29	26	21
Identify with Conservative or Labour	81	80	81	75	74	74
Very strongly Conservative or Labour	40	39	40	27	23	19

Note: Figures shown are percentages.
Source: BES surveys.

short-term considerations—such as the performance and personality of party leaders—and more open to the influence of mass media.

If class and party identification had lost much of their former impact, how was party choice in elections of the 1970s to be explained? The answer, according to Sarlvik and Crewe (1983), was 'issue voting'. Voters, it appeared, were increasingly able to pass the tests for issue voting established by Butler and Stokes, and described in Chapter 2. In 1979, when asked about a series of policy issues, it was found that the great majority of survey respondents (88 per cent on average) were aware of the issue concerned and had an opinion about it. Most (78 per cent) also perceived the parties as having different positions on these issues. Finally, there was a strong relationship between the voters' preferences and perceptions on issues and their choice of party. Sarlvik and Crewe also examined voters' evaluations of the competence of the parties in handling four 'valence' issues—those on which there is little disagreement about the end to be achieved—namely, in 1979, strikes, unemployment, rising prices, and law and order. Again, almost all respondents offered assessments of the ability of the Conservative and Labour parties to handle the problems, and again opinions correlated strongly with party preference.

Summing up on issue voting in 1979, Sarlvik and Crewe reported that the votes of 69 per cent of their respondents could be correctly predicted on the basis of their issue opinions and assessments. If only those predicted to vote for the two major parties are considered (it is notoriously difficult to predict third-party voting), 86 per cent of respondents actually voted for the party that was predicted on the basis of their issue opinions. Comparing the effect of policy opinions and assessments with the effect of social characteristics on party choice, the authors reported that 'the voters' opinions on policies and on the parties' performances in office "explain" more than twice as much as all the social and economic characteristics taken together' (Sarlvik and Crewe, 1983: 113). As with class dealignment, the BES team's inference that issue voting became predominant in the 1970s was rapidly corroborated by other scholars (Franklin, 1985; Rose and McAllister, 1986).

What was responsible for this dramatic increase in issue voting? 'Bottom-up' explanations focused on social change—the blurring of formerly quite rigid class boundaries and associated developments, such as improved educational opportunities. When combined with technological changes, especially television, which made political events more accessible to the voters, this amounted to a radical reshaping of the political landscape, transforming the fairly docile and deferential voters identified by Almond and Verba into demanding, disloyal, political 'consumers'. On the other hand, analysts could focus on 'top-down' factors. From this perspective, voters had become more truculent from the early 1960s onwards because there was much more to be annoyed about. Britain's politicians had always been fallible but, as the country's international status declined, their misjudgements seemed more glaring, leading to humiliating episodes such as de Gaulle's twin vetoes of EEC membership, the devaluation of sterling in 1967, and the IMF bail-out. It could be argued that even the old 'aligned' electorate would have been seriously shaken by such developments, leading to widespread questioning of previously unreflective allegiances.

The most likely explanation, as so often, is a complex mixture of the two factors. Whatever the country's fortunes in these years, social changes would have had a significant effect on voting behaviour, promoting a shift from long- to short-term motivations. However, the impression of incompetence among senior policymakers of both main parties can only have accentuated the tendency of voters to think more carefully before making their choice (or, indeed, to think twice before deciding that any of the parties was worth voting for). Ironically, British voters were becoming less fathomable at a time when the parties were taking unprecedented trouble to inform themselves about their vagaries. Highly trained experts in public opinion were now regarded as essential members of any serious political campaign. They arrived just at the time when their laborious findings were becoming less likely to serve as a reliable basis for action than the anecdote-based hunches of their political masters. Since not all of these hired experts possessed an instinctive feel for movements of opinion, seasoned politicians could often be a better guide than the professional pollsters. Hence, for example, in 1970 many Conservative candidates remained confident of overall victory when almost all the statistical evidence told them that they were sure to lose a third consecutive election.

Whatever the value of their surveys, the pollsters were well aware that the electorate was becoming more volatile, and in this respect their message was fully absorbed by most politicians. As a result, election campaigns were increasingly built on the assumption that voters were 'rational' decision-makers, whose support had to be sought through promises of a better tomorrow. To a limited extent, then, the idea of a volatile electorate was self-fulfilling; instead of trying to fire up the faithful, politicians were increasingly anxious to induce adequate enthusiasm among the crucial 'floating voters'. Needless to say, such strategies were unlikely to appeal to 'very strong' party identifiers. In addition, they tended to promote unrealistic manifesto pledges, leading to increased dissatisfaction with politicians of all parties. The rising young Conservative Douglas Hurd had good reason to call his memoir of the Heath government *An End to Promises* (Hurd, 1979), but in hindsight the title looks like a plaintive plea.

The 'Decade of Dealignment' had witnessed major changes in elections and electoral behaviour. The old certainties involving a stable two-party system sustained by two large 'tribes' of loyal supporters had come under serious threat. Margaret Thatcher was the beneficiary of a more issue-oriented, volatile, and unpredictable electorate in 1979: but that very volatility would make it difficult for any governing party to retain popularity in the 1980s.

Appendix: Campaign Polls

Figures 3.A1–3.A3 relate to Great Britain, as Northern Ireland is not included in national opinion polls (data from https://www.markpack.org.uk/opinion-polls/).

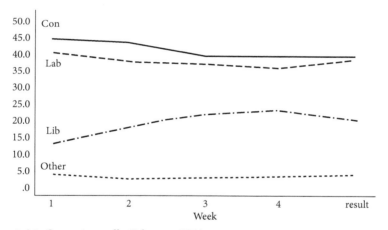

Figure 3.A1 Campaign polls, February 1974

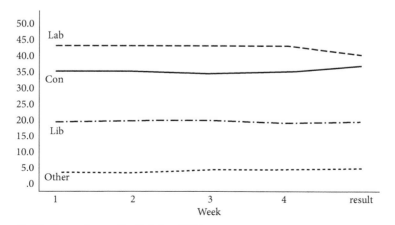

Figure 3.A2 Campaign polls, October 1974

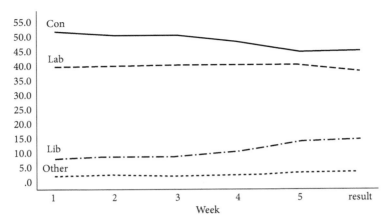

Figure 3.A3 Campaign polls, 1979

4

Conservative Hegemony?

Elections, 1983–92

Mrs Thatcher's First Term, 1979–83

In terms of the ebb and flow of popular opinion, the period between the 1979 and 1983 general elections was one of the most remarkable in British political history to that point (Table 4.1). The new government under Margaret Thatcher did not even have the normal honeymoon with the electorate. Instead, after the 1979 general election it became steadily more unpopular until the spring of 1982. The Falklands conflict, which began in April of that year, transformed the situation, and thereafter the Conservatives maintained a commanding lead over their opponents. In addition to this prodigious turnaround in the fortunes of the governing party, a new party of the centre-left—the Social Democratic Party (SDP)—was founded in March 1981, and evoked a very considerable response among the electorate. The 'Alliance' between the new party and the Liberals rose rapidly in the polls, and for a time in late 1981 and early 1982 it was clearly leading the old major parties. Although the initial surge was not sustained, the new force in the centre was vying with Labour for second place in voting intentions for the rest of the parliament.

It is not difficult to understand the initial unpopularity of the Thatcher government. It sought to make a decisive break with the post-war collectivist consensus (shared by the leaderships of both major parties) by reducing the role of the state. This strategy demanded rigorous restraint of public expenditure. In addition, the government sought to contain inflation by pursuing a monetarist economic policy—controlling the money supply—in the full knowledge that, in the short term at least, this would have a major impact on jobs. Sure enough, under a party which had lambasted Labour's record on unemployment the jobless figures rose rapidly from the end of 1979. In May 1979, 1.2 million people were out of work; by December 1981, the figure was 2.7 million, and it broke through the 3 million barrier in January 1982. Such figures had not been seen since the 1930s, and they would have been worse had the government not introduced creative new methods of defining and counting the numbers out of work. Heavy unemployment was generally regarded as a major contributory factor to the rioting which afflicted many urban areas of England in the spring and summer of 1981.

British General Elections Since 1964: Diversity, Dealignment, and Disillusion. Second Edition. David Denver and Mark Garnett, Oxford University Press. © David Denver and Mark Garnett 2021. DOI: 10.1093/oso/9780198844952.003.0004

Table 4.1 Election results (UK), 1983–92

	1983		1987		1992	
	Votes	Seats	Votes	Seats	Votes	Seats
Conservative	42.4	397	42.3	376	41.9	336
Labour	27.6	209	30.8	229	34.4	271
Lib/SDP*	25.4	23	22.6	22	17.8	20
Others	4.6	21	4.3	23	5.9	24
Turnout	*72.8*		*75.4*		*77.8*	

Notes: Figures for Votes are percentages. * Figures are for the Liberals and Social Democratic Party (SDP) combined in 1983 and 1987, and for the Liberal Democrats in 1992.

While the pain was perceptible to all observers, it was more difficult to discern any tangible benefits from this 'heroic' initial period of 'Thatcherism'. After a year in office, the government was presiding over a rate of inflation more than double (21.9 per cent) that of May 1979 (10.3 per cent); and, although it declined during 1981, the rate nonetheless remained higher than it had been towards the end of the previous Labour government. Moreover, the rise in unemployment, which reduced the tax base and increased social security spending, meant that—despite cuts in a variety of areas including education, housing, and defence—public expenditure actually rose as a proportion of GNP.

The overall picture of the British economy in these years was one of recession, with manufacturing industry suffering particularly acutely. A sharp rise in world oil prices was at least partly the cause but, thanks to North Sea reserves, Britain was now an oil-exporting country. Rather than improving the outlook for manufacturing, North Sea oil boosted the value of sterling, making British exports less competitive. In accordance with their interpretation of monetarist prescriptions, Treasury ministers accentuated the squeeze on manufacturing by maintaining high interest rates. Although the damaging effect of this policy was eventually recognized, in public the government (and particularly the Prime Minister) seemed inflexible, apparently unmoved by the plight of the unemployed and even by the protests of traditional allies in the business community. It is little wonder, then, that in the Gallup poll of October 1981 only 24 per cent of respondents were satisfied with Mrs Thatcher as Prime Minister—the smallest proportion approving the performance of any Prime Minister to that date. In the following December, only 18 per cent expressed satisfaction with the government's record—another all-time low.

Fortunately for the Conservatives, a residual respect for hierarchy limited the protests of Mrs Thatcher's internal opponents to coded messages. The Labour Party was not so inhibited. Jim Callaghan resigned as leader in October 1980 and, rather than replacing him with a politician who could start rebuilding public confidence in the party, Labour MPs opted for the candidate who was most likely to prolong their period in opposition. The polls consistently reported that Denis Healey was far more popular in the country (and also with Labour supporters) than his rival in the leadership contest, Michael Foot. The former duly won the first leadership ballot (also contested by Peter Shore and John Silkin) by a comfortable margin, but in the run-off his vote barely increased and he was beaten by Foot, by 139 votes to 129. Both of the leading candidates were tainted in the eyes of Labour's radicals on the left by their loyal service under Callaghan, with Healey as Chancellor having been forced to defend his government's most unpopular policies. Foot retained some of his old left-wing credentials, however, notably through his long-standing commitment to unilateral nuclear disarmament. He was a compelling platform and public orator of the old school but his style was unsuited to the television age. Partially sighted and physically frail, he was disdainful of any attempt to 'market' him or to modernize his image. He was pilloried in the media, for example, for wearing what appeared to be a green donkey jacket to the national Remembrance service of November 1981. When he was chosen as party leader, one shadow minister was reported to have remarked that 'Labour had decided to lose the next election' (Mitchell, 1983: 51). So it proved. Foot's poll ratings were consistently poor, and he was widely regarded as unelectable as a Prime Minister.

In the aftermath of 1979, left-wing activists in the Labour Party (with Tony Benn rather than Foot as their figurehead) sought revenge for what they perceived as 'betrayal' by their parliamentary leaders. For a time, they clearly enjoyed the upper hand in the party's internal battles. Resolutions to leave the European Community, to abandon nuclear weapons, and to close American bases in Britain were passed at successive conferences. Labour's National Executive Committee (NEC) refused to take action against Trotskyists (most notably the 'Militant' organization) alleged to be infiltrating the party. Conference demanded that the NEC should have the last word on the contents of the party's election manifesto. In addition, 'mandatory re-selection' of MPs by their constituency parties (a device to eject moderate Labour MPs, which in practice was used in relatively few cases for this purpose) was introduced, and the right to elect the party leader was removed from MPs and vested in an electoral college in which trade unions would have 40 per cent of votes, constituency parties 30 per cent, and MPs 30 per cent. Under the new rules, both the leader and deputy leader could be forced to stand for re-election every year at the party conference. Benn and his supporters gave a trial run to this new system at the 1981 conference, challenging Healey, who had won the deputy leadership unopposed the previous year. Although Healey's victory over Benn was wafer-thin, in hindsight it could be seen as a turning-point in the battles between the left and right for control of the party. At the time, however, it looked very different; while the trade unions and Labour MPs supported Healey, the party's constituency activists favoured Benn by an over-whelming margin.

A virtual civil war between left and right had been raging in the party since the early 1970s. The constitutional changes were the final straw, provoking the most damaging Labour split since the formation of Ramsay MacDonald's National Government in 1931. During 1980, leaders of the Labour right, including David Owen, Bill Rodgers, and Shirley Williams linked up with Roy Jenkins, the former Labour Home Secretary and Chancellor of the Exchequer, who had called for a realignment of British politics in an influential televised lecture in November 1979. With varying degrees of reluctance, the members of this so-called 'Gang of Four' concluded that the Labour Party had moved decisively in an uncongenial direction, so that further resistance would be futile. The SDP was finally launched in March 1981, supported by thirteen defecting Labour MPs and a solitary Conservative. The Liberals were now joined in the centre by a party offering nov-elty, apparent dynamism, a respectable number of MPs, and experienced leaders who enjoyed a high media profile. Although relations between the constituency organizations of the two parties were not always amicable, three months later an electoral agreement had been sealed, and the SDP–Liberal Alliance was established.

The effect on public opinion was dramatic. Given the unpopularity of the gov-ernment, and with Labour seemingly tearing itself apart in bitter left–right strug-gles, the electorate gave the new moderate force a warm welcome. Its share of voting intentions in the polls swiftly increased, and it was in first place by October 1981 (Figure 4.1). In July, Roy Jenkins narrowly failed to seize a safe Labour seat (Warrington) in a by-election. In November, Shirley Williams took the equally 'safe' Conservative seat of Crosby, and in March 1982, Jenkins was returned for Glasgow Hillhead. At the Liberal assembly in the autumn of 1981, David Steel, the party's leader, called on his troops to 'go back to your constituencies and pre-pare for government'. Hindsight has exposed Steel's speech to considerable mock-ery but, although it would have been wise to curb his euphoria to some extent, his optimism at the time can be excused. After all, the initial success of the Alliance confirmed that old party attachments would no longer mean so much to a more volatile electorate, and both Labour and the Conservatives appeared disinclined to return to the 'middle ground' of British politics.

In the first week of April 1982, however, Argentina invaded the Falklands Islands and the political scene was transformed again. A task force was des-patched to the South Atlantic. British troops landed on 21 May and defeated the Argentine forces, forcing the latter to surrender on 15 June. These dramatic events produced an immediate upsurge in support for the government. In March, the Conservatives' mean share of voting intentions was 33.3 per cent. This climbed to 37.8 in April, 45.8 in May, and 47.0 in June. It did not fall below 40 per cent for the remainder of the parliament. The Prime Minister's reputation also soared. On

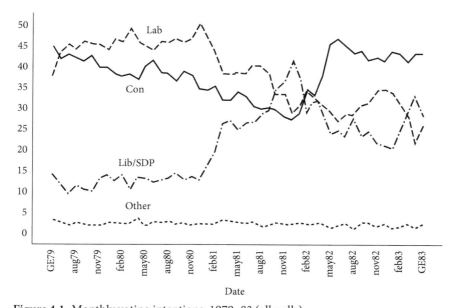

Figure 4.1 Monthly voting intentions, 1979–83 (all polls)

Notes: The 1979 and 1983 election results in Great Britain form the starting and finishing points. The data shown are the monthly means for all published polls. From February 1981, voting intentions for the SDP and 'Alliance' are combined with those for the Liberals.

Gallup's figures, her net satisfaction ratings rose from −21 to +23 over the same four months, and were rarely negative thereafter. Both Labour and the Alliance suffered from the resurgence of Conservative support.

The 'Falklands factor' so manifestly affected public opinion that it is tempting to attribute the re-election of the Conservatives in 1983 to this reason alone. For the government's opponents—the so-called 'wet' Conservatives, as well as supporters of other parties—such a verdict is particularly unpalatable. The government had previously implemented a programme of defence cuts in a way which suggested a lack of British interest in the Falklands and can only have encouraged the initial invasion. After the event, however, a controversial academic article suggested a more subtle interpretation of the 1983 election (Sanders et al., 1987). This was a contribution to an established literature on inter-election popularity trends. As previously noted, the first serious analysis of the subject had suggested that, over the period from 1947 to 1968, the level of government popularity in opinion polls could be predicted with considerable accuracy by just two economic indicators: the level of unemployment and the rate of inflation. In combination, these factors were dubbed the 'misery index' (Goodhart and Bhansali, 1970). As time passed, however, this index became less and less useful. Indeed, on the basis of unemployment and inflation rates at the time of the 1983 general election, the Conservatives would have been predicted to win *minus 156* per cent of the vote (Crewe, 1988: 28)! With an increasingly dealigned electorate, it appeared, not even misery was a good predictor of the popularity of the parties.

David Sanders and his colleagues used a more sophisticated model involving interest rates, inflation, and economic expectations (the 'feel-good factor') to explain the cycle of government popularity. They concluded that the 'Falklands factor' provided only a temporary fillip for the Conservatives (a 'random shock') and that it was the improving economy that enabled the government to maintain its opinion poll lead. This ensured that it entered the 1983 campaign in a well-nigh unassailable position. Improving economic optimism did help, no doubt. However, it seems likely that Mrs Thatcher's self-portrayal as a patriotic, resolute, and determined leader was strongly reinforced by the Falklands episode, and played a significant part in bolstering her popularity and hence that of her party.

The 1983 Campaign

If the Conservatives entered the election campaign with a significant lead, Labour took the field saddled not only with a hopelessly unpopular leader but also with a radical manifesto commonly referred to as 'the longest suicide note in history' (a description usually attributed to the former Labour minister Gerald Kaufman). Over the campaign the party's standing declined further (see Appendix, Figure 4.A1), while that of the Alliance improved. The handsome lead held by the Conservatives was never threatened.

As a result, the election campaign induced little excitement. Perhaps the most dramatic incidents occurred when, at the start of June, Denis Healey, Labour's deputy leader and shadow Foreign Secretary, accused Mrs Thatcher of 'glorying in slaughter' in the Falklands, while a few days later the shadow Education minister, Neil Kinnock, responding on television to a heckler who shouted that Mrs Thatcher had guts, remarked that people had left their guts on the Falklands battlefield to prove it. These verbal indiscretions were trivial compared with the governmental gaffes which had helped precipitate the war; but they provided easy targets for Mrs Thatcher's powerful press allies, who were well aware that most members of the public remembered the victorious close of the Falklands campaign rather than its inglorious beginning.

The Conservative Party chairman, Cecil Parkinson, had decided in advance that the issues on which the government could be vulnerable ('unemployment, the Health Service, the economy, and caring') should be confronted at the outset of the campaign. These were sensible precautions, but they were not strictly necessary. As Parkinson later reflected (1992: 227), 'Our opponents never, at any stage, forced us off our agenda and on to ground of their choosing'. Rather than making the Conservatives defend their record in office, Labour strategists allowed the campaign to focus on their own manifesto proposals, which, in keeping with conference resolutions, included leaving the EC, a non-nuclear defence policy, and considerable increases in public expenditure. The SDP's Shirley Williams described such pledges as 'an abuse of the common sense of the British voter' (Butler and Kavanagh, 1984: 91), while Conservative advertisements made point by point comparisons between Labour's manifesto and that of the Communist Party. Labour's own internal divisions over the commitment to scrap Polaris submarines became clear when Denis Healey and Jim Callaghan openly contradicted the new party line. When Mr Foot averred that he would never press the nuclear button in any circumstances, Mrs Thatcher promptly responded that she would be quite willing to do so if necessary.

Although Mrs Thatcher spoke only in the last of the party's four televised election broadcasts—which were more like commercial advertisements than ever—she dominated the Conservative campaign, taking charge of almost all press conferences, and being by far the most prominent Conservative in media news coverage. She also defended her record vigorously against (male) television interviewers, and was only once knocked off her stride when challenged by a persistent female voter, in a televised question and answer session, about the sinking of the Argentinian ship the *General Belgrano* during the Falklands conflict.

On the Labour side, although Foot attracted large and enthusiastic audiences of the faithful—and his dog, Disraeli, who accompanied him on walkabouts, received more sympathetic coverage than most leading politicians—Labour strategists were well aware that he was not going down well with the mass of voters. Accordingly, Denis Healey and the moderate shadow Home Secretary, Roy Hattersley, took prominent roles at national level. It was to no avail, however. By polling day, only 13 per cent of the voters thought that Foot would make the best Prime Minister (behind Thatcher on 46 per cent and Steel on 35 per cent). Fully 63 per cent thought he would be the worst Prime Minister (with Thatcher and Steel scoring 25 per cent and 2 per cent respectively in this particular unpopularity contest). As Ivor Crewe commented (1985: 181), 'Not since the war (probably much earlier) had a major party leader been regarded as so implausible a prime minister as Michael Foot. The more he appeared on television the more implausible he seemed.' Apart from Foot, however, it was widely agreed—even among Labour supporters—that the party's campaign was shambolic, contrasting sharply with the media-savvy and professional Conservative operation, masterminded once again by Saatchi and Saatchi. The Labour backbencher, Austin Mitchell, tried to ignore the national picture as he fought to retain his Grimsby seat. Later, he was scathing about Labour's national campaign which, far from helping his efforts, 'undermined candidates, contradicting what they were saying, generating embarrassing questions' (Mitchell, 1983: 129).

The Alliance parties confidently expected that their support would increase during the campaign—this, after all, had been the usual Liberal experience. Moreover, the Alliance would receive more television coverage than the Liberals alone in previous elections (the ratio 5-5-4, rather than the previous 5-5-3 for the three major contestants, was imposed by the broadcasters—the Alliance being reluctant to accept anything less than parity—at the outset of the campaign). In fact, the polls suggested little movement until the fourth week (see Appendix, Figure 4.A1). In part, the problem appeared to be that the electorate was confused by the Alliance's dual leadership, and, in addition, Roy Jenkins, the SDP leader and 'Prime Minister designate', was less popular than David Steel. There were, indeed, attempts to persuade Jenkins to step down from his leading role—but nothing came of this, and difficulties were forgotten as later polls showed a steady improvement in Alliance support.

The 1983 Results

In the popular vote, although the Conservatives fell below expectations, their lead over Labour was still decisive. At 27.6 per cent, this was Labour's worst vote share since 1918, with Tony Benn among the casualties (in Bristol South East). The Alliance improved still further on their opinion poll figures and ran Labour close for second place. In terms of seats won, of course, the story looks very different. The Conservatives increased their overall majority in the House of Commons as Labour slumped to 209 MPs—the smallest contingent since 1935. Their diminished ranks included, as the youngest Labour MP, one Anthony Blair, the newly elected member for Sedgefield. Despite their creditable score in votes, the Alliance parties between them elected only twenty-three MPs—seventeen Liberals and six SDP (including a surprise package in the shape of the 23-year-old Charles Kennedy in Ross, Cromarty, and Skye). Shirley Williams lost the by-election gain of Crosby and Bill Rodgers was defeated in Stockton North, leaving only a 'Gang of Two' in the Commons. In both Scotland and Wales, support for the nationalist parties declined, to 11.8 per cent and 7.8 per cent, respectively, but both the SNP and Plaid Cymru held on to their two seats apiece.

Extensive constituency boundary changes were implemented in 1983 (among other things, making life much more difficult for Benn in Bristol). These left only sixty-six constituencies unaltered and increased the total number from 635 to 650. However, 'notional' 1979 results for the new constituencies, compiled by academics, were commissioned, published, and used by the media—an innovation that was to become standard practice when boundaries were redrawn in future—thus allowing reasonably accurate estimates of constituency-level changes. In terms of conventional swing, 1983 saw a movement of 4.1 per cent from Labour to the Conservatives across Britain. This was much less uniform than normal across constituencies, however. There were, indeed, sixty-four seats in which there was a swing to Labour, and the pro-Conservative swing varied from just above zero to more than 10 per cent in nine cases. In fact, when more than two parties are in serious contention the concept of swing is a much less useful measure of electoral change than in the two-party case. Looking simply at changes in the vote shares obtained by the parties between 1979 and 1983, however, clear geographical patterns emerge. First, the pre-existing differences between the north and south of the country were accentuated. While Labour's vote share fell by 10.7 points in the three southern regions outside London (East Anglia, South East, South West), the decline was 8.2 points in the three northern regions (North, North West, Yorkshire and Humberside) and only 6.4 points in Scotland. The Conservatives also lost more support in Scotland (−3.0) than across Britain as a whole (−1.4). The second geographical pattern was also a long-term trend—more urban areas were tending to move towards Labour, and more mixed and rural areas to the Conservatives. In 1983, the Conservative share fell by 3.2 and 2.0 points in very and predominantly urban constituencies, respectively, but by only one point in mixed areas. In rural seats it increased by 0.5 points. We shall return to these geographical divisions (and their consequences) below.

Overall, support for the Alliance was 11.6 points greater than the Liberals alone achieved in 1979. Variations in their performance had little to do with socio-economic or geographical factors but, rather, reflected varying political circumstances. Thus, notwithstanding the ousting of Williams and Rodgers, sitting MPs who had defected from the Labour Party tended to do relatively well—David Owen held his vulnerable Plymouth Devonport seat, for example—but where they came up against strong nationalist opposition in Scotland and Wales, Alliance candidates fared very poorly.

By 1983, the context in which general elections were contested had changed a good deal compared with the early 1960s. Constituency boundaries had been redrawn twice, the electorate was less strongly aligned with parties, class voting had declined in importance, and the Alliance was much stronger than the Liberals had been. Yet, when we analyse party support across constituencies in the light of 1981 census data (Table 4.2) the results are not just similar to those reported in Chapter 2 for the 1964 election but suggest a greater polarization in Conservative and Labour support. All the relevant coefficients are statistically significant and almost all indicate stronger relationships than in 1964. Thus, Labour' s performance weakened more sharply than before in constituencies with large numbers of professional and managerial workers, owner occupiers, and car owners, while improving more rapidly as the density of population, and proportions of manual workers, council tenants, and households without a car increased. It is worth noting, too, that the ethnic minority population was now affecting the levels of party support in some constituencies—the larger the local ethnic minority population, the better Labour's performance and the poorer the outcome for the Conservatives

Table 4.2 Correlations between party shares of vote and constituency characteristics, 1983

	Conservative	Labour	Alliance
% Professional & managerial	0.78	−0.80	0.43
% Manual workers	−0.71	0.73	−0.28
% Owner occupiers	0.69	−0.60	0.28
% Council tenants	−0.75	0.67	−0.31
% Private renters	0.18	−0.20	0.11
% Aged 65+	0.23	−0.28	0.17
% In agriculture	0.28	−0.48	0.33
Electors per hectare	−0.27	0.37	−0.26
% With no car	−0.75	0.78	−0.43
% Ethnic minority	−0.15	0.26	−0.24

Notes: All coefficients are statistically significant. N=633 for all three parties.

Table 4.3 Correlations between turnout and constituency characteristics, 1983

% Professional & managerial	0.394	% Manual workers	−0.167
% In agriculture	0.312	Electors per hectare	−0.666
% Owner occupiers	0.514	% Council tenants	−0.343
% Aged 65+	0.059*	% Private renters	−0.321
		% With no car	−0.627
Constit. marginality 1979 (notional)	0.273	% Ethnic minority	−0.504

Notes: All coefficients are statistically significant except the one asterisked. N=618. Marginality is defined as 100 minus the difference in percentage share of votes between the top two parties.

and the Alliance. The appeal of the Alliance more generally—like that of the Liberals in 1964—was a paler reflection of that of the Conservatives. The coefficients for the two parties are all in the same direction, but mostly weaker for the Alliance.

Overall turnout in 1983 fell back to 72.7 per cent, although it increased in the very different context of Northern Ireland, where Gerry Adams, the Sinn Fein leader, was elected as MP for Belfast West in the wake of a hunger strike by IRA prisoners. Measuring turnout change at constituency level is difficult when boundaries are altered; but the pattern of variation across constituencies remained much as before. As with party support, however, analysis suggests a greater polarization between higher- and lower-turnout areas (Table 4.3). While turnout correlated positively with the proportions of solidly middle-class households, of owner occupiers, and of people employed in agriculture, on the one hand, on the other, more urban, working-class, poorer areas with larger proportions of council tenants and ethnic minority residents tended to have lower turnouts. Although boundary changes inevitably made for some uncertainty among voters about the political status of constituencies, the correlation between notional marginality and turnout remained positive and significant in 1983.

Mrs Thatcher's Second Term, 1983–7

The years between 1983 and 1987 saw fluctuating party fortunes, but the fluctuations were less violent than had been experienced in the previous inter-election period. The trend in opinion was by now a familiar one, however. The Conservatives gradually lost their advantage over Labour, although the government's lead was re-established for a time in late 1984, following the IRA's attempt to assassinate the Prime Minister and many members of her cabinet by bombing the hotel where they were staying during the Conservative Party conference in Brighton.

From the autumn of 1986, however, the Conservatives began to pull clear again. Labour had received a fillip from a change of party leader in October 1983; but thereafter, support for the party fluctuated within a very narrow range, never reaching 40 per cent or falling below 32 per cent until the last few months of the parliament. The Alliance, on the other hand, fell back after the 1983 election, only to rise steadily until mid-term when, for a brief period, all three parties were running neck and neck. As so often in previous inter-election cycles, this proved to be a false dawn, and support began to fall away in the spring of 1986. Despite a last-minute boost following a spectacular by-election victory at Greenwich at the end of February 1987, the Alliance entered the election clearly in third place (Figure 4.2).

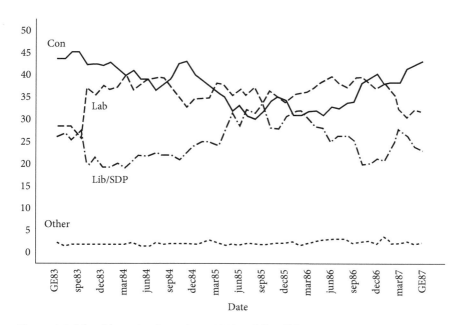

Figure 4.2 Monthly voting intentions, 1983–7 (all polls)

Notes: The 1983 and 1987 election results in Great Britain form the starting and finishing points. The data shown are the monthly means for all published polls. Throughout, voting intentions for the SDP and 'Alliance' are combined with those for the Liberals.

Mrs Thatcher continued to dominate her government and British politics generally in this period. Whatever individual voters might have thought of her personality and style, her leadership qualities were generally (if often grudgingly) acknowledged. Unemployment remained at more than three million throughout but this was offset, to some extent at least, by relatively low inflation and interest rates. For those in employment, living standards slowly improved. This allowed many to take advantage of cut-price offers of shares in newly privatized companies such as British Telecom (BT, 1984) and British Gas (1986). Thus, while Mrs Thatcher's first term had been overshadowed by a lengthy economic recession, the story between 1983 and 1987 was one of slow and steady recovery.

However, in Mrs Thatcher's second term there were two significant developments which overshadowed the routine matters of policy and might have derailed the fairly serene progress of the government. The first was a national strike by coal miners which began in March 1984. This was called by the National Union of Mineworkers (NUM), led by Arthur Scargill, without having held a ballot of the membership. The strike divided the union—with miners in Nottinghamshire particularly opposed—and involved many violent (and televised) clashes between strikers and police on picket lines. The government was determined to win a trial of strength with the NUM, and had ensured that coal stocks were high before embarking on a series of pit closures which were likely to provoke a showdown with the union's sabre-rattling leadership. In the event, after a year-long struggle, the NUM was comprehensively defeated and Scargill humiliated in a manner which served to discredit the left-wing militancy which he had come to symbolize. Although the strike intensified the existing divisions of opinion regarding Margaret Thatcher herself, it also caused serious friction within the Labour Party. The polls suggested that the government's hard-line stance was generally supported by the voters. In five Gallup polls between July and December 1984, for example, an average of 86 per cent of respondents disapproved of the methods being used by the miners; on average, 48 per cent said that they sympathized with the government-backed employers, and 28 per cent with the striking miners. Apart from this spectacular dispute, the number of working days lost through industrial action was the smallest it had been for many years.

The second incident which threatened the government was the so-called Westland Affair. In late 1985 the Westland company—Britain's sole surviving producer of helicopters—was in financial trouble. However, the Defence Secretary, Michael Heseltine, and the Prime Minister openly disagreed about whether it should be rescued by a European consortium or an American company. After protracted arguments, Heseltine resigned in 1986, claiming that Mrs Thatcher had not allowed him to put his case to the full cabinet. Two weeks later, it was alleged that one of the Prime Minister's allies in the affair, the Trade Secretary Leon Brittan, had engaged in dirty tricks on her behalf and he was forced to resign. Thatcher feared that she might have to follow suit; but in the key parliamentary debate, Neil Kinnock (by this time Labour leader) fluffed the chance of exploiting his unexpected opportunity.

The 'soft-left' Kinnock and Roy Hattersley, from Labour's social democratic wing, had been the only two candidates who mattered when the party chose a successor to Michael Foot in October 1983. In contrast to the anguished post-mortem which Labour was continuing to conduct on events since 1974, the leadership election was marked by an absence of rancour. Kinnock coasted to a comfortable victory, securing 71 per cent of the electoral college vote. Hattersley was then overwhelmingly elected deputy leader, and Labour members congratulated themselves on having chosen a 'dream team'.

Kinnock set about getting a grip on his party and forcing it to face electoral reality. In October 1985, he appointed a television producer, Peter Mandelson, to head a new Campaigns and Communications department at party headquarters; in turn, Mandelson established a Shadow Communications Agency, headed by Philip Gould, who had worked in advertising, to advise on media strategy and associated matters. The NEC was simply sidelined on these issues. As a result, compared with the situation under Callaghan and Foot, Labour's conferences were presented with greater polish and professionalism—in other words, they exchanged potentially damaging drama for risk-free dullness. Campaign preparations were very much more thorough and detailed compared with the shambles of 1983. For example, sympathetic television professionals were asked to find suitable locations for photo opportunities which would associate Kinnock and his allies with 'progress, youth, enterprise and dynamism' (Butler and Kavanagh, 1988: 61). Unlike his predecessor, Kinnock was also willing to listen to and act on advice concerning his dress and personal appearance.

The neutralization of the party's doctrinaire members was vital to Kinnock's strategy, and he did his best to turn a major problem into a public relations success. He lambasted Militant in an uncompromising speech at the 1985 conference and, eventually, secured the expulsion of leading members of that much-publicized group. The hard left was reduced to a small minority on the NEC. This helped to ensure the dropping of unpopular policies such as reversing council house sales, re-nationalizing the companies privatized since 1979, and leaving the European Community. Kinnock's campaign earned him bitter enemies. Indeed, some on the left of the Labour Party now hated him more than they did Mrs Thatcher. Nevertheless, by the time of the 1987 general election it was no longer so easy for the Conservatives to depict the main opposition party as an undisciplined, dogmatic rabble.

On the other hand, problems remained for Labour. There was little the party leadership could do about so-called 'loony left' councils, in London and elsewhere, which continued to provide the Tory-supporting tabloid newspapers with irresistible copy by, for example, inviting representatives of Sinn Fein to speak and banning books considered racist or sexist from local libraries. The electorally damaging unilateralist policy on nuclear weapons was retained; although he was responsive to opinion polls on key domestic policies, Kinnock took more persuading on defence issues, where his instincts were close to those of Michael Foot. The overall impression—cruelly reinforced by the depiction of Kinnock in the satirical television programme *Spitting Image* (ITV, 1984–96)—was that Labour was prepared to do almost anything to win office, but had saddled itself with a leader who was inclined to make long-winded speeches in defence of the few principles he retained.

Since Labour was now clearly determined to put its house in order, life became correspondingly more difficult for the Alliance. Immediately after the 1983 election, Roy Jenkins resigned as leader of the SDP. He was replaced (without a contest) by David Owen, one of the original 'Gang of Four' and formerly Foreign Secretary in the Callaghan government. Owen was much less favourably disposed to the Liberals than Jenkins had been—despising the anti-nuclear tendencies of many party activists, for example—and was determined to maintain the separate identity and policies of the SDP. In fact, defence policy was a recurring problem for relations between the two Alliance parties, with the Liberal Assembly voting against nuclear weapons in 1986. Nonetheless, following a post-election dip, the Alliance progressed steadily in opinion polls and enjoyed considerable success in local elections and parliamentary by-elections. There were sixteen of the latter between 1983 and 1987 and, taking them together, the Alliance won more votes than either the Conservatives or Labour, gaining four seats in the process. As we have noted, the most spectacular of these victories came in Greenwich in February 1987, at a point when the Alliance was trailing in the national polls. Rosie Barnes for the SDP soundly defeated a left-wing Labour candidate in a seat that Labour had held since 1945. This provided a last-minute boost for the Alliance, and optimistic supporters once again began to think about overtaking Labour in the popular vote in the coming election. Those who had been sobered by the experience of 1983 limited their ambitions to holding the balance of power between the two major parties. Even this prospect caused problems for the Alliance, however, as David Steel and most Liberals were much more favourably inclined towards Labour than the Conservatives, while the opposite was true of David Owen and his numerous supporters within the SDP.

The 1987 Campaign

More than ever, reporting of the 1987 campaign focused on opinion polls. *The Times*, for example, had a poll-related story as its main headline in five of its ten issues from 1 June to polling day, while television news and current affairs programmes regularly reported and analysed poll results. This is somewhat surprising, because, to say the least, the polls were not telling a very exciting story (see

Appendix, Figure 4.A2). There was no Alliance surge, despite the fact that for the first time a third party was granted broadcasting parity with its rivals. Labour's standing improved a little, but the party failed to make significant inroads on a solid Conservative lead throughout. There was a spasm of excitement in the penultimate week of the campaign, when a BBC *Newsnight* poll in marginal seats suggested that the Conservatives were not doing as well as expected, and a simultaneous Gallup poll reported a Conservative national lead of just four points. These findings induced 'wobbly Thursday' (4 June) among Conservative strategists, bringing to a head divisions between those who wanted a more 'presidential' campaign, exploiting Mrs Thatcher's recent successful visit to Moscow, and others who preferred to present the government as a team. The 'presidentialists' prevailed, but it is doubtful whether their input made any difference to the election result. Despite the chaotic scenes at Conservative Central Office on 'wobbly Thursday', before the end of that day the warring factions received advance intelligence of a new poll which placed the party ten points ahead of Labour. Lord (David) Young, whose importance in the campaign rivalled that of the titular Party Chairman, Norman Tebbit, exaggerated only slightly when he reflected that for those in the pressure-cooker atmosphere at campaign headquarters 'paranoia is the order of the day and the world is seemingly always about to end' (Young, 1990: 191). Presumably tempers frayed more easily because the strategists were further removed from the real action than they had ever been before.

As well as being the latest in a long line of 'television elections'—'only more so', in the words of Martin Harrison (1988: 139)—the campaign was personalized to an unprecedented degree. This reflected conscious decisions by the parties themselves. Labour, in particular, sought to capitalize on the personable and relatively young Neil Kinnock. The party's first election broadcast—immediately christened 'Kinnock: The Movie'—was made by Hugh Hudson, who had directed the award winning film *Chariots of Fire*. Shot in soft focus, with a mellow soundtrack borrowed from Brahms, it was all about the party leader—his origins, career, aspirations, and dedication. At the end, after another shot of the soaring seagull which had opened the film, the single word 'KINNOCK' appeared on the screen. The 'movie' was credited with having an immediate positive effect on Kinnock's personal ratings, and the Labour campaign team were so delighted that a repeat showing replaced the party's planned fourth broadcast.

All the party leaders virtually abandoned public walkabouts. Partly this was a matter of security concerns but it was also felt that the inevitable media melees rendered such events rather pointless. Instead, the campaigns concentrated on devising photo opportunities and coverage of these was extensive. As before, both the BBC and ITV assigned a reporting team to each leader. The most photographed Labour figure after Neil Kinnock was his wife, Glenys. In the evenings both Kinnock and Thatcher addressed rallies of the faithful. The days of open election meetings addressed by party leaders—and hence the possibility of audience heckling—now seemed dead and buried. The Alliance offered 'Ask the Alliance' sessions, at which the two Davids took questions from the audience. These were less successful than they might have been, as David Owen's magisterial style could only remind viewers of *Spitting Image* sketches which featured a large, deep-voiced Owen with a small puppet Steel squeaking admiringly from the former's top pocket.

After her initial lower profile, as the campaign progressed Mrs Thatcher began to dominate press conferences (held, as usual, in London, while Kinnock took about half of Labour's beyond the capital) and starred in the final party broadcast. The Conservative attack on Labour (seconded by Conservative-supporting newspapers) focused on defence policy, extremists, and spending plans. On defence, Labour's position was undermined when, in a television interview, Kinnock used words which implied that a non-nuclear UK might be occupied by enemy forces. The US President Ronald Reagan, who had already helped Mrs Thatcher's bid for re-election by treating Kinnock and his colleagues with well-publicized discourtesy during a visit to Washington, seized this further opportunity by referring to Labour's 'grievous errors' on defence (Shaw, 1994: 78). The Conservative onslaught included a vivid poster, which was also extensively featured in heavy press advertising by the party. Headlined 'Labour's Policy on Arms', it showed a soldier holding his arms aloft in surrender. Tory success in raising the salience of this issue is illustrated by the fact that, after opinion polls, defence was the topic most frequently covered in the lead stories of daily papers and also the most prominent issue in broadcast news. Among the electorate, whereas only 20 per cent considered defence to be an important election issue at the beginning of the campaign, by the penultimate week 60 per cent thought the same, with 66 per cent thinking Labour would handle the issue badly. On spending, MORI reported that 46 per cent of voters believed that Labour was making promises that couldn't be afforded, compared with 18 per cent thinking the same of Conservatives and 16 per cent of the Alliance. Painting Labour as the party of extremists and/or 'loonies' was less effective, thanks to Kinnock's well-publicized efforts to crack down on groups like Militant and, perhaps, to a suspicion among voters that tabloid stories about the 'excesses' of left-wing councils had been exaggerated.

It was generally agreed that Labour's national campaign was well organized and professional. To some extent, at least, this verdict was coloured by the tendency of the new breed of Labour advisors to exaggerate their own achievements. At this time, commentators in the media and academia were less accustomed to 'spin' and hence more receptive to self-advertising claims, whether on or off the record. Nevertheless, those involved did as well as could reasonably be expected, given the deficiencies in the product that they were trying to sell to the electorate. If the campaign flagged a little in its latter stages, this was unsurprising given the morale-sapping failure of the polls to move in Labour's favour. Despite Mrs Thatcher's uneven performance and the faction-fighting among her strategists, the Conservatives also seemed slick and hard-hitting. In the end, however, national campaigning appeared to make little difference other than to reinforce existing pre-dispositions among voters. The result of the election was remarkably similar to the state of the polls in the first week after the election date was announced (see Appendix, Figure 4.A2).

The election was contested by a record number of women candidates repre-senting the major parties—243 in all, comprising 46 Conservative, 92 Labour, and 105 Alliance. There was also the largest ever number of ethnic minority can-didates—28, of whom four were elected (all for Labour). In the constituencies, the Nuffield study noted the beginnings of change in what the authors had long considered to be 'the anachronistic local rites' of campaigning. Targeting, of groups of voters as well as constituencies, was much more effective than before; personal computers were starting to be used to assist with routine campaign tasks; communications between the centre and key seats were better organized than ever. Even the Nuffield authors—for long sceptical about the impact of local organization and activity—conceded that 'to some degree' local campaigning probably made a difference to the outcomes in some constituencies (Butler and Kavanagh, 1988: 211–12).

The 1987 Results

Across the UK, turnout in the election rose from 72.7 per cent in 1983 to 75.3 per cent. Interestingly, in Northern Ireland the change was in the opposite direc-tion, from 72.9 per cent to 67.0 per cent. Doubtless this reflected a degree of 'voter-fatigue', especially among the Unionist community. In protest at the 1985 Anglo-Irish Agreement, all MPs representing Unionist parties (fifteen out of Northern Ireland's seventeen MPs) had resigned their seats in order to trigger by-elections. These contests, held in January 1986, had done little to boost the unionist cause; indeed, the Ulster Unionist MP for Newry and Armagh had been defeated by Seamus Mallon of the nationalist SDLP. If the deflating effect of the gesture were not enough to reduce turnout, a new regulation meant that would-be voters now had to produce evidence of identity, making the practice of personation (such as voting on behalf of dead people) much more difficult.

In Britain only a few constituencies defied the upward trend in turnout. This broadly uniform pattern across the country probably reflected a revival of morale among Labour supporters, and possibly also a perception that the outcome this time was going to be at least a bit closer than in 1983. The pattern of variation across constituencies remained much as before, however.

Compared with 1983, over the country as a whole the Conservatives' vote share was almost identical (−0.1), while Labour's increased by 3.2 points, and support for the Alliance fell by 2.8. However, these averages concealed a detailed pattern that was far from uniform. Indeed, the widening of the North–South electoral gap was the main focus of commentary on the election results. We shall discuss this topic in more detail later in the chapter; for the moment it is enough to note that whereas there was virtually no swing between the Conservatives and Labour in the South of England outside London (0.3 per cent to Labour), the figure was 3.6 per cent in Northern England and 5.9 per cent in Scotland. In Scotland, the SNP rose from 11.8 per cent to 14.0 per cent of votes and from two to three seats (one of which was won by Alex Salmond, future leader of the party and First Minister of the devolved Scottish government). Plaid Cymru also added a seat in Wales, although the party's vote share declined a little (from 7.8 per cent to 7.3 per cent).

During the campaign there had been much discussion of tactical voting. The emergence of something approaching a three-party system in the country (if not in Parliament) meant that in many constituencies the combined votes of second- and third-placed candidates easily outweighed the winner's tally. If supporters of the trailing party disliked the leading party more than the one in second place, and were persuaded to switch to the latter, they could help to defeat their least favoured party. A pressure group, TV87, campaigned to urge Labour and Alliance supporters to do just this in order to defeat Conservative incumbents, and some newspapers published lists of seats where this could be effective. In the event, however, although there was certainly some tactical voting, it did little to unsettle the Conservatives. Curtice and Steed (1988) calculated that tactical voting won Labour just a single additional seat. On the other hand, tactical voting probably contributed to the seven Alliance and Nationalist gains in the election.

Labour recovered somewhat from the debacle of 1983 and at least easily held off the Alliance's bid for second place, thus shoring up the position of Kinnock, which some at the top of the party saw as their main concern. Nonetheless, in historical perspective, the 1987 result was still a poor one for the party, which now faced major challenges if it hoped to compete seriously for office again. In many respects, 1987 bears comparison with the contest of 1959, in which Labour had also suffered a hat-trick of defeats. The 1959 result had led many commentators to wonder whether demographic changes were making it impossible for Labour to win, and in 1987 it was not difficult to draw equally pessimistic conclusions. Since a reversion to the left-wing programme of 1983 seemed to be a sure recipe for electoral oblivion, the post-mortem this time round was dominated by those who wanted Labour to return to the middle ground. Conveniently for them and for Kinnock, who stayed on as leader, consultations with 'focus groups' could be spun to minimize tactical mistakes during the 1987 campaign and emphasize the extent and electoral significance of social changes. The predetermined conclusion, to adopt parlance which became fashionable in the following decade, was that while 'Old' Labour was doomed, a refashioned party which embraced the consumerist society could still hope to win. Meanwhile, the message of the election for leaders of the Alliance (except David Owen) was that the Liberals and the SDP had not been able to capitalize on their potential support as separate parties, and should contemplate merger in a last attempt to seize the middle ground before their opponents were forced to recollect its importance.

For Mrs Thatcher, things seemed set fair. However, after so many radical changes in her second term, the failure to secure an enhanced share of the vote compared with 1983 constituted less than a resounding vote of confidence. Indeed, with 43.8 per cent of the vote in 1959, Hugh Gaitskell's defeated Labour Party had performed better and, although the electorate had expanded by almost eight million since that election, the number of voters who chose the Conservatives in 1987 was almost precisely the same as in 1959 (13.76 million compared to 13.75 million). Notwithstanding the significant contextual differences, such figures suggest a more sober reading of the 1987 election than the one provided by government critics, some of whom, notably those associated with the periodical *Marxism Today*, were beginning to embrace 'revolutionary defeatism' by concluding that the Conservatives had established 'hegemony'. Even so, the government had retained a very comfortable majority in the House of Commons, and Mrs Thatcher had consolidated her position within her party and her government. As things turned out, however, in just over three years she was ousted from office—not by the electorate but by her own MPs.

The Demise of Margaret Thatcher (and the SDP): 1987–92

Things started brightly for the Conservatives after the 1987 victory. Nigel Lawson's Budget of March 1988 slashed income tax for higher earners and also cut the standard rate. Although the overall tax burden was still comparable to that which had provoked so many complaints when Labour was in office, Lawson had at least broken free of a discreditable post-war tradition by announcing a give-away Budget *after*, rather than before, an election. In the short term, low interest rates were also apparently advantageous to mortgage payers, although some of them would eventually suffer the consequences of an overheated housing market. With some equally overheated supporters proclaiming an 'economic miracle', the Conservatives maintained a clear lead over Labour in opinion polls for almost two years (Figure 4.3).

During 1989, however, the government's aura of invincibility began to dissipate. Mostly, the damage was self-inflicted, although the downturn in popularity cast doubt on any notion that the Conservatives had ever enjoyed 'hegemony'. In January 1989, as heralded in its 1987 manifesto but not seized upon by Labour, the government introduced a new method of raising finance for local government. Previously, households and businesses had paid rates to their local councils based on the value of the properties that they lived in or their business premises.

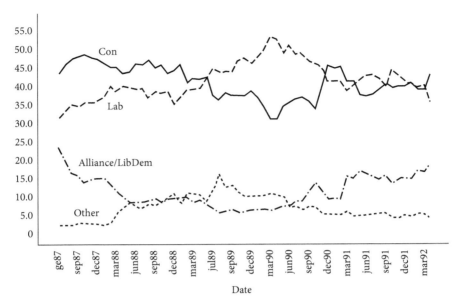

Figure 4.3 Monthly voting intentions, 1987–92 (all polls)

Notes: The 1987 and 1992 election results in Great Britain form the starting and finishing points. The data shown are the monthly means for all published polls. Up to March 1988, voting intentions for the Liberals, SDP, and 'Alliance' are combined. Thereafter, SDP support is included with 'Others' until May 1990, after which the party ceased to exist.

Domestic rates were unpopular, and were likely to become more so once a long-delayed revaluation of properties had taken place. Accordingly, the government decided to alter the system to one in which individuals rather than households paid a new levy, the so-called Community Charge. Having canvassed a number of options for local government finance, the government had plumped for the system which was most obviously unfair—it was literally true that under its terms a duke would pay no more than a dustman—and one with uncanny parallels to the Poll Tax which had provoked the Peasants' Revolt of 1381. Like the fourteenth-century tax, the Community Charge had nothing to do with the right to vote, but many people decided not to put their names on the electoral register in the hope of evading payment. According to one estimate, about a million voters disfranchised themselves in this way between 1987 and 1992 (Pugh, 2010: 385). Such confusions meant that the third Thatcher government managed to offend democratic sentiment, as well as enraging those who were already bewailing the widening of economic inequality since 1979.

As if determined to maximize its own difficulties, the government capitulated to pressure from Scottish Conservatives and gave the system a trial run north of the border. This decision activated a population which had played no part in the 1981 riots; the Community Charge inspired a campaign of civil disobedience in

Scotland and generated increased support for the SNP. These troubles were less spectacular, however, than the reaction when the tax was introduced in the rest of Britain in the spring of 1990. Violent disturbances occurred in London and elsewhere. The tax was strongly identified with Mrs Thatcher personally and she maintained her stout defence, despite the mounting evidence that it was a domestic 'policy disaster' unparalleled in post-war Britain (Butler et al., 1994).

The government was also damaged by retirements, resignations, and re-emerging divisions. In January 1988, William Whitelaw—a seasoned, shrewd, and trusted aide to the Prime Minister—retired from the cabinet on health grounds. In October 1989, the Chancellor, Nigel Lawson, resigned because the Prime Minister clearly preferred the judgement of an academic economist, Alan Walters, to his own policy of bearing down on inflation by linking the value of sterling to that of the German Deutschmark. Whether or not the electorate grasped the essentials of this dispute, it showed that Mrs Thatcher's adherence to the 'free' market, and her hostility to 'Europe', were now so strong that they could allow her to risk losing the services of a kindred spirit, who had served the party in varying capacities for a quarter of a century. Mrs Thatcher's unconcealed antipathy to the EC also provoked Geoffrey Howe, the former Chancellor and Foreign Secretary, to resign from the government in November 1990 and to attack the Prime Minister personally in his resignation speech from the backbenches. A speech by Howe was once compared by Denis Healey to 'being savaged by a dead sheep'. On this occasion, the content of Howe's address (if not the delivery) was rather more wolfish than usual. Lawson had also criticized the Prime Minister in language which was at least as deadly, even if the context was less dramatic, when he stood down the previous year.

To add to the government's woes, by the middle of 1990 the economy was once again in poor shape. GDP was declining, unemployment was rising, and inflation increasing. To address the latter, the government raised interest rates, which affected those with mortgages who had previously benefitted from the dizzy rise in house prices. Discontent with Mrs Thatcher's leadership had been simmering on the Conservative backbenches for some time, as MPs suddenly appreciated the flimsy nature of their party's hold on the electorate. At the end of 1989, a 'stalking horse' candidate, Sir Anthony Meyer, took advantage of rules which had been adopted in 1975 (in order to facilitate the deposition of Edward Heath), and challenged Mrs Thatcher in a leadership election. He received only twenty-four votes to her 314 but, given Sir Anthony's limited leadership potential, this was an ominous outcome, not least because there were also thirty-one abstentions. A year later, the outlook for the government was much bleaker. A more substantial figure, Michael Heseltine, challenged Mrs Thatcher after calculating that Howe's resignation speech had left her mortally wounded. On the first ballot of the election among MPs, Mrs Thatcher won 204 votes, compared with 152 for Heseltine. Her total was only two short of the 15 per cent majority required by the 1975 rules. Following individual interviews with members of the cabinet, however, Mrs Thatcher resigned amid emotional scenes and allegations of 'betrayal'. A week later, John Major, who had replaced Howe as Foreign Secretary before stepping into Lawson's shoes as Chancellor, was elected as the new Conservative leader and hence Prime Minister. The positive effect on support for the Conservatives was immediate (Figure 4.3) but, despite moves to abandon the poll tax, the recovery proved to be short lived. The ejection of Mrs Thatcher was a classic example of a short-term 'random shock' on public opinion, with the underlying pattern soon being reasserted. As the election approached, the two major parties were running virtually neck and neck in the polls.

The changes in the Labour Party under Neil Kinnock continued apace after 1987. The party had staved off catastrophe, and the task now was to rebuild so that Labour could mount a serious challenge to the Conservatives at the next election. As the 1992 Nuffield study has it, Labour was 'seeking electability' (Butler and Kavanagh, 1992: ch. 3). A major policy review was quickly established with the aim of getting rid of the 'negatives' which were seen as barriers to people voting Labour. Outright re-nationalization of any public utilities was renounced and replaced by a commitment to regulation. As part of a general attempt to appear more 'free-market friendly', spending commitments were limited; and the previous hostility towards the EC was replaced by something akin to a warm embrace. The influence of trade unions in the party was reduced (by cutting the proportion of votes that they cast at the party conference), and some of the Thatcher government's reforms relating to unions and industrial relations were accepted. Perhaps most significant, given Kinnock's views, the party's unilateralist policy on nuclear disarmament was ditched in favour of a multilateral approach. In addition, the campaign to root out dissidents within the party had made considerable progress. Well over a hundred members of Militant were expelled, including two MPs, and the leadership showed astute judgement in refusing to endorse (while clearly benefitting from) a campaign of civil disobedience against the poll tax.

In the terms of ideological engagement laid down during the years of post-war 'consensus', both of the main parties had been 'unelectable' in 1983. Of the two, the voters had judged Labour to be the more 'extreme' and, as a result, the party had almost been beaten by the Alliance, which represented consensual politics but lacked a distinctive social base. Although the process had been protracted and painful, by the late 1980s Labour had begun to turn itself into the kind of party which the SDP defectors would never have left. The remaining question was whether or not Neil Kinnock was the appropriate leader to sell that strategy to the voters.

The years after 1987 were dramatic ones for the political centre in Britain (see Denver, 1993). Immediately after the election, David Steel floated the idea of a full merger between the SDP and Liberals. Predictably, David Owen of the SDP made his opposition clear, but he found himself in a minority within his own party and subsequently resigned as leader. After tortuous negotiations beginning in September 1987, the new party—initially called The Social and Liberal Democrats and shortened by the press to 'salads'—was launched in March 1988. In the following July, Paddy Ashdown was elected leader, and in the autumn of 1989 the name was changed to Liberal Democrats.

Initially, the new party struggled. Membership recruitment and retention were poor and the financial position was precarious. Electoral prospects also looked forlorn. From May 1988 to August 1990 the Liberal Democrats never reached 10 per cent in the monthly voting intentions averages. In the 1989 European Parliament elections, the party came fourth, behind the Greens, with a miserable 6 per cent of votes. There was a limited upturn following a dramatic victory in a by-election in what had been a safe Conservative seat (Eastbourne) in October 1990. The unsentimental Sussex voters had supported the Liberal Democrats even though the vacancy had been created by the IRA's assassination of Mrs Thatcher's close personal friend, Ian Gow, who had been returned with a majority of over 16,000 in October 1987. The fear which spread among Conservative MPs after the Eastbourne result was a major factor in Mrs Thatcher's deposition in the following month. Things really began to look up for the newly merged Liberal Democrats, however, during 1991 (after the SDP had departed the scene), when they made progress in local elections and improved in opinion polls. In part this may be attributable to the considerable exposure that Paddy Ashdown (a charismatic ex-Royal Marine commando who had also served in the elite Special Boat Service) received during the first Gulf War in January and February of that year. There was a further marked improvement in both the party's standing and Ashdown's personal ratings in early 1992, coinciding with (and, possibly, caused by) his enforced but very frank admission that in the mid-1980s he had had an affair with a secretary. The new party could, then, enter the general election campaign without fearing that it might be eradicated, as had seemed possible in 1989.

What of the SDP? The minority in the party which opposed merger with the Liberals decided to keep a 'continuing SDP' in being (a rump of die-hard merger 'refuseniks' followed suit on the Liberal side). A good second place was achieved in a by-election at Richmond, Yorkshire, in February 1989 (relegating the Liberal Democrats to third place behind the winner, the future Conservative leader William Hague), but this proved to be a temporary relief. In the first six months of 1989, the party averaged just under 5 per cent of voting intentions; in the second half of the year, the figure was less than 3 per cent. The *coup de grâce* was administered by the voters in the Bootle by-election of May 1990, when the SDP candidate garnered only 155 votes (0.4 per cent), coming sixth out of seven candidates, behind not only the three major parties but also a Green, a (continuing) Liberal, and the Monster Raving Loony candidate. For Dr Owen, defeat by the Monster Raving Loonies was probably less hurtful than being worsted by the non-merged Liberal. Within two weeks the SDP voted itself out of existence. (For a full history and analysis of the SDP, see Crewe and King, 1995.)

In this inter-election period, support for 'others' reached a higher level than in any of those that we have examined so far. Previously, 'other' voting intention figures mainly reflected support for the nationalist parties in Scotland and Wales and hence made only a minor difference to the scores for Britain as a whole. In this period, however, support for others peaked at 16.5 per cent, in July 1989. This was mainly due to a sudden increase in support for the Green Party, which shot to prominence on the political scene in the 1989 European elections. Although it did not win any seats—these elections were then contested under first-past-the-post—the party came third in terms of the popular vote, with a 14.9 per cent share. This achievement took the major parties and political pundits by surprise. Doubtless it reflected the early travails of the Liberal Democrats, which prompted voters discontented with the main parties to look elsewhere for a vehicle through which to express their alienation. Although the Greens lost their bloom as time passed, the combined support for 'others' remained at a historically high level as the 1992 election loomed.

In Scotland, meanwhile, the SNP remained in the electoral doldrums (relatively speaking) during 1987. After that, however, support began to pick up, and in the last six months of 1989, with anger over the poll tax at its peak, the party averaged 26 per cent in polls conducted by System Three. Thereafter, the SNP only occasionally fell below 20 per cent, and in January/February 1992 stood at 26 per cent in Scotland once again.

The 1992 Campaign

As election campaigning became ever more professional, any notion that it would be confined to the few weeks before polling day had to be abandoned. Although there was, of course, a dramatic increase in the *intensity* of campaign activity after the announcement of an election date, by the 1990s it was easy to identify a separate 'long' campaign. In 1992, for example, the major parties mounted advertising blitzes well in advance of the election. In January, the Conservatives launched a poster entitled 'Labour's Tax Bombshell', which was widely credited with shoring up support for the party and was used again in the weeks before polling. Labour replied, somewhat belatedly, with 'VATMAN', featuring a caricature of the Chancellor, Norman Lamont, dressed as Batman. In hindsight, the party's strategists might have reconsidered the wisdom of associating Lamont, whose public *persona* was never very positive, with a heroic, comic-book crime-fighting figure.

When the 'short' campaign arrived, the Conservatives could not feel confident of a fourth consecutive victory. Labour held a small but persistent lead in the polls, the economy had not recovered as hoped from the deep recession that

Mrs Thatcher had bequeathed to Major, and both inflation and unemployment were heading in the wrong direction. The parties worked harder than ever to wrest control over the agenda. The Conservatives undoubtedly made progress by hammering away at Labour on taxation, especially after Labour's 'shadow Budget' proposed to raise the top rate of tax from 40 to 50 per cent. This attempt by Labour to appear competent and fully prepared for a return to government back-fired badly. Ironically, if Nigel Lawson and Mrs Thatcher had published their respective memoirs before rather than after the 1992 general election, the public would have known that the ex-premier had initially preferred a 50 per cent higher rate before Lawson cut it to 40 per cent in his controversial 1988 Budget (Lawson, 1992: 824; Thatcher, 1993: 623–4).

Labour, meanwhile, focused relentlessly on the National Health Service (NHS). The latter, indeed, gave rise to one of the few incidents of note during the campaign—the so-called 'War of Jennifer's Ear'. On the Tuesday of the third week, a Labour election broadcast featured a child in severe pain whose ear operation was repeatedly delayed by the NHS while another, with well-to-do parents, was treated almost immediately in the private sector. It emerged that this vignette was based on an actual case of a girl called Jennifer, and the press soon uncovered her iden-tity. There followed a series of furious rows about such matters as who leaked the family's name, whether Labour had exploited a child, and the ethics of the press in hounding the family. The net effect was to make it more difficult for Labour to capitalize on one of their most promising issues.

While any potential gain from the shadow Budget and Jennifer's ear were nulli-fied by clever Tory tactics, another Labour initiative resulted in a gratuitous self-inflicted wound. In the penultimate campaign week, the party organized a mass rally in Sheffield which was stage-managed to a degree never before seen in a British election. In an updated version of the 1987 'KINNOCK' broadcast, the Labour leader was presented in rock-star guise, along with suitable music, billow-ing flags, lighting effects, and a roaring audience of 10,000 people. With Labour's poll lead looking solid—if not terribly large—the mood seemed unpalatably tri-umphalist to some television viewers. Even the Labour MP Giles Radice described the occasion as 'vulgar' (Radice, 2004: 268). The event has acquired notoriety as the turning point that cost Labour the election. Actually, there is little direct evi-dence for this view. In the seven polls preceding the rally, Labour's lead over the Conservatives averaged 2.5 points; in the seven after the rally, it was exactly the same. Quite possibly, however, the effects of the Sheffield rally were felt later, when in the tranquillity of the polling stations voters asked themselves whether they would like to give Neil Kinnock the opportunity to celebrate in earnest. In this context, it is significant that when Labour entered the 1997 election cam-paign with far more realistic prospects of returning to office, there was no sign of premature celebration—and the victory party was more subdued than the Sheffield rally had been.

In comparison, the Conservative campaign appeared routine and dull, if well organized and professional. John Major began with a planned series of 'Ask John Major' events, at which the Prime Minister sat on a stool in the middle of an audience and answered unscripted questions. This format was soon abandoned, however, and Major adopted a more spontaneous approach. He took to standing on a soapbox in the open air brandishing a megaphone, declaiming—with sincerity rather than oratorical wizardry—to crowds which were sometimes hostile. A veteran of numerous local elections before embarking on his meteoric ministerial career, Major hoped that this conscious return to old-style campaigning would make a refreshing contrast to Labour's carefully choreographed efforts (Major, 1999: 289). Major was also persuaded to 'do a Kinnock' by appearing in a party broadcast called 'The Journey', produced by the film director John Schlesinger. This showed the 'classless' Prime Minister revisiting his early haunts and expressing his (apparently genuine) surprise when he discovered that many landmarks of his youth still existed. It is doubtful whether the film converted many voters to the Conservative cause and it embarrassed Major himself (Major, 1999: 300–1). One unimpressed viewer was the MP Edwina Currie, who recorded in her diary in the last hours of the campaign that the Prime Minister had 'turned out to be a very dull, wooden and incompetent performer'. As Major's former lover, Currie was not the most objective witness; but, although she thought that her party was 'heading for an ignominious defeat' nationally, her forecasts of results in and around her Derbyshire constituency erred on the optimistic side (Currie, 2002: 324–7).

Constrained by legislation and hampered by the intense news management activities undertaken by the parties (which explain to some extent the scramble triggered off by Jennifer's ear), the broadcast media provided their usual range of programming, with news reports focusing on the party leaders. Coverage was virtually round the clock—literally so in the case of Sky News, which was reporting an election for the first time. The press was as partisan as ever, with most papers lining up behind the Conservatives. *The Sun* was particularly ferocious, having sensed that Labour's focus on the party leader was a serious tactical blunder. On the day before polling, its front page announced 'NIGHTMARE ON KINNOCK STREET', and elaborated this spine-chilling scenario on 'Pages 2, 3, 4, 5, 6, 7, 8, 9 and 34'. On polling day itself, over a picture of Kinnock's head inside a light bulb, *The Sun*'s headline ran: 'IF KINNOCK WINS TODAY WILL THE LAST PERSON IN BRITAIN PLEASE TURN OUT THE LIGHTS'. Other papers were more restrained, with even Conservative-supporting publications expressing reservations and disquiet about what they perceived as unimpressive campaigning by Major and his party.

Local campaigning in the 1992 election received much more detailed academic consideration than had been the case hitherto (Denver and Hands, 1997). For the first time, a survey-based measure of the intensity of campaigning was developed, which was applicable across constituencies. Previously, the Nuffield studies had relied on informal advice from party insiders. Using the new approach, it was found that the Conservatives had the strongest campaigns overall but that Labour efforts were more successfully targeted. In the latter's marginal and 'possible' seats the party had the strongest campaigns of all. The analysis also showed that stronger Labour and Liberal Democrat campaigning had a positive effect on performance (although this was not the case for the Conservatives). Differential local campaign intensity, therefore, probably explains why the election results showed Labour performing more strongly in marginal seats than elsewhere (see below).

The 1992 Results

Despite all the huffing and puffing of the campaign, the popularity of the major parties barely shifted (see Appendix, Figure 4.A3). While the Liberal Democrats inched steadily forward and ended up three points ahead of where they started, Labour and the Conservatives both declined by just over one point. The final polls all indicated that there would be a hung parliament and even the exit polls conducted on polling day for the BBC and ITN suggested the same conclusion: both organizations forecast a hung parliament at the start of their results programmes. Although the presenters and analysts were slow to react to early results, when Labour failed to gain the Essex seat of Basildon (which was a key marginal as well as symbolizing the uneven geographical impact of 'Thatcherism'), it was clear that the Conservatives would hang on to office. As the satirist and Labour activist John O'Farrell lamented, 'The BBC had spent £20,000 on a huge 16-foot swingometer and it hardly swung at all' (O'Farrell, 1998: 268–9).

In fact, over the country as a whole there *was* a swing—of just 2.0 per cent from Conservative to Labour, which saw the latter gain forty-two seats compared with 1987. However, this was only half of the swing required to deny the Conservatives an overall majority for the fourth successive election. The Liberal Democrat vote share (17.8 per cent) was down by almost five points compared with the Alliance in 1987, but the number of seats won (twenty) was little different. In Scotland, the SNP advanced to 21.5 per cent of votes but remained at three seats. In contrast, a modest advance by Plaid Cymru in Wales (from 7.3 to 8.9 per cent) earned an additional seat, making a total of four. In their first major foray into a general election the Greens failed to repeat their success in the very different European elections of three years previously—their 253 candidates averaged just 1.3 per cent of votes (0.5 per cent of the total).

Once again there were marked regional variations in swing, but on this occasion there was a slight reversal of the long-term divergence between North and South. While the swing to Labour was only 0.9 per cent in Scotland and 2.1 per cent in the North of England, it was 2.8 per cent in the South East (including London).

Commentators suggested that this was because the recent economic recession had hit hard in the South but had a less dramatic impact in already-depressed Scotland and the North. More pertinently, in Labour's long-established heartlands, support was already so solid that there were far fewer potential supporters to be converted.

Even given regional variations, however, Labour did better, and the Conservatives worse, in terms of winning seats than would have been expected on the basis of the national swing. This was because Labour was more effective in capturing (or holding on to) target seats. In 168 constituencies that were marginal or 'possibles' from Labour's point of view, the swing to the party was 3.5 per cent. In the remainder (very safe, comfortable, or hopeless), it was only 1.6 per cent.

Turnout in the election rose significantly (see Table 4.1), no doubt reflecting anticipation of a close outcome. However, it seems to have been Conservative-inclined people who were scared into voting by the prospect of a change of government. In seats won by the Conservatives in 1987, turnout rose by 3.5 points, whereas in those won by Labour, there was hardly any change. Indeed, the increase was greatest where it was least relevant, in very safe Conservative seats (+4.2). In Britain, turnout ranged from 53.9 per cent in Peckham to 86.1 per cent in Leicestershire North West.

The election result provoked much soul-searching in various quarters. While the pollsters mounted investigations into why they had come unstuck so spectacularly, Labour politicians wondered what they had to do to win the trust of the electorate. Media commentators struggled to explain John Major's victory, and even academics were nonplussed. As we have seen, following the demise of the Butler–Stokes model of voting, 'issue voting' had found favour with electoral analysts. However, in 1992 the issues that were mentioned most by poll respondents as influencing their vote—health, unemployment, education—were all ones on which Labour enjoyed large leads as the best party. Theories linking elections to the economic cycle also looked doubtful, as the Conservatives had triumphed in the teeth of a serious recession (although it could be argued that the electorate blamed Thatcher rather than Major for the problems of the economy). Most commentators came to the view that the electorate had voted for their 'pocket book'. When times were difficult enough already, voters feared high(er) taxes and great(er) inflation under Labour—and that eclipsed their preferences on social issues.

This argument has superficial attractions. But Labour's shadow Chancellor, John Smith, asserted that 80 per cent of voters would benefit from his tax proposals. If such a widely respected figure was disbelieved, the most likely problem for Labour was a general lack of credibility rather than narrower economic considerations. The obvious (with hindsight) reason for Labour's lack of credibility was that Major, despite his limitations, was clearly preferred to Kinnock as Prime Minister. In July 1991—more than eight months before the election—the shrewd Conservative Chairman Chris Patten told the journalist Hugo Young that his two campaign issues would be leadership and economic competence, adding that 'The two are subsumed in the question, Would you trust N[eil] K[innock] with the economy more than you would trust J[ohn] M[ajor] with the NHS?' (Young, 2008: 330).

Patten's strategy paid off. Given that media coverage of the campaign (and of politics more generally) had been strongly focused on personalities for many years, negativity towards Kinnock (rather than overwhelming affection for Major) was probably the chief explanation for the surprising Conservative victory. In four polls conducted by MORI during the campaign, Major was nominated as best Prime Minister by 40 per cent of respondents on average, Kinnock by 28 per cent, and Ashdown by 21 per cent. Apart from its deterrent effect on voters in key Labour/Conservative marginals like Basildon, the Kinnock factor might also have persuaded wavering government supporters against giving 'tactical' support to Liberal Democrat candidates. The Liberal Democrat leader Paddy Ashdown certainly feared that this was the case. Tellingly, he noted on polling day that Conservative 'scare stories about a hung parliament meaning Kinnock in Downing Street' were 'beginning to have some effect' (Ashdown, 2000: 157). Undoubtedly, this harsh but plausible judgement on Kinnock has been resisted because sympathetic journalists and academics often developed a considerable personal affection for him and, if anything, this tendency has been reinforced by the feeling that Tony Blair's later electoral success would have been impossible without Kinnock's courage (see, for example, Morgan, 1992: 333–43). Kinnock himself recognized the problems that he had in appealing to a large swathe of voters and, according to Philip Gould (1998: 144) considered resignation 'on more than one occasion' before the election.

Voting in the 1980s

The Controversy Over Class Voting

The authors of the BES report on the 1983 election (Heath et al., 1985) stimulated a lively (and occasionally ill-tempered) debate among British electoral analysts by denying that there had been a steady weakening of class voting in Britain. Their argument involved, first, devising a new way of allocating respondents to classes, rejecting the traditional manual/non-manual dichotomy as inadequate, and substituting a five-category alternative. Second, they suggested that 'absolute class voting' (the percentage of the electorate who support their 'natural' class party) is not a useful way of either thinking about or measuring the level of class voting. The key indicator, rather, is the *relative* support for the parties in the different classes. Third, they argued that the most appropriate way of measuring this is to calculate the odds of voters in different classes voting (say) Labour and using the ratio of these odds as the measure of class voting. When this was done, the figures from 1964 to 1983 suggested not a progressive class dealignment but, rather, nothing more than 'trendless fluctuation' in the extent of class voting.

This argument was subjected to some very strong criticism in the academic world (see especially Crewe, 1986, and Dunleavy, 1987). Each stage in Heath et al.'s argument was attacked, but their use of odds ratios to measure class voting attracted particularly searching criticism, with Dunleavy describing the measure as, among other things, 'quite inappropriate', 'eccentric', 'peculiar', 'distorting', and 'virtually meaningless'. Nonetheless, with some modifications, the BES team reasserted their conclusion in their report on the 1987 election (Heath et al., 1991) and also, in more muted form, after the 1992 election (Heath et al., 1994), By 1997, however, a re-analysis by members of the BES team, using advanced statistical techniques, had revealed a decline in class voting which was very similar to the trend in the simple Alford index (Evans et al., 1999). Effectively, the class dealignment controversy was over, and it was agreed all round that the relationship between class and party support had indeed become markedly weaker after the 1960s.

Sectoral Cleavages

As discussed in Chapter 3, evidence of a weakening association between class and party preference among voters during the 1970s led most academic analysts to argue that 'issue voting' was on the increase and to downplay the role of socioeconomic factors. An alternative perspective was offered by Patrick Dunleavy (1980), however. He suggested that social location was still an important influence on voters but that the old cleavage based on occupational class had been replaced by new ones based on the sectors of production and consumption. The major parties had very different approaches to the public sector—especially after Mrs Thatcher became Conservative leader, her party seemed to regard the sector as little more than parasitic on the real wealth creators in the private sector. Labour, of course, remained a strong believer in the public sector after 1979. It would have been odd if those working in the different sectors of the economy did not recognize and act on this. On the consumption side, Dunleavy argued that people who lived in social housing, relied on public transport, and depended on the NHS for medical care, needed these services to be provided collectively and would be likely to vote Labour. On the other hand, owner occupiers, car owners, and those with private medical insurance were consumers in the private sector, and would be likely to favour the Conservatives.

In the 1983 election, party choice was indeed influenced—although to a limited extent—by sector of employment. According to BES data, employees in the private sector voted 47 per cent Conservative, 29 per cent Labour, and 23 per cent for the Alliance parties; among employees in the public sector the figures were 38 per cent Conservative, 32 per cent Labour, and 28 per cent Alliance. Although the Conservatives clearly did better among the former, Labour support was not significantly different among the two groups. On the other hand, the evidence for a consumption cleavage is weak. Part of the problem is that almost everyone uses the NHS, car ownership is widespread, and social housing rapidly became the preserve of a relatively small minority of the population. Overall, the public/private cleavage could never be seen as more than a partial explanation for voting behaviour in the era of dealignment.

'The North–South Divide'

In discussing the 1983 and 1987 elections, we noted that the Conservatives tended to do better in the south of the country, and Labour in Scotland and the north. There was nothing new in this geographical pattern to party support—similar differences existed in the nineteenth century. However, the apparent widening of the gap—reinforced by the obvious differences in the economic fortunes of North and South in the 1980s—attracted much interest and comment (see Johnston et al., 1988).

Figure 4.4 illustrates the extent of regional (and Scottish and Welsh) distinctiveness by showing, for each election from 1964 to 1992, the difference between the Conservative 'lead' over Labour in vote share (which could, of course, be a deficit) in the area in question and the same measure for Britain as a whole. In other words, the graph illustrates the extent of regional deviation from the national pattern. Over this period, Scotland was always more Labour-inclined, but the gap widened significantly in 1979 and through the 1980s before closing slightly in 1992. The North of England moved less sharply, but nonetheless significantly, away from the Conservatives. In contrast, the South of England outside London always deviated towards the Conservatives, and the extent of this deviation increased gradually throughout the period (although again with a slight reduction in 1992). In 1964, Wales was clearly the most pro-Labour/anti-Conservative part of the UK and it generally remained so, although the extent of its deviation from national patterns of support did not change very much in the elections covered in this chapter. Finally, the lines on the graph referring to London and the Midlands are consistently very close to the horizontal line which indicates no deviation at all. Throughout, relative support for the two major parties in these regions closely resembled the national picture.

Over this period, support for the Liberals and their successors also varied a good deal across regions. In the 1960s, they were known as the party of the 'Celtic fringe'. This gives a misleading impression, however, in that across Scotland and Wales the centre party always had *smaller* vote shares than in Britain as a whole from 1964. Liberal successes were very much on 'the fringe of the fringe'—in

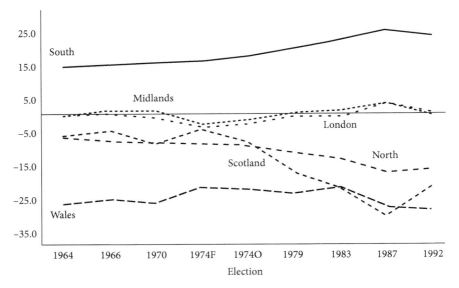

Figure 4.4 Regional deviations from national (GB) Conservative lead over Labour, 1964–92

Notes: The names and boundaries of English regions were revised in 1994. For the period covered here 'North' includes the North, North West, and Yorkshire and Humber regions; 'Midlands' comprises East and West Midlands; and 'South' covers East Anglia, South East and South West.

constituencies such as Orkney and Shetland and Montgomeryshire, for example. The North and Midlands were also lacking in enthusiasm for the centre parties. The two regions where the Liberals, the Alliance, and then the Liberal Democrats consistently did best were the South East (outside London) and what might be regarded as their heartland area of the South West (especially in Devon and Cornwall).

A less frequently noted geographical divergence in party support during the 1980s related to predominantly urban as opposed to rural areas. Figure 4.5 shows how the Conservative 'lead' over Labour varied from 'very urban' areas (mainly cities) through to rural areas in elections from 1964 to 1992. The figures show remarkably clear and steady trends. Very urban areas moved more strongly towards Labour at every election in the series. From the mid-1970s, 'mainly urban' areas also moved towards Labour. In contrast, mixed and rural areas increasingly deviated towards the Conservatives. By 1992, the divide was such that while the Conservatives led Labour by 47.9 per cent to 21.3 per cent in rural areas, they trailed by 37.0 per cent to 45.3 per cent in those that were very urban.

Various explanations for the geographical polarization of party support in Britain have been advanced. They include slow changes in the socio-economic make-up of different areas because of migration trends, and uneven economic development. Curtice and Steed (1982) also suggested a purely political

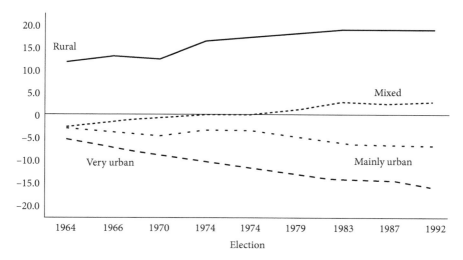

Figure 4.5 Urban/rural deviations from national (GB) Conservative lead over Labour, 1964–92

Notes: Constituencies are categorized according to the number of electors per hectare. Very urban is defined as greater than 24, mainly urban as 8 to 24, mixed as 1.3 to 7.9, and rural as less than 1.3.

explanation. As the Liberals and their successors (and the nationalists in Scotland and Wales) increased in popularity from the 1970s onwards, they generally gained at the expense of the locally weaker major party. Since the Conservatives were already weaker in the North and Scotland (and urban areas), their vote was squeezed by the increase in support for 'minor' parties. Thus they performed more poorly than Labour. In the South and rural areas the picture was reversed, with Labour being the party to suffer.

Like some other explanations, including the differential regional impact of economic policy, this certainly sheds light on regional trends in the 1980s. It is worth remembering, however, that regional differences in party support are not new (see Field, 1997). In the nineteenth century, the Conservatives did best in the south of England while the Liberals were strong in Scotland, Wales, and the North. This suggests that a more general explanation is required than the regional effects of the policies of particular governments. Field suggests a version of 'core–periphery' theory. The 'core' (London and the South East in this case) dominates the periphery culturally, economically, and politically. Peripheral regions tend to be poorer, suffer more in times of economic depression, have worse housing conditions, and less good services. Consequently, people living in these regions often resent the domination of the core and tend to favour radical, non-establishment parties. This theory does not fit the British case perfectly—London is the 'core of the core' but has not disproportionately favoured the Conservatives—but it does offer some clues to understanding the long-term geographical pattern of voting.

Nonetheless, in trying to explain regional electoral differentiation, analysts often invoke even vaguer ideas, such as distinctive social, cultural, religious, or political traditions.

The widening of geographical divisions in party support during the 1980s had significant consequences for the operation of the electoral system. In crude terms, Labour seats in the North and in cities became more safely Labour, while Conservative seats in rural areas and the South became more safely Conservative. Fewer and fewer constituencies were marginal. As a result, fewer seats changed hands on any given national swing. Curtice and Steed (1986) calculated that between 1955 and 1983 the number of constituencies that could be defined as marginal fell from 166 to 80. At least to some extent, this trend was reinforced by the reluctance of increasingly professional (and cash-limited) parties to expend resources in apparently pointless constituency contests. Previously, the shares of seats accumulated by the leading parties on the basis of their vote could be described by a 'cube law'—that is, if vote shares were in the ratio A:B, then seats would be in the ratio $A^3:B^3$. Thus, if the ratio of the two-party vote were 3:2, seats would be in the ratio 27:8. This exaggerative effect was held by its supporters to be one of the strengths of the first-past-the-post system. Gradually, however, the exaggerative effect declined, and by 1992 there was no effect at all. The ratio of Conservative to Labour votes in Britain that year was 55:45, and the ratio of seats won was also 55:45.

Conservative Hegemony?

When the Conservatives left office in 1997, they had been in power continuously for eighteen years. This was the longest period of single-party rule since the Great Reform Act of 1832. The 1992 BES study was entitled *Labour's Last Chance?* (Heath et al., 1994) and, after the election, Anthony King reflected on 'The implications of One-Party Government' (King, 1993). Superficially, then, there seem to be good grounds for describing this period as one of Conservative 'hegemony'.

In the first place, however, such a conclusion involves focusing exclusively on general elections. At local level things looked rather different. In 1990, for example, across Britain, Labour had about the same number of councillors as the Conservatives and controlled more councils, including fourteen of the thirty-two London boroughs, thirty-one of the thirty-six metropolitan boroughs and the four most populous Scottish regions (compared with, respectively, 12, 0, and 0 for the Conservatives).

Even at national level the 'Conservative hegemony' description can be queried. The party's victories were achieved on relatively modest shares of the vote by post-war standards. During the winning run of the 1950s (1951, 1955, and 1959), the Conservative vote share was never *smaller* than 48 per cent; in the four wins from 1979, it was never *greater* than 44 per cent. Conservative success owed much to the fragmentation of the opposition forces and the fact that in these circumstances the electoral system made it easier for them to win seats with smaller shares of votes. The Conservatives also had a great deal of luck, in that after 1979 their main opponent, Labour, almost tore itself apart after lurching to the left and chose leaders who lacked electoral appeal. Although Labour's position gradually improved, desertions by MPs and supporters to what became the Liberal/SDP Alliance weakened the party, and meant that a potential anti-Conservative majority in the country was hopelessly fractured. The Conservatives would have had to be accident-prone to the point of carelessness not to win elections against such weak and divided opponents. Finally, it is clear that the electorate did not endorse the main elements of 'Thatcherism' with any enthusiasm (see Crewe, 1988). In 1986, for example, by large majorities the electorate thought that reducing unemployment was more important than curbing inflation, and opposed the privatization of utilities. In late 1979, Gallup had reported that, by a margin of 44 per cent to 25 per cent, voters favoured extending government services even if this meant tax increases, as opposed to cutting taxes at the expense of services. By March 1992, the respective figures were 66 per cent and 10 per cent, suggesting at the very least that even the beneficiaries of previous Conservative cuts in direct taxation were disinclined to admit that they wanted more of the same. Such data make awkward reading for those who assume in hindsight that Mrs Thatcher was propelled to power by a nationwide revulsion against a confiscatory state and maintained in office by a popular ideological 'counter-revolution' until less resolute individuals brought her down.

The Conservatives won all four general elections between 1979 and 1997—thanks in large part to a divided opposition and a demoralized Labour Party. The bare voting figures, backed by evidence drawn from surveys of public opinion, cast doubt on any notion of a Conservative hegemony, however. The survival of the Liberal Democrats as a significant electoral force, confirmed by their respectable performance in the 1992 general election, ensured that, among those who voted, Conservatives remained in a minority. To some seasoned Labour strategists, all that was needed was to sit quietly and wait for the Conservatives to run out of luck. Others, however, were convinced that something more radical was required—and that Labour could never hope to return to office unless it started to act as if Conservative hegemony had been real.

Appendix: Campaign Polls

Figures 4.A1–4.A3 relate to Great Britain, as Northern Ireland is not included in national opinion polls (data from https://www.markpack.org.uk/opinion-polls/).

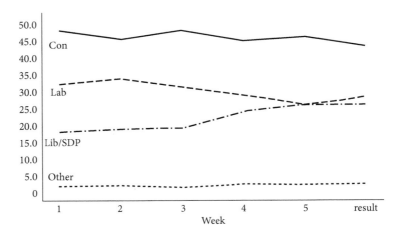

Figure 4.A1 Campaign polls, 1983

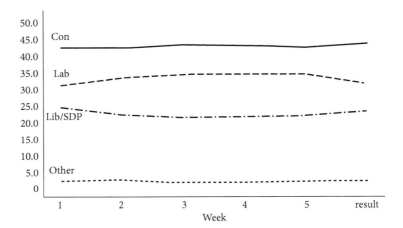

Figure 4.A2 Campaign polls, 1987

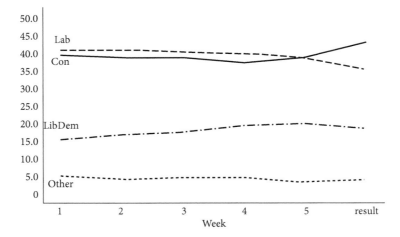

Figure 4.A3 Campaign polls, 1992

5

The Triumph of New Labour

Elections, 1997–2005

The Longest Parliament: 1992–7

The parliament elected in 1992 was the longest lasting since the maximum time between elections was fixed at five years in 1911. There was one simple reason for this—at no point after September 1992 was the Prime Minister, John Major, in a position to call an election which his party had any serious prospect of winning. Before that date, the government had every reason to be pleased with its position in the country's estimation. Flushed with their unexpected general election success in April, in the May local elections the Conservatives reversed a long series of losses, gaining more than 300 seats and easily leading the other parties in terms of vote share. Afterwards, Chris Patten (who had lost his seat in the general election) reflected that 'the conventional wisdom... says that everything in the garden is rosy. It seldom is. Things crop up that nobody expects' (Young, 2008: 344). That particular political cliché was vividly verified in the second half of 1992.

In late 1989, John Major (as Chancellor) had eventually persuaded Mrs Thatcher that the UK should join the European Exchange Rate Mechanism (ERM), so that the value of the pound was fixed in relation to other European currencies and was allowed to 'float' only within narrow margins. In the currency markets, however, the pound was thought to be overvalued, and during the summer of 1992 it came under intense pressure as dealers began to divest themselves of their holdings in sterling. On 16 September ('Black Wednesday') the exchange rate of sterling against other currencies plummeted despite the Bank of England intervening to buy pounds on a massive scale. Successive panic-driven hikes in interest rates—from 10 per cent to 12 per cent and then 15 per cent in the space of a few hours—were unavailing. That evening, the Chancellor, Norman Lamont, was forced to announce that the government had conceded defeat; sterling's membership of the ERM had been suspended.

At a stroke, the central plank of the government's counter-inflation policy had splintered and the long-standing reputation that the Conservatives enjoyed as the party of economic competence was wrecked. In trying to shore up sterling the government had wasted billions of pounds and ended up with an effective devaluation of the currency. The *Times* headline of 17 September left no room for doubt: 'Beaten Lamont Devalues Pound'. It was perhaps a bit unfair to single out the

British General Elections Since 1964: Diversity, Dealignment, and Disillusion. Second Edition. David Denver and Mark Garnett, Oxford University Press. © David Denver and Mark Garnett 2021. DOI: 10.1093/oso/9780198844952.003.0005

Chancellor for blame. In fact, ERM membership was the Prime Minister's policy, so this was really a 'Nightmare on Major Street'. The episode had plainly been a fiasco, with the media emphasizing the huge sums that had been spent to no effect, and the government was humiliated. Although the other two main parties had also favoured ERM membership, the impact on public opinion was swift and dramatic. In early September, Gallup reported that the Conservatives enjoyed a lead of five points over Labour as the party best able to handle Britain's economic difficulties. A month later, Labour had taken an eighteen-point lead on this question, which then stretched to twenty-one points in November. This was despite the fact that Labour's alleged incompetence in economic matters had just cost the party dear in the 1992 election. During the rest of the parliament, the Conservatives never regained their reputation for sound economic management. In terms of voting intentions, in polls during August and early September, Labour held a single point lead over the Conservatives, on average. Just weeks after 16 September, that lead had widened to seventeen points.

The ERM disaster had further, indirect effects that impinged on the government's popularity. It emboldened the Eurosceptics among Conservative MPs. Twenty-two diehard opponents of European integration had voted against ratifying the Maastricht treaty in May; but the experience of the ERM hardened opinion and the question of Europe divided the party with increasing bitterness. Secondly, the Prime Minister and his government lost the support of the Tory press. With the Eurosceptic *Sun* in the vanguard, Major was portrayed as a weak and indecisive muddler. He never regained even lukewarm support, far less the significant personal backing that he had enjoyed before the election.

If this were not bad enough for the Conservatives, in various ways they succeeded in making things worse for themselves and came to be regarded as a government that could get nothing right (Denver, 1998). Having mercilessly pilloried Labour as the party of high taxation during the election campaign, in the March 1993 Budget the Chancellor increased taxes on alcohol and tobacco by more than inflation, raised national insurance contributions, reduced tax allowances for married couples and mortgage holders, froze other allowances (an effective cut in real terms) and extended Value Added Tax (VAT) to domestic fuel and power. The latter, in particular, was a direct betrayal of a campaign promise and—a year too late—authenticated Labour's portrayal of Lamont as 'Vatman'. The VAT increase was widely thought to be instrumental in the loss of two previously safe seats (Newbury and Christchurch) to the Liberal Democrats in by-elections in May and July, respectively. Later in 1993, Lamont's replacement, Kenneth Clarke, further restricted income tax allowances and introduced two new taxes—on insurance premiums and air travel. The Conservative advantage on taxation— they led Labour by 49 per cent to 27 per cent as the party best on taxation during the 1992 election—was squandered along with the party's reputation for sound economic management. After the March 1993 Budget—which was thought to be unfair by a record margin of 75 per cent to 19 per cent according to Gallup's figures—Labour was viewed as the best party on taxation by 42 per cent to 33 per cent, and the Conservatives did not regain the lead on this issue before the 1997 election. When the long-promised cuts in the standard rate of income tax finally arrived—by one penny in both 1995 and 1996—it was a case of much too little too late. It was almost as if, having accepted that the Conservatives were set for a period in opposition whatever he did, Clarke decided that he might as well leave office untainted by accusations of trying to buy back the approval of alienated supporters. The result was the bequest of an enviable economic outlook to Labour and no noticeable improvement in Clarke's career prospects.

The Major government also came to be associated with 'sleaze'. This took two main forms, involving either sex or money. Between September 1992 and June 1996, no fewer than nine members of the government resigned (and another died) in the context of a sex scandal, ranging from straightforward adultery to bizarre auto-erotic sexual practices. Although most of those involved were relatively minor figures in the government, the Conservatives had cast themselves as the champions of family values and, in 1993, Major had launched a 'Back to Basics' initiative—actually a call for the application of practical common sense to policy decisions but widely interpreted as an attempt to reassert traditional moral values. Even in its intended form the slogan was ill conceived, implying that the Conservatives had lost sight of 'the Basics' at some point during their protracted spell in office. But once the media decided to interpret Major's initiative as a moral crusade, exposure of the ensuing sexual scandals could be justified as evidence of breath-taking hypocrisy within the governing party (Baston, 2000).

Financial sleaze was probably even more damaging to the government's reputation. In some cases, this involved revelations concerning MPs who were willing to take cash from lobbyists in return for asking specific questions in the House of Commons. In others, ministers were discovered to be accepting hospitality and cash payments from prominent businessmen, and were forced to resign their positions. The most notorious, perhaps, was Jonathan Aitken, who resigned as a defence minister in April 1995 in order to sue the *Guardian* newspaper for libel. Although he claimed to bear 'the simple sword of truth' against 'twisted' journalists, his real weaponry turned out to have been forged from more mundane metal. His libel case collapsed, and after the 1997 election he was jailed for perjury. A different sort of financial sleaze related to the so-called 'revolving door' through which leading Conservatives were whisked from the cabinet to city boardrooms. Many of these lucrative positions were offered by firms that had featured in the privatization programme carried through by these self-same ministers. 'What is really sleazy', said *The Sun*—itself hardly a paragon of traditional morality—'is the number of Tories sticking their snouts in a trough of their own making' (19.01.1993).

Partly as a consequence, the programme of privatization, which had been a central and apparently successful element of Thatcherism during the 1980s, itself became unpopular. The people running the newly privatized utilities were paid vastly more than those who had managed them when they were publicly owned, yet did not seem to perform very differently; indeed, they were often the same individuals. In the summer of 1996, for example, despite increased charges for consumers, large management salaries, and healthy profits, Yorkshire Water was unable to keep its customers supplied, and its executives urged the local population to cut down on baths. For weeks on end, the company (and by implication the whole privatization policy) was vilified and ridiculed in the press. Despite the change in public sentiment, the government pressed ahead, against strong opposition, with the privatization of British Rail. This was completed in 1996, and was followed by hundreds of train cancellations by one company which had sacked too many drivers. For a significant body of opinion, this was a privatization too far. Not inaptly, Robert Adley (1992: 6–7), Conservative chairman of the Commons transport committee, warned that it would become 'a poll tax on wheels'.

Finally, as mentioned previously, the Conservatives were plagued by divisions over Europe. During 1993, securing ratification of the Maastricht treaty by the House of Commons proved a nightmare for the government as indefatigable Eurosceptics, encouraged from the sidelines by Baroness Thatcher, fought it all the way. In November 1994, in a vote on the European Finance Bill which was made an issue of confidence, eight backbench rebels abstained and John Major deprived them of the Conservative whip—in effect expelling them from the parliamentary party. They were joined by another MP who resigned the whip voluntarily. These nine proceeded to embarrass the government at every opportunity. In the following April, however, in a humiliating climb-down by Major, the whip was restored unconditionally.

The sniping on Europe continued to frustrate the Prime Minister, and in June 1995, he dramatically resigned as Conservative leader in order to force a leadership contest, challenging his critics to 'put up or shut up'. John Redwood resigned his post as Welsh secretary to 'put up', and ran on a Eurosceptic platform. Major was duly re-elected by his MPs, with 218 votes to 89 for Redwood and 22 abstentions. However, despite energetic attempts to 'spin' this outcome as a triumphant vindication of Major's manoeuvre, one-third of the parliamentary party had withheld support from the Prime Minister, and the European issue continued to cause ructions in the party, both in Parliament and in the country. The public recognized the reality beneath the spin. In their monthly polls over 1995 and 1996, Gallup reports show that, on average, 79 per cent of respondents thought that the Conservatives were divided, with only 12 per cent describing them as united. Voters generally prefer parties to be united, and there seems little doubt that Conservative disunity made the party and the government look shambolic.

With such a dismal record, any government would have struggled to maintain a reasonable level of popularity among the electorate. The Conservatives' difficulties were compounded, however, by changes on the Labour side. Immediately after the 1992 general election, Neil Kinnock announced that he would resign as Labour leader and, in July, John Smith was elected to replace him. Regarded as a right-winger in the early 1980s but firmly in the centre of the post-Kinnock party, Smith was a reliable and cautious Scottish lawyer, whose forensic debating skills made him more of a political heavyweight than his predecessor. He inclined to the not unrealistic view that Labour needed just 'one more heave' to oust the Conservatives. Rather than embark on further changes in addition to those initi-ated under Neil Kinnock, the party could rely on government mistakes to secure victory. Following Smith's elevation, Labour's standing in the polls improved steadily, especially after the ERM debacle (Figure 5.1). Smith's sudden death in May 1994 robbed Labour of its first widely respected and popular leader since 1979; even *The Sun* (13.03.1994) marked the occasion by mourning the loss of 'Britain's next Prime Minister'. In the following July, Tony Blair was chosen as the new leader and he proved to be even more popular with the public.

Blair did not believe in 'one more heave' but, rather, that his party still needed root and branch reform. Specifically, it had to alter the perceptions which deterred people from voting Labour—such as its reputation as a party wedded to high taxation and indiscriminate public spending. Blair proceeded to transform the Labour Party and make a decisive victory at the next election even more likely. The role of the party conference in policy-making was further reduced, as was the influence of trade unions in the party. Policy changes—notably a pledge to

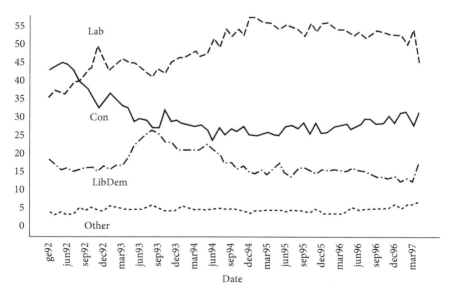

Figure 5.1 Monthly voting intentions, 1992–7 (all polls)

Notes: The 1992 and 1997 election results in Great Britain form the starting and finishing points. The data shown are the monthly means for all published polls.

introduce no increases in income tax or in spending by the shadow Chancellor Gordon Brown, following Blair's earlier promise to be 'tough on crime'—moved the party decisively to the right. The formerly all-conquering left, having been softened up by Kinnock and Smith, was reduced to impotence. Most spectacularly of all, Blair persuaded the party to accept the rewriting of Clause IV of its constitution, which had affirmed the commitment to public ownership of the means of production and exchange. The replacement could be criticized as an anodyne statement of vague generalities ('to create for each of us the means to realise our true potential and for all of us a community in which power, wealth and opportunity are in the hands of the many, not the few') but it signalled a hugely symbolic change. The party could now depict itself as 'New' Labour, unencumbered by the baggage of the past.

Under Blair, Labour's campaigning and relations with the mass media became much more professional and, indeed, increasingly independent of party headquarters, with a 'campaign and media centre' being set up in Millbank Tower late in 1995. Peter Mandelson remained a key figure in this process, together with political strategist Philip Gould and Blair's press secretary, Alastair Campbell. Labour spokespeople, however senior, were ruthlessly kept 'on message' by the campaign team. The centrepiece of the operation was a much-admired computerized 'rapid rebuttal' system', which provided leading party figures with the material to challenge government and Conservative Party arguments (sometimes even before the arguments themselves were made). A less frequently noted consequence of the new approach was the skill and thoroughness with which Labour made submissions to the public enquiries held by the Boundary Commissions which were engaged in a redrawing of constituencies. This attention to detail resulted in the party achieving favourable outcomes in a significant number of disputed cases, so that the expected advantage accruing to the Conservatives from boundary changes implemented in advance of the 1997 election was largely nullified.

The impact of Blair on popular opinion was immense. From August 1994 to January 1997 Labour's share of voting intentions never fell below 50 per cent, and Blair easily outscored his opponents as the best person to be Prime Minister, being preferred on average by 41 per cent compared with 19 per cent for John Major. With the government and its leader floundering, and Tony Blair on the crest of a wave, it is no surprise that in polling and mid-term elections various 'worst ever' records for the Conservatives were shattered. They lost all seven seats that they defended in by-elections over the parliament, with swings of 35 per cent against them in Christchurch (lost to the Liberal Democrats in July 1993 following the death of the incumbent Conservative, Robert Adley, who had spoken out against rail privatization) and 29 per cent in Dudley West (lost to Labour in December 1994). In the European elections of 1994, the Conservatives slumped to their lowest vote share of the century in a nationwide election (27.9 per cent).

In addition, enormous losses were sustained in local elections (including worst-ever performances in both Scotland and England in 1995). Personally, John Major notched up the worst-ever satisfaction ratings for a Prime Minister. Over the inter-election period as a whole, since regular polling began no party had maintained so large a lead for so long as Labour did from October 1992.

Soon after the 1992 election, the Liberal Democrat leader, Paddy Ashdown, announced a significant change in the party's stance. Previously, the Liberal Democrats had claimed to maintain a posture of 'equidistance' relative to the Conservatives and Labour—willing to work with either in exchange for some concession—*any* concession, it might be thought—on changing the electoral system. Now Ashdown firmly positioned the party in opposition to the Conservatives and willing to cooperate only with Labour. As the Conservatives declined, the Liberal Democrats at first improved their position, in the process gaining three seats in by-elections in 1993 and 1994 and also making significant strides in local elections. Their numbers in the House of Commons were also boosted by two MPs defecting from the Conservatives. However, the extraordinary popularity of Blair affected the Liberal Democrats as well as the Conservatives, and support ebbed away in the second half of the parliament.

Some new parties emerged in this period. Perceived as the most important at the time was the Referendum Party, which was founded and funded by millionaire Sir James Goldsmith. As its name suggests, the party's sole *raison d'être* was to secure a referendum on Britain's relationship with the European Union, and its most potent tactic was to pressurize Tory MPs in vulnerable constituencies. The United Kingdom Independence Party (UKIP) was founded in August 1993, but made few ripples and no headway at this stage.

In relation to the course of support for the parties in this inter-election cycle, there was one very unusual feature. From 1993 until 1997 there was a steady and sustained improvement in the economy. GDP rose significantly, inflation and interest rates were low, real personal disposable income increased, and unemployment fell steadily. Having reached a peak of just under three million in December 1992, the number registered as unemployed fell to 1.75 million by February 1997. According to some electoral analysts, these successes would be expected to increase the 'feel-good factor' among voters and feed through into increased support for the government. But the Conservatives waited in vain for the reviving economy to work its electoral magic. Clearly, the improved economic performance was outweighed in voters' minds by the negative factors already discussed.

After years of introspection, the Conservatives finally woke up to the threat posed to them by Tony Blair. Their response, just before the election, was to launch a poster campaign with the slogan 'New Labour: New Danger'. One of the controversial posters famously showed Blair with the eyes of a demon. However, the electorate was unimpressed by this blatant attempt literally to 'demonize' Blair; it won plaudits from the advertising industry but very few votes. If anything, the campaign might have helped to persuade some radical voters who disliked New Labour's unthreatening image that the party was worth voting for after all.

The 1997 Campaign

On 17 March, John Major announced that the 1997 election would take place on 1 May. Less than three weeks previously, in the last by-election of the parliament, Labour had taken the Conservative seat of Wirral South—previously thought to be fairly safe—on a swing of over 17 per cent. The outlook for the government could hardly have been bleaker, and the ensuing campaign was bereft of 'glad, confident mornings'. Although the Conservatives inched forward and Labour declined from its initial stratospheric heights, in historical perspective the gap between the two major parties remained enormous (see Appendix, Figure 5.A1). Consequently, the national campaign was almost a matter of going through the motions, with Labour's well-oiled machine, led by a youthful and confident Tony Blair, being relatively untroubled by a divided Conservative Party under a Prime Minister perceived to be well past his sell-by date.

Some people's dream of televised debates between the party leaders edged a little closer in 1997. John Major declared himself in favour, and discussions with ITV and the BBC over the best format reached an advanced stage. However, the Conservatives presumably calculated that Labour—as the party with most to lose—would scupper the idea on some pretext or other. Accordingly, even while negotiations were taking place, senior Conservatives claimed that Blair would refuse to take part because he feared a verbal drubbing from Major; to emphasize the point the Conservatives proceeded to hire an actor to dress up as a chicken and follow Blair around the country. Some senior Labour strategists were unsettled by this cheap gimmick, which threatened to distract attention from the launch of the party's manifesto. A Labour pantomime chicken—this time a headless specimen, to symbolize Major's alleged lack of direction—was duly recruited to pester the Prime Minister. The *Daily Mirror* hired another actor to dress up as a fox, resulting in a series of scuffles between 'what appeared to be the bedraggled inhabitants of a deranged zoo' (Jones, 1997: 183, 190; Campbell, 2010: 692, 694).

Apart from the chickens, the national campaigns of the parties followed the usual routine—press conferences, leaders' tours, photo opportunities, television appearances, and election broadcasts. Unusually, however, in the last week John Major made speeches in a single day in Northern Ireland, Scotland, Wales, and England. This was meant to emphasize his plea to voters to 'save the union'—a stratagem which was never likely to resonate even with the English, and, incidentally, caused him to miss appearing on *ITV 500*, the most watched political programme on ITV during the campaign apart from *News at Ten*. Behind the routine activities, however, Labour's campaign organization and management reached new peaks of thoroughness and professionalism. The adjective most frequently used in connection with the party's campaign was 'ruthless'—ruthless targeting of constituencies and voters, ruthless adherence to the dictates laid down at the centre, ruthless management of the media, ruthless marketing. The result was a campaign which—while doubtless effective in its own terms—was oddly lifeless. There were no gaffes to speak of. On the contrary, the press complained of a situation in which 'Labour candidates all sounded like programmed Daleks, mechanically intoning platitudes' (Scammell and Harrop, 1997: 181). This, as well as the inevitable weariness, probably explains why Alastair Campbell, a key architect of the campaign, was in a 'flat mood' even as the scale of the landslide became apparent on election night (Campbell, 2010: 742).

The 'sleaze' issue was kept alive during the campaign by the fact that Labour and the Liberal Democrats stood down in the Cheshire constituency of Tatton. Here, the Conservative incumbent, Neil Hamilton, had been implicated in financial misdemeanours and was opposed by Martin Bell, a disgruntled BBC correspondent standing as an 'anti-sleaze' Independent, in a contest which attracted considerable national attention.

The issue which received most coverage both in broadcast news and the press, however, was Europe; and this presented John Major with a painful dilemma. Negotiations over monetary union—a single European currency—were imminent. On the one hand, many in the Conservative Party—both in Parliament and in the country—were strongly opposed to any move in this direction. On the other, Major could not afford to alienate Kenneth Clarke and Michael Heseltine, respectively his strongly pro-European Chancellor and Deputy Prime Minister. His response was basically 'wait and see'—that is, to go into negotiations with an open mind and then decide what to do when agreement was reached. During the campaign, however, increasing numbers of Conservative candidates (the *Daily Mail* listed 308) made clear their opposition to monetary union; presumably many would have done so even without the intrusion of the Referendum Party. In response, Major made an emotional televised plea to his party 'not to tie my hands' in negotiations. There were more photographs of assorted Eurosceptics in the national daily press than there were of Major himself. The contrast with Blair's mastery within his own party was plain.

Another novel aspect of the national campaign in 1997 was that Labour enjoyed the backing of a clear majority of the press. The most significant and sensational switch was by *The Sun* and, as a result, the readership of Labour-supporting papers was double that of those advocating a Conservative victory (the *Daily Express*, *Daily Mail*, and *Daily Telegraph*). Even among the latter, support for the government was, at best, lukewarm, with the *Daily Mail*, for example, being highly critical of Major. *The Times*, meanwhile, urged its readers to vote not for a specific party but for Eurosceptic candidates, helpfully supplying a list on polling day. Also on polling day, the two biggest circulation papers (*The Sun* and the *Daily Mirror*) each emblazoned their front pages with photographs of Tony Blair and the respective headlines 'It Must be Him' and 'Your Country Needs Him'. Neither needed to say who 'he' was—and neither mentioned his party.

Refinements in national campaigning were mirrored at constituency level in 1997. The extent to which all three major parties concentrated resources on target seats was even greater than before, with special organizers being despatched to the key battlegrounds well before the election. Not content to focus on individual constituencies, the Conservatives and Labour identified specific groups of voters within these seats, showering them with direct mail, promotional videos, and frequent telephone calls. One estimate suggests that Labour's local campaign effort (code-named Operation Victory) actually targeted only about 900,000 electors out of 42.6 million (Denver et al., 1998). In terms of activities, public meetings declined further; but canvassing became more sophisticated (and renamed 'voter ID') through greater use of telephone contact and computerized records. Computers were also widely used to facilitate routine campaign tasks, and email dominated intra-party communication. Unsurprisingly, all parties' campaigns were much more intensive in their target seats than elsewhere, and, as in 1992, more vigorous campaigns were rewarded with better performances by the Liberal Democrats and Labour but not the Conservatives (Denver and Hands, 1998). Overall, Labour led the way in planning, organizing, and executing a local campaigning strategy. Rather than a series of separate campaigns reliant on local initiative and effort, those in target seats were now treated as an integrated aspect of the larger national and nationally planned campaign. The other parties sought to emulate this successful approach in later elections.

The 1997 Results

New constituency boundaries came into effect in 1997, and the number of seats continued to creep upwards (to 659). There was, once again, a record number of candidates (3,724 across the UK), but this failed to stimulate the electorate (possibly wearied by a longer than usual campaign period and the seeming inevitability of a Labour victory). Turnout duly fell from 77.7 per cent to 71.4 per cent, a new post-war low. As on previous occasions, the boundary revisions make analysis of changes in turnout at constituency level problematic, but there is ample evidence that decline was all but universal, although smaller than average in Northern Ireland (−2.4) and Scotland (−4.1) than elsewhere.

In terms of party support, the Conservatives maintained their string of 'worst-ever' records as Labour won the election in a landslide (see Table 5.1). The Tories' vote share was its lowest in modern times; the number of seats won was the smallest since 1906; the swing to Labour (10 per cent) was the biggest since 1945. In

Table 5.1 Election results (UK), 1997–2005

| | 1997 | | 2001 | | 2005 | |
	Votes	Seats	Votes	Seats	Votes	Seats
Con	30.7	165	31.7	166	32.4	198
Labour	43.2	418	40.7	412	35.2	355
Lib Dem	16.8	46	18.3	52	22.0	62
Others	9.3	30	9.3	29	11.4	31
Turnout	*71.6*		*59.6*		*61.6*	

Note: Figures for Votes are percentages.

Scotland (for the first time ever) and Wales (for the first time since 1906), the Conservatives won no seats at all. The drubbing was made even more emphatic by widespread anti-government tactical voting, which was much more prevalent than in 1992. As for the other parties, Labour won more seats (418) than even in its famous triumph of 1945 (393), while the Liberal Democrats, despite a small decline in vote share, more than doubled their tally (to 46) (thanks to tactical voting and carefully targeted local campaigning). In Scotland, the SNP vote share rose only slightly, to 22.1 per cent, but this enabled the party to capture six seats. In Wales, on the other hand, Plaid Cymru's one point increase in voting support left them, as before, with four seats. The Referendum Party, contesting 547 constituencies, won 2.7 per cent of the votes while the Independent Martin Bell—known to the public as 'the man in a white suit' from his days as a television reporter—overturned a notional majority of more than 22,000 votes to oust Neil Hamilton in Tatton by more than 11,000. The willingness of large swathes of voters to desert their traditional parties could hardly have been more convincingly demonstrated.

As in 1992, there was a slight reversal of the North–South divide in that the pro-Labour swing was stronger in London (13.3 per cent) and the South East (12.1 per cent), where Labour had most ground to make up, and smaller in its established heartlands of Scotland (7.4 per cent), Wales (7.1 per cent), and the North (9.8 per cent). Except for two unusual cases (Bradford West and Bethnal Green and Bow, where the Conservative candidates were from the largest local ethnic minority group and the Labour candidates were not), every constituency showed a Conservative to Labour swing.

While the Conservatives slunk off to nurse the wounds they had suffered since 1992, Tony Blair entered 10 Downing Street in triumphant fashion. Professional to the last, his campaign team ensured that the street was packed with party supporters and their families waving Union flags when he returned from seeing the Queen. The anthem of the Labour campaign (another somewhat irritating,

American-inspired innovation) had been D:Ream's optimistic 1994 hit, 'Things can only get better'. At least Labour's thumping majority meant that Blair and his government would have every chance to prove that they could live up to this claim.

Blair's First Term, 1997–2001: Riding a Wave

In terms of trends in party support, the period between the 1997 and 2001 general elections was another remarkable one. This was the first inter-election cycle since regular polling began in which the governing party never relinquished its advantage in monthly voting intentions (on the basis of the average of all published polls). It was also the first in almost fifty years in which the governing party did not lose any seats in by-elections. As Figure 5.2 shows, after an initial post-election slump, the Conservatives very slowly improved their position without ever really threatening Labour's lead. They did come within hailing distance in September and October 2000, when oil tanker drivers, farmers, and others caused widespread disruption in protests over fuel taxes. Five individual polls put the Tories in the lead at this time, but the boost proved temporary. In the last polls

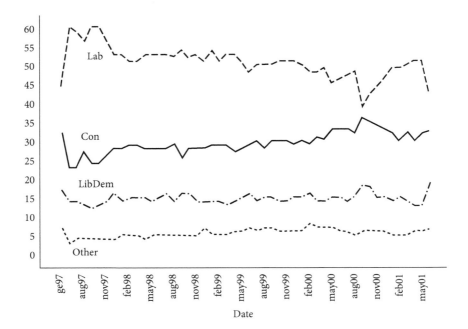

Figure 5.2 Monthly voting intentions, 1997–2001 (all polls)

Notes: The 1997 and 2001 election results in Great Britain form the starting and finishing points. The data shown are the monthly means for all published polls.

before the 2001 election was called, the Conservatives stood at 32 per cent of voting intentions—almost identical to their share in the 1997 disaster. Liberal Democrat support in voting intention polls was very consistent across the inter-election period, only twice straying outside a very narrow band of 13 per cent to 16 per cent. Like the Tories, the party benefitted from government unpopularity at the time of the fuel protests—despite Liberal Democrat enthusiasm for 'green' taxes—but this did not last long. From November 2000 until the election was called, Liberal Democrat poll ratings were stuck at or near a level that had been sustained from late 1997.

For a governing party, Labour's support between the two elections was remarkably strong and consistent. The government hit 60 per cent of vote intentions three times during its honeymoon with the electorate in the second half of 1997, and the party's worst rating was a very respectable 39 per cent in the fuel crisis month of September 2000. After that, things improved steadily and in the last few pre-election polls Labour stood at 51 per cent of voting intentions. This was well up on the party's 1997 vote share and seemed to presage another stunning victory. There is a common assumption, after all, that elections are not won and lost in the four weeks of the official campaign but in the four years that have gone before.

One of the main reasons for Labour's popularity was the relatively strong performance of the economy. The Chancellor of the Exchequer, Gordon Brown, made 'prudence' his watchword, and stuck rigorously to the tax and spending plans laid down by the previous government. His caution was rewarded with steady economic growth, falling inflation, and a reduction in unemployment. By the start of 2001, the latter was at its lowest level for twenty-five years—a source of understandable pride for a chancellor who constantly extolled the character-bolstering effects of paid work. However, to placate Labour supporters who felt that he was being too prudent by half—and, no doubt, with the party's re-election prospects in mind—in his April 2000 Budget Brown signalled that public spending would rise significantly if the government was given a second term (Smith, 2005: 170).

Despite Brown's record, an even more important factor sustaining Labour's position in the country was the extraordinary popularity of the Prime Minister, Tony Blair. 'New Labour' was clearly identified with him, and his style of governing—'sofa government'—emphasized his personal role in leading the government and the country. This was reinforced by the continuation of an immensely professional and thorough media operation now masterminded from Downing Street by Alastair Campbell, the 'spin doctor' in chief. Blair's response to the death of Diana, Princess of Wales, at the end of August 1997, for example, was skilfully tailored to the occasion, in comparison to the efforts of the Leader of the Opposition and the Queen.

Throughout the parliament, Blair led his Conservative and Liberal Democrat rivals as the best person to be Prime Minister by huge margins. His advantage over William Hague, now Conservative leader, on this question averaged fifty-two points in 1997, forty-four in 1998, forty-one in 1999, and twenty-seven in 2000. No previous Prime Minister had a sustained record of popularity remotely approaching that achieved by Blair (Denver and Fisher, 2009). In view of such figures it was pardonable for Blair to liken the election, when it came, to 'getting into the boxing ring and then finding there was no opponent' (Seldon, 2004: 461).

Not everything went smoothly for the government, of course. Apart from the fuel blockades mentioned above, there were still tensions in the Labour Party between the remaining 'traditionalists' and 'Blairite' modernizers. It gradually became clear that the latter group were not on the most amicable personal terms, and they jostled incessantly to advance themselves. The media and public were tiring of the apparently endless 'spinning' of facts and stories even before the 1997 election. Afterwards, having performed so successfully, it seemed that the party could not kick the habits that it had acquired in opposition. It lost ground in local elections, did not do particularly well in the first elections to the newly devolved institutions in Scotland and Wales, and came second to the Conservatives in the 1999 European elections (albeit on a derisory turnout of 24 per cent). Nonetheless, Labour's eyes were fixed on the next general election and, in that context, the government appeared untroubled. The strong economy and a personally popular Prime Minister were backed up by virtually continuous campaigning, both nationally and in the constituencies, which began almost as soon as the 1997 election was over.

In the Conservative Party, John Major resigned as leader immediately after the 1997 election—escaping, with undisguised relief, to watch a cricket match. He was succeeded in June by William Hague, then aged just 36. Essentially, Hague won the leadership because he bore fewer battle-scars than his opponents, Kenneth Clarke, John Redwood, Peter Lilley, and Michael Howard. Before the final run-off against Clarke, Hague won the key endorsement of Baroness Thatcher, but it was clear that this reflected the latter's antipathy towards Clarke rather than an appreciation of Hague's own abilities. Nevertheless, Hague's tenure was not without successes. By general consent, his performances in the House of Commons—especially at Prime Minister's Questions—were at least as effective in themselves as Blair's sallies against Major. He also pushed through significant changes in party organization which effectively made the Conservatives a single party (rather than separate parliamentary and voluntary parties) and gave members the right to participate in the election of the party leader. On the other hand, Hague was mercilessly caricatured by cartoonists, and did indeed look rather foolish when he was photographed in a baseball cap. For reasons that, as in Kinnock's case, are difficult to pin down—his relative youth, baldness, and northern accent may have played a part, along with a lack of *gravitas* exemplified by a boast about his youthful drinking exploits—he simply failed to impress the electorate and was never taken seriously as a potential Prime Minister.

Having done so well (in terms of seats) in 1997, the Liberal Democrats might have hoped to make more of an impact in national politics afterwards. In fact, any hopes they might have entertained of influencing Labour were dashed by the government's huge majority. A commission under Roy Jenkins to investigate an alternative electoral system for general elections was set up by the government; but its report advocating a more proportional system was promptly shelved—proving, as many had already suspected, that Blair would only push for constitutional reform insofar as it suited his interests. Paddy Ashdown resigned from the Liberal Democrat leadership in 1999 and, in the August of that year, was replaced by Charles Kennedy, an emollient and likeable Scottish MP. In terms of popular support, the Liberal Democrats made little headway nationally (Figure 5.2) but they made steady progress in local elections, including winning control of Liverpool in 1998 and Sheffield in 1999. Following the first Scottish Parliament elections in 1999, the party entered a governing coalition with Labour in Edinburgh, and a spectacular by-election win in the formerly safe Conservative seat of Romsey in May 2000 also boosted spirits.

There was change among the 'others' following 1997. The Referendum Party disappeared following the death of Sir James Goldsmith in the July following the election, thus leaving the anti-European field to UKIP. The latter was itself riven by disputes among its leaders, but still won 7 per cent of the votes and three seats in the 1999 European elections (which were now fought under a proportional electoral system). The nationalist parties in both Scotland and Wales were emboldened by significant support in their respective devolved elections, and both also changed their leaders. Ieuan Wyn Jones replaced Dafydd Wigley at the head of Plaid in 2001, and, following the (temporary) retirement of Alex Salmond in 2000, the relatively obscure John Swinney became leader of the SNP.

The 2001 Campaign

By 2001, although the campaign period was still legally defined for the purposes of regulating election expenditures by candidates, campaigning was not just a matter of long-term and short-term activities but could reasonably be described as continuous. For months and years before the election was called, the major parties had used phone banks to contact voters in key seats, sent out millions of pieces of direct mail, and invested resources in local campaigning. This ongoing campaigning was not just a matter of national advertising and media strategies to promote national leaders and achievements. It now included the 'ground war' activities—canvassing, street stalls, local publicity, and the like—which had once been crammed into a three- or four-week period. Nonetheless, there remained, of course, a step change in the intensity of campaigning after the Prime Minister announced on 8 May that the election would be held on 7 June.

It had been widely expected that the election would be held on 3 May to coincide with local elections in England. This would have enabled Labour to capitalize on Gordon Brown's March Budget (which included a cut in petrol duty and an increase in pensions, as well as more spending on schools and the NHS). Polls suggested that this was the best-received Budget, and Brown the most popular Chancellor, since the war. However, an outbreak of foot-and-mouth disease which became more widespread through March and April forced Blair to delay. The government was initially criticized for complacency in dealing with the outbreak but, in any event, it was soon realized that campaigning against a background of animals being burned in the countryside was not appealing, especially to rural voters whose emotions had already been stoked by the prospect of a legal ban on hunting.

When the short campaign did get under way, it was more planned and orchestrated from the centre than ever. Technology enabled the centre to keep in constant touch with spokespeople and candidates, so that they could be kept on message; teams of spin doctors advised the leaders and sought to control media reporting of the campaign. As an illustration of the extent of preparedness and professionalism, the Conservatives were able to despatch 10,000 leaflets to target voters in each marginal seat on the day after the election was called. For its part, Labour commissioned two or three private polls per week during the campaign, while Philip Gould conducted focus groups almost every night to monitor popular feeling.

Such professionalism in election campaigning is admirable, no doubt; but a consequence of things being orchestrated from the centre is that modern election battles lack spontaneity. Everything—leaders' tours and interviews, press conferences, speeches, election broadcasts—is practised and predictable. Thus, no major party election broadcast in 2001 featured just 'talking heads'. All were made by professionals, none lasted more than five minutes, and most were less than three minutes long.

Despite (or perhaps because of) these attempts to pander to perceived modern tastes, the public and the media found the 2001 campaign even more boring than ever. It is also unsurprising that the media seized on any departure from bland and pre-packaged campaigning as a blessed relief. One such incident, which featured prominently in news broadcasts, involved Tony Blair being harangued about the NHS by an angry voter in Birmingham. The undoubted highlight, however, came in the second campaign week when the Deputy Prime Minister, John Prescott, retaliated with an effective punch against a man who had hit him with an egg thrown at point-blank range. Outside genteel metropolitan liberal circles this did Prescott's reputation nothing but good and, after initial consternation, Blair was wise to laugh off the affair.

Campaigning in 2001 presented the Conservatives with serious problems. They were well behind in the polls, and Labour's move to the centre gave them little scope to attack the government on the policy issues that mattered most to voters. Moreover, Labour's apparent success in running the economy meant that allegations of incompetence were unlikely to carry much weight. To compound the difficulty, all national daily newspapers except the *Telegraph* and *Mail* (and including, for the first time, the *Express* and *Times*) backed Labour. In what most observers interpreted as a 'core vote' strategy, the Conservatives focused on keeping the UK out of the euro and on what they claimed were a large number of 'stealth taxes' introduced by Gordon Brown. The former was a popular policy, but the euro was well down most voters' list of concerns—far below the NHS, education, and law and order, for example—while the latter was perhaps too subtle to resonate with the electorate.

In any event, it didn't seem to matter what the Conservatives said or did. Under a more effective leader, they might have made the election into a more meaningful contest. As it was, even if Labour's record had been open to serious question, the Opposition's attacks would have been blunted given the difficulty their leader experienced in trying to establish some rapport with an unimpressed electorate. Over the course of the campaign, the Conservative poll rating changed very little (see Appendix, Figure 5.A2). Inevitably, Labour's share of voting intentions declined steadily from the commanding heights at which it started—an average of well over 50 per cent in the second week. Even so, at no time was there a remote possibility that Labour would lose the election. The beneficiaries of Labour's partial decline were the Liberal Democrats. From week two their share of voting intentions rose steadily, reflecting the growing personal popularity of Charles Kennedy and the unconvincing efforts of the Tories. At the start of the campaign Kennedy received a lukewarm reception, averaging 4.8 on a 'likeability' scale (scoring from 0 to 10) used by the BES. His ratings improved more sharply than Blair's, however—while Hague's were static—and he ended at 5.5 (see Clarke et al., 2004: 147).

The 2001 campaign was another considerable challenge for broadcasters. The electorate was very far from being entranced and the result seemed a foregone conclusion. The response, according to the 2001 Nuffield study, was 'offering less of the same' (Harrison, 2002: 134). The proportion of news bulletins devoted to the election declined as compared with previous elections, although there was ample coverage in special programmes across television and radio for those who wanted it. Perhaps emblematic of this campaign, a news programme aimed at younger viewers on Channel 5 wired up volunteers to see if their interest was more aroused by exposure to election coverage or watching paint dry. The latter proved more exciting for the unlucky participants (Harrison, 2002: 135).

As far as the techniques of campaigning are concerned, however, 2001 again saw major innovations which capitalized on technological developments. All of the major parties hosted national websites, which proved to be important (and relatively cheap) ways of communicating with candidates and activists, as well as providing information for journalists and the (relatively few) ordinary electors who were interested enough to visit. In a much-discussed initiative, over the last weekend of the campaign Labour sent text messages to the mobile phones of young people after 10 p.m., urging them to vote Labour in the expectation that it would introduce legislation to extend pub licensing hours. The party also distributed a million videos to key voters.

In the localities, around 20 per cent of candidates or local parties had dedicated websites, and the use of computers to assist printing and canvassing was almost universal. In all but a small minority of seats the traditional public meeting was now extinct. In most seats, however, the party workers undertook familiar tasks, such as distributing leaflets, canvassing, and 'knocking-up' on polling day. In the seats on the parties' target lists, Labour's strategy of central direction was now adopted by others. Labour's approach on this occasion was codenamed Operation Turnout—not reflecting concern about the *overall* level of citizen engagement but rather a fear that *Labour* supporters would be insufficiently motivated. Although voters in safe seats now received little attention from parties, those in marginals were targeted by the parties as never before. The centre in both main parties was involved in importing organizers well in advance of the election, undertaking 'voter identification' via national telephone banks, arranging volunteers from neighbouring constituencies, and sending out personalized direct mail to specific voters.

The sophistication now evident in both local and national campaigning may have had unforeseen consequences, however. Election campaigns resembled professional marketing operations, and the public became increasingly sceptical and cynical about the endless 'spin', photo opportunities, instant rebuttals, electors in safe seats being taken more or less for granted, and election broadcasts that were difficult to differentiate from commercial advertisements. Blair's campaign launch, in which he delivered a political message in front of uncomprehending schoolchildren, was particularly ill-judged; even the Prime Minister later acknowledged that it had been 'inappropriate', and confessed to experiencing 'an almost irresistible desire to giggle at the absurdity of it' (Blair, 2010: 314). This confession was delivered long after the event. At the time, it was easy for those outside the Westminster 'bubble' to see that 'professionalism' might serve simply to turn voters off party politics.

The 2001 Results

In 2001 there were two important innovations in the administration of elections. First, whereas electors had previously been able to put themselves on the electoral register only in the October of each year, 'rolling registration' now allowed this to happen up until a few weeks before polling day. Second, voting by post was now allowed 'on demand'. Previously a good reason—such as illness or absence on business—had to be given for requesting a postal vote, and the relevant form had to be signed by a 'responsible person', such as a doctor or Justice of the Peace. Now, however, anyone could apply to vote by post, and the proportion of votes cast in this way (5.2 per cent of the total) was more than double the 1997 figure (2.4 per cent). In the longer term, however, on-demand postal voting was to give rise to significant problems involving electoral corruption.

These changes—intended to make voting easier—did nothing to prevent a dramatic decline in turnout in 2001. At 59.4 per cent, UK turnout was at its lowest level since 1918: and the latter contest, held in the immediate aftermath of the First World War, had obvious limitations for comparative purposes. Apart from Northern Ireland (where, in the first general election since the Good Friday Agreement, turnout actually increased a little, to 68 per cent), participation fell in every UK constituency. Only eleven constituency contests attracted turnouts in excess of 70 per cent, while sixty-seven were below 50 per cent, including three which failed even to reach 40 per cent—Liverpool Riverside (34.1 per cent), Manchester Central (39.1 per cent), and Glasgow Shettleston (39.7 per cent). In 1964, in comparison, no constituency had a turnout below 50 per cent, and the vast majority (548) exceeded 70 per cent.

These figures shocked many political commentators, and over the next few years there was much agonized discussion about what should or could be done to improve matters. However, very few politicians were seriously discomfited; for them, as Churchill had once pointed out, a majority of one was enough, no matter how many people cast a vote. In part, the specific circumstances of the 2001 election contributed to the low turnout. From the outset there was no doubt about which party would win. In addition, turnout fell most heavily in traditionally strong Labour areas, suggesting that some Labour supporters had been unimpressed by the party's move to the centre under Tony Blair. From an international perspective, sharply falling turnout was not confined to the UK; and, over the longer term, the trend was clearly associated with weakening attachments to parties among voters in mature liberal democracies. It was obvious that there could be no quick fix, restoring turnout to the kind of levels that had previously been normal over the post-war period. Yet non-voting on such a scale could not be a welcome development within any healthy liberal democracy, and mass abstention could quickly become as habitual as unthinking voting on 'tribal' lines had been in the days of partisan alignment.

In terms of vote share, 2001 saw very little change from the previous election. Although there was a small swing in votes (1.8 per cent) from Labour to the Conservatives across the UK, this resulted in a net gain of just one seat for the latter and a net loss of six for the former. The Liberal Democrats increased their vote share by 1.5 points, earning six additional seats. Across Britain, however, only twenty-one seats changed hands—the smallest number since 1955. In Scotland, the SNP again secured second place in terms of votes (the Conservatives coming fourth), but dropped back a little to 20.1 per cent and lost a seat, to end up with five. In Wales, Plaid enjoyed its best ever general election performance, with 14.3 per cent of votes, but remained at four seats. One other remarkable result is worthy of note. In the Wyre Forest constituency (based on Kidderminster, Worcestershire), a local doctor (Richard Taylor), standing as an Independent and campaigning on the issue of cuts at the local hospital, took the seat from Labour with a majority of almost 18,000 votes. Martin Bell's 1997 victory at Tatton had been assisted by the decision of both Labour and the Liberal Democrats not to run candidates; at Wyre Forest four years later, only the Liberal Democrats (who had finished a distant third in 1997) stood aside. Bell himself stood down from Tatton, in accordance with his promise to serve for only one term, but was persuaded to stand for the Essex seat of Brentwood and Ongar, where he came a very respectable runner-up. He was succeeded at Tatton by the youthful George Osborne.

Blair's Second Term, 2001–5: Hanging On

During the 2001–5 parliament, the New Labour government tasted serious unpopularity for the first time, and Tony Blair's status as an electoral talisman was called into question. This was mainly due to the Iraq War and its aftermath, which dominated political debate in the second half of the parliament.

Initially, Labour enjoyed the usual honeymoon with the electorate after the 2001 election. In September of that year, however, the terrorist attack on the twin towers in New York acted as a sensational reminder that the fall of Communism had not ushered in a peaceful and prosperous 'New World Order'. The UK gave full backing to the 'war on terror' announced by the US President, George W. Bush, and, thereafter, foreign affairs played a much larger role than normal in British political discussion and activity. British and American troops were involved in Afghanistan from October 2001, but attention then turned to Iraq. In addition to his well-deserved reputation as a murderous dictator, Iraq's leader, Saddam Hussein, was suspected of conducting a clandestine operation to produce 'weapons of mass destruction' (WMD). The government of the USA, backed by the UK and others, was determined to remove him (although deliberate 'regime change' was not stated as an official policy). After a long period of unavailing negotiation aimed at securing the endorsement of the United Nations, British military action was approved by the House of Commons, and British troops participated in the invasion of Iraq in March 2003. Before the war began, public opinion was strongly against British involvement unless it was sanctioned by the UN, and huge numbers joined a protest march in London. Once UK forces went into action, however, there was a predictable turnaround in opinion. Moreover, there was a 'Baghdad bounce' in support for Labour which had been declining fairly steadily for about a year (Figure 5.3).

Militarily, the Iraq invasion appeared to come to a speedy and successful conclusion, but Blair's problems were just beginning. The Leader of the Commons, Robin Cook, resigned over the issue just before the vote on military action, followed by two junior ministers, three Parliamentary Private Secretaries, and (later) by another cabinet minister, Clare Short. In the vote itself, almost half of all Labour backbenchers (139) voted against the government—at that point the biggest backbench rebellion in living memory and, numerically, the largest against any Labour government. In Iraq, despite exhaustive searches, no WMD were found, and the aftermath of military success proved to be bloody and unstable. At home, doubts grew about the intelligence reports used to make the case for the invasion. In July, Dr David Kelly, an expert on WMD, who had confided to a BBC reporter his concern about the role of Labour spin doctors in 'sexing up' a dossier reviewing the evidence against Saddam, committed suicide. Subsequently, the government involved itself in a furious row with the BBC over its reporting of the issue, and a later inquiry forced the resignation of the Director-General, Greg Dyke (a known Labour supporter). Not only the Prime Minister's judgement but also his integrity were now called into question, and opinion swung decisively back against the war. From May 2004, YouGov consistently found pluralities saying that the intervention had been wrong.

Long before that, however, many voters had lost their faith in Blair. In March 2003, according to MORI, the Prime Minister's rating among the electorate (per cent satisfied with how he was doing his job minus per cent dissatisfied) stood at −5, while in April it was +5. Thereafter, rather than the Iraq intervention emulating Mrs Thatcher's 'Falklands Factor', Blair experienced a 'Baghdad Boomerang'. His popularity slumped to −16 in May, −30 in June and an average of −28 from July to December. Partly as a consequence, Labour found itself running almost neck and neck with the Conservatives in the polls from the middle of 2003 through to the autumn of 2004.

The government's difficulties with its own parliamentary party spilled over into other areas. Proposals to introduce tuition fees for university students and to establish 'foundation hospitals' met with stiff opposition from Labour MPs (and passed the Commons only thanks to the votes of Scottish members, although the policies would not apply in Scotland since these matters were now the responsibility of the devolved administration in Edinburgh). In addition, the public became increasingly aware of tensions at the very top of government, where the Chancellor, Gordon Brown, was increasingly resentful of the Prime Minister. Feuding between the two and their supporters made for a poisonous atmosphere, and in Blair's second term became a national joke (at least among those interested in politics) following the publication of a well-informed and vividly written exposé by the journalist Andrew Rawnsley (2001).

William Hague resigned as Conservative leader on the day after the 2001 election. After a lively contest, party members—participating in a leadership election for the first time—chose Iain Duncan Smith (over Kenneth Clarke) as their leader in September. Duncan Smith, whose name was widely (though not always affectionately) truncated to IDS, benefitted from the new system for electing the Conservative leader, which allowed party members to make the final choice between two candidates who had emerged from a series of ballots among Tory MPs. The outcome of the system's first trial raised serious doubts about its wisdom; IDS was not the preferred candidate of MPs in any of their three preliminary rounds of voting, making it difficult for him to establish his legitimacy as a parliamentary leader. Equally damaging was the fact that among the general public IDS was far less popular than the defeated Clarke, for reasons which went beyond his relative obscurity. A committed Eurosceptic, IDS had consistently rebelled against John Major's compromise position on the EU. Thus, IDS epitomized the divisions which had helped to bring his party to grief in 1997, and, although he was by no means a right-wing caricature on domestic matters, some of his views were highly controversial among Conservatives who were hoping to establish a more 'liberal' image for the party. Although the Conservatives slowly improved their position in the polls under his leadership (Figure 5.3), he was never personally popular among the voters and never headed Tony Blair—even at the latter's lowest point—as the best person for Prime Minister. In the first half of 2002, Duncan Smith's satisfaction ratings averaged −6 on MORI figures, but fell to −23 from July to December and then −27 for January–October 2003.

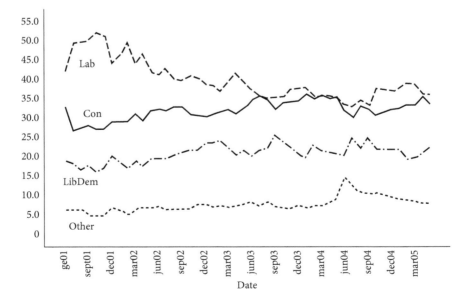

Figure 5.3 Monthly voting intentions, 2001–5 (all polls)

Notes: The 2001 and 2005 election results in Great Britain form the starting and finishing points. The data shown are the monthly means for all published polls.

At the end of October—after a much-ridiculed speech to the annual conference which earned IDS '17 patently stage-managed standing ovations' (Bale, 2010: 187)—Conservative MPs passed a vote of no confidence in their leader, thus ensuring his dismissal. Duncan Smith was succeeded (without a contest) by Michael Howard, who significantly closed the gap on Blair as a potential Prime Minister and, for a time, maintained his party's improving standings in the polls. Although he was by any contemporary reckoning a significant political figure— suggesting that Conservative MPs, at least, had learned from the inappropriate elevations of Hague and Duncan Smith—Howard was not perceived by the electorate as particularly likeable. Moreover, as a prominent advocate of unpopular policies such as the poll tax, he was seen as a throwback to Thatcherism. As a result, his honeymoon with the voters was brief.

The Liberal Democrats, meanwhile, also held steady, and were generally at a slightly higher level of support than they had achieved in 2001. 'Other' parties— in particular UKIP—experienced an upsurge of support at the time of the European elections in June 2004, but this tailed off in the following months.

The government's travails were reflected in mid-term elections. In the six parliamentary by-elections that were held, Labour's vote share dropped by an average of almost 20 percentage points, and two seats that had previously been held were lost (Brent East and Leicester South). The beneficiaries were the Liberal Democrats, campaigning on an anti-Iraq War platform. Thus, for example, at Hartlepool in July 2004 their vote share rose by 19 percentage points compared with 2001, and their candidate moved from third to second place behind Labour, which retained the seat previously held by Peter Mandelson. The pro-war Tories, by contrast, saw their vote share fall by 11 percentage points, consigning the party to fourth place behind UKIP (and a lost deposit).

In local elections, too, there were significant losses of seats for the government, with Labour trailing the Conservatives in 'national equivalent' vote share each year from 2001 to 2004.[1] As in 1999, the European Parliament election of 2004 produced poor results for the government. The fact that this contest coincided with local elections in England and Wales meant that the turnout (38.2 per cent) was more respectable than in 1999. Even so, Labour received only 22.6 per cent of the Great Britain vote, while the Conservatives won 26.7 per cent. Labour took just nineteen of the seventy-five available seats. There had been further bad news in the Scottish Parliament elections of 2003. Although still easily the largest party, Labour's share of the vote in the constituency contests dropped from 38.8 per cent to 34.6 per cent, leading to a loss of seven of these seats. Nonetheless, the Labour–Liberal Democrat coalition continued in office. In Wales, on the other hand, there was a recovery compared with 1999. Labour's vote share increased both in the constituency (to 40 per cent) and list voting (to 36.6 per cent), and the party was able to form a Welsh administration on its own.

In some ways, the 2001–5 inter-election cycle represented a return to normality in British politics, since the incumbent government ran into rough weather, electorally speaking. It was not entirely 'normal', however, because, as Hartlepool had illustrated, the official Opposition was not necessarily the chief beneficiary. In the European elections UKIP (and, to a lesser extent, the Green Party), in Scotland the SNP, Scottish Socialists, and Greens, and in the opinion polls the Liberal Democrats and others, prevented the Conservatives capitalizing fully on Labour's relative unpopularity. In a normal cycle, however, the government would be expected to stage a recovery as the next general election approached—and so it proved this time. (Note that the upturn in Conservative support for April 2005 apparent in Figure 5.3 is slightly misleading. It is based on only five polls completed before the election date was announced and includes one—widely considered a 'rogue'—which showed the Conservatives in a five-point lead.) Nonetheless, the two major parties were clearly closer together entering the election than had been the case in 1997 or 2001, while, ominously for both of them, the Liberal Democrats were in a relatively strong position.

The 2005 Campaign

The announcement of the election date and the dissolution of Parliament signalled an upgrading and intensification of the parties' campaigning efforts that had been going on throughout the previous four years. Moreover, campaign activities, slogans, speeches, policy statements, broadcasts, photo opportunities, and all the rest were designed and fine-tuned in the light of exhaustive research into the likely reactions of the voters. Both the Conservatives and Labour conducted extensive polling operations in the years before the election. During the formal ('short') campaign both had access to polls conducted almost every day, plus special polls of target seats and 'swing' voters, supplemented by analysis of the views of nightly focus groups. Apart from the formal Conservative polling effort, the party's generous supporter Lord (Michael) Ashcroft launched a freelance operation to monitor opinion in crucial seats. Even the Liberal Democrats—normally too poor to afford such luxuries—organized a tracking study in their own target constituencies. The plethora of polling might have been good news for the companies which were paid for the work, but, as the 2005 Nuffield study wryly commented, 'the parties could have shared much of their data' since they were all telling more or less the same story about voting intentions and the strengths and weaknesses of the parties' images (Kavanagh and Butler, 2005: 92). There is, of course, no chance of such an obvious money-saving idea being adopted.

'Dreary', 'trivial', and 'nasty' were among the epithets used in the press to describe the 2005 short campaign. Apart from Mr Howard calling the Prime Minister 'a liar' (and the Conservatives backing this up with a poster to the same effect), there were remarkably few newsworthy incidents and the polls were mostly flat (see Appendix, Figure 5.A3). On the Labour side, Blair and Brown papered over their differences, and spearheaded the campaign. Their new spirit of unity was symbolized by a photo opportunity which showed them enjoying ice-creams together; the amicable mood melted away just as quickly after the election, however. The national campaign was again ruthlessly managed. Recognizing that Blair would not be allowed to escape awkward questions about Iraq and other issues, Labour strategists decided to make a virtue out of necessity and exposed their leader to a punishing round of media appearances (Seldon, 2007: 339). Inevitably, this 'masochism strategy' was itself carefully stage-managed. Whenever Blair was shown on television surrounded by 'ordinary voters', it was no surprise that the latter in fact turned out to be Labour members and supporters specially drafted in for the purpose.

The Conservative campaign—managed by Lynton Crosby, a seasoned (if controversial) Australian tactician—was equally professional and thorough. It concentrated on 'humanizing' the much-maligned Howard, as well as emphasizing issues on which the Conservatives were strong—crime and immigration—and attacking the government (in particular Tony Blair) as arrogant and untrustworthy ('all spin and smirk'). For most of the campaign, the Iraq War remained in the background as an issue. Less than two weeks before polling, however, the Attorney General's advice to the Prime Minister in 2003—initially expressing doubts about the legality of the war and later giving only guarded approval—was leaked. The issue then dominated the news agenda until the end of the campaign. This was a boost for the Liberal Democrats who had opposed the war outright, unlike the Conservatives, whose current leader (Howard) had been as supportive of Blair's policy as his predecessor (IDS), before experiencing what seemed an opportunistic change of mind. The Iraq pot was kept boiling by the death of (yet another) British soldier two days before the election.

The emergence of the Iraq War as a campaign issue (and hence the question of trust in the Prime Minister with which it was entwined) duly coincided with a slight improvement in support for the Liberal Democrats. Nevertheless, although the Conservatives drifted gently downwards, voting intentions for the three parties remained broadly stable throughout the campaign (see Appendix, Figure 5. A3). The fact that after the election was called only one poll out of forty-seven showed the Conservatives in the lead doubtless contributed to the general absence of excitement. This time there was no Prescott punch to enliven proceedings; revelations about the burly Deputy Prime Minister's affair with his diary secretary might have spiced up the campaign, but it was not until the following year that the public got to know about this.

For the first time in a general election, a large proportion of the population had access to digital TV channels and could, therefore, easily avoid viewing anything to do with politics if they were so minded. At the other extreme, election 'junkies' could glut themselves on round-the-clock coverage on channels such as BBC Parliament and Sky News. In the face of these challenges, the main terrestrial channels provided, in Martin Harrison's words, 'a vast and varied effort' (Harrison, 2005: 110). In the run-up to the election, party leaders continued the recently established trend of subjecting themselves to appearances on popular, but not explicitly political, programmes. Mrs Thatcher had pioneered this approach with her patronage of the *Jimmy Young Show* (BBC Radio 2). Young had been forced into retirement by the BBC in 2002, leaving no obvious heir-apparent in the key middle-brow market. To hedge their bets, during February all three leaders appeared on *Woman's Hour* (BBC Radio 4), *Richard and Judy* (ITV), and *Steve Wright in the Afternoon* (BBC Radio 2). Serious observers might have found these encounters excruciating, but campaign strategists viewed them as valuable means of connecting with 'ordinary people' or, at least, the nearest approximation to contact with average voters.

The major innovation in broadcast coverage of the campaign was another step towards televised leaders' debates. All three main party leaders appeared one after the other before a BBC *Question Time* audience, and the programme was watched by over four million viewers. Tony Blair clearly came off worst, facing a barrage of hostile questions and finding himself wrong-footed by a woman who insisted that NHS targets made it more difficult to get an appointment to see a doctor. This was clearly a disagreeable surprise to the Prime Minister (and the exchange generated much newspaper comment next day), but at least it made a change from interminable discussion about Iraq.

While the 'air war'—dull though it seemed to be—took the lion's share of publicity, the 'ground war' in the constituencies received at least as much attention from the parties themselves. Organizers and volunteers on the ground still went through the old drills that we have listed in previous chapters—delivering leaflets, checking the intentions of voters through door-to-door canvassing, and 'knocking up' supporters on polling day. However, central involvement in local campaigning—or 'the integration of the national and local campaigns' as the parties preferred to describe it—again reached new heights (Fisher et al., 2007). In both main parties strategy was determined at the centre, where important activities were organized and implemented. Labour sent out ten million communications to named voters; all the main parties had central telephone 'banks'; and the location of advertisements on hoardings was centrally planned, as was the production of 'local' campaign literature. Labour also produced and distributed a quarter of a million campaign DVDs (showing a creditable awareness that videos were now old hat), although it is unclear how many were actually watched.

In 2005, most voters reported having no contact with their local campaign beyond receiving the candidates' election addresses through the post. Their relative exclusion from the national democratic debate reflected conscious decisions by the parties, which focused their efforts more than ever on handfuls of voters in a minority of seats. These were identified by party headquarters well in advance of the election, thanks to sophisticated computer software. Thus, at the start of the year, the Conservatives targeted 2.4 million swing voters in key seats; by the end of the campaign, they had narrowed their fire to 1.6 million in 190 seats (Barwell, 2007). Even then, the research sponsored by Lord Ashcroft suggested that the Opposition's precious resources were being spread too thinly (Ashcroft, 2005). As if to confirm Ashcroft's delineation of the crucial election battleground, Labour made (or tried to make) seven separate contacts (email, post, or telephone) with their target voters in just 107 seats. As in previous elections, more intense local campaigning was associated with higher turnouts, and the evidence also suggests that parties (especially the Liberal Democrats) reaped an electoral payoff in that they fared better where their campaigns were strongest (Fieldhouse and Cutts, 2009).

The 2005 Results

Labour emerged from the election with a much reduced but still comfortable parliamentary majority of more than sixty over all other parties. The party's vote share dropped sharply, however, to 35.2 per cent—the smallest ever share for a party winning an overall majority in Parliament (Table 5.1). As in the mid-term elections, it was not the Conservatives who benefitted but the Liberal Democrats and 'others'. The increase in the Conservatives' share of the votes was minuscule (+0.7). Nevertheless, the net swing from Labour (3.1 per cent) helped the Conservatives take thirty-one seats from the government; the party also made a net gain of two (won five, lost three) from the Liberal Democrats. In addition to the seats won by the Conservatives, Labour lost twelve to the Liberal Democrats, two to the SNP, one to Respect, and one to an Independent in Blaenau Gwent. The latter was a very safe Labour seat in South Wales, where Labour's national headquarters had insisted upon an all-women shortlist when a new candidate was being chosen. A female lawyer from London was duly selected, and the local Labour Welsh Assembly member stood against her in protest. Despite suffering from a terminal illness, the Independent (Peter Law) won easily. The campaign in the London constituency of Bethnal Green and Bow was like a mini-referendum on the Iraq War, contested by two colourful characters (Labour's Oona King and George Galloway of the Respect Party, who had been a Labour MP until his expulsion in 2003). The anti-war Galloway won, but the seat returned to its traditional Labour allegiance in 2010.

The Liberal Democrats' vote share advanced to 22 per cent and they reached a post-war record of sixty-two seats. The party did particularly well (and Labour particularly badly) in seats with significant Muslim populations, and also in seats with larger than average proportions of students. The Iraq War, coupled with Labour's decision to impose tuition fees for those in higher education, thus had clear electoral consequences for the government. Among the minor parties, the British National Party (BNP) and the Greens recorded their best-ever (though still modest) performances, while UKIP—with almost 500 candidates—came fourth in terms of the popular vote (2.2 per cent). In Scotland, where the number of constituencies had been reduced from seventy-two to fifty-nine as a consequence of devolution, the SNP fell back to 17.7 per cent of votes, but added an extra seat to make six in total. In Wales, Plaid also declined—to 12.6 per cent of votes and from four to three seats.

As had by now become normal, there were considerable variations in the changes in party performance across constituencies. Indeed, the veteran commentator, Anthony King, suggested at the time that analysing the results was 'like trying to discern patterns in a shattered mosaic' (*Daily Telegraph*, 07.05.2005). Excluding Scotland (where boundary changes complicate matters), the Conservative vote share rose in 323 constituencies and declined in 245; Labour was up in 31, while the Liberal Democrats fell in 72. The differences between each party's best and worst performances were huge. The Liberal Democrats, for example, improved by more than 20 percentage points in four constituencies, but dropped by more than nine points in five.

As well as being affected by the presence of Muslims and students, these sorts of variations were also influenced by differences in the electoral context across constituencies. Thus, the Conservatives fared worse in seats where Labour and the Liberal Democrats were the two leading parties than where they themselves were serious contenders. In contrast, Labour did least badly in Conservative/ Liberal Democrat contests; the Liberal Democrats themselves did best where they were in competition with Labour—not unexpectedly since the government was more unpopular than before—while making little headway in seats in which they were the best-placed opponents of the Conservatives. Thus, their well-publicized 'decapitation' strategy, whereby they aimed to oust leading Conservatives, was a complete flop. One other factor making for variations in major party performances in 2005 was the presence or absence of minor party candidates. There are significant negative correlations between the changes in vote shares for both the Conservatives (−0.21) and Labour (−0.08) and change in support for the BNP, suggesting that both major parties may have suffered to an extent from defections in that direction. Although Labour's performance was also negatively affected by support for the Green Party, none of the three leading parties was affected systematically by the local performance of UKIP.

When we move from changes in party support between 2001 and 2005 to absolute levels of support across constituencies we reach rather more familiar territory. Table 5.2 updates for 2005 the analysis for 1983 presented in Chapter 4 (see Table 4.2). Although more than twenty years separate the two cases, they present a broadly similar picture of how the parties' support varied according to the social make-up of constituencies. As in 1983, the Conservatives clearly did better in more rural areas as well as where the proportions of people with professional and

Table 5.2 Correlations between party shares of vote and constituency characteristics, 2005

	Conservative	Labour	Lib Dem
% Professional & managerial	0.57	−0.57	0.32
% Manual workers	−0.62	0.63	−0.33
% Owner occupiers	0.61	−0.46	0.04*
% Social renters	−0.68	0.61	−0.19
% Aged 65+	0.31	−0.37	0.14
% In agriculture	0.31	−0.50	0.22
Persons per hectare	−0.31	0.31	−0.02*
% With no car	−0.73	0.65	−0.16
% Ethnic minority	−0.22	0.24	−0.05*

Notes: All coefficients are statistically significant except those asterisked. N=626 for Conservative and Labour, and 625 for Liberal Democrats.

managerial occupations, owner occupiers, and older people were greatest. They did worse in urban areas, and where there were more manual workers, social renters, households without a car, and voters from ethnic minorities. The correlations with Labour support are a mirror image of those for the Conservatives. In the case of the Liberal Democrats, the pattern remained similar to that for the Conservatives, but the associations were generally weaker.

It is worth noting, however, that compared with 1983 the variables relating to occupational class and housing were more weakly associated with levels of party support in 2005, as was the proportion of households with no car. On the other hand, the relationships involving the urban/rural dimension were generally stronger, as were those involving the proportion of older people and of members of ethnic minorities.

Turnout in 2005 recovered a little from the abysmal level of 2001. Nevertheless, at 61.4 per cent it was still well below the post-war norm, despite the fact that about 12 per cent of the electorate were issued with postal votes, and these eventually accounted for 15 per cent of the ballots cast. The change to postal voting on demand was clearly not, as advocates had claimed (or hoped), an effective antidote to low turnout, although it may have prevented a further fall from the depths plumbed in 2001. For the third election in a row, Liverpool Riverside recorded the lowest turnout (41.5 per cent); but it was not without rivals for the electoral wooden spoon, since thirty-five seats failed to reach 50 per cent, almost all of them in big cities. At the other extreme, turnout was 70 per cent or greater in thirty-one constituencies, headed by rural Leominster on 77.3 per cent. There was a significant difference between the average turnout in seats won by the Conservatives (65.3 per cent, N=197) and those won by Labour (57.9 per cent, N=355)—a difference which contributed to the bias of the electoral system in Labour's favour (see Chapter 7).

Table 5.3 Correlations between turnout and constituency characteristics, 2005

% Professional & managerial	0.54	% Manual workers	−0.57
% In agriculture	0.45	Persons per hectare	−0.54
% Owner occupiers	0.70	% Social renters	−0.72
% Aged 65+	0.43	% Private renters	−0.16
% with degrees	0.24	% With no car	−0.79
Constit. marginality 2001	0.71	% Ethnic minority	−0.40
		% Aged 18–24	−0.42

Notes: All coefficients are statistically significant at the 0.01 level. Glasgow North East (Speaker's seat) and Staffordshire South (delayed election) are excluded from all calculations and Wyre Forest (Independent victory in 2001) from that for marginality. N=626. Marginality is defined as 100 minus the difference in percentage share of votes between the top two parties.

A more general indication of turnout variation across constituencies is provided in Table 5.3. This can be compared with Table 4.3, which gives similar information for the 1983 election. As in the latter contest, turnout in 2005 was higher in constituencies with more professional and managerial households, owner occupiers, older people, agricultural employees, and also people with degrees. It was lower where there were more manual workers, persons per hectare, social and private renters, households with no car, people from ethnic minorities, and young people. It is striking, however, that most of the correlation coefficients for 2005 are considerably stronger than those for 1983. By 2005, Britain was very clearly divided into relatively low turnout and high turnout seats, and the two were very different in terms of their social make-up. The table also shows that 2005 turnout was strongly related to the previous marginality of individual seats. This election, indeed, produced the strongest correlation of any postwar contest between constituency marginality and turnout, reflecting the intense targeting of the parties' campaigning efforts on marginal seats. Those that were safe or hopeless for the party concerned were now being almost ignored.

Voting Behaviour

In Chapter 3 we presented data drawn from 1964 to 1979, showing the decline in the 'twin pillars' of the Butler–Stokes model explaining party choice—class voting and party identification. In Tables 5.4 and 5.5 the figures are updated to 2005. In 1983, the long-established Alford index of class voting was clearly smaller than it had been in the 1960s and 1970s. Despite a few fluctuations thereafter, the decline broadly continued, and the index reached its lowest-ever level in 2005. A similar tale is related by the figures for 'absolute class voting'—the combined percentages of working-class Labour and middle-class Conservative voters. From this

Table 5.4 Measures of class voting, 1960s–2005

	1960s	1970s	1983	1987	1992	1997	2001	2005
Alford index	39	31	25	25	27	20	23	18
Absolute class voting	63	55	49	49	52	46	45	41

Note: The figures for '1960s' are means for 1964, 1966, and 1970 while '1970s' are for the three elections from 1974 to 1979.

Source: BES surveys (Denver, 2007: 69).

Table 5.5 Party identification, 1960s–2005

	1960s	1970s	1983	1987	1992	1997	2001	2005
Identify with a party	90	87	86	86	94	93	89	81
Identify with Conservative or Labour	81	74	67	67	78	76	73	63
Very strong identifiers	42	25	20	19	19	16	13	10
Very strongly Conservative or Labour	40	23	18	16	18	15	11	9

Notes: Figures shown are percentages. The figures for '1960s' are means for 1964, 1966, and 1970 while those for the '1970s' are for the three elections from 1974 to 1979.

Source: BES surveys (Denver, 2007: 72–4).

perspective there was an upward blip in 1992, but by 2005 only about two-fifths of voters supported their 'natural' class party at the polls. This evidence might appear to conflict with the analysis in Table 5.2 which showed that the class composition of constituencies remained strongly correlated with levels of support for the major parties. The conflict is more apparent than real, however. The crucial point is that in more working-class areas *everyone* (including the middle class) is more likely to vote Labour, while in more middle-class areas *everyone* (including the working class) is more likely to vote Conservative. Polarization at the aggregate constituency level is thus perfectly compatible with the well-attested class dealignment among individual voters.

Partisan dealignment also continued throughout the period covered by this chapter (Table 5.5). The trend is complicated by the fact that in the 1992 BES survey (and subsequently) the positioning of the questions on party identification was altered as compared with the earlier studies, making it easier for respondents to testify to a party identity which they might not really feel. Even so, the decline in the proportion identifying with a party resumed, and by 2005 was about ten points lower than in the 1960s. A similar pattern—but a steeper fall—is evident in the case of those identifying specifically with the Conservatives or Labour. The two major parties commanded the loyalties of four-fifths of the electorate to some extent in the 1960s, but by 2005 this had been reduced to three-fifths at most.

More striking, however, is the decline in the proportion of those whose declared commitment to their party was 'very strong'. In this case, the changed question-order in 1992 made little difference. Among all identifiers, and also among those identifying specifically with the Conservatives and Labour, 'very strong' identifiers fell from about two-fifths to about one in ten. This emotional disengagement from parties which were once 'loved and trusted' has had enormous consequences for electoral behaviour, campaigning and much else.[2] For example, it is a major cause of the decline in turnout noted in Chapter 1, and has made those who *do* vote more volatile in their choice of party. Far from being relatively rigid as in the past, the distribution of party support among voters had steadily become fluid and unpredictable from the 1960s onwards.

These developments had cast doubt on the explanatory value of the Butler–Stokes model of party choice as early as the 1970s, and in the next two decades it was increasingly clear that alternative explanatory frameworks were required. Electoral analysts agreed that voters' assessments and judgements were playing a bigger part in their decisions, but there was no consensus on which particular assessments were the key ones, and even less on how to describe the changed approach to voting. 'Issue voting', 'instrumental voting', 'retrospective voting', 'consumer voting', and 'judgemental voting' were among the terms suggested. In their report on the 2001 and 2005 elections, however, the BES team elaborated a model of 'valence politics' which quickly came to be accepted as the best way of explaining party choice in the dealigned era (Clarke et al., 2004, 2009). As explained in Chapter 1, among other things this approach gives much more weight to opinions about party leaders than was previously the case. From that perspective there is no difficulty in explaining Labour's victories from 1997 to 2005. As we have seen, Tony Blair was much preferred to John Major in 1997 and William Hague in 2001 as the best person for Prime Minister. In 2005, Blair's lead over Howard was smaller than he had enjoyed over his rivals in previous elections—in five YouGov campaign surveys Blair was preferred by between 34 and 37 per cent, while Howard's scores were between 23 and 25 per cent—but his advantage was still clear and consistent. In addition, however, Labour easily outscored the Conservatives as the best party to run the economy—not always decisive in itself, but a classic, highly salient valence issue. Over the five surveys previously cited, the proportion opting for the Conservatives on the economy averaged 28 per cent, compared with 47 per cent choosing Labour. Strongly favoured on the major valence issue and with the highest-rated leader, it is hard to resist the conclusion that Labour simply couldn't lose in 2005, despite the lingering ill-feeling over Iraq and the inevitable domestic grievances which the government had accumulated since Blair had hailed a 'new dawn' in 1997.

Non-Voting

In Chapter 3 we looked briefly at explanations for non-voting in the 1970s, noting that turnout was significantly lower among those with weak or non-existent party identification, young people, the unmarried, the residentially mobile, and those living in privately rented accommodation. In those days, of course, there were many fewer non-voters than was the case at the start of the twenty-first century. In the 1960s and 1970s, a persistent problem for survey studies of non-voting was that many respondents—whether through forgetfulness or guilt—claimed to have voted in an election when they had not in fact done so. This was overcome by researchers for the BES at the 1987 election, who consulted the marked electoral registers that had been used in polling stations to determine which of the survey respondents had recorded a vote in reality and which had not. This practice continued in subsequent elections and allowed much more accurate and reliable analysis of non-voting. Nonetheless, as Table 5.6 shows, the patterns noted by Ivor Crewe and his colleagues in the 1970s were still evident in 2005. There was no significant difference in turnout between men and women, and age remained the single most important variable influencing propensity to vote. By the latter election, however, the differences between age-groups had widened considerably, with the over 65s being about twice as likely to vote as 18–24-year-olds. This had obvious policy implications for parties in relation to pensions and other benefits for the over 65s. Length of residence in a neighbourhood also continued to be associated with variations in the likelihood of voting, and those living in privately rented accommodation were still less likely to turn out than owner-occupiers. However, the unenviable record of private renters was now rivalled by the reduced ranks of 'social renters' (local authority or housing association tenants). Married and widowed people were clearly more likely to vote than those who had never married, those whose marriages had otherwise come to an end, and those living together as partners—the latter being a group that had expanded dramatically since 1964. Indeed, the decline of traditional marriage and the increase in cohabitation could be additional factors contributing to the long-term decline in turnout in British elections (Denver, 2008). It is important to note that these differences identified in Table 5.6 persist even when controls for other variables are introduced.

The importance of strength of party identification is clear from the data. In 2005, those with a very strong identification were almost as likely to vote as they ever had been. The problem, as previously noted, was that there were fewer of them around. Finally, the table shows that by 2005 a clear difference in turnout had emerged between broadly middle-class groups and manual workers. Those with professional and managerial occupations and having professional qualifications or a degree were much more likely to vote than others. No such socio-economic

Table 5.6 Turnout in 2005

Sex		Housing	
Men	59	Owner-occupiers	68
Women	63	Private renters	44
Marital Status		Social renters	44
Married/widowed	70	*Highest education qualification*	
Live with partner	47	None	57
Separated/divorced	53	School	57
Single/never married	45	Vocational	59
		Professional	74
Occupation		Degree	74
Professional and managerial	75	*Years spent in neighbourhood*	
Other non-manual	60		
Manual	51	1–2	55
		3–9	63
Age		10–19	69
18–24	38	20+	75
25–34	48	*Party identification*	
35–44	61		
45–54	64	None	33
55–64	74	Not very strong	57
65+	76	Fairly strong	70
		Very strong	79

Note: Figures given are percentages. The original data have been weighted to reflect the actual turnout in the election.

Source: Data from BES 2005 cross-section survey.

differences were found in the 1960s and 1970s, and their emergence suggests that a significant section of the working class—to the extent that the latter still existed—had become alienated from, or apathetic about, a political system in which, to the casual observer, the major parties and the major politicians all looked pretty much alike.

Conclusion

Tony Blair dominated British politics from 1997 to 2005. At first, he was 'Teflon Tony', but the attractive veneer had worn away long before the end of his second term. Labour's 2005 election slogan—'Britain Forward not Back'—was both uninspiring and remarkably defensive, implying that Labour's best card was residual fear of a return to Conservative rule rather than pride in its own achievements during eight years of overwhelming parliamentary majorities. Blair was undoubtedly assisted by the inability of his main opponents to produce a leader who could combine weight and popularity among the voters and it is, of course, fascinating—if ultimately futile—to speculate about what might have happened had the Conservatives chosen Clarke rather than IDS in 2001. What is undeniable, however, is that—whatever the public's reservations—Blair remained an important electoral asset for Labour. As he entered his third term, the question was whether he retained the vitality and the vision to move Britain 'forward'.

Appendix: Campaign Polls

Figures 5.A1–5.A3 relate to Great Britain, as Northern Ireland is not included in national opinion polls (data from https://www.markpack.org.uk/opinion-polls/).

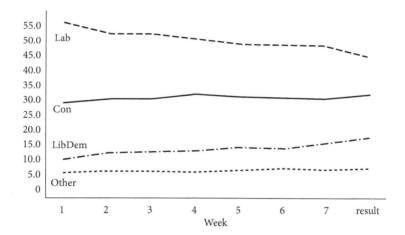

Figure 5.A1 Campaign polls, 1997

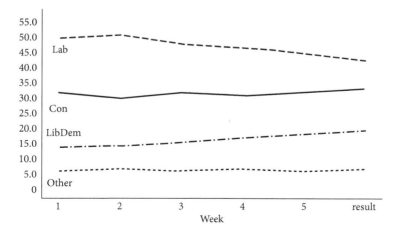

Figure 5.A2 Campaign polls, 2001

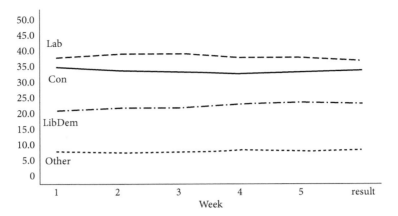

Figure 5.A3 Campaign polls, 2005

Notes

1. The cycle of local elections in Britain is such that different numbers and types of local authorities are elected each year. Actual vote shares in these elections are not, therefore, an accurate guide to the national popularity of the parties but have to be adjusted to provide 'national equivalent' shares. Throughout we use the national equivalent shares calculated by Colin Rallings and Michael Thrasher of the Local Government Elections Centre at the University of Plymouth.

2. In *Human Nature in Politics*, Graham Wallas (1910) described parties as 'something that can be loved and trusted and can be recognised at successive elections as the same thing that was loved and trusted before' (cited in Denver, 2007: 84).

6

Conservative Revival and the Rise of 'Others'

Elections, 2010–15

Despite a troubled inter-election period and a marked decline in vote share, Labour emerged from the 2005 election still holding a very clear overall majority of seats in the House of Commons. Contemporary observers could have been forgiven for thinking that politics at the top would continue much as before. In fact, however, over the next five years the political scene—and, in particular, the electoral outlook for the parties—was transformed. To a large extent this was due to changes in the leadership of all three major parties. Blair, Howard, and Kennedy had led their respective forces in 2005; by 2010, the leaders were Gordon Brown, David Cameron, and Nick Clegg.

The End of the Affair: The Demise of Tony Blair

Although Tony Blair had led Labour to an unprecedented third successive election victory in 2005, the next two years were as difficult for him as 1988–90 had been for Margaret Thatcher. The 2005 result did nothing to quell speculation about when Blair would resign and give way to Gordon Brown. This was not just generated by mischievous media; it was fuelled by plotting and anti-Blair briefings by Brown's supporters, both on the backbenches and in the government itself. This unhappiness among Labour politicians was partly provoked by the policies being pursued by the government—involvement in Iraq continued and the terms of the 2006 Terrorism Act irritated Blair's liberal detractors. The party leadership also became embroiled in allegations of 'sleaze', bringing a dramatic end to a story which had started with the 'Ecclestone affair' of 1997. In that year, shortly after talking with Bernie Ecclestone—the billionaire in charge of Formula 1 motor racing who had recently given £1 million to the Labour party, despite not being known for pro-Labour opinions—Blair announced that new rules forbidding the advertising of tobacco products would not apply to motor racing for four years. This did not sit well with Blair's previous argument that Labour in office needed to be 'purer than pure' in order to restore public trust in politics after the sleaze of the Major years. Now, after 2005, it was claimed that rich Labour

British General Elections Since 1964: Diversity, Dealignment, and Disillusion. Second Edition. David Denver and Mark Garnett, Oxford University Press. © David Denver and Mark Garnett 2021. DOI: 10.1093/oso/9780198844952.003.0006

supporters had been offered peerages in return for financial contributions to the party. A police investigation followed, during which the party's chief fundraiser, Lord Levy, was arrested and the Prime Minister himself formally interviewed, although no charges were laid.

The main problem for Blair, however, was simply that his popularity among the electorate was fading fast (Figure 6.1). In July 2005, the Prime Minister's satisfaction rating among the voters, according to Ipsos MORI, stood at −3: far below his peak, but still highly creditable for someone who had been leader of his party for more than a decade. For the next five months the average was −20; for 2006 it was −34; for the first four months of 2007 the score was −41. To make matters worse, in December 2005 the Conservatives acquired a new, young, and previously almost unknown leader, David Cameron, who quickly made a favourable impression. Blair soon found himself running neck and neck with (and occasionally trailing) Cameron on the 'best Prime Minister' question in the polls—a novel experience for the former. In terms of voting intentions, for the first time since 1992 the Conservatives held a sustained lead over Labour from the spring of 2006.

Not unexpectedly, these ratings were reflected in mid-term election results. In the 2006 local elections, Labour lost a further 350 seats—the national equivalent vote shares being 39 per cent for the Conservatives, 26 per cent for Labour, and 25 per cent for the Liberal Democrats. In 2007, the vote shares were similar, but Labour lost around 550 seats while the Conservatives gained 900. Also in that

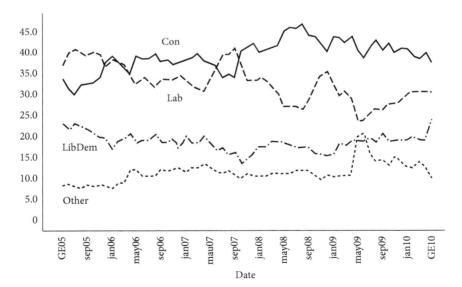

Figure 6.1 Monthly voting intentions, 2005–10 (all polls)

Notes: The 2005 and 2010 election results in Great Britain form the starting and finishing points. The data shown are the monthly means for all published polls except the daily polls undertaken by YouGov for Sky News in September/October 2009 and for *The Sun* in March 2010.

year, the elections for the devolved institutions in Scotland and Wales caused embarrassment for Labour in two countries where they normally dominated. In Scotland, Labour came second to the SNP in terms of votes, lost nine constituencies, and was ousted from control of the Scottish Executive (as the Scottish government was then known). In Wales, Labour mustered less than a third of the vote, lost six constituency seats (while gaining one), and no longer had overall control of the Assembly. In four parliamentary by-elections during 2005–6, the party's vote share declined and the formerly safe seat of Dunfermline and West Fife was lost to the Liberal Democrats (February 2006). In Blaenau Gwent (June 2006), an Independent once again denied the party victory in what until 2005 had been one of its safest seats.

These poor performances increased the pressure on Blair. Celebrating ten years in office in May 1989, Margaret Thatcher had disappointed her critics (and even some of her well-wishers) by showing no sign of impending retirement; indeed, after the 1987 general election she had declared her wish to go 'on and on'. Within a few days of reaching the same anniversary, Blair announced that he would leave office on 27 June 2007. It was a wretched departure for someone who had been the darling of the electorate for so long. A YouGov poll in April 2007 found clear majorities of respondents believing that Blair had not cleaned up politics (78 per cent); was not able to unite the nation (72 per cent); had lost touch with ordinary people (66 per cent); had played fast and loose with the truth (66 per cent); could not be trusted (63 per cent); was ineffective (60 per cent); was too influenced by the rich and powerful (59 per cent); was concerned only for himself and his party (57 per cent); and did not stick to principles (51 per cent). The only bright spot for Blair in this report was that 51 per cent still thought that he was likeable as a person—which, in view of the other details, probably said more about Britain's addiction to a 'celebrity culture' than it did about Blair's perceived human qualities. Aged only 54 at the time of his resignation, Blair could have expected a prolonged political 'afterlife', if not as a 'backseat driver' in Lady Thatcher's mould then at least as a significant player in subsequent election campaigns. But his absence from the spotlight did not make British hearts any fonder; in the eyes of most voters, he had undergone an abrupt transition from icon to irrelevance.

Gordon Brown in Office

Gordon Brown was elected unopposed as Labour leader—and hence Prime Minister—in the month of Blair's departure. The absence of any other candidate prevented party members from providing Brown with a 'mandate', allowing critics to accuse him of lacking legitimacy. This was just the first of Brown's many misfortunes. If Blair's final term was uncomfortable, Brown's tenure of Number 10 turned out to be torrid. Initially he seemed to have adapted well to the role he had coveted for so long, responding decisively to widespread flooding and to terrorist incidents at Glasgow airport and in London. He certainly offered a different style from that of his predecessor—'Not Flash, just Gordon', as a poster put it—and there was a marked 'Brown bounce' in Labour's poll ratings (Figure 6.1).

Given that Labour had re-established its lead in the polls, there was mounting speculation—fanned by the media but at least partly encouraged by Brown's entourage—that a snap election would be called in the autumn of 2007. Initially intended as a ruse to spread panic in Conservative ranks, the idea soon gave rise to some serious preparations for a poll. During Labour's party conference in September the speculation reached fever-pitch and Brown himself dropped a public hint that he might soon be asking the Queen to dissolve Parliament. At the subsequent Conservative conference, however, David Cameron gave a characteristically confident performance while George Osborne, the shadow Chancellor, announced that a Conservative government would greatly increase the threshold at which inheritance tax became payable. The effect was a sharp and speedy increase in support for the Conservatives in the polls; a simultaneous visit by Brown to British forces in Iraq was derided as a cynical attempt to deny the Opposition 'the oxygen of publicity' (Rawnsley, 2010: 500–8).

In the last five surveys before the Conservative conference, Labour held an average lead of 9.6 points; in the first five after the conference ended, the parties were neck and neck. Brown announced that there would be no election, disingenuously claiming in a press conference that his decision had not been influenced by the polls. The authors of the 2010 Nuffield study (which, for the first time since 1951, did not include David Butler) identified 'the election that never was' as a key turning point in Gordon Brown's term of office, and the change of mood was obvious at the time (Kavanagh and Cowley, 2010: ch. 1). The press dubbed the dithering Prime Minister 'Bottler Brown' but his handling of the matter also left some of his colleagues unimpressed. In particular, relations steadily deteriorated between Brown and his Chancellor, Alistair Darling, a respected but uncharismatic politician who had been appointed at least in part because Brown expected that under his stewardship the Treasury would cause far less trouble for Number 10 than it had done during his own spell as Chancellor.

Whatever critics might say about Brown's political courage or tactical judgement, he could at least fall back on the reputation for financial acumen which he had gained as Chancellor. However, in the same month that he ruled out an election the first indications of serious problems in the financial sector began to emerge, thanks chiefly to the irresponsible lending strategies of US institutions but falling with particular severity on Britain where American practices had been copied. The Northern Rock bank was the first to experience difficulty in funding its own reckless operations, prompting a rush by its customers to withdraw their cash. The government sought to prevent a panic by guaranteeing bank and building society savings up to £35,000, but worse was to follow. In September 2008, the collapse of the US-based Lehman Brothers investment bank triggered a full-scale international financial crisis. In Britain the stock market tumbled, banks had to be bailed out and then taken into public ownership in all but name, interest rates were lowered successively to reach 0.5 per cent in March 2009, and there was large-scale 'quantitative easing' (i.e. printing money) to maintain the flow of credit. The effects soon spread to the rest of the economy—firms went out of business, unemployment rose significantly, and GDP declined. Moreover, the state was now piling up enormous debts and amid an international 'credit-crunch' its own ability to borrow came into question.

At first, Brown (and consequently his party) received some praise for his response to the crisis (Figure 6.1). He was decisive and authoritative on the issues and played a key role in coordinating international action to stave off an economic disaster similar to the Great Depression of the 1930s. Opinion gradually changed, however, as the economy failed to recover and people came to resent Brown's previous boast that he had abolished 'boom and bust'. The crisis also began to be perceived as at least partly his fault. Only voters well versed in high finance could comprehend how he had contributed to the problem by establishing a 'light-touch' regulatory regime for the banks, but it was easier to equate Britain's plight with the yawning gap in the public accounts, which was at least partly attributable to the spending increases he had authorized during his last term as Chancellor. Moreover, bank bailouts were widely criticized for appearing to rescue greedy and incompetent financiers from the consequences of their own actions. In previous times of national crisis, Prime Ministers had broadcast to the nation in the hope of maintaining morale, but Gordon Brown was clearly not cut from the same viewer-friendly cloth as Harold ('Pound in Your Pocket') Wilson. Inevitably, the upturn in Labour support proved to be very short-lived, and the party had declined to a new low by the summer of 2009.

The unpopularity of the Prime Minister and his government were reflected in elections as well as opinion polls. In the 2008 round of local elections, Labour's share of the national equivalent vote was just 24 per cent, compared with 43 per cent for the Conservatives and 23 per cent for the Liberal Democrats. In the following year, Labour came third, with support at around 22 per cent. In both years, Labour lost hundreds of seats and control of many councils. Indeed, after the 2009 round of county council elections, the Conservatives were by far the largest party in local government in England and Wales, holding 48 per cent of all council seats (compared with 23 per cent for Labour and 21 per cent for the Liberal Democrats) and controlling 209 of the 373 councils (Rallings and Thrasher, 2009). The cumulative council election gains notched up by the Conservatives had an importance beyond the merely local, since advances of that kind can invigorate a party's membership nationwide—as well as encouraging activists in the localities concerned—while damaging the morale of opponents.

The 2009 European elections brought even worse news for Labour. The party came third with just 15.2 per cent of the votes, behind the Conservatives (27.7 per cent) and UKIP (16.5 per cent). In percentage terms, it was Labour's worst result in a nationwide poll since 1910. In parliamentary by-elections the government lost Crewe and Nantwich to the Conservatives in May 2008. This was the latter's first by-election gain since 1982, when a quixotic battle between Labour and an SDP defector had presented Mitcham and Morden to the Tories. Labour also lost Glasgow East to the SNP in July and Norwich North, again to the Conservatives, a year later.

The last year of the parliament was dominated by revelations in the *Daily Telegraph* concerning the expenses of MPs. Some of their claims for reimbursement were fraudulent (eventually resulting in the arrest and punishment of offenders); others were plainly attempts to play the system (switching the designation of second homes to 'main residence' in order to maximize payments); while the rest attracted ridicule as well as outrage (biscuits, dog food, and a floating duck island). As the details emerged after May 2009, the public became incandescent about this apparent confirmation of previous suspicions about Britain's legislators. When MPs appeared on a BBC *Question Time* programme later in the same month, they were met with open hostility which crossed the border into contempt.[1] The issue was badly handled by the Speaker of the House of Commons, Michael Martin, who attracted criticism from all sides and was forced to resign—the first Speaker to do so since 1695. Another probable consequence of the affair was that before the 2010 election 149 MPs decided not to contest their seats—the largest number for any post-war election. Although there were serious offenders in all three main parties, David Cameron appeared more decisive in dealing with the culprits on his side than Brown, and he was certainly more fulsome in his apologies to the voters. Since the governing party was always likely to suffer from a scandal which had broken out on its watch—and since most of the press now backed Cameron and the Conservatives—the steady stream of revelations certainly did nothing to improve Labour's re-election prospects.

From the summer of 2009, however, the government's standing with the electorate recovered steadily, if slowly, and the upward trend was maintained until March 2010. There were no political developments at the time which could explain this partial revival. Although governments usually experience some recovery in popularity as an election approaches, this is often accompanied by an economic upturn which they themselves have engineered. Over the months in question, however, the economic news remained gloomy—unemployment reached its highest level for fourteen years in late 2009 and early 2010, for example. Miller and Mackie (1973) argued some time ago, however, that the relationship between government popularity and economic performance is largely spurious. Whether or not a government tried to boost the economy as an election approached, there would still be an upswing in its favour. Even when the electorate was broadly aligned with the major parties, it was relatively easy for less committed supporters to 'defect' in mid-term (even if only in answer to pollsters' questions or in local elections). When a real general election was in prospect, however, voters had to ask themselves if their discontent with the government was such as to warrant letting the other side win—and in many cases the answer was 'no'. That is presumably why Labour crawled to within hailing distance of the Conservatives as the 2010 election campaign got under way. The improvement certainly owed nothing to the Prime Minister's belated attempts to soften his dour public persona. Unfortunately for him, Gordon Brown found it difficult to display a natural smile in front of a camera. This was a mystery to those who had seen his genial side in private, and may have been partly a result of a youthful sporting injury which had badly impaired his eyesight. Whatever the source of his gauche on-screen persona, the result was considerable mockery when his attempts to smile in an internet video appearance turned out to be both unconvincing and invariably ill-timed.

Cameron and the Conservatives

As previously noted, David Cameron took over as Conservative leader in December 2005. Michael Howard had intimated his intention to stand down immediately after the election, triggering a hard-fought campaign to succeed him. The front-runner, initially, was David Davis, a former minister whose service in the Commons dated back to 1987, with Cameron—who had first been elected as an MP in 2001 and was little known outside Westminster—acting as the standard bearer for 'modernizers' within the party. The key event of the campaign was at the party conference, where Cameron dazzled his audience by speaking for twenty minutes without notes. Davis—like 'Rab' Butler and Reginald Maudling in the similar speaking contest of 1963—failed to inspire even his own supporters. In the ballot of party members, Cameron, then aged 39, won with 134,446 to Davis' 64,398. Even if some were doubtful about the former's plans for updating and improving the party's image, they voted for the person they thought more likely to appeal to the wider electorate. In this respect, the party had taken a long time to learn from New Labour, but had got it right at the fourth time of asking. As we have seen, Cameron's positive impact on Conservative poll ratings meant that, within a year, the Opposition had over-taken Labour and this lead was maintained—apart from the few months of the 'Brown bounce'—for the rest of the cycle. We have also noted that promising results were achieved in local, European, and by-elections, although there was little improvement in Scotland, where the SNP was best placed to benefit from Labour's unpopularity.

Another promising electoral portent for the Conservatives came in 2008 when Boris Johnson defeated the Labour incumbent, Ken Livingstone, to become Mayor of London. However, for Cameron this was a mixed blessing. Although it was clearly a very good outcome for the party, Johnson's unconventional ways (and appearance) earned him considerable popularity across the country. 'Boris' was probably the only British politician who could be recognized by a majority of people without having to mention his surname. Johnson had resigned his Commons seat to fight the mayoral election, but soon well-placed cronies in the party and the media were promoting him as a rival to Cameron for the Conservative leadership.

Cameron and his team quickly set about 'detoxifying' the Conservative 'brand'. Evidence showed that, in the abstract, Conservative policies were reasonably popular. When they were linked to the party by name, however, support for them dropped sharply. Cameron and the modernizers were right when they argued that the problem lay in 'the brand'. The image of being the 'nasty party'—a description quoted at the 2002 annual conference by Theresa May, then the Conservative Chair—had stuck. Accordingly, the Thatcherite past was played down (if not quite disowned), and issues such as tax cuts, immigration, and Europe relegated to the back burner. Rather, Cameron emphasized social liberalism and, in particular, his personal commitment to environmentalism: for the 2006 local elections the party slogan was 'Vote Blue Go Green'. In addition, the central party made strenuous attempts to promote the selection of female and ethnic minority candidates, especially in winnable seats. While the use of this 'A-list' of candidates backfired in some cases (the people on the list were mocked as 'Tatler Tories' and some constituency associations resented the imposition of 'outsiders') it is indicative of the modernizing approach pursued by Cameron and his coterie ('Cameroons'). Naturally there was considerable resistance to the new direction being taken, on the back benches as well as in the constituencies. There was a more serious reaction when Cameron's modernizing manoeuvres turned to specific policies, such as the announcement that the party would not allow the establishment of any new grammar schools.

What party activists love most, however, is a winner. Given Cameron's poll ratings he could get away with a good deal—although not as much as his role model, Tony Blair—when he made decisions which irritated grass-roots opinion within his own party. From April 2008, the polls reported that he consistently led Gordon Brown as the leader who would make the best Prime Minister. In terms of satisfaction with the performance of the Leader of the Opposition—in effect a measure of popularity—the three previous Conservative leaders had all registered impressively negative scores over their period of office (Hague averaged −24.8, Duncan Smith −16.4, and Howard −11.7). Cameron averaged +5.0 over fifty months. Although unspectacular, this was at least a positive score; for rank and file Conservatives it must have made a pleasant change to speak about their incumbent leader without at least some degree of embarrassment.

Liberal Democrats and Others

Not to be outdone, the Liberal Democrats changed leaders twice between 2005 and 2010. After 2005, Charles Kennedy remained popular with the voters and ordinary party members. However, now that the party seemed to be a more serious force, thanks to its electoral success under Kennedy, its leading figures became increasingly critical of the latter's alleged heavy drinking and 'relaxed' approach to aspects of the job. The pressure on Kennedy was compounded (and in some cases caused) by ideological differences; while the centre of gravity within his party had moved to the right, he had barely changed from his SDP days and clearly relished the experience of attacking New Labour from the left. After his enforced resignation (January 2006), Kennedy was succeeded by another Scottish MP, Sir Menzies Campbell, who defeated the ill-fated Chris Huhne in the leadership ballot. A former Olympic athlete and one-time holder of the British record for the 100 metres, Campbell was now widely seen as an elder statesman (he was almost 65 when he became leader). He was a safe pair of hands whose relative lack of interest in ideological matters made him unlikely to fall foul of the emerging quasi-Thatcherite 'Orange Book' faction or to anger MPs and party members who, like Kennedy, continued to see the Liberal Democrats as a left-leaning party. Campbell's age quickly came to be seen as a problem, however, and his performances in the House of Commons were less scintillating than his youthful exploits on the track. His reluctant departure in October 2007 proved that his party was now prepared to rival the Conservatives (and easily beat Labour) in its unsentimental attitude towards under-performing leaders. Another leadership election produced a narrow victory for Nick Clegg, who defeated Huhne by just 511 votes out of more than 41,000 cast and took over in December. Clegg, a multilingual former journalist who had served in the European Parliament, had been an MP only since 2005, and was thus even less experienced than David Cameron. However, he was closely identified with the Orange Book group, and duly led the Liberal Democrats back to a stance of 'equidistance' between the major parties rather than lining up on the 'progressive' side as had been the case since 1995, when Paddy Ashdown went public with his barely concealed preference for a coalition deal with Labour.

The two leadership changes each produced a small fillip in popularity for the Liberal Democrats (probably owing to the attendant publicity for the party), but the effects were not dramatic or enduring (Figure 6.1). Shortly after Kennedy's departure, as previously noted, the party notched up a spectacular by-election gain by taking Dunfermline and West Fife (which was geographically close to Menzies Campbell's own seat as well as that of Gordon Brown) from Labour in February 2006, but their performance in other elections over the period was very ordinary. The position of the Liberal Democrats slowly improved from early 2009 but as the election drew near they were still some way short of the level of support that they had achieved under Kennedy in 2005.

The most remarkable aspect of Figure 6.1 is the popularity of 'others' (mainly UKIP, the BNP, Greens, and nationalists in Scotland and Wales). In the 2005 election, this miscellaneous group had accumulated just 8 per cent of the votes. From then until 2010, however, they averaged 11 per cent of voting intentions. This was easily the best ever sustained performance by the minor parties (counting the nationalists as 'minor' in the overall British context), and compares with an average of only 7.7 per cent over the 2001–5 cycle. As in that period, there was a sharp spike in support coinciding with European Parliament elections (June 2009). On this occasion, however, the spike was from a higher base, and the subsequent decline still left the 'others' in a stronger position than in the run-up to the 2005 election.

In the European elections, as already noted, UKIP came second in terms of vote share and won thirteen seats. On 8.6 per cent of the vote, the Green Party took two seats, while the BNP (6.2 per cent) also returned two MEPs—one each in North-West England and Yorkshire and Humberside. Across Britain, the three major parties together won only 57 per cent of the votes. In local elections, too, the three 'major minor' parties enjoyed some success, winning some council seats in England and Wales (although these were in only a few geographically widely dispersed local authorities). Most notably, in 2006, the BNP won twelve seats in the London borough of Barking and Dagenham, thus becoming the second largest party on that council. In general, however, the first-past-the-post system continued to make it difficult for small parties to win seats in local elections. Nonetheless, it remains the case that 'fringe' parties were more popular in this period than ever before. This was in part a consequence of long-term partisan dealignment—many voters no longer being strongly tied to the 'old' parties—but it can also be attributed to widespread disillusion with mainstream politics, especially in the context of the expenses scandal that enveloped MPs of all parties during this parliament.

In Scotland, what SNP leader Alex Salmond described as 'a historic moment' occurred in May 2007 when his party defeated Labour in the Scottish Parliament election and went on to form a minority Scottish government. There were other notable successes—the party became the largest in Scottish local government (also in 2007), when the relevant elections were contested using the single transferable vote (STV) system for the first time. Most remarkably, in July 2008 the SNP won a by-election in Glasgow East—previously considered one of Labour's safest Scottish seats. In polls of Westminster voting intentions, however, the SNP generally trailed behind Labour. In 2008, for example, Labour averaged 34 per cent and the SNP 32 per cent among Scottish voters; in 2009, the relevant figures were 34 per cent and 29 per cent. This disjunction between voters' preferences in devolved and UK elections was also apparent in Wales, and was then a regular feature of party support in the two countries. Nonetheless, the SNP entered the 2010 general election with a higher level of support than it had achieved in 2005.

As ever, Plaid Cymru was not as strong in Wales as the SNP in Scotland. It remained, however, a significant player in the Welsh party system. Following the Assembly elections in 2007, when three additional seats were gained, the party entered a ruling coalition with Labour. Otherwise, its electoral performances were unspectacular, making little headway in local elections and coming third in the European Parliamentary election in Wales behind Labour and the Conservatives.

The 2010 Campaign

After a prolonged series of what casual observers might have thought relatively humdrum general election campaigns, the 2010 version proved to be in some ways the most remarkable of our period to that point. This is because—following a media campaign and discussions initiated by Sky News during 2009—the parties and their leaders finally agreed to participate in live broadcast debates. As we have seen, it had become almost a tradition for the party lagging in the polls as an election approached to call for a live televised confrontation. Just as traditionally, the leader of the party which was ahead in the opinion polls would spurn the invitation, for the good reason that there was nothing to be gained and, possibly, a lot to lose. However, David Cameron had spoken in favour of debates during the contest for the Conservative leadership—as part of his modernizing agenda—and to back down in the heat of battle would have made him look like a 'bottler' of Brownite proportions. In any case, Cameron's advisors expected that he would perform much better than his rivals. On the Labour side, although it was recognized that Gordon Brown was not a great television performer, he did have the authority of being Prime Minister and, in any case, the party's prospects were already too dismal to be seriously damaged. For those Liberal Democrats who had wielded the knife against Kennedy and Campbell, the decision to go ahead with the debates provided the perfect post hoc justification. A performer with the twin attributes of eloquence and obscurity, Clegg was being offered the chance of sharing a platform with Cameron and Brown in front of a mass audience. This virtually guaranteed that the Liberal Democrats would receive media attention throughout the campaign, offering an unparalleled opportunity for the party to put its case to the voters.

Although the televised debates dominated the national campaign—and for many commentators effectively *were* the national campaign—other activities continued as normal. All the parties swung into action at the start of January. The Conservatives, in particular, launched the first of a series of poster campaigns. However, this backfired to an extent. The posters featured a photograph of David Cameron, casually dressed and looking suitably concerned, but it was clear that the leader's picture had been airbrushed and those on sites around the country and on the Internet began to attract graffiti artists who vied with each other to furnish humorous and/or obscene alternatives to the intended political message. Later, in March, Cameron launched his 'Big Society' theme—his stab at a 'big idea' which, whatever its inherent merits, left most voters perplexed (Dorey and Garnett, 2016). Lord (Peter) Mandelson, meanwhile, was back in his old harness, taking charge of Labour's campaign. His efforts were hampered, however, by an acute lack of resources, donations to the party having dwindled following the sleaze allegations under Tony Blair. Nonetheless, staff at the respective party headquarters busied themselves making the usual plans for the campaign—drafting the manifestos, planning leaders' tours, updating targeting strategy, preparing campaign materials. In addition, target voters were inundated with direct mail and calls from national telephone banks. Private polling and the use of focus groups—which had been going on throughout the parliament—increased in intensity.

This time, however, there was a new element—the debates—and from the start of 2010 all parties began their preparations. Both the Conservatives and Labour hired American media consultants to advise the leaders on how to present themselves most effectively. All three party leaders were forced to undergo several rehearsals at which colleagues acted the parts of their opponents in the debates—usually very convincingly, it seems. Crisp answers to the expected questions were prepared and practised, along with 'spontaneous' ripostes to the anticipated comments of the other party leaders.

When the short campaign finally got under way in April, the looming prospect of the debates dwarfed other aspects of campaigning that had long been considered part of the furniture of general elections. National press conferences held by each party in turn, which used to structure each campaign day, were virtually abandoned. Election broadcasts became relatively minor matters for the major parties (although no fewer than twenty different parties now qualified for a broadcast) and were produced relatively cheaply, at short notice. Although the leaders did visit marginal seats, their travels were seriously curtailed because of the need to prepare for the debates. Even so, Gordon Brown's visit to Rochdale in the week before polling turned into a media sensation. After chatting to a lady pensioner (Gillian Duffy), he got into his car and, forgetting that his microphone was still attached and turned on, described her as a 'bigoted woman'. Soon the recording was being replayed on radio and television, and the story was splashed all over the newspapers the next day. Brown returned to Rochdale to apologize personally to Mrs Duffy. Despite the media frenzy over this incident, it had no discernible impact on voting in the election. Those who were outraged didn't much like Brown in any event; those who liked him didn't seem to care, or sympathized with his obvious embarrassment. Perhaps the most important (and depressing) lesson of this tawdry episode was that the mainstream British media had become a platform which discouraged voters and party leaders from saying what they really thought about sensitive political issues—and each other. In the televised debates, both Brown and Cameron competed to intone repeatedly 'I agree with Nick'—doubtless for purely tactical reasons.

Despite Brown's off-screen contretemps with Mrs Duffy, the debates dominated the media's campaign agenda. As noted in Chapter 1, they were broadcast on three consecutive Thursdays in April, in the second, third, and fourth weeks of the campaign. Each programme lasted ninety minutes and the first (on ITV1) was watched by almost ten million viewers, the second (on Sky) by four million, and the last (on BBC1) by about 7.5 million. The clashes between the leaders were followed immediately by jousting among the rival spin doctors, each trying to claim victory for their respective champion. Polls provided almost instantaneous indications of audience reactions, which were then unpicked for days in the media. Thus, another consequence of the debates was to crowd out to a greater extent than ever any residual reporting of issues, policy announcements, and the like.

The organization of the debates and the performances of the participants have been discussed in detail elsewhere (Kavanagh and Cowley, 2010: ch. 8; Wring et al., 2011). For our purposes, it is enough to note that by general consent the Liberal Democrat leader, Nick Clegg, made by far the best impression in the first debate, Cameron and Clegg were neck and neck in the second, while Cameron was adjudged the clear 'winner' of the third. The latter's disappointing start might actually have worked to his advantage, forcing him to sharpen his act so that he reserved his best performances for the encounters closer to the election.

The impact of the first debate on public opinion was electric. The Appendix (Figure 6.A1) shows the trend in voting intentions over the campaign, splitting those for the second week into polls completed before and after the debate. The first week of campaigning was generally thought somewhat lacklustre by commentators. There was little change in support for the major parties, although there appears to have been a slight improvement in the position of the Liberal Democrats and marginal slippage in support for others, as compared with the situation just before the election was called. Following the first debate, however, the Liberal Democrats shot up into second place, and, indeed, two polls published over the following weekend put them in the outright lead. Although they declined from this peak during the next week, they largely held on to their new-found eminence and were consistently running second to the Conservatives. The latter's ship steadied somewhat and inched forward in the last two weeks of campaigning—partly, no doubt, thanks to Cameron's improved performance in the second and third debates—but Labour failed to make a significant recovery.

The 'Cleggmania' that followed the first debate resulted in more intense scrutiny of the man and his party. Even if Brown and Cameron professed to 'agree with Nick', their journalistic cheerleaders evidently disliked his policies and were contemptuous of his personal qualities. The right-wing press lashed the Liberal Democrats on policy grounds, singling out their support for the euro, their defence policy, and the proposal to offer British citizenship to illegal immigrants who had been in the country for ten years or more. At least these obvious targets provided some relief from personal vituperation questioning Clegg's patriotism and integrity. While such tactics were hardly a novel feature of British election campaigns, there was an unmistakable edge of desperation this time round. No doubt this reflected the impact of the debates, which reinforced the feeling that this was simply a contest to determine the identity of the next Prime Minister. The same consideration ensured that the three party leaders featured in front-page headlines twice as often as their counterparts in 2005.

In terms of partisan orientation, this time the national press was heavily weighted against Labour and its leader. With the deliberate intention of wounding the Prime Minister, *The Sun* had come out decisively against the party on the day of Brown's speech to the Labour conference in September 2009. By the time of the election, only the ever-faithful *Mirror* remained from the impressive list of Labour-supporting papers assembled by Tony Blair. *The Guardian* joined *The Independent* in backing the Liberal Democrats. All other papers (excepting the *Daily Star* which, as usual, concentrated on sex and celebrities) supported the Conservatives with varying degrees of enthusiasm. Although the ability of newspapers to sway their readers' opinions (as opposed to merely reinforcing or even following them) is open to debate, it must have been reassuring at this time for a party to have the bulk of the press—especially, perhaps, *The Sun*—on its side. At a minimum, this ensured that the leader of the party concerned was spared the draining experience of a relentless rubbishing in the headlines of mass-market newspapers.

The 'Ground War'

Another consequence of the sudden increase in support for the Liberal Democrats after the first debate was that all three main parties immediately adjusted their constituency targeting strategies. That is just a small indication of the thoroughness and professionalism—which was by now normal—that the parties brought to the constituency 'ground war' of 2010. Indeed, in most marginal seats it was now misleading to talk about 'local' campaigning at all, if by that we mean campaign activities planned, implemented, and staffed at the local level. As had been the case for some years, in key seats almost all the planning and organization was done at the centre, and (in addition to telephone banks) nationally appointed staff were usually drafted in to lead the constituency battles. In part, the greater involvement of professionals and other paid staff at the centre in constituency campaigning was a response to steep declines in local party membership, which deprived all the parties of volunteers willing to do the necessary 'foot slogging'. In addition, however, the sophisticated technology available enabled central organizers to target voters more precisely than perhaps even local campaigners could manage. All major (and some minor) parties in 2010 used commercial (MOSAIC) databases for this purpose. Moreover, whereas this system had previously allowed targeting at postcode level, by 2005 individual households could be selected. Five years later, the parties had individual voters in their sights.

As noted above, the massive direct mailing effort before and during the campaign emanated entirely from national level. Between 2008 and early 2010, Labour sent out more than eight million letters to voters in 138 constituencies. Another 7.4 million were despatched during the campaign itself. This was surpassed by the Conservative effort, which involved sixteen million items of direct mail from 1 January plus four million localized letters. The Liberal Democrats, despite trailing the other parties in terms of financial resources, also contributed substantially to the mountains on the nation's doormats, sending about twenty million items of direct mail between the start of the year and the end of the campaign. The party headquarters also operated telephone banks, although even this campaigning tool now appeared outdated given the ubiquity of mobile phones and the far from complete coverage of telephone directories. All the parties boasted new facilities, enabling local party workers to upload their canvass returns to headquarters (although it has to be said that this might not have been very useful to campaign managers, as canvass returns can be notoriously unreliable guides to subsequent voting behaviour).

For obvious reasons, Labour conducted a defensive strategy, seeking to hold on to seats rather than gain any, while the Conservatives were on the offensive. The latter's 'ground war' operation had been going on for some years, and was planned in meticulous detail. Special grants (so-called 'Ashcroft money', since the wealthy Deputy Chairman of the party, Lord Ashcroft, channelled large donations to local campaigning) were made to local parties in target seats, provided that they were well organized and enthusiastic. Research confirms the contemporary impression that the Conservatives fought the strongest local campaigns, focusing efforts on their target seats more rigorously than before (Fisher et al., 2011). Even so, some observers detected an upsurge in Labour activity towards the end of the campaign as volunteers appeared to be galvanized by the prospect of a heavy defeat.

Despite all the attempts to identify, contact, inform, persuade, and reinvigorate individual voters in 2010, not even the most inventive campaigners at party headquarters could ensure that people turned out on polling day. For that crucial finale to a campaign, willing volunteers were still required to take the electoral registration numbers of voters at polling stations and knock on the doors of laggard supporters. In that respect, the sharp end of the 2010 campaign resembled that of 1964. Over the intervening years, the combined effects of new techniques, central direction, and the chequered careers of the main parties made it a marvel that so many were still prepared to offer their services on the big day.

The 2010 Results

Another new record number of candidates (4,150) contested the 2010 election, which was fought on revised constituency boundaries in England and Wales. All nine final polls published on the eve or morning of the election suggested that no party would win a majority in the new parliament, and, to that extent, their forecasts proved correct (Table 6.1). On the other hand, while the Conservative performance was in line with their predictions, all polls underestimated Labour's vote share—although not by much in most cases—while the aftershocks of 'Cleggmania' were registered in a consistent tendency to overestimate Liberal Democrat support. Indeed, two polling firms placed the latter second behind the Conservatives in their final surveys, while another two had them disputing the runner-up spot with Labour.

In fact, contrary to expectations, the Liberal Democrats increased their vote share by only one point and lost five seats—a stunning disappointment for the party. There was widespread disbelief when analysis of the exit poll commissioned jointly by the BBC, ITN, and Sky News suggested just such an outcome immediately after voting finished at 10 p.m. In fact, the exit poll prediction of the overall result proved to be remarkably accurate.

The apparent evaporation of support for the Liberal Democrats in 2010 is still something of a mystery (see Atkinson and Mortimore, 2011). There is some evidence, however, that those most attracted to the Liberal Democrats by Clegg's performance in the debates tended to be young people and those with a limited interest in politics. Both of these groups were renowned for their tendency not to turn out at the moment of truth, which probably accounts for much of the gap between declared support for the Liberal Democrats in opinion polls and the votes of those who turned out in the election itself.

Across the UK, the Conservatives increased their vote share by 3.7 points while Labour dropped by 6.2 points, resulting in a swing of 5 per cent in favour of the former. The substantial 7.1 point lead gained by the Conservatives over their

Table 6.1 Election results (UK), 2010–15

	2010		2015	
	Votes	Seats	Votes	Seats
Con	36.1	306	36.8	330
Labour	29.0	258	30.4	232
Lib Dem	23.0	57	7.9	8
Others	11.9	29	24.9	80
Turnout	*65.3*		*66.4*	

Note: Figures for Votes are percentages.

nearest rivals was not enough, however, to win an overall majority of seats, as they fell short by twenty. This reflects the bias in the electoral system, which is considered below.

'Other' parties took almost 10 per cent of the votes outside Northern Ireland—a post-war record. In terms of vote share, the most successful of these was UKIP, with 3.1 per cent. Its most prominent candidate, Nigel Farage, stood down as leader in order to contest the Buckingham seat held by the Commons Speaker, John Bercow, but, following an accident during the campaign when his light airplane crashed into a field, he was beaten into third place behind Bercow and another ex-Tory standing on behalf of the Buckinghamshire Campaign for Democracy. The BNP took 1.9 per cent of the vote and the Green Party 1.0 per cent, although both of these parties had many more candidates than in 2005—the BNP contingent rising from 119 to 338 and the Greens from 203 to 335. Despite losing support, the Green Party won its first ever seat in the House of Commons (Brighton Pavilion) in the person of its leader, Caroline Lucas.

In Scotland, the SNP—now forming a minority government in Edinburgh—advanced to 19.9 per cent of votes, regaining second place in popularity. The party retained its six Westminster seats (while losing Glasgow East, which it had won from Labour in the 2008 by-election). In Wales, Plaid fell back to 11.3 per cent of the vote, but again held on to its (three) seats.

The pattern of change in party support was broadly similar across the country, with two significant exceptions. The first was London. Here—in the territory of Boris Johnson, the controversial Conservative mayor—there was only a small decline in Labour's vote share (−2.3) and a small Conservative increase (+2.6). In addition, uniquely, there was a drop in support for 'others', as rises for the BNP and UKIP were offset by sharp falls in votes for the Green Party and 'other others', such as Respect. The limited damage that Labour suffered was due probably in part to the large concentrations of ethnic minority and Muslim voters in the city, especially given that the Iraq War, a highly salient issue in 2005, was no longer such a potent negative factor. Across England there was a significant positive correlation (0.50, N=531) between change in Labour's vote share and the percentage of ethnic minority residents in a constituency. The more there were of the latter, the less badly Labour did.

The other exception to the national pattern was Scotland. Here, in a remarkable contrast to the rest of the UK, Labour actually *improved* upon its 2005 performance (+3.1 points) and there was a reduction in support for the Liberal Democrats (−3.7). The Conservatives advanced, but by very little (+0.9). This marked deviation in terms of Labour and Liberal Democrat support is not difficult to explain. In 2005, under a Scottish leader, Charles Kennedy (who was more popular in Scotland than elsewhere, according to BES data), the Liberal Democrat share of Scottish votes had improved by much more than in other parts of Britain. Having disposed in rapid succession of Kennedy and another Scottish leader (Menzies

Campbell), ending up with a manifestly 'posh' southerner in the shape of Nick Clegg, the Liberal Democrats were always likely to struggle in Scotland in 2010. Labour, meanwhile, had replaced Tony Blair—whose seat in the North-East of England belied his outlook and accent—with Gordon Brown, a Fifer, son of a Church of Scotland minister, with deep roots in Scottish society, and a Scottish intonation which was as ingrained as his inability to smile on cue for the cameras. Since they recognized the Prime Minister as one of their own, Scottish voters were disinclined to desert him despite his various travails. In the final YouGov campaign poll in Scotland, for example, 43 per cent of respondents thought that Brown was doing a good job as Prime Minister, compared with 39 per cent who found him unequal to the task; contemporaneously across the UK as a whole, only 38 per cent thought that he was doing well, and 57 per cent rated his performance as bad.

Notwithstanding the impression given by the leaders' debates in 2010, general elections are still more than national contests between party leaders. Local personalities, contexts, issues, events, and traditions, as well as on-the-ground campaigning, all play a significant part. With the days of 'uniform swing' long gone, in 2010 there was considerable variation in the extent of change—and, in some cases, its direction—even allowing for the need to use 'notional' 2005 votes in the new constituencies in order to measure changes in party support since the previous contest.

Outside Scotland, Conservative support declined in thirty-six constituencies while Labour's rose in thirty-seven. Over the UK as a whole, the Liberal Democrat vote share fell in 252 seats, was unchanged in three, and increased in the remainder. Even when support moved in the expected direction, the magnitude of the changes varied hugely. Conservative increases, for example, ranged from less than 1 percentage point to more than 16 (in Hartlepool, scene of the party's 2004 by-election disaster), while Labour decreases peaked at almost 24 percentage points in Barnsley East (which might partly be explained by a miscalculation of original Labour strength in the estimated 2005 results). The range of outcomes for the Liberal Democrats was truly spectacular—from a drop of 16 percentage points in Orpington, which the Liberals had gained in sensational style in a 1962 by-election but was now an impregnable Tory seat held by Boris Johnson's brother Jo—to an increase of 25 points in Redcar. The latter result exemplifies the continued importance of local issues; the Labour candidate was punished by the voters because of the government's inability to prevent the closure of the Teesside steelworks.

An unusual degree of local variation had been anticipated in 2010 because of the scandal over MPs expenses, which had dominated headlines in the preceding year. All incumbents, it was suggested, could be tarred with the expenses brush and suffer at the polls. As we have seen, a record number of sitting MPs decided that this was an opportune moment to retire from the fray. It is clear, however, that the most apocalyptic fears or hopes raised by the expenses scandal simply failed to materialize. Indeed, it is hard to detect any significant evidence of the expenses scandal affecting voting patterns. Overall, incumbents from all parties out-performed new candidates selected to defend seats where the previous MP had decided not to contest the election. Those who decided to fight on under the shadow of scandal might have been regarded as more sinned against than sinning but, in any event, expectations that anyone who sat in the 2005–10 parliament would incur at least some displeasure from the voters were not fulfilled.

There is clear evidence, however, that variations in the intensity of campaigns by the major parties across constituencies affected local results (Fisher et al., 2011). The arduous Conservative effort in targeted seats yielded positive results (even if they were not as spectacular as strategists might have hoped). The Liberal Democrats also fared best where they campaigned hardest. Perhaps most surprisingly in the circumstances, Labour's local campaigning was most effective of all and helped the party stave off defeat in a number of constituencies.

The presence of large numbers of UKIP, BNP, and Green candidates enables us to explore the impact of these parties on the fortunes of the major contenders. Table 6.2 presents correlation coefficients which show the inter-related effects of changes in support for the various parties. Not unexpectedly, the Conservatives fared worse where the other main parties performed better, and vice versa. There was, however, no significant relationship between changes in Conservative support and the performance of UKIP—or, indeed, that of any of the minor parties. The assumption that UKIP cost the Conservatives votes and seats is simplistic— although that did not deter commentators (and some politicians) from making it. Indeed, on the basis of these data it is more plausible to claim that UKIP cost *Labour* votes—the more the former improved its position, the worse the performance of the latter. The BNP and Greens also seem to have weakened Labour (the coefficients are negative and statistically significant), the former party presumably drawing support from elements of the white working class which felt alienated from Labour. Unsurprisingly, the Liberal Democrats also suffered where the Greens contested the election, while changes in their support were unaffected by the performance of either UKIP or the BNP.

Table 6.2 Correlations between changes in vote shares, 2005–10

	Change % Con	Change % Lab	Change % Lib Dem
Change % Lab	−0.29	–	–
Change % Lib Dem	−0.27	−0.52	–
Change % UKIP	0.06	−0.13	0.07
Change % BNP	−0.01	−0.27	0.04
Change % Green	0.04	−0.27	−0.13

Notes: Significant coefficients are printed in bold. The N for coefficients involving Conservatives, Labour, and Liberal Democrats only is 630; for these parties and UKIP it is 589, for the BNP it is 246, and for Greens 368. The Speaker's seats in 2005 and 2010 are excluded.

Turnout

During the 2010 election campaign, there were predictions in some quarters of a 'bumper' turnout. These were fuelled partly by the increased proportions of poll respondents saying that they were 'certain' to vote and also by reports that large numbers of people were downloading electoral registration forms from the Electoral Commission's website. On 6 May long queues formed at some polling stations, and in a few places there was even a reported shortage of ballot papers. In fact these were isolated incidents, due more to the incompetence of election officials than to insatiable demand from voters. Turnout did increase to 65.1 per cent, but this was still markedly lower than at any general election between 1950 and 1997.

Turnout rose most where it had previously been lowest—in other words, where there was plenty of scope for improvement. Understandably, elections in which a close outcome is predicted usually have higher turnouts than those which look to be easy victories for one side or the other, and this is surely the main reason for the increase in 2010. Any expectation that the televised leaders' debates (and the ensuing 'Cleggmania') would stimulate a notably higher level of participation by voters was not borne out.

There remained, however, something of a North–South divide in turnout, with Scotland (63.8 per cent) and the three northern English regions (North-East, 60.9 per cent; North-West, 62.3 per cent, Yorkshire and Humber 63.2 per cent) polling below the unimpressive average. At constituency level, the turnout wooden spoon was seized by Manchester Central (44.3 per cent) after being held by Liverpool Riverside for the previous three elections. At the other end of the scale, the highest turnout (77.3 per cent) was recorded in East Renfrewshire, a constituency which includes affluent suburbs to the south of Glasgow. To put this aspect of the 2010 election into perspective, the *best* constituency turnout was lower than the *overall average* for the 1992 election (77.9 per cent), and would not have been in the top half of turnouts in 1964. More generally in 2010, five constituencies had turnouts in the 40s, 109 in the 50s, 370 in the 60s, and 146 in the 70s. In 1964, in contrast, only seventy constituencies had a turnout of less than 70 per cent while a figure of 80 per cent or over was recorded in 205 seats.

Turnout variations across constituencies displayed what was now a long-familiar and predictable pattern. Despite the overall increase and changed boundaries, Britain continued to be divided into low turnout and high turnout constituencies, and the two remained very different in social terms. The former are mainly urban, working class, and poor; the latter rural and suburban, middle class, and relatively affluent. In addition, the perceived closeness of the constituency contest (based on the result in the previous one) once again was positively and significantly associated with turnout. However, the relevant correlation coefficient with marginality (0.46) was smaller than in some previous elections. This probably reflects uncertainty among some voters as to the status of the new constituencies in which they now found themselves, and suggests that, in addition to differential campaigning, electors' awareness of the 'safety' or 'marginality' of their seat played some part in determining whether or not they voted.

The Outcome and the Aftermath

The Conservatives secured a clear lead over Labour in terms of the popular vote, and, in line with the theory of valence politics, that can be explained to a large extent by the electorate's evaluations of the party leaders. From the start of 2009, David Cameron clearly led Gordon Brown and (even more clearly) Nick Clegg as the most preferred Prime Minister. As reported by the BES rolling campaign survey (see http://bes2009-10.org/), Cameron maintained a comfortable lead on this question throughout the campaign, despite the outburst of 'Cleggmania' following the first leaders' debate. In the final campaign week, YouGov reported that Cameron was the preferred choice of 32 per cent of voters compared with 26 per cent for Brown and 22 per cent for Clegg. It is hard to escape the conclusion that had the election been decided on the basis of personalities alone, Cameron's Conservatives would have won decisively.

However, the performance of the government more generally and the prospective performance of its rivals are also aspects of valence politics. In this respect, the electorate continued to harbour doubts about the Conservatives. Perhaps the best evidence of this is the failure of their campaign to convince the voters that they were clearly the best party to deal with the country's problems. The BES rolling campaign survey shows that the Conservatives maintained only a narrow lead over Labour as the party best able to deal with the issue nominated by respondents as the most important. On the key valence issue of the economy (rated as by far the most important by the electorate), during the campaign Labour had steadily whittled away the Conservatives' lead as the 'best party'. By election day the two parties were running neck and neck on this question.

While continued misgivings about the Conservatives help to explain their relatively disappointing share of the votes, the party's failure to secure an overall majority was largely a result of the anti-Conservative bias in the electoral system. After all, in 2005 Labour had won 56.5 per cent of the seats in Britain with just 36.1 per cent of the votes; in 2010, the Conservatives had a slightly larger vote share (36.9 per cent) but secured 'only' 48.4 per cent of the seats. We explore the sources of this bias in the concluding chapter. Here it suffices to note that Conservative strategists, as well as media commentators, were well aware of the facts of electoral life before May 2010 and made no secret of the task facing them.

During the latter part of the campaign, the leaders were questioned relentlessly about what they would do if no single party could command a majority in the

House of Commons. The stock answer of Brown and Cameron was to warn against the dangers of a 'hung' parliament. Clegg obviously faced the greatest dilemma, since the Liberal Democrats would be likely to hold the balance of power. Initially, his line was that the party coming first in votes and seats would have a moral mandate to govern even if it fell short of an overall majority. As Clegg himself had good reason to know, however, the peculiarities of the British system meant that Labour could easily have finished behind the Conservatives in votes but ahead in seats. Eventually, however, Clegg conceded that he would not keep Gordon Brown in power if the latter lost the popular vote.

The Conservatives' failure to defeat the electoral system as well as their opponents led to an indecisive outcome. There followed an extraordinary period of intense manoeuvring and negotiation among the parties, under continuous media scrutiny, which ended with the formation of a coalition government between the Conservatives and Liberal Democrats (see Fox, 2010; Kavanagh and Cowley, 2010: ch. 10; Laws, 2010). The civil service was prepared for this eventuality and senior officials were on hand to offer advice. The Liberal Democrats, who hoped for a hung parliament, had also considered all the options; their two main rivals, who viewed the necessity for any deal with distaste, started to think about their strategies at a relatively late stage of the campaign. Although some Conservatives favoured forming a minority government and defying the other parties to precipitate another election, David Cameron preferred a coalition, and offered to open talks with the Liberal Democrats—an offer accepted by Nick Clegg on the basis that the Conservatives, as the most popular party, deserved to be consulted first. An arrangement between Labour and the Liberal Democrats was favoured by people who had voted for the two parties—and by their respective members. However, the parliamentary arithmetic meant that other parties would have to be involved in a Labour–Liberal Democrat coalition; an additional problem was the uneasy personal relationship between Brown and Clegg. Some discussions between the two parties took place, during which the Liberal Democrats detected a lack of enthusiasm on the Labour side.

Finally, on the Tuesday after the election, Brown resigned as Prime Minister and David Cameron was installed in Number 10. The coalition agreement between the two parties—which included holding a referendum on electoral reform—was quickly published, and on the Wednesday, Cameron and Clegg held a joint press conference in the garden of 10 Downing Street. The rapport between the two leaders was such that the BBC's political editor Nick Robinson described the occasion as 'a political civil partnership ceremony' (Kavanagh and Cowley, 2010: 226). In Britain's first coalition government since the Second World War, Clegg became Deputy Prime Minister and four other Liberal Democrats were given Cabinet positions. Any euphoria surrounding the 'civil partnership' was soon to be dissipated, however, as events revealed that coalition governments are no less vulnerable to the costs of governing than those formed by a single party.

As will be seen in the next section, however, the major threat to the coalition came not, as might be expected, from the official Opposition but from rising support for UKIP, which was to have dramatic consequences.

The Costs of Governing: 2010–15

It is normal for governing parties to encounter periods of unpopularity among the electorate. Running modern Britain is a difficult business and things never turn out as well as aspirants for office and their supporters pretend, expect, or (more commonly) hope. Inevitably, unpopular decisions have to be taken. Given the perilous state of the British economy and the enormous deficit in public finances inherited by the new government this was clearly going to be the case after May 2010. It is rarer, however, for governing parties to alienate their own supporters quite to the extent that the coalition partners proceeded to do.

The big losers in this inter-election period were the Liberal Democrats. Simply entering a coalition with the Conservatives offended a significant segment of those who had perceived them as a radical party and, on that basis, voted for them in the 2010 election. The BES post-election survey found that, when asked which party would be their first choice under an Alternative Vote system, 11 per cent of those who had voted Liberal Democrat made Labour their first choice while only 4 per cent nominated the Conservatives. Of those who stuck with the Liberal Democrats as their first choice, 35 per cent opted for the Conservatives as second choice while 34 per cent went for Labour and 19 per cent for the Greens. When asked to indicate their feelings about the Conservatives, 41 per cent of Liberal Democrat voters placed themselves on the 'dislike' side of the scale. It was little surprise, then, that having garnered almost 24 per cent of the (British) vote in May the Liberal Democrats fell to 19 per cent of voting intentions in June and 16 per cent in July. The slump continued to the end of the year before settling at around 10 per cent—less than half of their support in the 2010 election—for the next few years (Figure 6.2).

As the authors of the 2015 Nuffield study point out, this decline in popularity largely *preceded* what some commentators believed was a particularly damaging decision by the party leadership: to support a tripling of university tuition fees, which they had promised to abolish altogether during the election campaign (Cowley and Kavanagh, 2016: 103–6). Nonetheless, this about-turn did nothing for the reputation of Nick Clegg who had given a very public pledge to vote against any increase in fees. Having risen dramatically in public estimation during the election campaign, Clegg's reputation now sank like a stone. Starting with a positive rating of +40 in May 2010 (per cent saying he was doing well minus per cent thinking he was doing badly) according to YouGov data, he was down to single figures (+5) by September and well into negative territory (−27) by

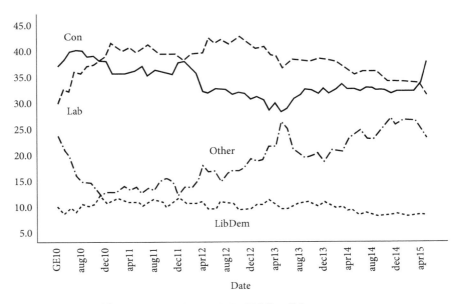

Figure 6.2 Monthly voting intentions, 2010–15 (all polls)

Note: The 2010 and 2015 election results in Great Britain form the starting and finishing points.

December. This was just the beginning: Clegg's average ratings over the next four years were −54 (2012), −52 (2013), and −56 (2014). These were by far the worst scores for any of the party leaders. Similarly, the percentages choosing Clegg as the best person to be Prime Minister, which had stood at over 20 per cent during the 2010 campaign, was down to 5 per cent by the end of the year and remained around that level for the rest of the parliament (Figure 6.3). Evidently, even the shrunken band of loyal Liberal Democrat supporters doubted the Prime Ministerial calibre of their leader.

The dismal showing of Clegg and his party in the polls was borne out in mid-term elections. The Scottish Parliament election in 2011 was a disaster, with only five seats won (compared with sixteen in 2007, under Menzies Campbell's short-lived leadership). Local election results went from bad to worse. The party's national equivalent vote shares fell from 16 per cent to 11 per cent between 2011 and 2014, and more than 1,700 council seats—over two-fifths of the number held in 2010—were lost. In parliamentary by-elections—in which they used to be the party to watch—the Liberal Democrats lost their deposit in ten of the nineteen contests that were held outside Northern Ireland. Indeed, in Rotherham in November 2012, the party contrived to come in eighth place behind an assortment of other candidates while in South Shields (May 2013) it suffered the sort of result which had driven the SDP out of existence, coming a humiliating seventh

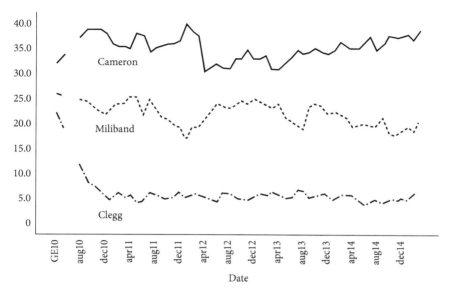

Figure 6.3 Best person for Prime Minister, May 2010–March 2015

Note: The initial figure for the Labour leader relates to Gordon Brown.

Source: YouGov.

(behind even the BNP and only just beating the Monster Raving Loony Party). Finally, in Rochester and Strood (November 2014) the Liberal Democrat candidate failed to reach 1 per cent of votes. The sole by-election bright spot was Eastleigh in February 2013. The seat had been held by Chris Huhne who resigned from parliament after pleading guilty to a charge of perverting the course of justice. In these circumstances the Liberal Democrats hailed their holding on to the seat as a near-miracle but, even in this case, the party's vote share declined by 16.6 points. In the European Parliament elections in May 2014 the Liberal Democrats won less than 7 per cent of votes and lost ten of their eleven seats.

To add serious injury to these various insults, in May 2011 the cherished goal of the Liberal Democrats—to reform the electoral system used for Westminster elections—had been dealt a crushing blow when a proposal to adopt the Alternative Vote (AV) system was comprehensively rejected in a national referendum, by 68 per cent to 32 per cent of the votes. The only constitutional crumb proffered to the Liberal Democrats was the passage, in 2011, of legislation which decreed that future general elections would be held at fixed five-year intervals, unless a government lost a vote of confidence or MPs voted to dissolve parliament by a two-thirds majority of the whole House. Although to some extent the Fixed-Term Parliaments Act limited the power of the executive to call an election at a time of its choosing, it was obvious that it had been forced through by the government because it suited the interests of both coalition parties, giving them a realistic expectation that their partnership would last a full five years. In the absence of dramatic and unexpected happenings, all aspiring parliament candidates could put a ring round 7 May 2015 as the date of the next general election—a luxury which had not been afforded to any of their predecessors. However, in other circumstances it was obvious that the 'escape clauses' in the Act would leave plenty of electoral cards in the hands of the executive. It is not surprising that, far from hailing it as a major step towards a 'modernized' constitution, in his lengthy account of the coalition government the Liberal Democrat minister David Laws dismissed the Act in a single, brief paragraph (Laws, 2016: 87–8).

During the general election campaign the main parties had disagreed over the most effective way to reduce government debt, while accepting that some harsh decisions would have to be taken. The Liberal Democrats had joined Labour in arguing for spending cuts which, though severe, would take place over more than one parliament. The Conservatives, by contrast, had proposed more radical measures, involving significant reductions in spending which would have an immediate effect on (almost) all government departments, but particularly in the areas of welfare and local government (Dorey and Garnett, 2016: 137–78). This programme of 'austerity' was bound to generate negative reactions from those likely to be affected, along with interest groups claiming to speak on their behalf. Although to some extent their new coalition partners could be used as a shield to deflect some of the criticism, it was inevitable that the Conservatives—as the major party in the coalition—would take most of the blame. In addition, the government quickly ran into serious trouble with its plans for reforming the NHS. The state of the health service is very clearly a valence issue; the NHS is strongly supported by almost everyone, and is an institution of which British people as a whole are very proud. 'Don't mess with the NHS' would be a sensible posture for any prudent government to adopt—or at least 'don't be *seen* to mess with the NHS'. On this occasion, however, having promised during the election that there would be no more top-down reorganizations, once in office the Conservatives set out plans for wholesale change which attracted strong criticism.

On top of these difficulties, however, the Conservative leadership—in their drive to 'modernize' the party's image and 'decontaminate the brand'—appeared to go out of their way to alienate their core supporters. As well as the tripling of student tuition fees, following a speedy defence review the armed services were subject to severe cuts in personnel and equipment, with soldiers reportedly receiving notices of potential redundancy while serving in Afghanistan. The police, too, were subject to budget cuts. At the same time, the Justice Secretary (Kenneth Clarke) embarked on a programme of rehabilitating convicted offenders, aiming to reduce the prison population. This was one area in which penny-pinching measures were unlikely to enthuse core Conservative voters. Meanwhile, child benefit was removed from families paying the higher rate of income tax, while the overseas aid budget was ostentatiously protected from cuts and even set to increase significantly. David Cameron's earlier 'cast-iron' promise of a referendum on the EU's Treaty of Lisbon had been abandoned before the election; ironically, the ensuing outcry among Eurosceptics only increased the pressure on Cameron to resort to the 'nuclear option' of a referendum on Britain's membership of the EU, thus going much further than his party's 2010 manifesto, which had merely argued that a referendum should be held to decide the British attitude to any future treaty changes. In January 2013 Cameron capitulated to demands from within his own party, as well as the electoral pressure from UKIP (see below), and to promise that an in/out referendum would be held during the next parliament if the Conservatives won the next election. In his first conference speech as leader, Cameron had expressed the hope that members of his party would stop 'banging on' about Europe; far from inducing a period of quiet from his Eurosceptic critics, by opening the prospect of British withdrawal Cameron had extended to them an unlimited banging licence.

Although some of Cameron's decisions after assuming office provoked waves of anger amongst contributors to the *Telegraph* letters page, support for the Conservatives remained relatively buoyant for some time (see Figure 6.2). Through to March 2012, the party's share of voting intentions in the polls remained close to or just above the level achieved in the general election. Indeed, in the first major electoral test for the Conservatives—in May 2011—when there were widespread local elections in England (outside London) as well as elections to the Scottish Parliament and Welsh Assembly, they did surprisingly well (apart from in Scotland). Their vote-share in Wales increased to 25 per cent (+2.6) in the constituency contests, bringing them two additional seats in the Assembly. In the English local elections, the Conservatives were braced for losses since they had made significant gains in 2007, when the seats at stake had last been contested. In the event, the number of Conservative councillors actually increased by eighty-five, and the party took control of four additional councils. The national equivalent vote shares were: Conservative 38 per cent, Labour 37 per cent, and Liberal Democrats 16 per cent. Given the tough decisions that had been taken by the government and the unpopularity of some of its policies, this was a notable achievement for the Conservatives. The electorate, it appeared, was still willing to give them the benefit of the doubt in their efforts to do something about the deficit in public finances bequeathed by Labour.

Less than a year later, however, the Conservatives began to experience serious popularity problems when George Osborne's Budget was poorly received. Among the measures introduced were a reduction in the top rate of income tax, a freezing of tax allowances for older voters (dubbed a 'granny tax' by the popular press), the extension of VAT to hot snacks (a 'pasty tax'), and the promised withdrawal of child benefit from better-off families. In the weeks and months that followed, various corrections, clarifications, and qualifications to the Budget proposals had to be issued. Ed Miliband labelled the whole operation an 'omnishambles' (later named 'word of the year' by the *Oxford English Dictionary*), and this description began to be applied to various aspects of the government's performance. The electorate appeared to agree with Miliband, on this subject at least. In April, according to Ipsos MORI, Osborne had the poorest satisfaction ratings (−30) of any Chancellor since Kenneth Clarke in 1994 and the Conservative share of voting intentions slid sharply downwards. The effects were felt in the local elections of May 2012, when the party lost over 400 seats and fell to 33 per cent of the national equivalent vote, although this outcome was still far from a disaster.

For the remainder of 2012 the Conservatives were plagued by their apparent inability to engineer economic growth or even—despite all the talk of cuts and austerity—to do much about reducing the deficit in public finances (Dorey and Garnett, 2016: 49–81). In the background, however, another issue was simmering away—the legalization of same-sex marriage. David Cameron had sprung his support for such a move on an unsuspecting party towards the end of his conference speech in October 2011. Although his personal pledge was greeted with loud applause in the hall, this attempt to 'detoxifying the brand' was a step too far for many. Subsequently, there were frequent reports of members and activists resigning over the issue, including, eventually, the long-serving (female) chair of Cameron's own local Conservative association (*Daily Telegraph*, 25.02.2013). When the relevant legislation came before the House, in February 2013, on a free vote, more Conservative MPs (136) were opposed—including two cabinet ministers, eight junior ministers and eight whips—than supported it (127).[2]

Three weeks later, the above-mentioned by-election at Eastleigh took place. The Conservatives initially had hopes of taking the seat from the Liberal Democrats, but came a humiliating third behind their coalition partners and UKIP. Although reports suggested that concern about immigration was a major factor influencing defections to UKIP, same-sex marriage was also an issue and the Coalition for Marriage (a group opposed to change) actively campaigned in the constituency. Nigel Farage, who had resumed the leadership of UKIP, later highlighted the 'disconnect' between traditional Conservative supporters and their party in colourful terms: 'Tory voters are historically used to a party of free enterprise and wealth creation, but all it wants to talk about is gay marriage, wind turbines and metropolitan Notting Hill claptrap' (*Daily Telegraph*, 16.03.2013).

From April 2012 through to March 2015, support for the Conservatives varied within very narrow limits (see Figure 6.2). On these data, the party's share of voting intentions fell (just) below 30 per cent only once but never exceeded 33.6 per cent. Heavy losses were sustained in the county council elections of 2013 (with a national equivalent vote share of just 26 per cent) and again in the 2014 local elections, although in the latter case the national equivalent vote share improved to 30 per cent. The party's failure to move any higher in the public's estimation, even when there was tangible evidence of a growing economy and the next election approached, was doubtless due to a variety of factors—including, probably, an inability to control immigration, stagnant living standards, and growing concern about the state of the health service. It is hard, however, to resist the conclusion that Cameron's modernization strategy had alienated many Conservative-minded people. Upsetting core supporters is risky at the best of times. When there is a viable alternative party for the disaffected to embrace (viz. UKIP) and no evidence of new supporters being attracted in any great numbers, then the strategy begins to look distinctly unwise. Cameron himself seems to have realized this danger at least in respect of his earlier expressions of concern for the environmental agenda, which he now reportedly referred to as 'green crap'. Although he remained more popular than his party—and generally performed well in the Punch and Judy show of Prime Minister's Questions—Cameron had good reason to doubt whether he would leave a constructive legacy, even if his party secured an overall majority in the 2015 election. A few days before the dissolution of parliament, he revealed that whatever his fortunes in the coming contest he would not serve a third term as Prime Minister. It was a very odd thing to announce at this time, complicating the Conservative campaign with speculation about his likely successor and making him seem something of a 'lame duck' even before the election result was known; but it is unlikely to have made much difference to 2015 voters.

Labour(ing) Under Miliband

Given their inability to please even their natural supporters, it is surprising that the Conservatives were not further behind Labour in the polls between 2010 and 2015. The latter spent the first few months of opposition electing a new leader. The favourite was David Miliband, the broadly (and rather blandly) Blairite former Foreign Secretary. His challengers included his brother Ed and three other candidates. After a campaign that (inevitably) featured televised debates, David Miliband won the support of most Labour MPs and party members. He lost out to his brother, however, on the votes of affiliated trade unions, and Ed squeezed home as the new Labour leader in September 2010. The victorious sibling struggled to make a positive impact with the electorate, however, and the impression among the latter that he had not only stabbed his brother in the back but was also in hock to the unions, was never dissipated. Miliband tended to be portrayed by the media—and to come across—as a geek with a charisma by-pass—an identikit 'career politician', with limited experience of 'real life'. Throughout the inter-election period, he never once headed David Cameron as the best person for Prime Minister in YouGov's regular polls (Figure 6.3). Although Labour was doing well enough electorally—retaining ten of the eleven seats defended in parliamentary by-elections and gaining one (Corby, in November 2012, which was vacated by one of Cameron's 'A'-list women MPs), while also making sweeping gains in the 2012 and 2013 local elections—there were also disappointments. The loss of Bradford West to the Respect party in a by-election in March 2012 was a major setback and the party also suffered a morale-sapping defeat in the 2011 Scottish Parliament elections, falling from forty-six to thirty-seven seats, and leaving the SNP with an overall majority.

Labour support peaked in the latter half of 2012 before drifting gradually downwards throughout 2013 and 2014 to a point where the two major parties were neck and neck as they entered the election year. It seems likely that this trend was largely due to the increasingly negative view of Miliband held by the electorate. Whereas during 2011 his personal ratings according to YouGov had averaged −22, this figure fell to −30 in 2012, −31 in 2013, and −42 in 2014. In the latter year, Labour's performance in the local elections was very modest and Miliband's reputation was not enhanced by a much-criticized speech at the party conference in which he failed to mention the deficit in public finances or immigration—two of the biggest issues worrying the electorate. Nonetheless, it is also the case that the public remained unconvinced that the party as a whole had learned from the financial mess of 2007–10 and continued to associate it with economic mismanagement.

The Rise of the 'Others'

If the Liberal Democrats were the clearest losers after the 2010 general election, then the unmistakeable winners were the 'others'. By December 2010, the opinion polls recorded a higher collective tally for these assorted minor parties than for the Liberal Democrats, and that remained the case until the 2015 election. The score for 'others' in Figure 6.2 includes support for a number of parties but the dominant features were the progress made by the SNP in Scotland and UKIP in England. In Wales, Plaid dropped back somewhat in the 2011 Assembly elections and made no progress in terms of Westminster voting intentions in Welsh opinion polls. The BNP, which had attracted considerable attention in the 2010 election, was engulfed by internal feuding afterwards and faded from view. For most of the inter-election period the Green Party hovered around 2 per cent in the polls and made no headway in by-elections or local elections. Things changed around the time of the 2014 European Parliament elections, however. In that contest, the Greens won almost 8 per cent of the vote and increased their representation from two to three seats. Thereafter, their support in the polls inched upwards to reach 7 per cent in December but during the first three months of 2014 it eased back to stand at 5 per cent in March.

As already indicated, the SNP won a stunning victory in the Scottish Parliament elections in 2011, securing an overall majority of seats despite a proportional electoral system adopted in part to prevent such an outcome. Notwithstanding this success, the SNP generally lagged behind Labour in voting intentions for Westminster until the aftermath of the independence referendum in September 2014. In 2011, the average shares of Westminster voting intentions in Scottish polls was 30 per cent for the SNP and 42 per cent for Labour, while in 2012 the respective figures were 30 per cent and 41 per cent. This variant of 'split-ticket' voting, in which people who had come to regard the SNP as their preferred party to run the Scottish government nevertheless continued to support Labour in Westminster elections, was transformed by the independence referendum. The three major UK parties had campaigned together for a 'no' vote. Despite independence being rejected (by 55 to 45 per cent) the SNP—led by Nicola Sturgeon after Alex Salmond resigned in the wake of the vote—could now argue with some force that their Labour and Liberal Democrat opponents were in cahoots with the Conservatives, so that only a vote for the nationalist party could advance Scotland's interests.

The effect was registered in opinion polls in the months before and after the referendum. In the first nine months of 2014 Labour averaged 37 per cent to 33 per cent for the SNP. However, after the event there was a huge turnaround. In the six months from October to March 2015, Labour trailed well behind the SNP with an average share of 28 per cent to the latter's 45 per cent; there was also a surge in applications for membership of the SNP. Whatever the reason for Labour's decline in Scotland—and complacency resulting from decades of dominance was clearly a factor—the polling figures led to speculation that the SNP could virtually sweep the board in the general election, thereby seriously damaging Labour's chances of forming a government at Westminster.

The main driver of variations in support for 'others' in England and Wales was UKIP, led by Nigel Farage. The remarkable change in the party's share of voting intentions from the 2010 election to 2015 is charted in Figure 6.4. After gaining 3.2 per cent of the Great Britain vote in 2010, UKIP at first made little progress in by-elections, although the party did come a distant second to Labour in Barnsley Central in March 2011. In a clutch of by-elections in November 2012, however, increases in vote shares were generally larger than before and the Liberal Democrats were pushed into fourth place in two contests—Corby and Croydon North—while in another two (Middlesbrough and Rotherham) UKIP came second. The attendant publicity for the party helped to increase its poll ratings in late November and December. Another sharp improvement came in early 2013, following the Commons vote on same-sex marriage and accompanying the Eastleigh by-election. The second place achieved in that contest gave UKIP—and Nigel Farage—yet more valuable publicity and a further boost in the polls. In the county council elections in England and Wales in May 2013, UKIP won almost 150 seats, and on the same day came second in a parliamentary by-election in South Shields. That seat was easily won by Labour but the Conservatives trailed badly in third place. In the county elections, Labour led in terms of national equivalent vote shares with 29 per cent, followed by the Conservatives on 26 per cent, but UKIP

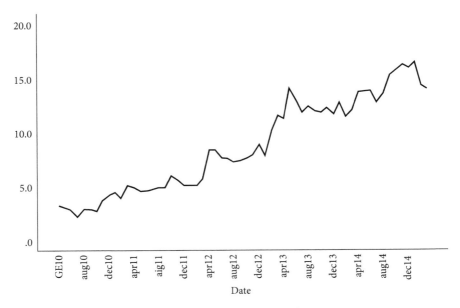

Figure 6.4 UKIP share of voting intentions, 2010–March 2015
Source: YouGov.

was on 22 per cent while the Liberal Democrats mustered only 13 per cent. These were poor results for all three major parties but represented a notable success for UKIP, gleefully exploited by Farage in frequent media appearances. A year later, UKIP exceeded all its previous results, coming out top in the European Parliament election with 27.5 per cent of the votes and twenty-four seats. This was the first time in more than a century that a nationwide election did not result in either the Conservatives or Labour coming first in terms of popular support. There was a further sting in UKIP's tail, however. Late in 2014, two Conservative MPs resigned from the House of Commons, fought by-elections on behalf of UKIP and were comfortably re-elected. By January 2015, the party stood at around 16.5 per cent of voting intentions.

Although Labour was not doing as well as might be expected and the Liberal Democrats were manifestly in deep trouble, most attention in the run up to the 2015 general election focused on the problems of the Conservatives arising from the unhappiness among their grass-roots supporters at the direction in which their party was being led and the opportunities that this presented to UKIP. Cameron must surely have regretted his claim (back in 2006) that those who supported UKIP were 'a bunch of fruitcakes, loonies and closet racists', as this became a sort of badge of honour for defectors to the party. Although both UKIP and the Greens had fallen back from their peak by the start of the election campaign, there was no sign of their support evaporating rapidly as had been the experience of minor parties in the past. The stage was set, therefore, for an unusually unpredictable election. This arose not just from the fact that the two major parties were almost equal in (un)popularity by the first months of 2015. In addition, there was uncertainty surrounding the impact of the decline in Liberal Democrat support, as well as the prospects for the SNP, Greens, and UKIP, and how the performances of the latter would affect the votes of the 'big two'.

The 2015 Campaign

The 2015 general election campaign was variously described by commentators as 'turgid', 'antiseptic', 'sham', 'bloodless', 'plodding', and, even 'Sisyphean' (for those well-versed in classical literature). In part, this was because the relative popularity of the parties hardly changed despite all the bluster and efforts of the campaigners. Figure 6.A2 (in the Appendix) shows the trend in voting intentions from 30 March (the date of the dissolution of Parliament) on the basis of the ninety-three polls undertaken until the eve of the election. The weekly average for the Conservatives was always between 33 and 34 per cent while Labour fell outside that range just once—to 34.1 per cent. The Liberal Democrats also 'flatlined' at between 8 and 9 per cent while the 'others' held steady on just under a quarter of voting intentions. On the basis of these figures, almost everyone involved—commentators, party professionals, politicians, and academics—assumed that the election would once again produce a House of Commons in which no party enjoyed an overall majority and some sort of coalition or inter-party agreement would be necessary.

That assumption, combined with the fact that campaign polls in Scotland continued to suggest that there would be a massive swing from Labour to the SNP, thrust the nationalists and their new leader, Nicola Sturgeon, to the centre of the national campaign. The latter had suggested that some kind of deal with Labour was a possibility and, consequently, the Conservative campaign argued relentlessly that the SNP could put Miliband into 10 Downing Street and exert a malign influence thereafter. One poster, for example, showed Sturgeon with a tiny Miliband peeping out of her pocket. For many English voters this prospect was a coalition too far, and, despite Labour's denying that there would be any deal, the issue certainly did no harm to the Conservative cause. Amongst many Scottish voters, the undisguised Conservative animosity towards the SNP could be seen as a backhanded compliment and another reason to vote for nationalist candidates rather than Labour or the Liberal Democrats.

The 'SNP problem' became more prominent after the first televised leaders' debate. The rise of the 'others'—and Cameron's reluctance to risk the kind of setback he had suffered in 2010—had made it difficult for the broadcasters and major parties to agree the format of the debates this time around (Cowley and Kavanagh, 2016: 279–83). In the end, there was only one debate in which Cameron, Clegg, and Miliband faced one another (on 2 April) and this was something of a farce since it also involved the leaders of UKIP, the SNP, Greens and Plaid Cymru (the DUP having failed in its bid for inclusion). The television audience of 5.9 million was well down on the 2010 viewing figures. There was no clear 'winner', but Nicola Sturgeon made a favourable impression with her forceful debating style. While Miliband was anxious to live down the sobriquet of 'Red Ed', which his media critics had bestowed on him, Sturgeon's uninhibited approach invited voters in the UK as a whole (let alone Scotland) to regard the SNP as the leading 'progressive' force in this election. A 'challengers' debate followed (without Cameron and Clegg) on 16 April and a BBC *Question Time* special allowed the audience to interrogate the three main party leaders separately (30 April). Viewers numbered 4.4 million and 3.8 million, respectively, for these programmes.

As well as attracting less interest from the electorate, the 2015 debates had much less impact on the course of the campaign than their counterparts in 2010. Although they did provide valuable publicity for the minor parties, none of the major party leaders registered a resounding success and all avoided disaster. Nevertheless, if Miliband had possessed outstanding Prime Ministerial potential, televised debates of any kind would have given him an opportunity to burnish his credentials at Cameron's expense. As it was, his advisors just seemed relieved that he had emerged without perpetrating any egregious gaffes.

Digital campaigning assumed a new level of importance in this election. In their chapter on the media in the 2015 version of *Britain Votes*, Wring and Ward (2015) devoted more space to the Internet and social media than to the press, radio, and television combined. The Conservatives spent £100,000 per month on Facebook in the run up to the election while Labour spent about £10,000 per month. All parties engaged in large data-gathering exercises to enable them to identify and contact individuals with tailored messages on Twitter and other forums. In addition, according to Wring and Ward, there was 'a tidal wave of noise' online (2015: 233) related to the campaign—generated by people such as internet bloggers outside the formal party structures—which provided an alternative, often satirical and sometimes subversive, view of the election. Perhaps the most noteworthy social media event of the campaign was an interview given by Ed Miliband to the comedian turned social commentator Russell Brand. The latter had previously urged his YouTube followers (numbering around one million and mostly youthful) not to vote. However, the interview, for the purposes of which Miliband seemed to adopt a sort of 'Estuary English' inflection, was streamed through Brand's YouTube channel and he subsequently encouraged followers to vote Labour. Whatever its effect on the newly enfranchised and those who were still too young to vote, to opponents of more advanced years this episode served only to demonstrate Miliband's unsuitability to become Prime Minister.

Although online campaigning and discussion relating to the election was greater than ever before in 2015, it is not at all clear whether it made any difference to voters' behaviour. It is salutary to note, for example, that while David Cameron was the most searched for politician on Google over the campaign, the questions most frequently asked about him were 'whether he was rich, dead, left-handed or, indeed, a Labour politician' (Wring and Ward, 2015: 239). Identifying and measuring the impact of online activity on turnout or party choice is well beyond the capability of current political science. However, its chief effect is likely to be the energizing of existing supporters—either to vote or to donate money to a pre-chosen cause— rather than to secure any 'conversions' from one party to another.

The final predictions of the election outcome produced by the polling companies did nothing to dispel the widespread expectation that, in terms of votes at least, the election was too close to call. Five of them predicted a dead heat between the Conservatives and Labour; four gave the Conservatives a one point advantage; two put Labour in a narrow lead. Members of the public who had remained engaged throughout the process prepared themselves for another prolonged period of post-election horse-trading, resulting in another coalition of some kind.

The 2015 Results

As Table 6.1 shows, the electorate confounded the pollsters and pundits by giving the Conservatives a significant lead over Labour in the popular vote and, as a result, they secured a narrow but sustainable overall majority in the House of Commons. A slump in support for the Liberal Democrats was not unexpected, but its extent was a surprise to many observers: the party whose leaders had seen the coalition as an opportunity to confirm its renaissance as a serious political force found itself reduced to just eight MPs. The Liberal Democrats were replaced as third party in terms of the popular vote by UKIP, which advanced by almost ten points but won just one seat—a poor return for almost four million votes— while taking second place in 120 constituencies. The Green Party also improved its vote share, if rather less dramatically; but there were no additions to the single seat it already held. In Scotland, in what Alex Salmond aptly described as 'an electoral tsunami', the SNP amassed 50 per cent of the votes and fifty-six of the fifty-nine seats. Having won forty-one Scottish constituencies in 2010, Labour was reduced to a solitary MP (Ian Murray, who actually increased his majority in Edinburgh South). This was an unparalleled thrashing for Labour in an election in Scotland; suddenly, the party's supporters knew how Scottish Conservatives had felt when they experienced their own electoral wipe-out in the wake of Thatcherism.

On polling day, there was the usual ill-founded speculation in the media about the level of turnout. For example, the next day's *Daily Telegraph*, which was published after only a few results had been declared, reported that 'turnout was forecast to be at its highest for almost two decades'. Elsewhere, a betting firm was rumoured already to have paid out on wagers that turnout would exceed 68.5 per cent. If true, this proved to be premature generosity on the part of Paddy Power, since the overall UK turnout was 66.4 per cent. Despite the fact that the outcome was expected to be very close and claims that the combined endeavours of UKIP and Russell Brand would mobilize previous non-voters, this was an increase of just 1.1 points on the 2010 figure. On the positive side, 2015 was the third general election in succession which registered an increase in turnout; on the other hand, it remained significantly lower than at any election between 1950 and 1997.

As before, it is useful to analyse the interactions between changes in support for the various parties at constituency level. Table 6.3 shows the relevant correlation coefficients for England and Wales. It can be seen that both the Conservatives and Labour benefitted from the decline in Liberal Democrat support—the more the latter fell in a constituency, the better the major parties fared. As in 2010, it was commonly assumed before the election that an advance by UKIP would hurt the Conservatives more than Labour. In fact, although better UKIP performances were indeed associated with worse results for the Tories, the effect was actually stronger when changes in the UKIP and Labour vote shares are analysed. Changes in support for the Greens were not significantly related to Conservative performance but tended to be similar to the pattern for Labour. The coefficient measuring the relationship between changes in vote shares for the Greens and the Liberal Democrats is the most strongly negative of all, however. The collapse in Liberal Democrat support helped the Green Party to its best-ever general election result.

Although changes in support from 2010 varied somewhat from place to place, there was an impressive level of continuity in the distribution of votes for the major parties across constituencies. This is indicated by the correlation coefficients measuring the strength of the association between the parties' shares of votes in 2010 and 2015. Excluding Scotland, these are 0.97 for the Conservatives, 0.96 for Labour

Table 6.3 Correlations between changes in vote shares, 2010–15 (England and Wales)

	Change % Con	Change % Lab	Change % Lib Dem
Change % Lab	**−0.16**	–	–
Change % Lib Dem	**−0.38**	**−0.39**	–
Change % UKIP	**−0.30**	**−0.36**	0.13
Change % Green	0.02	**0.26**	**−0.53**

Notes: Significant coefficients are printed in bold. The N for coefficients involving Conservatives Labour, and Liberal Democrats only is 572; for these parties and UKIP it is 529, and for Greens 368. The Speaker's seat is excluded.

Table 6.4 Correlations between party shares of votes and constituency characteristics, 2010–15 (England and Wales)

	Lib Dems		UKIP		Green	
	2010	2015	2010	2015	2010	2015
% Prof./managerial	0.30	0.31	−0.19	−0.59	0.00*	0.27
% Manual workers	−0.32	−0.30	0.17	0.58	−0.02	−0.32
% Owner occupiers	0.04*	0.09	0.28	0.33	−0.19	−0.35
% Social renters	−0.19	−0.22	−0.19	−0.06*	0.10*	0.15
% Aged 18–24	0.11	0.04*	−0.33	−0.25	0.24	0.42
% Aged 65+	0.18	0.17	0.36	0.37	−0.05*	−0.20
% In agriculture	0.23	0.22	0.25	0.09*	−0.03*	0.03*
Persons per hectare	−0.05*	−0.06*	−0.35	−0.44	−0.09*	0.28
% With degrees	0.31	0.31	−0.41	−0.74	0.14	0.39
% No qualifications	−0.40	−0.34	0.19	0.65	−0.10*	−0.38
% Students	0.19	0.09*	−0.37	−0.41	0.25	0.46
% With no car	−0.17	−0.17	−0.32	−0.26	0.17	0.25
% Ethnic minority	−0.11	0.12	−0.36	−0.44	0.02*	0.11
(N)	*(572)*	*(572)*	*(529)*	*(572)*	*(311)*	*(536)*

Notes: All coefficients are significant at the 0.01 level except those asterisked. The Speaker's seat is excluded.

and 0.89 for the Liberal Democrats (N=572 in all cases). Support for UKIP and the Greens was rather less predictable on the basis of their performance in 2010, the relevant coefficients being 0.58 (N=529) and 0.76 (N=306), respectively.

Unsurprisingly, the relationships between the social and demographic characteristics of constituencies and level of support for the Conservatives and Labour (as well as for turnout) were much as before. Given the collapse experienced by the Liberal Democrats and the advances by UKIP and the Greens, however, it is worth examining the distribution of support for these parties in 2010 and 2015. This is shown in Table 6.4.

The Liberal Democrats (and Liberals before them) have always done better in more middle-class and rural areas and this remained true in both 2010 and 2015, notwithstanding the sharply contrasting overall performance of the party in these contests. It is worth noting, however, that while there were positive associations between the proportions of young people and students and support for the Liberal Democrat in 2010, the relationships were not significant in 2015. The U-turn on student tuition fees evidently cost the party some support when the day of reckoning arrived, and threatened to have a lasting effect given the age-profile of the voters (and voters-to-be) who had turned against the Liberal Democrats.

The coefficients for UKIP are an unusual mixture. In both 2010 and 2015 the party did best where there were more manual workers, older voters and people lacking educational qualifications but also, rather paradoxically, its vote share was positively related to the proportion of owner occupiers in a constituency. On the other hand, the party fared worse in metropolitan areas and constituencies where there were more professionals, students, young people, ethnic minorities, residents with degrees, and people with no car. The difference between the two elections is that in 2015 these patterns were much more clear-cut, as indicated by the strength of the correlation coefficients. The Green Party clearly appealed to very different sorts of people. In 2010, the only factors which had any noteworthy associations with variations in Green support were the proportions of students and young people. In 2015, those correlations strengthened considerably but in addition the Green vote acquired a more metropolitan, middle-class profile.

Within Scotland, the big story was the astonishing advance of the SNP. This featured staggering increases in vote share of between 30 and 40 percentage points in twenty-seven constituencies and of more than 40 points in three Glasgow constituencies. The performances of the Conservatives and Liberal Democrats were unrelated to that of the SNP but the rivalry between the latter and Labour as the leading parties in Scottish politics is underlined by the fact that changes in their vote shares were strongly negatively related (coefficient = −0.71). Even a cursory reading of the election results reveals that the greater the gain by the SNP across the constituencies, the bigger was Labour's loss of support.

Did these seismic shifts reflect changes in the socio-economic bases of SNP support? In 2010, only two variables were significantly and positively (if modestly) associated with SNP vote share—per cent manual workers (0.40) and per cent with no educational qualifications (0.28). In 2015 the comparable coefficients were 0.51 and 0.57 while per cent in social housing and per cent with no car also became significant at 0.67 and 0.41, respectively. Although SNP leaders would probably dislike the comparison, these data made the party seem like the Caledonian counterpart of UKIP. Moreover, as in UKIP's case there were strong negative relationships with standard middle-class indicators—professional and managerial workers (−0.68), those with degrees (−0.63) and owner occupiers (−0.41). Clearly, the distribution of the SNP vote was much more structured in this election by occupational class and class-related variables than previously, underlining the depth to which the nationalists had mined Labour's traditional seams of support. Despite winning 50 per cent of Scottish votes, then, the SNP had evidently failed to establish itself as a 'catch all' 'Party of Scotland', without a distinctive social base. For any remaining pessimists within the SNP, it might have been preferable if it had enjoyed a high tide rather than a 'tsunami' in 2015; as the governing party at Holyrood it would be forced to defend its record, while in terms of Westminster elections it now had precious little to gain and much to lose.

Explaining the Outcome

There is little difficulty in accounting for the poor performance of the Liberal Democrats in the election. This was merely the latest in a series of electoral disasters stemming from the decision to enter a coalition with the Conservatives. Nick Clegg had sought to reposition his party, from offering a radical alternative to Labour to serving as a more 'progressive' version of the Conservatives. Fleetingly, in the aftermath of the 2010 general election, Clegg's strategy seemed to be vindicated, and the coalition looked like a union of two parties who were converging on the centre-right of British politics from different ideological directions. However, if the coalition interlude between 2010 and 2015 witnessed David Cameron's failure to 'modernize' the Conservative Party, thanks to grass-roots opposition, over the same period Nick Clegg managed to 'toxify' the Liberal Democrat brand amongst potential supporters to an extent which would have dumbfounded his inoffensive predecessors.

The surge in support for UKIP was not unexpected in the light of the party's performance in polls and elections over the preceding five years. To some extent, this represents a British version of the increased support for so-called 'populist' parties in other European countries including France, Germany, Austria, and Italy (Goodhart, 2017; Richards, 2017). In these cases the electorate had become increasingly resentful of the policies pursued by political elites (especially in relation to immigration) and less favourably inclined towards the EU. In Britain during the 2015 election, according to YouGov, the voters ranked immigration second only to the economy as the most important issue facing the country—the latter being nominated by 52 per cent of respondents compared with 51 per cent for the former. Strikingly, more thought that UKIP was the best party to deal with this issue (27 per cent) than placed their trust in the Conservatives (22 per cent) or Labour (16 per cent).

In Scotland, as previously noted, the independence referendum changed everything. Although the SNP lost that battle, the campaign had galvanized supporters of the nationalist cause and brought floods of new recruits. This, allied to Labour's lacklustre campaign and the impressive performance of Nicola Sturgeon in the televised debates, was sufficient to persuade many erstwhile Labour supporters to desert their traditional allegiance and turn to the SNP.

Turning to the question of why the Conservatives managed to defeat Labour so soundly across Britain as a whole, there are good grounds for thinking that, to a considerable extent, the former's victory was another vindication of the 'valence voting' approach which we outlined earlier. According to YouGov, the three issues considered most important by the electorate in 2015 were the economy (mentioned by 52 per cent of respondents), immigration (51 per cent) and the Health Service (45 per cent). These easily outstripped other policy areas and can be defined as valence issues because everyone wants a healthy economy and a first-class health service while the great majority of people favoured 'managed' (rather than 'uncontrolled') immigration. As to the party judged best to handle these issues, although Labour led the Conservatives by 14 percentage points on the Health Service, the Conservatives were ahead by 18 on the economy and 6 on immigration (an issue on which, as we have seen, the largest proportion of respondents preferred UKIP). Overall, then, the Conservatives appear to have had the edge on the key valence issues in the election. However, if general elections can be seen as verdicts on detailed aspects of a government's record (as opposed to more general perceptions of 'governing competence') an 'objective' observer might have reached a more damning verdict on the coalition, and, in particular, on the performance of Cameron's Conservatives. After all, far from exerting themselves to reduce Labour's traditional advantage on health, they had reneged on their promise to refrain from 'top-down' reorganization of the NHS. Having argued that their programme of 'austerity' would save Britain from bankruptcy and put things right within a single parliament, they ended up pursuing a course which bore considerable similarity to the more gradual approach recommended by Labour in 2010. Finally, in 2010 the Conservatives had pledged a radical reduction in net migration, even tying themselves to the goal of reducing current levels to below 100,000 per year. By the time of the 2015 general election, far from reducing net inward migration, the Conservative-dominated coalition had presided over a significant increase (more than 300,000 during 2015). Overall, then, the outcome of the 2015 election is probably best understood as a vote of no confidence in the Opposition, rather than an endorsement of the main party of government—a case of 'this government hasn't done well, but we haven't been given any reason to think that their opponents would have done any better'.

When it comes to assessments of the party leaders, however, there is no room for doubt. David Cameron heavily outscored Ed Miliband as the most preferred Prime Minister. As already noted (see Figure 6.3), the latter never once headed the former from the time he became Labour leader until the start of the campaign. During the campaign itself, although there was some improvement in Miliband's position, he still lagged well behind Cameron. On the eve of the election, Ipsos MORI reported that Cameron was thought to be the most capable Prime Minister by 42 per cent of respondents compared with 27 per cent thinking this of Miliband. Miliband not only lagged Cameron in this respect but the proportions thinking that he was doing a good job as Leader of the Opposition were consistently smaller than those who took a negative view of his performance. Had pundits and the media paid a little more attention to the background data produced by the polls on party preferences on issues and preferred Prime Minister, rather than being obsessed by the 'horse race', they might have been a little more cautious in accepting the headline messages that the election result would be close to a dead heat.

Those who concentrated on the relative fortunes of the two main parties would also have missed the significance of the rise of 'others' in the two elections covered in this chapter. Although the electoral system prevented changes in popular support being reflected in seats in the House of Commons, it was obvious that the old two-party (or two-and-a-bit-party) system was facing a serious challenge in this period. The combination of dealignment and disillusion among the electorate resulted in the three parties that had dominated British elections throughout the post-war period receiving historically small shares of the popular vote. Although in combination they cobbled together 88.1 per cent of the UK vote in 2010, this proportion slumped to 75.1 in 2015. In 1964 the relevant figure had been 98.7 per cent.

Whether the two elections discussed in this chapter deserve to be described as a 'Conservative revival' is perhaps more open to debate. To be sure, the party emerged from the wilderness of the Opposition benches to govern first in coalition and then on its own. Nonetheless, electoral problems remained. Although the vote shares obtained in 2010 and 2015 represented a marked improvement on the scores recorded in the three previous general elections, they were still significantly worse than those that had been achieved from 1979 to 1992. In addition, the Liberal Democrat refusal to endorse the latest report of the Boundary Commission—in retaliation for Cameron's failure to make progress on reform of the House of Lords—meant that the Conservatives still suffered from the outdated constituency boundaries that remained in place, at an estimated cost of around twenty seats in 2015. Finally, the issue of Britain's membership of the EU was becoming increasingly dangerous to the party leadership, whose essentially pragmatic outlook was now clearly out of step with backbench opinion as well as the mood amongst grassroots supporters.

As mentioned above, to placate the Eurosceptics in his party and to counter the threat from UKIP, Cameron had committed himself to holding an 'in/out' referendum on the issue in the next parliament, leaving time for what he hoped would be a 'proper reasoned debate' and (in his best-case scenario) a chance for the EU to reform itself along congenial lines (see https://www.gov.uk/government/speeches/eu-speech-at-bloomberg). He had presided as Prime Minister over two referendums (on electoral reform and Scottish independence), both of which were forced upon him, but in which a majority of voters had backed his preferred option—a re-affirmation of the status quo. On those occasions, Cameron could feel confident that he enjoyed overwhelming support from within his own party. In respect of EU membership, however, he could feel no such certainty—indeed, his own previous posturing on the subject had done nothing to dissuade fellow-Conservatives who thought that it was high time to part company with the EU. Accordingly, the text of Cameron's Bloomberg speech of January 2013 was dominated by an argument for continued membership of the EU (suitably reformed); implicitly, even at this stage he was telling British voters that they would have the chance to leave the EU if they really wanted to, but they would be fools if they took advantage of that opportunity.

When the votes had been counted in the 2015 general election and the Conservatives had defied expectations with their overall parliamentary majority, David Cameron effectively became the prisoner of his own promise. In terms of referendum campaigns, during the coalition government of 2010–15 his record was 'played two, won two'. Thanks at least in part to his personal popularity, he was now free from his dalliance with the Lib Dems: but he was hardly master in his own house, and it was about to become third time unlucky.

Appendix: Campaign Polls

Figures 6.A1 and 6.A2 relate to Great Britain, as Northern Ireland is not included in national opinion polls (data from https://www.markpack.org.uk/opinion-polls/).

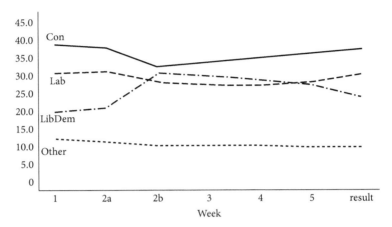

Figure 6.A1 Campaign polls, 2010

Note: Week 2 of the campaign is split into the days before (2a) and after (2b) the first televised debate involving the party leaders.

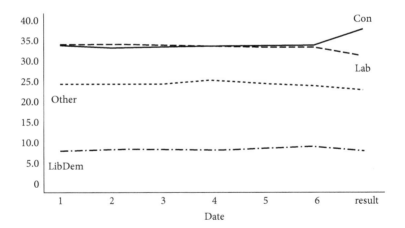

Figure 6.A2 Campaign polls, 2015

Notes

1. See http://news.bbc.co.uk/1/hi/programmes/question_time/8051222.stm.
2. Different sources give slightly different figures. These are from the BBC News website.

7

The Brexit Elections, 2017–19

David Cameron made good on his pre-election promise and did not serve another full term as Conservative leader and Prime Minister. However, the next election took place rather sooner than he had expected, and his hopes of a graceful hand-over to his friend, Chancellor Osborne, were dashed. Indeed, although the parliament elected in 2015 lasted only two years, all three of the main UK parties changed their leaders during that brief interlude—and one of the newcomers, Labour's Jeremy Corbyn, would not have lasted until 2017 if the views of his parliamentary colleagues had been decisive. It was not unprecedented for all three main UK parties to field 'rookie' leaders in a general election: indeed, this had happened as recently as 2010—but that election had taken place five years after the previous one, giving the new leaders some time to 'bed in'. In this respect the decade after 1964, during which Harold Wilson and Edward Heath faced off against each other in four successive contests (while the Liberals changed leader only once) seemed very distant indeed by 2017. The recent high wastage rate among British political leaders is vivid testimony to the importance placed by parties on the vote-winning abilities of their chief standard-bearers—and the high cost of perceived failure.

By any standard the election of 2017 was remarkable, beginning with the fact that it was triggered by a Prime Minister who had repeatedly and emphatically argued that Britain required a period of stability rather than a new election. Whatever Theresa May's private thoughts, the 2011 Fixed-Term Parliaments Act was supposed to free Prime Ministers from the temptation to call 'snap' elections. In practice, however, the obvious flaws in the legislation were exposed at its first test; fearing that they would look cowardly in the eyes of voters if they denied the government the necessary two-thirds majority, opposition MPs allowed the relevant motion to pass virtually uncontested. This was not the first time in the 2015–17 parliament when MPs thought it advisable to vote against their private convictions. In June 2015 the Commons agreed (by 544 votes to 53) to the second reading of a Bill which paved the way for a referendum on UK membership of the European Union, despite the fact that a clear majority in the House of Commons (let alone the Lords) thought a poll on this subject would be ill-timed at best.

British General Elections Since 1964: Diversity, Dealignment, and Disillusion. Second Edition. David Denver and Mark Garnett, Oxford University Press. © David Denver and Mark Garnett 2021. DOI: 10.1093/oso/9780198844952.003.0007

The 'Brexit' Referendum of 2016

The use of the referendum as a device to help resolve specific political questions is another reminder of the radical changes in British democratic practice since 1964. It is, of course, possible to justify such departures from the normal procedures of representative democracy when an important question arises which, for one reason or another, those elected to govern the country feel themselves unable to resolve. Arguably, in a history of general elections, referendums should be treated much like other developments during the course of a parliament—that is, they are worth noting as expressions of public opinion on a single issue, but as such they are less reliable guides to *party* popularity than the regular opinion polls.

On this basis, an account of British general elections since 1964 which contained lengthy discussions of each of the ten (or eleven, if one counts the 1998 London poll on the introduction of an elected mayor) significant referendums would suffer from repeated distractions. However, as we have seen, it is impossible to explain the outcome of the 2015 general election without reference to the Scottish independence referendum of the previous year. Significant as they were, the 'spill-over' effects of that referendum were mainly confined to Scotland; and although the balance of party forces in parliament would almost certainly have been different had the referendum never happened, the Conservatives would still have enjoyed an overall majority. The 'Brexit' referendum of 2016 was an entirely different matter. The voting patterns exhibited at that referendum appeared to reflect new cleavages in the British electorate which threatened to destabilize the Westminster party system. Indeed, it is not fanciful to claim that it had more significant consequences for students of British elections than any other single event over the years since 1964. Certainly the next contest we consider—the general election of 2017—would never have taken place had it not been for Brexit.

David Cameron's decision to promise an in/out EU referendum, announced in January 2013, had overridden a 2010 manifesto pledge to call a poll on the terms of any subsequent EU Treaty. There was no such treaty in prospect in January 2013. Cameron's announcement was, in part, a recognition of the failure to quell unrest within his party over 'Europe'; this combined with division on other issues, was starting to threaten the ability of his coalition government to command consistent parliamentary majorities. Cameron also feared that, unless UKIP's demand for an in/out referendum was conceded, disgruntled Conservative supporters might defect. While Labour also had good reasons to fear Nigel Farage, it was far less likely that any defections of supporters would include its elected representatives— or, more importantly, its financial donors. Whatever his calculations, Cameron's announcement did nothing to stem the rise of UKIP which topped the poll in the 2014 European parliamentary elections and won nearly four million votes in the 2015 general election despite retaining only one of the two MPs who had deserted the Conservatives (see Chapter 6).

To reverse this tide Cameron pinned his hopes on a meaningful renegotiation of Britain's terms of membership, allowing him to claim that the EU was flexible and that he could be trusted to stand up for the national interest. The negotiations duly began shortly after the 2015 election and extended over several months. Unfortunately for Cameron, he was unable to convince voters (even those on his side of the referendum question) that the talks had produced significant concessions. A similar scenario had not proved fatal to the hopes of the Wilson government for a positive outcome in the 1975 referendum (see Chapter 3); but in those days the press had been almost unanimous in supporting UK membership of what was then the EEC, and things were very different in 2016. Far from extinguishing the Eurosceptic threat to Cameron's position, the ill-starred negotiations made matters worse; by the time of the 2016 referendum UKIP's average share of voting intentions had climbed to 16.6 per cent.

In retrospect, it can easily appear that British politics was in a state of suspended animation between the 2015 general election and the EU referendum. There had, indeed, been little change in the popularity of the major parties, although the Conservatives experienced a slight dip and Labour a brief upward movement following George Osborne's March 2016 Budget which did not impress the voters (even if it was not as maladroit as the 2012 'omnishambles'). Cameron himself was still popular and was clearly preferred as the best person to be Prime Minister. However, such ratings are relative to the 'competition', rather than being absolute measurements of a politician's public standing; and even when judged against the controversial Jeremy Corbyn, Cameron's weaknesses were exposed by an Ipsos MORI poll of April 2016, which found that he was regarded as more 'out of touch' and less honest than Corbyn, who was perceived as doing a better job as a party leader despite Labour's manifest disunity.

This was an inauspicious context for Cameron's own part in the referendum campaign, which began officially on 15 April 2016. Clearly anticipating a victory for 'Remain', after which he would have to mend fences with the Eurosceptics in his party, Cameron decided not to indulge in the kind of personal attacks on his opponents which, in 1975, had been perpetrated by the press while also denying a proper hearing to those who were concerned about national 'sovereignty'. In 2016—although in the intervening years of 'globalization' the concept of sovereignty had been rendered far more questionable—the Eurosceptic case against interference from Brussels gained much greater traction, not least because large-scale immigration from within the EU provided a practical illustration of the need to 'take back control'.

The outcome of the referendum, held on 23 June, was a victory for 'Leave' by 51.9 percent to 48.1 per cent on a turnout of over 72 per cent. The latter figure was comfortably above that in any recent general election and also significantly higher than in the 1975 poll, when, despite the best efforts of the pro-EEC press, it had been less than 65 per cent. Detailed research suggested that in 2016 the rival campaigns had not been equally successful in energizing potential supporters; 19 percent of the electorate who had leaned towards 'Remain' did not vote, compared to just 11 per cent of those who preferred 'Leave' (Evans and Menon, 2017: 81). The 'binary' question—'Leave' versus 'Remain'—proved particularly congenial to tacticians on both sides, most of whom had worked in the previous general election and were familiar with the most sophisticated techniques for targeting voters, notably the potential for 'data mining' offered by social media, like Facebook. While the precise impact of such media—and the extent to which unfriendly powers like Russia exploited them to affect the overall result—can never be measured, it seems reasonable to suppose that social media provided a more effective medium to convey a message which was simple and positive (i.e. 'Leave') as opposed to one which was relatively complex and primarily intended to arouse fear of the alternative ('Remain').

Although opinion polls had suggested that a close result was on the cards, the win for 'Leave' surprised many. It was a devastating personal blow for Cameron who promptly resigned as Prime Minister. Although he claimed in his own defence that he had no alternative but to bow to UKIP's demand for an in/out referendum, in this instance his decision was swayed by the problems facing his party rather than the future of his country. In embarking on this gamble, he had chosen to overlook the solid evidence that British voters had become much more volatile since the 1975 referendum; that politicians of all parties were distrusted more than ever before in the wake of the 2009 expenses scandal; and that any attempt to 'prove' that Britain would be worse off if it left the EU would run up against evidence of turmoil within the Eurozone since 2008. To compound Cameron's difficulties, official statistics released during the referendum campaign showed that, far from reducing net migration into the UK to less than 100,000 as the Conservatives had promised, the annual figure was still around 300,000. This concrete evidence that the government was unable to control the country's borders was worth far more than apocalyptic 'Remain' predictions about the consequences of a 'Leave' victory.

David Cameron preferred to think that his own authority would still be strong enough to coax voters into an acceptance of the status quo, as in the previous referendums on electoral reform and Scottish independence. These precedents, however, were profoundly misleading. In the electoral reform case (2011), real enthusiasm was confined to a small minority of the population; in a contest marked by widespread public indifference, Cameron's interventions on behalf of 'first-past-the-post' were easily enough to tip the balance. In the 2014 'IndyRef' there were strong passions on both sides, yet a show of unity among pro-Union parties, combined with a promise of greater devolved powers, was reinforced by overwhelming support for a 'No' vote in the UK and Scottish press. The 2016 EU referendum was different, in that (almost) all of the *positive* arguments (whether factually based or otherwise) fell on one side: the leadership of the main opposition party offered no strong guidance to its supporters by holding itself aloof from the debate; and (in particularly sharp contrast to the 1975 vote) several national newspapers (e.g. *The Sun, The Daily Mail, The Daily Express, The Daily Telegraph* and their Sunday versions) not only endorsed 'Leave' on the day, but had been preparing the referendum battleground by attacking 'Europe' and all its works since Thatcher's 1988 Bruges speech (if not before).

The Aftermath of the Referendum

A contest for the Conservative leadership followed Cameron's resignation. In July, after a farcical few weeks in which other contenders were either eliminated by the votes of MPs or withdrew—and Michael Gove dished the chances of his fellow 'Leaver', Boris Johnson, by announcing his own candidacy—the Home Secretary Theresa May emerged as Conservative leader and Prime Minister without the direct participation of ordinary party members. This situation evoked parallels with Gordon Brown's succession in 2007, with the difference that whereas Brown was an (almost) inevitable choice to replace Tony Blair, Mrs May's claims only began to look irresistible because in various ways her rivals made themselves seem unelectable. Nevertheless, Mrs May generated her own version of the 'Brown bounce'; the effect on Conservative electoral fortunes was immediate and striking. Having inherited a situation in which it was hovering around 35 per cent in terms of voting intentions, the new Prime Minister's party was well into the 40s by October and the upward trend continued thereafter (Figure 7.1).

The repercussions of the referendum were not confined to the Conservative Party. Electorally speaking, the second most important event in these two years was the elevation of Jeremy Corbyn to the Labour Party leadership in September 2015. Ed Miliband resigned immediately after his party's defeat and in the subsequent contest Corbyn, a battle-scarred veteran of the Labour left and a well-known opponent of European integration, swept to victory. Partly this was because new rules endorsed by Miliband enabled anyone to become a 'registered supporter' of the party for a few pounds, entitling them to vote in leadership contests. There was a sudden spike in applications before Corbyn's victory (including at least one mischievous Conservative MP) although belated attempts were made to debar known members of rival left-wing organizations. Ominously, however, of the 230 MPs who voted in the ballot, only twenty supported Corbyn, compared to the thirty-six who had nominated him.

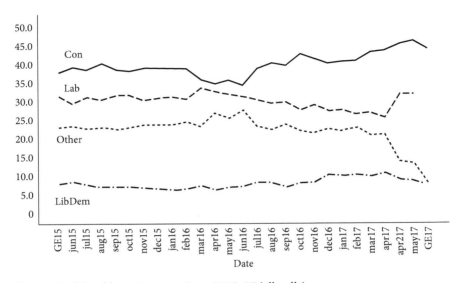

Figure 7.1 Monthly voting intentions, 2015–17 (all polls)

Note: The 2015 and 2017 election results in Great Britain form the starting and finishing points. The data shown are the monthly means for all published polls.

Corbyn's victory was a major surprise and in his policies and his age (66 at the time of his election) he differed markedly from recent leaders of the major parties. However, in at least one respect his leadership conformed to a familiar trend. Most new party leaders enjoy a brief honeymoon with the electorate as people take time to get to know about and assess the person concerned. So it proved in this case, as Labour support remained steady through late 2015 and early 2016. Nonetheless, as Figure 7.1 illustrates, the party consistently trailed well behind the Conservatives and the highest point reached was a paltry 33 per cent of voting intentions, in March 2016. Thereafter, it was downhill all the way to just over 25 per cent in the first half of April 2017. In these months, assorted front-benchers resigned from the Corbyn team and in the immediate aftermath of the June 2016 referendum Labour MPs passed a vote of no confidence in the leader by 172 to 40. The MPs, for the most part, had never been persuaded that Corbyn was a credible alternative Prime Minister and, backed by polling evidence, now expected that he would prove a disaster if he stayed in place until the next general election, whenever that was held. The local and Scottish Parliament elections in the spring of 2016 seemed to confirm these fears. In the locals in England, despite beating the Conservatives by 33 per cent to 32 per cent in the 'national equivalent vote' calculation, Labour became the first Opposition party in over thirty years to lose ground in local elections held separately from a general election. In Scotland, Labour languished as the third party at Holyrood with just twenty-four seats, behind both the SNP (sixty-three) and the Conservatives (thirty-one).

For Corbyn's opponents at Westminster, the final straw was his lacklustre (to say the least) contribution to the EU referendum campaign. From one perspective, the new Labour leader had played a hand worthy of Machiavelli. As the referendum proved, many traditional Labour seats (particularly in the north of England) favoured 'Brexit' by significant margins; so an unequivocal commitment to the 'Remain' camp would have been a risky proposition even for a leader whose heart was in the fight. Furthermore, rather than reaping an electoral reward from its support for the UK in the Scottish referendum, Labour had found itself almost wiped out in the 2015 general election in Scotland. Sharing a platform with Cameron and other pro-'Remain' Tories, in short, seemed like a one-way ticket to electoral oblivion—even worse for the 'Corbynistas', it would mean making common cause with the real enemy (Tony Blair). It seemed far more advisable for Corbyn to make vague pro-EU noises—which would not be remembered, let alone held against him, after the expected 'Remain' victory—while signalling disapproval of the nature of the Conservative-dominated campaign from the sidelines.

However, whatever Machiavelli might have thought of Corbyn's performance, to his parliamentary colleagues it was all too clear during the referendum campaign that he was trying to perform a balancing act while continuing to harbour a clear preference for 'Leave'. When the early voting returns indicated a defeat for 'Remain', dissident Labour MPs who sought Corbyn's removal for a variety of reasons began to prepare for a change of leader as a matter of urgency. However, in September 2016, Corbyn saw off their challenge by a more emphatic margin than his initial victory, thanks not least to the absence of a credible alternative. The 'Corbynistas' were now clearly ascendant in the party, if not among its representatives in the House of Commons; and the bad electoral news continued. In five parliamentary by-elections held from October 2016 to February 2017 (ignoring Batley and Spen which, following the assassination of the incumbent MP Jo Cox by an apparently unstable nationalist, the other major parties did not contest) Labour's vote share declined in all cases. The pattern was more characteristic of a governing party experiencing 'mid-term blues' than of an Opposition with realistic prospects of a return to office. This was particularly true of the February 2017 Copeland by-election. The Conservative victory in a Cumbrian seat which Labour had held since 1935 was the first by-election gain by a governing party from the Opposition in thirty-five years.

There is little doubt that the changing fortunes of the Conservative and Labour parties between the 2015 and 2017 elections reflected the relative popularity of their leaders. Figure 7.2 shows that in this respect there was not much to separate David Cameron and Jeremy Corbyn—the former became more unpopular fairly quickly after the 2015 election, while the latter's 'honeymoon' did not last long. With the advent of Theresa May, however, the situation was transformed. Her ratings were consistently—and strongly—positive while Corbyn continued to

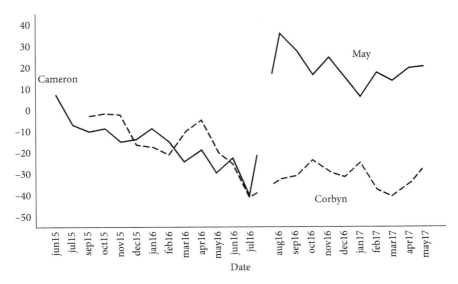

Figure 7.2 Popularity of party leaders, June 2015–May 2017

Note: The data are net figures from the Ipsos MORI series measuring satisfaction with the performance of party leaders which can be interpreted as a measure of their popularity.

Source: Ipsos MORI.

languish in negative territory. In September 2016, Ipsos MORI reported that May easily outscored her rival on being perceived as a capable leader (68 per cent to 24 per cent). This overall preference for May reflected a high public regard for specific characteristics: she was seen as more patriotic than Corbyn (75 per cent to 49 per cent), better at handling a crisis (52 per cent to 18 per cent), blessed with sounder judgement (56 per cent to 30 per cent), and being inspired by a more attractive vision of Britain's future (55 per cent to 38 per cent). In addition, whereas her predecessor, Cameron, was regularly believed by 40 to 50 per cent of poll respondents to be 'more style than substance', only 25 per cent thought this of Theresa May. It looked as if the Conservatives, with their famous instinct for self-preservation, had alighted on the best person to guide them through their post-referendum difficulties.

The Others

Following his party's disastrous showing in the 2015 election, Nick Clegg resigned as leader of the Liberal Democrats and was succeeded in July of that year by Tim Farron, the personable MP for Westmorland and Lonsdale. Nonetheless, the party struggled to remind the electorate of its existence, let alone of its credentials as a potential party of government. Despite occasional reminders of the old glory days—such as winning the Richmond Park by-election in December 2016—there was not much solid evidence of progress. Richmond Park was an ideal opportunity for the Liberal Democrats, since the constituency had voted heavily for 'Remain' in the EU referendum and Zac Goldsmith, whose resignation had triggered the by-election, was a 'Leaver' whose controversial father, James, had established the short-lived Referendum Party in the 1990s (see Chapter 5). On less favourable terrain the Liberal Democrat performance was patchy at best; in terms of vote share in the 2016 local elections the party came a very distant third and in Scotland it held on to just five seats in the Parliament—down from sixteen, and behind even the Green Party. Although their position in the polls improved in the first months of 2017 this mini-revival raised the Liberal Democrats only a couple of points above their 2015 score.

As we have seen, UKIP's popularity reached a peak around the time of the EU referendum. However, the success of the Leave campaign immediately created a problem for the party. With its *raison d'être* apparently achieved, voters could legitimately ask whether there was any point in its continued existence. The ever-newsworthy Nigel Farage resigned as party leader soon after the referendum. There followed a period of confused infighting—including reported physical violence involving Members of the European Parliament—after which Diane James, an MEP since the 2014 European elections, emerged as party leader in September 2016. She resigned after just eighteen days in post, citing a lack of support for her plans to reform the party, and left UKIP altogether a few weeks later. Farage returned as caretaker leader until Paul Nuttall, another MEP, was elected by a comfortable margin. Barely more than 15,000 people cast votes in a contest to decide the leadership of a party which had precipitated one of the most significant developments in post-war British politics. Understandably, confusion about the party's leadership and future direction affected UKIP's performance in by-elections, culminating in the failure of Nuttall himself, after a notably chaotic campaign, to take Stoke Central from Labour on the same day as the Conservative victory at Copeland. The party sank slowly but steadily in the opinion polls and entered the 2017 election on around 11 per cent of voting intentions.

* * *

As we have seen, the evidence of its unpopularity with the voters was not enough to persuade the Labour Party to change its leader. On the other hand, the highly positive poll ratings for herself and her party had a profound effect on Mrs May's thinking on the subject of an early election. In April 2017, while on a walking holiday in Wales, she decided that the opportunity was too good to miss even if this entailed a contradiction of her oft-stated pledge to spare Britons from another election until 2020. On her return, she announced that an election would be held three years ahead of schedule, on 8 June 2017. What the *Daily Telegraph* headlined as 'May's Bolt from the Blue', and the *Sun* as 'May's Election Bombshell' took almost everyone by surprise. Presumably it also provoked mixed feelings within her own party since it meant that the (already delayed) changes to parliamentary seats being worked on by the Boundary Commissions—generally believed to favour the Conservatives—had to be aborted. Mrs May argued, however, that an election had become necessary to strengthen her hand in the forthcoming nego-tiations over Brexit and to prevent future parliamentary obstruction. The fact that the Conservatives (and she personally) enjoyed an apparently unassailable lead in the polls seemed to trump any of the attendant risks. Expectations of a Tory landslide had intoxicated the *Daily Mail*, which in November 2016 had branded senior judges as 'Enemies of the People' for their insistence on the principle of parliamentary sovereignty (against Mrs May's proposal to trigger the process of withdrawal from the EU without consulting MPs). Its report of May's decision to dishonour her previous promises about an election was adorned with the headline 'Crush the Saboteurs', and a large photograph of the Prime Minister which made her look like the kind of person for whom the 'crushing' would be a pleasure.

The surprise announcement caught all of the parties on the hop to varying extents but the 'others' were particularly disadvantaged. Nomination papers were required to be submitted by Thursday 11 May—just three weeks and a day after MPs had decided to make a mockery of the Fixed-Term Parliaments Act and acquiesce in the Prime Minister's decision to go for an election. Unsurprisingly, the number of candidates nominated in Great Britain declined sharply compared with 2015 (from 3,833 to 3,195); there were 460 Green Party candidates (down from 568), while the tally of UKIP aspirants slumped from 614 to 379, despite the presumed attractions of standing for a parliament which had a mandate to 'take back control' for Britain. Assorted independents, eccentrics, and inhabitants of the political fringe were also much less in evidence than usual, their numbers falling from 659 in 2015 to 366 in this election. The fall in the number of candidates possibly arose from difficulties in raising the £500 required for each candidate's deposit at short notice but the Greens and UKIP also claimed that there was a tac-tical element to their decisions—trying to help Labour in marginal seats in the first case and not standing against strongly pro-Brexit Conservatives in the second.

The 2017 Campaign

The 2017 campaign was disfigured by two indiscriminate terrorist attacks. The first occurred on 22 May when a suicide bomber struck at the Manchester Arena in the aftermath of a pop concert. Twenty-three people were killed and more than a hundred injured; more than half of the victims were children. In the second, at London Bridge on 3 June, a van was driven at high speed into pedestrians and the occupants subsequently ran amok with kitchen knives. Eight people were killed.

Following these horrific incidents public campaigning was temporarily suspended by all parties except UKIP, which argued that a truce would hand a tacit victory to the terrorists.

At a more mundane level, an unusual feature of the 2017 campaign was that it was punctuated by a major round of local elections. These contests, scheduled for 4 May, were for all councils in Scotland and Wales and for county councils, some unitary authorities and some mayors in England. Local parties were already heavily involved in these campaigns when the general election was called and they went ahead as planned. The last (and only previous) time that this happened was in 1955. There were June general elections in 1983 and 1987, as we have seen, but in each of these cases the Prime Minister (Margaret Thatcher) cannily waited for a detailed analysis and assessment of the results before calling the national poll.

Had Theresa May been as patient as Mrs Thatcher and waited to digest the results of the 2017 local contests she would have been even more confident that her government would benefit from a 'snap' national election. In England and Wales, the Conservatives gained almost 400 seats while Labour lost around 250 and UKIP was ousted from every one of the 143 seats that the party defended. In Scotland, the Tories came second in both votes and seats while Labour support plunged and the SNP—although still clearly the leading party—under-achieved compared to recent standards. The national equivalent vote shares for the UK as a whole, as calculated by Rallings and Thrasher, put the Conservatives on 39 per cent, Labour on 28 per cent, and the Liberal Democrats on 18 per cent (*Sunday Times*, 07.05.2017).

Another departure from recent practice in 2017 related to the televised debates involving party leaders. As we have seen (Chapter 6), in 2015 David Cameron took full advantage of his bargaining position with the broadcasters and refused to perform under any format which placed him on an equal footing with minor party leaders. Mrs May followed his example and, initially, Jeremy Corbyn also rejected the idea of appearing alongside the 'others'. As a result, the first debate on ITV on 19 May featured only six minor party leaders—not so much a case of 'Hamlet without the Prince', but rather Romeo and Juliet without either of the star-crossed protagonists. The broadcast attracted just 1.6 million viewers. As the Nuffield study notes, 'marginally fewer people tuned in than watched a programme about vets on Channel 4 at the same time' (Cowley and Kavanagh, 2018: 331). Just before the BBC debate scheduled for 31 May, however, Corbyn realized that he was missing an opportunity and took his place along with the minor parties and the Home Secretary, Amber Rudd, who stood in for the camera-shy Mrs May. Again the viewing figures for the programme were unimpressive (3.6 million according to BARB data) and, on the face of it, the exchanges appeared to have little impact on the trend in public opinion. By this time, however, May's limitations as a campaigner had been exposed (see below) and her non-appearances can only have reinforced the misgivings of voters who initially had regarded her as a dependable national leader for troubled times.

Figure 7.A1 (in the Appendix) shows the weekly averages for voting intentions during the campaign for the three main parties and 'others' (mainly UKIP). At the outset, the Conservatives enjoyed a huge lead over their rivals, apparently confirming expectations of a landslide victory for them and an electoral catastrophe for Labour. Support for the Conservatives remained unusually strong until the third week in May, although Labour was clearly already on an upward trend from its very poor starting point. After that, however, the popularity of the Conservatives dipped while Labour continued to close the gap, despite appearing to flag a little in the last week of campaigning.

As Figure 7.A1 makes clear, the 2017 election quickly developed into a two-horse race. When the election was called, UKIP immediately fell to around 8 per cent of voting intentions and as the campaign progressed its support drifted further downwards to stabilize at between 4 and 5 per cent. The Liberal Democrats also declined a little over the campaign. Having averaged over 10 per cent in the first two weeks they subsequently fell to just under 8 per cent. Since the clearest distinction between the Liberal Democrats and their Conservative and Labour rivals in this election was their unequivocal and long-established endorsement of continued EU membership, the slippage of support for Farron and his party could be explained by a lack of public appetite for a second Brexit referendum. Given their recent misfortunes, however, it is unlikely that the Liberal Democrats would have benefitted from *any* specific policy proposal, however popular—not least because Farron himself was unable to concentrate on Brexit because of constant media speculation about his religious faith and his approach to questions of personal morality.

In Scotland, meanwhile, there were eleven campaign polls and these suggested that, from a dire position at the start (less than 20 per cent of voting intentions), Labour had pulled level with the Conservatives by the end, with the average of the last three Scottish polls showing each of them on 26 per cent. They were vying for second place behind the SNP, which averaged 40 per cent in these later polls. Although this gave the SNP a very comfortable lead, its share of voting intentions was significantly smaller than the 50 per cent achieved in 2015 and the party was in danger of looking like a faltering electoral force in comparison to the giant stride it took in that year. In Wales, two early polls gave the impression of more dramatic stirrings, showing clear Conservative leads over Labour in a country which had failed to elect a single Tory MP as recently as 2001. Later in the campaign, however, surveys suggested that Labour had resumed its customary position as the dominant party; ultimately the Conservatives actually lost ground compared to 2015. As in Scotland, the Welsh polls reported that support for the nationalists was somewhat lower than in 2015.

The reversal of fortunes for the two leading parties over the course of the campaign was unprecedented. Never before had the gap between them narrowed so dramatically. The Conservatives went from looking set to break records, to struggling to break even; Labour initially seemed on course for a defeat of seismic proportions but ended the campaign with realistic prospects of winning next time round. In eight polls conducted in the first four days after the relevant Commons vote, the Conservative lead over Labour averaged 20 percentage points; in the final polls by nine companies the average was just 8 points. What explains this dramatic turnaround?

Put simply, the Conservatives ran a disastrous campaign (see Ross and McTague, 2017; Shipman, 2017; Cowley and Kavanagh, 2018: ch. 9). In the first place, the party machine was unprepared for the snap election its own leader had called. Lynton Crosby, the Australian campaigning wizard who had masterminded David Cameron's unexpected victory in 2015 and was to take charge of the 2017 effort, was on holiday in Fiji when the election was announced and only arrived in the UK a week later. Even if he had been present from the outset, he would have encountered serious divisions at the top of the campaign organization, mostly involving squabbles between Mrs May's close personal advisors, on the one hand, and the campaign professionals and cabinet ministers, on the other. Everyone agreed that the Conservatives should cash in on the popularity of the Prime Minister but she and her closest colleagues saw the election as an opportunity to promote a radical domestic policy agenda. Others (including Crosby) saw no reason to depart from clear and simple messages. Meanwhile, the staff at party headquarters suddenly found themselves in a frantic race to organize the campaign (as well as get candidates in place). In particular, arrangements for online campaigning—about the importance of which, astonishingly, May's advisors were sceptical—were particularly poorly developed (Shipman, 2017: 239). In addition, early complacency meant that campaigners on the ground—even including candidates—were diverted from supposedly 'safe' Conservative seats into marginal Labour-held constituencies. As it turned out, some of those apparently safe seats were lost, while none of the marginals held by Labour were gained.

Second, and more importantly, while the decision to focus the campaign on Theresa May's 'strong and stable leadership'—with local candidates being instructed to describe themselves as 'standing with Theresa May' in posters, leaflets, and so on—was not in itself a serious error, the Prime Minister's advisors undermined it by their insistence that, on domestic issues, she should be presented as a candidate for 'change' as much as 'continuity'. This twin-track approach left May with the considerable challenge of appealing to two different audiences—those who wanted a hard-nosed, business-like government as well as those who hoped for radical policies which would bring the 'age of austerity' to an end. If Mrs May had already secured (or inherited) an overwhelming parliamentary majority, it is possible that she could have left both of these audiences broadly satisfied. However, she and her advisors forgot that in order to reach that position, her party would have to win the election; and it turned out that, rather than relishing the prospect of enthusing voters from across the ideological spectrum,

May was reluctant even to play to her core supporters. Although she had a reputation for good campaigning in her constituency, it soon became apparent that Mrs May did not shine, to say the least, in this respect on the national stage. In highly stage-managed public appearances she appeared unable to empathize with ordinary voters and to do little more than recite the same soundbites, irrespective of the audience or any questions that she was asked. Journalists frequently described her efforts as 'robotic' and christened her the 'Maybot'.

At the planning stage, the 'continuity and change' strategy must have looked so persuasive that no one considered the possible consequences if it should go wrong. Other cabinet ministers with more proven vote-winning potential, such as the ebullient (albeit somewhat divisive) Foreign Secretary Boris Johnson, were relegated to minor roles. While the emphasis on Mrs May is understandable, given the message of the polls concerning the relative standing and public perceptions of the party leaders at the outset, the public's evaluations of individuals are very fickle. Politicians can go from the heights to the depths of popularity very quickly and so it proved in this case.

Thirdly, and most importantly, the Conservative election manifesto was a self-inflicted wound. It was drafted by two of Mrs May's key advisors—Nick Timothy and Ben Gummer—in great secrecy and with minimal consultation. Launched during the third week in May, it included policies cutting winter fuel payments for all but the poorest pensioners as well as complicated changes relating to the funding of social care for the elderly. Some reform of that system was long overdue, yet May's plan was bound to provoke an outcry, especially among some traditional Conservative supporters. It must have seemed a good idea to grasp this nettle while voters were distracted by Brexit, but the ruse backfired in spectacular fashion. The proposed funding system was dubbed a 'dementia tax' by critics and polls immediately began to indicate a significant slippage in Conservative popularity. Candidates across the country reported sharply negative reactions among the electorate. Cowley and Kavanagh (2018: 198) note that in the BES rolling campaign surveys 'social care' and 'dementia tax' began to emerge after the manifesto launch as reasons people gave for changing their minds about which party to support. By the following weekend 'care' was the single most significant issue. That same weekend, just four days after the announcement of the policy, the Prime Minister backtracked. In a speech in Wales she said that the social care proposals had been dropped while at the same time trying to argue that in this respect nothing had changed. Reporters gleefully noted that far from providing 'strong and stable leadership' Mrs May now appeared 'weak and wobbly'.

Labour had its own problems in terms of campaign organization at the centre, with divisions and disagreements between the full-time officials and the inner circle of Corbyn enthusiasts. Unlike the Prime Minister, however, the Opposition leader appeared more at ease with members of the public and came across as friendly and likeable. His public meetings (or, more accurately, rallies of supporters) attracted crowds of increasing size, packed with young people who testified to their 'Corbynmania' in a manner usually reserved for pop stars. It was unlikely that the Conservatives and their allies in the press would repeat their successful negative campaigns against previous Labour leaders like Foot, Kinnock, and Miliband; those who disliked Corbyn had probably made up their minds long before the election and drawing attention to his radical ideas ran the risk of increasing his appeal among voters who were growing tired of 'austerity'. In particular, Corbyn's record as an alleged 'friend of terrorists' might have been regarded as a crippling electoral liability for Labour in the aftermath of the attacks in Manchester and London. However, his continued insistence that, at least in part, the terrorist threat had arisen from mistaken British policy, combined with criticism of government cuts in expenditure on the police, ensured that the party's steady rise in the polls continued unabated.

Unlike the Conservative manifesto, the Labour version proposed large increases in public expenditure to be funded, it was claimed, by higher taxes on the rich and corporations. On previous form, the Tories would have focused their fire on Labour's promises and on this occasion the premature leaking of the manifesto, amid considerable publicity, seemed tailor-made for a campaign of that kind. However, this breach of security in the Labour camp worked to the party's advantage; after all, May had insisted that the country needed a radical change of direction, so her party was unable to gain traction with the usual argument that Corbyn and his colleagues were threatening to put the government's achievements at risk. Accordingly, the Conservatives made only a token attempt to discredit Labour's plans, even when senior Opposition figures seemed unfamiliar with the spending implications of their own policies. In effect, the Conservatives allowed Labour's claim to have 'costed' its manifesto to pass unchallenged. Among the consequences was a lack of critical attention to Labour's promise to abolish university student tuition fees and re-introduce grants. It was this policy which was credited with galvanizing support for Corbyn and his party among newly qualified voters, around 45 per cent of whom would either already be at university or be intending to enter higher education in the near future. Recent graduates who would not be affected directly (but who had campaigned against tuition fees since their introduction in 1998) were also likely to respond sympathetically to this policy pledge without looking too closely at the inevitable bill.

Another possible reason for Labour's success in narrowing the gap with the Conservatives was the party's online campaigning. As Cowley and Kavanagh bluntly assert (2018: 311): 'There is little doubt about Labour's victory on the social media front' (see also Ward and Wring, 2018). As already noted, Conservative preparations for digital campaigning were inadequate at best when the campaign began. The party's digital team concentrated on using adverts on Facebook, allocating more than £2 million for this purpose. Labour spent

£1.2 million—much more than in 2015—on their digital effort and, as before, also concentrated on Facebook. In addition, the party made extensive (and inexpensive) use of other platforms such as 'Snapchat' and Twitter, as well as developing software known as 'Promote' to assist local campaigns in targeting specific groups of voters. Labour's biggest advantage, however, was among 'outriders' or 'satellite campaigns'—groups which, while not part of the official campaign, generated masses of relevant online material which was widely shared among users. These were overwhelmingly pro-Corbyn; the most significant was Momentum, an organization formed specifically to support the leader (Dommet and Temple, 2018). As noted in Chapter 6, it is difficult to know whether and how online campaigning affects the probability of voters choosing one party over another. It is likely that those who view online adverts and the like are already inclined to vote for the party concerned. Nonetheless, even a reinforcement effect can be significant and it is difficult to believe that Labour's massive advantage in this respect was not a factor in the party's (and Corbyn's) increase in popularity during the 2017 campaign.

While campaign polls can be characterized as 'snapshots' of opinion at the time, the final polls produced by each company are routinely regarded as predictions of the election outcome. Given a relatively volatile electorate and problems concerning electoral registration and differential turnout among various sections of the electorate, this is not an easy business. Nonetheless, it is surprising that the nine established firms polling in the final week produced estimates of the Conservative lead ranging from one point (Survation) to thirteen points (BMG), with the rest averaging eight points. As it turned out, although most were reasonably accurate as far as the Conservatives (and the Liberal Democrats) were concerned, all (including Survation) underestimated the strength of Labour support—one (BMG) by eight points and two (ICM and ComRes) by seven.

The 2017 Results

While the pollsters had given their final predictions, their contribution to the drama of the 2017 general election was not over until the release of the election-day exit poll sponsored jointly by the BBC, ITV, and Sky News. If Theresa May's decision to call an election had surprised many, the exit poll result announced at 10 p.m. on 8 June evoked astonishment, disbelief, elation, and consternation among the various interested observers. It forecast that the Conservatives would lose their overall majority in the House of Commons while Labour would make around three dozen gains. Although the final tallies were not exactly as predicted, the general message of the exit poll was borne out when the real votes were counted (Table 7.1).

Over the country as a whole, the Conservatives emerged as the largest party in terms of the popular vote with a 42.3 per cent share—an increase of 5.5 points on

THE BREXIT ELECTIONS, 2017–19

Table 7.1 Election results (UK), 2017–19

	2017		2019	
	Votes	Seats	Votes	Seats
Con	42.3	317	43.6	365
Labour	40.0	262	32.1	202
Lib Dem	7.4	12	11.6	11
Others	10.3	59	12.7	72
Turnout	*68.9*		*67.5*	

Note: Figures for Votes are percentages.

their 2015 performance. In these terms this was the party's best result since 1983—a point often overlooked in subsequent commentary, which tends to give the impression that the Tory campaign was so bad that no rational individual would have voted for the party. Nevertheless, the outcome was dismal in comparison to initial expectations. By contrast, Labour's share of the vote compared with 2015 rose by 9.6 points, to 40.0 per cent. This 2 per cent swing to Labour—while certainly not sensational by historic standards—produced a net gain of thirty seats for the party, while the Conservative tally fell by thirteen. The result was hailed as a personal triumph for Jeremy Corbyn, partly because Labour's poll rating had been so low at the beginning of the campaign, but also because it was enough to deprive Theresa May of a majority in the House of Commons. Nevertheless, Labour had lost a third consecutive election, despite on this occasion fighting a party which had run a poor campaign and tacitly attacked its own record in office since 2010 by calling for radical change.

The Liberal Democrats' vote share declined even further from their 2015 debacle to just 7.4 per cent, although they managed to gain four seats. The party leader, Tim Farron, held on to his constituency of Westmorland and Lonsdale by only 777 votes (as compared with almost 9,000 in the difficult circumstances for Liberal Democrats that prevailed in 2015). After a very strong performance in 2015, the 2017 election reduced UKIP to insignificance with only 1.8 per cent of votes. The Greens also fell to just 1.6 per cent and, although the party's joint leader easily retained her seat in Brighton, they remained confined to the political fringe. Apparently, the 'rise of the others' which was discussed in Chapter 6 had gone sharply into reverse. Together, the Conservatives and Labour won 82.3 per cent of the UK vote—their largest combined share since 1970.

In terms of swing—which could now be resurrected as a meaningful measure of electoral change given the dominance of the two major parties—there were marked differences across English regions. In the North East there was actually a small movement to the Conservatives (0.3 per cent) while in Yorkshire/Humberside and the Midlands the swing to Labour was below the nationwide figure. In the South East (3.7 per cent) and South West (3.3 per cent) the pro-Labour swing was above average but the most 'deviant' English 'region' was London. In 2015, the capital had seen a much larger increase in Labour's vote share than anywhere else and in 2017 the trend continued with a swing of 6.3 per cent to Labour. There was clearly a yawning political rift between London and (most of) the rest of the country. This had been evident, of course, in the EU referendum in 2016 when London was the only 'region' of England and Wales that voted to remain in the EU (and did so by a large margin).

The most striking 'regional' result in 2017, however, relates to Scotland. Here, the Conservatives rose to second place with 28.6 per cent of votes and thirteen seats (twelve gained from the SNP) ahead of Labour on 27.1 per cent. Most unusually, the Scottish results did something to spare Conservative (and Theresa May's) blushes on election night. Nonetheless, Labour's small improvement in vote share enabled the party to take six 'low-hanging' seats from the SNP. Even the Liberal Democrats managed to cash in on the SNP's relative decline in popularity despite an almost unchanged vote share, taking three of the latter's seats to raise their total to four. Although the SNP boost following the 2014 referendum appeared to have petered out and the party now had to defend a contestable record in governing Scotland, the erosion of its 2015 electoral support (down from 50.0 to 36.9 per cent) could not be seen as a restoration of trust in the Westminster-based 'unionist' parties. In particular, the Conservative campaign in Scotland had been largely independent of the operation directed from London and the party's Scottish leader, Ruth Davidson, was considerably more popular there than Theresa May. In addition, the Conservatives were now clearly the most authentically and most strongly pro-union force and hence in a position to gather votes from other parties opposed to Scottish independence.

The 2017 election results in Northern Ireland are worth noting, especially in the light of subsequent events (for a detailed discussion, see Tonge and Evans, 2018). Here, there was confirmation of the pre-existing trend towards two-party dominance. The Democratic Unionist Party (DUP) led with 36.0 per cent of votes and ten seats followed by Sinn Fein on 29.4 per cent of votes and seven seats (with the remaining seat being taken by the Independent Unionist, Lady Sylvia Hermon).

The interactions between changes in the parties' vote shares at constituency level in England and Wales are explored in Table 7.2. Scotland is excluded due to complications arising from the strength of the SNP. As a reminder, negative correlation coefficients indicate that where one of the parties concerned fared better, the other had poorer results while positive figures mean that the two parties tended to rise and fall together. The Conservatives clearly benefitted from the decline in UKIP support and the relationship between Conservative gains and UKIP losses was very strong (coefficient = −0.80). There was a significant, if not very strong, tendency for Labour to poll less well where the Greens held up best, whereas the pattern of ups and downs across constituencies for the Conservatives and Greens

Table 7.2 Correlations between changes in vote shares 2015–17 (England and Wales)

	Change % Con	Change % Lab	Change % Lib Dem	Change % UKIP
Change % Lab	−0.25	–	–	–
Change % Lib Dem	−0.36	−0.45	–	–
Change % UKIP	−0.80	0.07*	0.10	–
Change % Green	0.32	−0.45	−0.05*	−0.34

Notes: Constituencies which the Greens did not contest in either 2015 or 2017 are excluded, as is the Speaker's seat. N=572 for all cases except those involving the Greens (N=547). All coefficients are statistically significant except those asterisked.

tended to be similar (although this was more a case of the Conservatives doing less well where the Greens were leaking more votes to Labour).

Not unexpectedly, changes for both major parties were negatively related to changes in the vote shares of the Liberal Democrats. However, the most surprising coefficient is that for the Conservatives and Labour. Although this is in the expected direction (−0.25) it is not large, meaning that changes in support for the two were not actually very strongly related. In the pre-dealignment days of overwhelming two-party dominance, an increase in vote share for one would have been matched almost exactly by a decline for the other. The relevant contextual considerations have long gone, however, and it is the comings and goings of large numbers of third, fourth, and fifth party candidates—as well as changes in their popularity—that makes the relationship between shifts in support for the two leading parties less than straightforward.

Table 7.3 shows how changes in support for the major parties in England and Wales were related to constituency characteristics. The coefficients for the Conservatives are generally much stronger than those for Labour, indicating that their fluctuating fortunes were skewed to a much greater extent by the factors involved. Mrs May's party fared much better in seats where there were more manual workers, owner occupiers, people with no educational qualifications and voters aged over 65. On the debit side for the Conservatives, they made less headway the more middle-class the constituency and the more people with degrees. They were also less successful in cities (persons per hectare) and in areas with more privately rented housing and larger ethnic minority electorates. During the campaign and after the election there was much comment suggesting that Labour (and Jeremy Corbyn in particular) was able to galvanise young people (and especially students) by promising to abolish university tuition fees. The evidence in the table supports this interpretation. Labour clearly did better and the Conservatives worse in constituencies with larger numbers of young people and students. The outstanding example of this was Canterbury—home of the University of Kent—where Labour overturned a Conservative majority of almost 10,000 to snatch the seat.

Table 7.3 Correlations between changes in Conservative and Labour shares of votes 2015–17 and constituency characteristics (England and Wales)

	Conservative	Labour		Conservative	Labour
% Manual workers	0.65	−0.11	% Prof./ Managerial	−0.64	0.03*
% Owner occupiers	0.34	−0.26	% Private renters	−0.52	0.36
% No qualifications	0.70	−0.16	% With degrees	−0.75	0.12
% Aged 65+	0.42	−0.24	% Aged 18–24	−0.20	0.34
			% Students	−0.35	0.34
			Persons per hectare	−0.45	0.22
			% Ethnic minority	−0.45	0.18
% Leave in EU ref.	0.79	−0.28			

Notes: N=572. All coefficients are statistically significant, except the one asterisked.

Initially, at least, this election was supposed to be about Brexit and, in keeping with this view, the English regions that moved more strongly to the Conservatives (North East, Yorkshire, and the Midlands) were those that had been most enthusiastic about leaving the EU in the 2016 referendum. The others—especially London—were much less strongly for 'Leave' and displayed bigger swings to Labour in 2017. In addition, the kinds of constituencies that moved more strongly to the Conservatives—those with more working-class and older voters—were reminiscent of the areas that had delivered larger 'Leave' votes in 2016. Although the counting areas used in the referendum were local councils, we can explore this issue at constituency level by using estimates of how constituencies voted in the referendum, prepared by the House of Commons Library (2017), to compare the two votes directly. Across England and Wales, there was a correlation of 0.79 between the percentage voting 'Leave' in 2016 and the improvement in the Conservatives' position between 2015 and 2017. For Labour, the figure is −0.28. Evidently, the more 'Leave' voters there were in a constituency, the greater the boost for the Conservatives. The other side of the coin is that the bigger the 2016 'Remain' vote, the worse was the result for the Conservatives. With some justification, therefore, the election outcome might be characterized as 'the revenge of the Remainers' (not that it did their cause any good).

We will postpone discussion of how the distribution of absolute levels of party support across constituencies was related to social and demographic characteristics (see Chapter 8) so that we can look at this election in comparison to those of 2015 and 2019.

Turnout

Moving from a discussion of party support during the campaign and in the election to patterns of turnout in 2017 is rather like entering a calm haven after battling through uncharted and stormy waters. In this case, there was relatively little change.

Over the UK as a whole, turnout increased from 66.4 per cent in 2015 to 68.9 per cent in 2017. This was the fourth general election in succession to record an increase in turnout from the low point of 2001. Participation by the electorate increased in Northern Ireland (+7.2), Wales (+2.7) and in every English region. Of the latter, the largest rise occurred in London (+4.7) and the smallest (+2.2) in Eastern England. In Scotland, however, the situation was reversed with turnout dropping back (−4.6) from what had been an unusually high figure in 2015. There was much greater variation in turnout change at constituency level, of course, and these fluctuations affected the fortunes of the parties. The correlation between change in turnout and change in Conservative vote share was −0.33—the more turnout rose, the more the Conservatives declined—whereas Labour tended to improve more the greater the rise in turnout (a coefficient of 0.20). This again suggests that 'Remain' supporters were more determined to turn out in order to 'avenge' the referendum result— or, more prosaically, that 'Leavers' who had been inspired to cast a vote on the binary referendum question were less motivated by the 2017 election campaign. In Scotland, a positive correlation of 0.50 (N=59) indicates that the extent of the SNP's decline across constituencies was quite strongly related to the extent to which turnout fell (although this was far from the whole story).

In absolute terms, within England the southern regions continued to record higher turnouts than those in the north. The highest UK figure was recorded in Twickenham (79.7 per cent) while the poorest was in Glasgow North East (53.1 per cent). There were, indeed, four Glasgow constituencies in the bottom ten. Analysis of turnout variations across constituencies in England and Wales in relation to their socio-economic characteristics produces a picture which has held more or less constant for more than fifty years. Seats that are more middle-class, are not in metropolitan areas, have greater proportions of older, more affluent, and better-educated voters once again registered higher turnouts. On the other hand, for the second election in succession there was no significant relationship between previous marginality and turnout. Worries that the sophisticated targeting of campaign efforts on key seats by the parties (and even individuals within them) might lead voters in others (the great majority) to become more apathetic have not been borne out. However, why the formerly strong relationship between marginality and turnout disappeared in 2015 and 2017 remains something of a mystery.

Voting in 2017

We now turn to individual-level data on voting in 2017 and begin by looking again at turnout. During the campaign, as we have seen, it was widely believed that Jeremy Corbyn's campaign struck a particular chord with young people. In addition, the social media effort of Labour and its online allies was credited with significant success in reaching these voters and motivating them first to enrol on the electoral register (with detailed instructions on how to do so) and then to vote (with many targeted individuals even being directed to their nearest polling station). After the election, Labour's relative success in constituencies with more young voters and in university towns, which also had larger than average increases in turnout, led commentators to conclude that there had been a 'youthquake' in terms of turnout in 2017 (see, for example, Whiteley and Clarke, 2017). Indeed, the polling firms themselves blamed their under-estimation of Labour's vote on assuming (understandably, on the basis of previous experience) that turnout among younger respondents would be much poorer than actually occurred. In due course, however, an analysis of BES data from the post-election cross-section survey appeared and effectively poured cold water on these claims (Prosser et al., 2018). The figures in Table 7.4 show the familiar pattern of turnout increasing steadily with age to reach more than 80 per cent among the over 65s. Comparing these with 2015 data suggests that there was actually a *decrease* in turnout between that election and 2017 among the youngest age-group. It was among those aged between 25 and 44 that the sharpest increases in participation were recorded. On the basis of these data, say Prosser et al., 'we can be confident that there was no dramatic surge in youth turnout'. They also illustrate the dangers of inferring individual behaviour from aggregate statistics, noting that although turnout change correlated positively with the proportion of young electors in a constituency there was an even stronger correlation with the proportion of children aged under four! The fact that *places* with more young people had higher turnouts does not mean that it was young people themselves who caused this.

As with age, for the most part Table 7.4 presents a familiar picture of differential turnout. It was higher among homeowners, married or widowed people, the more affluent, and graduates. On this occasion, however, it seems that men were significantly more likely to vote than women. We also show the figures according to vote in the EU referendum and our earlier surmise that 'Remainers' were keener to go to the polls than 'Leavers' is confirmed by the survey data.

In Table 7.5 we show how different groups in the electorate voted in 2017. It is striking, first of all, that occupational class had little impact on party choice. The Conservatives won more support than Labour from skilled manual workers while the reverse is true for 'other non-manual' workers. Among the solidly middle-class professional and managerial groups the Conservatives' lead was relatively narrow; Labour's lead among unskilled workers was even smaller. This weak relationship

Table 7.4 Turnout in 2017

Sex		Housing tenure	
Men	68	Owner occupiers	76
Women	63	Private renters	53
Marital status		Social renters	51
Married/widowed	78	*Highest education qualification*	
Live with partner	49	None	64
Separated/divorced	61	School	67
Single/never married	55	Vocational	61
Age		Professional	70
18–24	43	Degree	80
25–34	56	*Party identification*	
35–44	69	None	36
45–54	66	Not very strong	62
55–64	77	Fairly strong	78
65+	82	Very strong	82
Income		*Vote in EU referendum*	
Top third	78	Leave	74
Middle third	67	Remain	78
Lowest third	70	Did not vote	30

Note: Figures shown are percentages. The original data have been weighted to reflect the actual turnout in the election.

Source: Data from BES 2017 cross-section survey.

between class and party was amply confirmed by commercial polls conducted on or just after polling day (see, for example, the on-the-day poll published by Lord Ashcroft (https://lordashcroftpolls.com/2017/06/result-happen-post-vote-survey/) and the YouGov figures reported in Cowley and Kavanagh (2018: 420–1)). In line with these patterns, the differences in party support according to income level shown in Table 7.5 are very modest. In previous chapters (3 and 5) we have summarized the extent of class voting by using the Alford index and these figures are updated in Table 7.6. On this measure, class voting declined in every decade from the 1960s to the 2000s before falling sharply in 2010, plummeting in 2015, and virtually disappearing in 2017.

In contrast, in 2017 the impact of age on voter preferences was as pronounced as it was in relation to turnout. Labour enjoyed a huge advantage among the youngest age group and a clear majority among all aged less than 45. The Conservatives were the largest party in the 45–64 cohort and, as usual, had a commanding lead among the over 65s. These stark age differences led to talk of a realignment of British politics along generational rather than class lines.

The other variables in the table show that men were more inclined to vote Conservative than women, and homeowners more than those in rented properties. The Conservatives also retained their customary advantage among Anglicans

Table 7.5 Social characteristics and party choice, 2017

	Con	Lab	Lib Dem		Con	Lab	Lib Dem
Occupational class				*Housing tenure*			
Prof. & managerial	47	36	11	Owner occupiers	49	36	8
Other non-manual	41	43	8	Private renters	31	55	8
Skilled manual	46	41	5	Social renters	22	59	6
Other manual	38	45	5	*Highest education*			
				qualification			
Income				None	48	37	3
Top third	47	38	10	School	46	40	8
Middle third	42	42	8	Vocational	44	42	4
Lowest third	38	45	3	Professional	54	34	8
Age				Degree	35	46	13
18–24	22	67	4	*Religion*			
25–34	30	56	10	None	37	44	9
35–44	28	51	12	Anglican	66	22	7
45–54	45	41	8	Roman Catholic	45	47	3
55–64	41	39	8	Other Protestant	46	34	7
65+	62	26	5	'Christian'	47	41	6
Sex				Non-Christian	16	74	7
Men	44	38	9	*Ethnicity*			
Women	40	46	6	British/Irish	47	37	8
Vote in EU referendum				Mixed race	14	79	7
Leave	59	27	4	Asian	20	74	6
Remain	32	50	12	Afro-Caribbean	24	71	4

Notes: Figures shown are percentages. The original data have been weighted to reflect the actual turnout in the election. Rows do not total 100 per cent because votes for others are not shown.

Sources: Occupational class data are from the 2017 BES internet panel and the remainder from the BES 2017 cross-section survey.

Table 7.6 Alford index of class voting, 1960s–2017

	1960s	1970s	1980s	1990s	2000s	2010	2015	2017
Alford index	43	32	25	24	21	17	5	3

Sources: BES main surveys 1964–2010; BES internet panels 2015 and 2017.

and continued to have much less appeal among BAME voters than their main rivals. There was something of a change, however, in respect of education. Unusually, the Conservatives led—quite easily—among those with no educational qualifications while Labour outscored Mrs May's party among those with degrees. This contributed to the picture of a Britain electorally divided into younger, well-educated, metropolitan voters, on the one hand, and older, less well-educated 'provincials', on the other. This was the same sort of divide that had characterized voting in the EU referendum. Unsurprisingly, then, the Conservatives led by

32 points among those who had voted to leave the EU while 62 per cent of those who had chosen the 'Remain' option voted either Labour or Liberal Democrat.

Explaining the Result

In previous chapters we have suggested that 'valence voting' has become the most appropriate tool for explaining election outcomes. A significant element in this approach concerns the electorate's judgements about which party leader would make the best Prime Minister and Figure 7.3 shows the relevant data on this question during the 2017 campaign. As can be seen, although the proportion favouring Theresa May slipped over these few weeks while Jeremy Corbyn's standing improved dramatically, the former still retained a clear lead on election day. The changes in this respect over the campaign certainly help to explain the narrowing of the gap between the parties but, in the end, the party whose leader was the preferred Prime Minister 'won' the election, receiving most votes and winning more seats than any other party. Amidst the jubilation of Corbyn's supporters, the MPs who had failed to prevent him from leading the party into a general election can only have wondered what might have happened under a less divisive figure.

Thus, there certainly seems to have been a 'leadership effect' in 2017, albeit not in the direction one would expect on the basis of subsequent commentary. When we turn to issues, however, the valence voting approach runs into problems. Asked to nominate the most important issue facing the country, respondents to

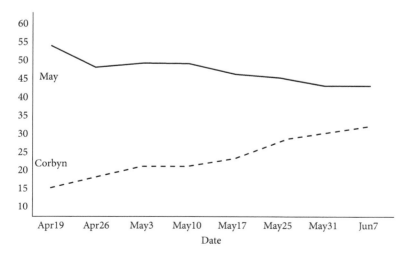

Figure 7.3 Best person for Prime Minister, April–June 2017
Source: YouGov.

the BES post-election survey named four which clearly outscored all others—Brexit (chosen by 35 per cent); immigration (13 per cent), the NHS (10 per cent), and terrorism (8 per cent).The NHS (or 'Our NHS' as politicians of all parties now feel compelled to say) and terrorism are clearly valence issues and Labour had a large lead among those nominating the former as most important (40 per cent, against 13 per cent for the Conservatives). On terrorism, the Conservatives had a surprisingly small advantage (3 points), with almost half of respondents expressing no preference for either party, or feeling that the problem was beyond the competence of any politicians. Previously, we have suggested that immigration could be seen as a valence issue on the grounds that the great majority of the electorate favours controlling and/or reducing the numbers involved. Especially in the context of Brexit, however, immigration also has 'position' elements in that people could disagree about the extent and nature of any controls. In any event, among those mentioning this issue, the Conservatives held a large lead (23 points) over Labour as the party best able to deal with it.

Brexit easily outscored the others as the most salient issue. In the immediate aftermath of the referendum, May (as a lukewarm 'Remainer') was regarded as the best candidate to turn this polarizing 'position' issue into a question of competence, by persuading the public that Britain had made its decision and it was now a matter of the best party to act on the nation's instructions. It is doubtful whether anyone could have surmounted this challenge, given the passions aroused in 2016. However, May (cajoled by her strongly-pro 'Leave' advisor Nick Timothy, and probably wishing to over-compensate for her referendum position) contrived to speak as if the issue had been settled ('Brexit means Brexit') while giving the impression that people who regretted the decision to leave the EU were no longer part of the nation. In this respect, the *Daily Mail* was speaking for the Prime Minister when it dubbed judges 'Enemies of the People'. Thus, in the months before the 2017 election, May pulled off the improbable feat of making 'Brexit' even more of a 'position' issue than it had been during the referendum. People were for it or against it and, as we have seen (Table 7.5) their position on the question in 2016 strongly influenced their choice of party in 2017.

However, if we take a closer look at the 2017 campaign, we might conclude that, far from undermining the 'valence' theory of voting, it is better understood as a dramatic exception which helps to clarify the rule. First, although Brexit provided the pretext for the election, the Conservatives based their campaign on the expectation that an impression of governing competence would be the crucial factor in securing them a crushing victory. So strong was their belief that they would run rings round Labour on this score that Mrs May and her advisers felt it was safe to include controversial policies on position issues—notably social care—in their manifesto. May's subsequent 'U-turn', combined with the initial negative impression created by the policy, undermined the Prime Minister's reputation for competence. It is even possible that this apparent evidence of *in*competence coloured public responses to the terrorist attacks in Manchester and London; certainly May's most direct criticism of Corbyn's attitude to terrorism, launched a few days after her U-turn, had no effect on his rising popularity and the subsequent incident in the country's capital just four days before the election did not inspire voters to rally around the incumbent government as would normally be expected. One can only conclude that if she had pronounced herself to be 'strong and stable', taken no domestic policy risks, and persuaded her media supporters to avoid inflammatory headlines, May might indeed have secured a mandate to 'Crush the Saboteurs'.

Second, Labour's strategists agreed with their Conservative counterparts; if the election was going to be decided by perceptions of relative competence, the government was set for a very clear victory, if not a landslide. As a result, for all their well-attested mutual suspicions, Labour strategists and Jeremy Corbyn's advisers were in accord in their preference for a campaign which focused on position issues—the former because they wanted Corbyn to lose on a radical manifesto, the latter because they believed (with good reason) that the country was crying out for an alternative to 'Tory austerity'. The party's only concession to 'valence voters' was the claim that its manifesto had been 'costed' by experts. Against all expectations, this ruse succeeded—but only because the Conservatives decided not to launch a concerted attack on the economic front. Once again, the overall impression is that 2017 was a position issue election, but only because of the unprecedented circumstances; and that even in this 'position' contest there was a 'valence election' struggling to get out.

All general elections are interesting; some are surprising; only a few can be described as 'astonishing'. The latter adjective certainly applies to 2017. No election in living memory had seen a party start so far behind and make up so much ground. Never had a party leader who started the campaign so low in the estimation of the electorate (not to mention his party colleagues in Parliament) so clearly confounded critics. Equally, however, there is no precedent for a British Prime Minister calling an election in order to capitalize on her presumed competence, then presiding over a campaign which at times seemed almost deliberately calculated to debunk her reputation as a safe pair of hands. Having bet on what seemed a racing certainty at the outset, Mrs May proceeded to hobble her own horse. If Margaret Thatcher really did think that her greatest achievement was forcing her opponents to abandon 'socialism' and re-brand themselves as 'New Labour', Theresa May went one better by making it possible for Jeremy Corbyn to look like a serious contender despite his abandonment of the election-winning New Labour formula. Prolonged exposure to Corbyn did not (as the Conservatives expected) drive the electorate into the Mrs May's arms. In the end, far from solving anything, the election sharpened Britain's ongoing political crisis.

A Return to Two-Party Politics?

The fact that the Conservatives and Labour together captured their largest share of votes in almost fifty years might appear to indicate that the old electoral duopoly made a comeback in 2017 and that the electorate was once again aligned behind the two giants. This would be a mistaken interpretation, however. With a dealigned and volatile electorate it was always possible that in certain circumstances the two big parties would be the ones to benefit. The point is that any gains in support would be driven by transient rather than long-term factors. There was, indeed, a good deal of volatility in 2017 as votes flooded from UKIP and, during the campaign, from the Conservatives to Labour. On this occasion, however, it was the minor parties (including even the SNP) which suffered rather than the major players.

Any idea that the 2017 election marked a return to stable two-party politics would have to be supported by evidence of a hardening of allegiances. Table 7.7 updates the data on party identification which we presented in Chapter 5. In 2017 there was indeed some recovery in the proportion of the electorate identifying to some extent with the two main parties (to 66 per cent) and in those identifying 'very strongly' with one of them. Even so, the latter contingent accounted for only 12 per cent of voters. Although their vote share increased sharply in this unusual election, the core support on which the two big parties could rely remained much smaller than it had been in the heyday of two-party politics. Traditional party loyalties were not reasserted and the scope for volatility remained huge. The next few years would show that anyone thinking that 2017 heralded a revival of traditional two-party politics was suffering from an excess of nostalgia for 'the good old days'.

2017–19: Brexit, Brexit, Brexit

Following the 2017 election, negotiations between the government and the DUP resulted in a promise that the latter's ten MPs would support the government on a

Table 7.7 Party identification, 1960s–2017

	1960s	1970s	1980s	1990s	2000s	2010	2015	2017
Identify with a party	90	87	86	94	85	82	85	84
Identify with Conservative or Labour	81	74	67	77	68	63	61	66
Very strong identifiers	42	25	20	18	12	12	15	16
Very strongly Conservative or Labour	40	23	17	17	10	8	10	12

Notes: Figures shown are percentages. The figures for '1960s' are means for 1964, 1966, and 1970; those for '1970s' are for the three elections from 1974 to 1979.

Source: BES surveys.

'confidence and supply' basis. That is, they would fall in behind the Prime Minister on any votes of confidence in the House and also support the Conservatives on key financial matters. In return, Northern Ireland was to receive increased public expenditure. This arrangement ensured that the government would normally enjoy a small majority (of five) over all other parties (although in practice it was a little larger since the seven Sinn Fein MPs did not take their seats). Mrs May was quick to remind voters of the historic ties between her party and Ulster Unionism, apparently forgetting the fact that under David Cameron the Conservatives had joined forces with the less confrontational Ulster Unionist Party (UUP) *against* her new DUP allies in Northern Ireland. In respect of its policies on a range of key issues, indeed, the DUP was a less natural partner for Theresa May than the pre-Corbyn Labour Party. By acting so quickly to ensure that the Conservatives remained in office, however, Mrs May secured herself a (temporary) period of silence from her internal party critics. Nonetheless, she was forced by cabinet colleagues to ditch her two closest personal advisors (Nick Timothy and Fiona Hill) who had alienated leading members of the government and whose role in the election campaign had been heavily criticized.

After the 2017 election, the government's agenda and the political scene was dominated by a single issue to an extent never before seen in peace time. Mrs May had set out her position on Brexit at Lancaster House in January 2017, when she suggested that the UK would leave the Single Market and the Customs Union as well as withdrawing from the European Court of Justice—an uncompromising position more characteristic of UKIP than of Conservative 'Brexiteers' up to that time. She went on to say that 'the preservation of our precious union' was a key objective of the negotiations, dismissed any 'half-in half-out' solution or the prospect of 'unlimited transitional status' which would resemble some kind of 'permanent political purgatory'; asserted that 'no deal for Britain is better than a bad deal for Britain'; and looked forward to 'a smooth and orderly Brexit'. In respect of the latter her prophetic powers could hardly have been more wayward. Nonetheless, the main elements of the speech had found their way into the Conservative election manifesto.

Although these themes were repeated in other speeches by the Prime Minister, in July 2018, at a meeting of the cabinet at Chequers (her official country residence), she presented ministers with terms for a transitional period after withdrawal which, while technically satisfying her repeated mantra that 'Brexit means Brexit', gave the impression that she had met the EU at least half-way. In other words, she was proposing to dash the expectations which she herself had raised among hard-line 'Brexiteers', who were now faced with the spectre of 'BRINO'— 'Brexit In Name Only'. The suspicion that Mrs May had been persuaded to back down from her previous hard-line stance, and was now hoping to force Brexiteers to fall into line behind a compromise deal, was reinforced by the circumstances of the Chequers meeting, whose attendees were held *incommunicado* and apparently threatened with having to take taxis home (rather than ministerial cars) if they indicated any intention of resigning. Shortly after the meeting, however, David Davis, the Brexit Secretary, resigned, followed swiftly by the Foreign Secretary Boris Johnson. Two junior ministers, two vice-chairs of the Conservative party and four parliamentary private secretaries also departed. Four months later, when May's proposed withdrawal agreement was revealed, along with a 'political declaration' laying down some guiding principles for a final deal, more resignations from the government followed, including those of Dominic Raab (who had replaced Davis as Brexit Secretary), Esther McVey (Work and Pensions Secretary) and (later) Sam Gynah, the universities and science minister. Eurosceptic back benchers were enraged and the agreement was widely and variously criticized as 'humiliating', 'calamitous', 'shambolic', and so on. In particular, Brexiteers (not to mention May's DUP partners), were agitated by the arrangements relating to Northern Ireland, which implied treating that part of the UK differently from Great Britain, and the fact that the UK could not unilaterally withdraw from these arrangements. The rallying cry of the (oddly named) European Research Group (ERG)—comprising strongly Eurosceptic backbench Conservative MPs—was now 'Chuck Chequers'.

Events moved rapidly and dramatically thereafter, although not rapidly or dramatically enough for a public which was clearly suffering from 'Brexit fatigue'. In early December 2018 the House of Commons demanded the publication of the legal advice given to the government in relation to the withdrawal agreement and when that was refused passed an unprecedented motion declaring the government in contempt of Parliament. Just a week later, the House was due to hold a 'meaningful vote' on the agreement but at the last moment the Prime Minister postponed it, claiming that she would seek changes from the EU. This produced a storm of criticism and on the next day Conservative malcontents (led by the ERG) gathered enough support to initiate a vote of confidence in Mrs May as Conservative leader. In the ensuing vote the Prime Minister prevailed, with 200 votes in her favour to 117 against. Although she survived, May was obviously seriously weakened; while she had fared markedly better than the last leader to face a vote of confidence (the arch-Brexiteer Iain Duncan Smith, who had lost by fifteen votes in 2003), her performance compared unfavourably with that of John Major, who in 1995 had won a tacit vote of confidence by 218 votes to 89. As in 1995, however, rather than 'clearing the air' within the party, the challenge to the leader left the Conservatives deeply divided with protagonists exchanging epithets such as 'extremists' and 'morons'.

The withdrawal deal that the Prime Minister had negotiated with the EU finally came before the House of Commons in January 2019 and was defeated by a historic margin—432 to 202. We will not attempt to detail the bizarre parliamentary manoeuvrings and to-ing and fro-ing with the EU that followed, save to note that they included numerous further defeats for the government (one of which involved it losing control of business in the House) and a day which saw the consecutive defeat of several motions recommending different ways forward. The original date set for withdrawal was 29 March 2019, but this was extended first to 30 June, after which the EU agreed that there could be a further postpone-ment until 31 October. None of this enhanced the reputation of Parliament (or its controversial Speaker, John Bercow), with people in the country being variously bewildered, saddened, and outraged that MPs could not reach agreement. Although there may have been some sympathy for Mrs May's predicament, her credibility plumbed new depths. She was forced to announce that she would not lead her party into the next election but calls for her immediate resignation revived when, in late March, she initiated discussions with Labour in order to find some compromise on Brexit. Backbenchers and Conservatives in the con-stituencies were aghast that May should engage with a party whose leader they had continuously lambasted as a terrorist-hugging Marxist. A letter calling for her position to be considered at an emergency meeting of a little-known body—the National Conservative Convention—attracted the necessary number of signa-tures from constituency chairs.

Meanwhile, the Labour party had problems of its own. In addition to discontent over the leadership's handling of Brexit, for some time there had been accusations that anti-Semitism had infected the party, with Jewish Labour MPs in particular being subject to abuse. The leadership, it was argued, had failed to deal adequately with these cases and later the party was subject to an investigation by the Equality and Human Rights Commission. As a consequence of these developments, in February 2019 seven Labour MPs led by Chuka Umunna, the member for Streatham, resigned the Labour whip and formed what they called 'The Independent Group'. They were shortly joined by another Labour MP and three Conservative 'Remainers'. By April the 'TIGS', as they were swiftly christened, had become a registered party named 'Change UK–The Independent Group'.

More worryingly for the Conservatives, a spectre from the past also re-emerged at this time in the shape of Nigel Farage. He had a hand in forming, and soon became leader of, 'The Brexit Party'—an organization with just three official members, to satisfy the Electoral Commission's criteria for recognition as a political party. He was backed by most of UKIP's MEPs (including Paul Nuttall, another former UKIP leader) and indicated that the party would contest the forthcoming European Parliament elections which the government was forced to hold due to its failure to leave the EU by the appointed date. The new party attracted more than 100,000 'registered supporters', who paid for the privilege, as well as substantial donations from former funders of the Conservative Party.

Despite all the impassioned and well-publicized Brexit battles at Westminster and beyond, the popularity of the major parties did not change very much from the 2017 election to the end of 2018. As Figure 7.4 shows, for a brief period after

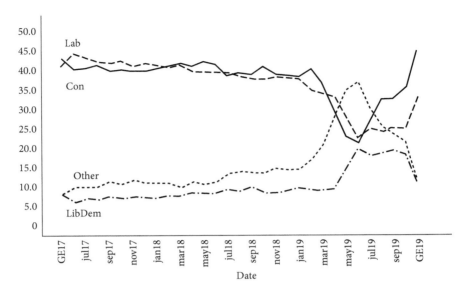

Figure 7.4 Monthly voting intentions, 2017–19 (all polls)

Notes: The 2015 and 2017 election results in Great Britain form the starting and finishing points. The data shown are the monthly means for all published polls.

the election Labour held a small lead but from the autumn of 2017 the main par-ties were running neck and neck in terms of their monthly polling averages, albeit with a slight downward trend for both. There was a small increase in support for 'others' in the summer of 2018 following the Chequers meeting, mainly due to a mini-revival by UKIP (from an average of 3.4 per cent from January to June to 5.2 per cent from July to November). However, the party was not well placed to receive even this modest improvement. The Farage act proved impossible for the party to follow; the next three leaders who made the attempt (Paul Nuttall, Henry Bolton, and Gerard Batten) lasted little longer than Diane James. Batten's appoint-ment of 'Tommy Robinson' (who had several other names, was associated with various extreme right-wing groups, and was ineligible for membership of UKIP) as an advisor prompted the resignations from the party of Nuttall and Farage. Within weeks, sensing that UKIP had become a 'tainted brand', Farage had helped to set up the Brexit Party.

Although she was struggling under unrelenting pressure by the end of 2018, Mrs May could take some comfort from her continuing lead over Jeremy Corbyn as the nation's preferred Prime Minister (Figure 7.5). As we have seen, Corbyn had closed the gap in this respect during the election and for the rest of 2017 May's lead remained relatively narrow. Throughout 2018, however, his appeal faded as his short-comings as a leader (as opposed to a campaigner) became more apparent. Even when the proportion plumping for Mrs May dipped at the time of

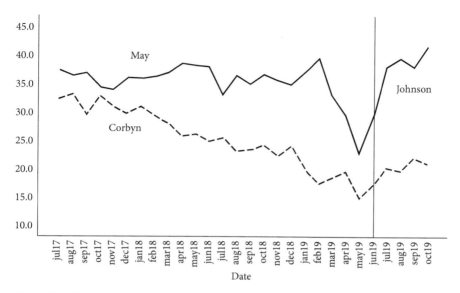

Figure 7.5 Best person for Prime Minister, July 2017–October 2019
Source: YouGov.

the fateful Chequers meeting, there was an increase in 'Don't Knows' rather than preferences for Corbyn. This trend accelerated as it became clear that the government was not going to deliver Brexit on schedule. The proportion of YouGov's respondents choosing Mrs May as the best person for Prime Minister plunged, with more than half refusing to plump either for her or Jeremy Corbyn by April. In the same month support for Farage's new single-issue party began to register and then increased rapidly to draw level with the Conservatives by June.

The poll results were reflected in local elections held across England in early May. Of the 248 councils involved, the Conservatives lost control of forty-four and Labour of six. In the process, the former lost 1,330 seats and the latter eighty-four. While UKIP also lost ground (and neither the new Brexit Party nor Change UK contested the elections), the gainers were the Liberal Democrats (+704 seats), Independents (+605) and Greens (+194). The BBC's 'projected national vote share' was 28 per cent for both the Conservatives and Labour, 19 per cent for the Liberal Democrats, and 25 per cent for others. Although the Liberal Democrats and Greens tried to claim that this represented a success for anti-Brexit forces, it seems more likely that the perceived failures of the 'big two' enhanced the attractions of the numerous alternatives.

After these catastrophic results—the worst for the party since the dire days of 1995—Conservative calls for Mrs May's resignation grew even louder. Showing more fortitude than tactical acumen, she proposed to table a new EU withdrawal bill but when its contents were revealed the leader of the House, Andrea Leadsom, resigned and other ministers made it plain that they would not support it. This time the game was up. On 24 May 2019 the Prime Minister announced her imminent resignation and the battle to replace her was now openly under way.

Mrs May's decision was made inevitable by the results of the elections for the European Parliament, which were held on 23 May. The fact that these contests were being held in the UK was in itself a vivid illustration of the government's failure to fulfil its promises to 'Leave' voters. The Conservatives duly came fifth with only 9.1 per cent of the votes in Great Britain—their worst performance in a national election since 1832. However, the results were at least equally grim for Labour, which managed just 14.1 per cent—the party's worst showing since 1910. In Scotland, indeed, Labour contrived to come fifth in votes, only narrowly ahead of the Scottish Greens. Across Britain, the Liberal Democrats (20.3 per cent) and the Greens (12.1 per cent) fared well but it was the newly formed Brexit party which topped the poll with 31.6 per cent of the vote. The latter led in every English region outside London, as well as in Wales, and even managed to win a seat in Scotland where it came second overall (14.8 per cent), albeit a long way behind the SNP (on 37.8 per cent). In sharp contrast, the other new party— Change UK—virtually sank without trace and six of its eleven MPs resigned from the party shortly afterwards. These results (and the attendant voting intention figures reported by the polls around this time) demolished any notion that 2017 had re-established two party politics and put an end to volatility.

Surprisingly, perhaps, there was no shortage of applicants to succeed Theresa May: thirteen MPs originally indicated a desire to enter the contest. To speed things up, however, the 1922 committee of backbench Conservatives, which was in charge of the first stages of the process, stipulated that contenders should have the backing of eight MPs (rather than just a proposer and seconder). By the deadline for nominations in early June, ten candidates had fulfilled this requirement. In a series of votes by MPs these were whittled down to two—Boris Johnson and Jeremy Hunt (the latter having replaced Johnson as Foreign Secretary). The choice was now down to Conservative party members in a postal ballot. Johnson was the overwhelming favourite and held on to win two-thirds of the 139,000 votes cast despite press attention to his colourful private life. He thus became the third Conservative Prime Minister in the space of three years and quickly formed a government which was avowedly pro-Brexit.

The change of personnel produced an immediate fillip in support for the Conservatives (see Figure 7.4) although Labour also benefitted a little as the popularity of the Brexit party subsided from its June peak and the Liberal Democrat improvement stalled. Entering the 2019 campaign, Johnson's Conservatives enjoyed a clear lead over their rivals (although not as large as that held by Theresa May at the outset of the 2017 campaign). Johnson also quickly opened up a commanding lead over Jeremy Corbyn as the electorate's preferred Prime Minister (Figure 7.5) although his approval rating fell consistently below that of his predecessor during her days of perceived 'strength and stability'.

Following Johnson's accession, Parliament was due to meet in early September. In advance of that, however, Johnson announced that after re-assembling Parliament would be prorogued for five weeks (rather than the usual three during party conferences) in order to allow the government to prepare its legislative programme. As Johnson had no doubt calculated, the ensuing outcry was lost on most voters, for whom 'prorogation' was an unfamiliar concept: although Speaker Bercow denounced the decision as a 'constitutional outrage', public responses were likely to reflect rather than alter existing attitudes to Brexit. A legal challenge was launched and the Supreme Court eventually (and unanimously) declared the plan unlawful, tacitly implying that the Prime Minister had misled the monarch. Under the Stuarts this would have been the prelude to impeachment proceedings but Johnson knew he had no reason to fear a one-way ticket to the Tower.

When the House of Commons did convene on 3 September there began a period in which MPs from various parties who had opposed Mrs May's deal (and who regarded Boris Johnson with considerable distrust) ransacked the parliamentary procedural locker in order to thwart the new government's desire to use the threat of a 'no deal' Brexit in the hope of forcing the EU to make further concessions. At the same time, they rejected the Prime Minister's attempts to call a general election at a time (and in circumstances) which would have allowed him to pose as 'the people's champion'. The Speaker once again allowed MPs to take control of the agenda and they passed a bill requiring the government to seek another delay to Brexit if no deal had been agreed by 19 October. In the key vote, twenty-one Conservatives opposed the government, including two former Chancellors and five members of Theresa May's last cabinet. Next day, all of them had the whip withdrawn (i.e. were expelled from the party). According to those affected, this was tantamount to transforming the parliamentary party from a broad church to a sect. Another MP had ostentatiously crossed the floor of the House to join the Liberal Democrats and at the end of the week two government ministers resigned including, remarkably, the Prime Minister's brother. In anything like 'normal' times, this would have been a devastating blow for a party leader but in the age of Brexit it was just another mundane day at the office.

On the second day of sitting the government introduced a bill to allow a general election to be called but this failed to obtain enough support. Another attempt to force an election, on Monday 9 September met the same fate. Amid tumultuous scenes Parliament was prorogued on this date, but not before Speaker Bercow announced that he would retire at the end of October. His speech was greeted with prolonged applause on the opposition benches and stony silence on the other side.

By mid-October, Johnson had negotiated a new Brexit deal with the EU— although to the casual observer it seemed little different to the one brought forward by Theresa May. However, MPs passed an amendment specifying that Brexit could not be implemented until all the necessary accompanying legislation had been considered. Since this would entail a lengthy delay the government withdrew its 'Brexit' bill. It was re-introduced on 22 October and on this occasion passed its second reading. The hopes of Brexiteers were dashed again as the Commons immediately rejected the proposed timetable for implementation. A final attempt to force a general election under the terms of the Fixed-Term Parliaments Act was made on Monday 28 October but once again this failed to obtain the necessary votes. Next day, however, the government brought forward a bill authorizing an election on 12 December. This required only a simple majority to pass and the Liberal Democrats and SNP indicated that they would support it. Since this made a majority inevitable, Labour reversed its position of the day before and also voted for an election. Once again, the Fixed-Term Parliaments Act had been exposed as a flawed and flimsy piece of constitutional tinkering.

The 2019 Campaign

As in 2017, the 2019 election campaign saw significant changes in levels of party support, underlining once again the volatility of the modern British voter. The October poll averages for voting intentions had the Conservatives on 35.4 per cent, Labour on 24.9 per cent, the Liberal Democrats on 18.2 per centm and the accumulated 'others' on 21.5 per cent. The latter included the Brexit party (11.4 per cent) and the Greens (4.1 per cent). Figure 7.A2 (in the Appendix) shows how the situation evolved over the ensuing seven-week campaign.

As in 2017, Labour's standing improved steadily throughout. Although it was apparent that Jeremy Corbyn was not emulating his crowd-pulling exploits of 2017, by the last week of the campaign the party's average share of voting intentions had increased by around nine points. This was despite the fact that, according to *The Guardian* (13.12.19), Labour insiders were complaining that the central campaign organization was marred by 'clashing egos, confused messaging, and an infuriating lack of clarity about both day-to-day planning, and where the party's battleground lay'. It was not even clear who was in charge (although Seumas Milne, Corbyn's chief advisor, John McDonnell, the Shadow Chancellor and Karie Murphy, a party official, played leading roles) and Labour stuck with an optimistic offensive strategy despite the story being told by the polls.

Also as in 2017—but this time under Jo Swinson who had been elected as the party's first female leader in the preceding July—the Liberal Democrats trended downwards, falling from the high teens to around 12 per cent of voting intentions. Ms Swinson herself attracted some ridicule at the outset by suggesting that she could become Prime Minister, while the party's most distinctive policy—simply to set aside the referendum result and stay in the EU—caused some disquiet among her colleagues and evidently did not resonate with the voters as it became more widely known. The final trend reminiscent of the 2017 experience was a decline in support for others. In the national British context, the most significant of these at the outset of the campaign was the Brexit Party and there was speculation about an electoral pact between the latter and the Conservatives. A formal arrangement was firmly rejected by Boris Johnson, however. After initially declaring that the party would contest almost every seat, Nigel Farage announced that it would not oppose incumbent Conservative MPs. In part because it had many fewer candidates than originally envisaged, the party slid to around 3 per cent in the polls, similar to the levels recorded by UKIP in 2017.

In one respect, however, the 2019 campaign was very *unlike* its predecessor. As already described, the Conservative campaign in the previous election had been singularly inept and this enabled Labour to close the gap between the parties in dramatic fashion. On this occasion, the Conservative campaign strategy—spearheaded by Isaac Levido, an Australian associate of Lynton Crosby specially appointed for the purpose—was ultra-cautious, despite the assumption of party members that their new leader would be far more attractive to voters than the 'Maybot'. The manifesto was uncontroversial and Johnson stuck to a simple script whose main feature at all times was the mantra 'Get Brexit Done'. On one occasion the Prime Minister showed his reluctance to elaborate on his slogan by taking refuge from reporters in an industrial refrigerator. Evidently Johnson's team thought that antics of this kind were preferable to the risk of campaign-wrecking verbal gaffes. Despite Labour's progress over the campaign, support for the Conservatives also increased and their lead was never seriously threatened.

In Scotland, meanwhile, five campaign polls indicated that the SNP was poised to improve upon its 2017 performance (averaging 42 per cent of voting intentions) mainly at the expense of Labour. The latter (average 18 per cent) consistently lagged in third place, far behind the Conservatives (28 per cent). In contrast, the few Welsh polls published once the campaign was in full swing reported that Plaid Cymru was making no headway and that, although Labour was losing support, it continued to be the most popular party.

Although this was the first election to be held in December since 1923, the short daylight hours and wintry weather did not deter local campaigners. The Corbyn-supporting 'Momentum' group claimed, for example, that there were 700 Labour activists over one weekend in the (marginal) Chingford constituency held by Iain Duncan-Smith. Inevitably, however, local campaigning was less visible and less distinguishable from national campaigning as the parties focused more and more on online activity via Facebook, Twitter, Instagram, and so on. For this aspect of campaigning the Conservatives appointed two New Zealanders, with links to Lynton Crosby and a record of successful campaigning abroad.

At national level, party leaders engaged in their usual tours, meeting carefully selected voters and addressing rallies of supporters in the evenings (when not hiding from representatives of the media). Once again, however, televised leaders' debates were the main events of the national campaign and these gave rise to the customary controversy. ITV announced that the first debate would feature only Johnson and Corbyn. This move was challenged in the courts by the Liberal Democrats and SNP but their objections were over-ruled and the broadcast went ahead on 19 November (attracting a very respectable seven million viewers). Another debate involving the two major party leaders alone was shown by the BBC on 6 December, but drew only about 4.4 million viewers. By this time, it would appear, the Brexit-fatigued voters were losing their appetite and just wanted to Get the Election Done. Johnson also appeared on a BBC *Question Time* special (22 November) with Corbyn, Swinson, and Sturgeon, but otherwise refused to appear with minor party leaders. Controversially, this led Channel 4 to replace him (and Nigel Farage who also declined) with an ice sculpture in a multi-party debate on climate change. In addition, the BBC had scheduled one-to-one interviews of all the party leaders conducted by the pugnacious Andrew Neil. Neil's grilling of Jeremy Corbyn was widely thought to have discomfited the Labour leader and Johnson refused to submit himself to the same treatment. Despite all the passion, energy, and column inches devoted to them, however, it seems unlikely that the televised debates, discussions, and interviews greatly influenced voters. No matter how the leaders performed or whether (in Johnson's case) they appeared at all, the trend in party support continued relentlessly on its path.

As in numerous previous elections there was a good deal of discussion concerning tactical voting in 2019, with websites offering relevant advice. Unusually, however, this had practical effects. In the first place, as we have seen, Nigel Farage decided not to oppose incumbent Conservatives with the unconcealed implication that his supporters should do nothing to undermine a government which promised to 'deliver' Brexit at last. For their part, the Liberal Democrats, Plaid Cymru, and the Greens agreed not to oppose one another in sixty constituencies, leaving the best-placed of them to carry the anti-Brexit standard.

An unusual feature of the 2019 election was the number of incumbent MPs who entered the contest under a different label from the one they had sported when winning their seats just two years previously. From the Conservative side, four stood as Liberal Democrats, three as Independents, and one for the Independent Group for Change. Two ex-Labour MPs also represented the latter (the party formerly and briefly known as Change UK) while four were now Liberal Democrats and three Independents. Further evidence of the 'Brexit effect' on past party loyalties included John Major's recommendation of a tactical vote against the party he once led and Michael Heseltine's advice for Conservatives to vote Liberal Democrat. Meanwhile, a number of ex-Labour MPs with a variety of grievances publicly urged people to vote against their former party on the grounds that Jeremy Corbyn was not fit to be Prime Minister.

At the start of the last week of the campaign, three opinion polls suggested a narrowing gap between the Conservatives and Labour. While this encouraged optimists in Labour quarters to think that the 'miracle' of 2017 could be repeated, a degree of panic in Conservative circles was suggested by a warning from the *Daily Telegraph* (11.12.19)—the 'house journal' for Johnson supporters—that the election was 'on a knife edge'. Unfortunately for the paper's editorial team, of the ten firms which undertake political polling regularly in Britain and produced final predictions, the one used by the *Telegraph* (Savanta Com Res) was the least accurate, underestimating the Conservatives' vote share by five points and over-stating that of Labour by three (see https://ukpollingreport.co.uk/). Nonetheless, the averages for all ten final polls (Conservative 43.3 per cent, Labour 33.9 per cent, and Liberal Democrats 11.6 per cent) suggested that the Conservatives were on course for a clear victory.

Despite this solid Conservative lead in the polls, commentators were reluctant to extrapolate from voting intention figures to predictions of the election out-come in terms of seats in the House of Commons. In part this caution derived from the serious underestimation of Labour's performance by all polls in 2017, but there were also worries about the potential impact of the Brexit Party and uncertainties relating to tactical voting, especially in marginal seats. However, the much-vaunted 'Multiple Regression and Post-Stratification model' developed by YouGov, which had proved spectacularly successful in 2017, finally predicted an overall Conservative majority of twenty-eight seats, although the relevant report was hedged with numerous cautionary warnings. In the event, the Conservatives far out-performed these expectations.

The 2019 Results

Not for the first time, the eagerly-awaited BBC/ITN/Sky News exit poll, unveiled as soon as voting was over, provoked the usual violent and conflicting emotions among the various partisans although, on this occasion, there were few expres-sions of outright disbelief or pledges by politicians to consume items of headgear if the forecast proved correct. The poll predicted a substantial overall Conservative majority of eighty-six seats in the House of Commons. As Table 7.1 shows, the actual majority was eighty seats—easily enough to guarantee five years in govern-ment barring some unforeseen catastrophe. Labour ended up with sixty seats fewer than in 2017 while the SNP racked up forty-eight of the fifty-nine seats in Scotland (with Plaid Cymru retaining its four seats in Wales).

In terms of vote shares, the Conservatives improved somewhat on their 2017 tally but Labour fell back sharply, giving an overall swing of 4.6 per cent from the latter to the former. The Liberal Democrats achieved a healthy increase in vote share but the total (11.6 per cent) was a serious disappointment given their per-formances in the local and European elections only some seven months previ-ously and the fact that as recently as October they had averaged over 18 per cent in the polls. The party recorded a net loss of one seat and their defeated candidates included Jo Swinson herself, who was unseated (for the second time in five years) by the voters of East Dunbartonshire.

As expected, the Greens and the Brexit Party were fringe players in terms of votes and seats although Caroline Lucas, the only Green MP, easily retained Brighton Pavilion. The apparently weak performance of Nigel Farage's party was a predictable result of the leader's decision not to contest Conservative-held seats, which apart from other things was sure to deter any potential voters who harboured fantasies of Farage in Downing Street. In the 275 constituencies where it fielded candidates, the Brexit Party's share of votes was 5.1 per cent (the respective figure for the Greens being 3.5 per cent in 494 seats).

In advance of polling day, there were fears that a pre-Christmas election would result in a significant drop in turnout but, although the weather was indeed wet and windy across much of the country, the UK-wide figure of 67.5 per cent was only slightly down on 2017. At constituency level it varied in Britain from 49.5 per cent in Hull East to 80.4 per cent in Jo Swinson's East Dunbartonshire. The pattern of variation across constituencies remained much as before, although it is perhaps worth noting that on this occasion there was something of a return to normality in that there was a positive (though not particularly pronounced) correlation between marginality and turnout (0.13).

Although the shift from Labour to the Conservatives was evident in every English region and Wales (and also in Scotland although the swing calculation is not very meaningful in that case), its extent varied substantially. It was most marked in the North East (8.3 per cent) and above average in the rest of the North of England and the Midlands. In the South East (3.3 per cent) and South West (3.6 per cent), on the other hand, the Conservatives fared less well but the swing was smallest of all in London (2.6 per cent). The more pronounced swing to the Conservatives in the North and Midlands resulted in the party gaining in spectacular fashion some seats which had long been considered very safe for Labour. In Bolsover, for example, the veteran Labour Brexiteer Dennis Skinner was ousted after almost fifty years as MP while Blyth Valley went Conservative for the first time since the seat's creation in 1950. In Scotland, Labour's partial 2017 recovery fizzled out, as its 2019 vote share slumped by ten points (to 18.6 per cent), leaving Ian Murray in Edinburgh South as once again the party's sole Scottish-based representative at Westminster. The Conservatives also fell back (to 25.1 per cent), losing seven seats, but nonetheless retained second place while the Liberal Democrats (9.3 per cent) won four seats (gaining North East Fife to balance the loss of Jo Swinson). The beneficiary of these developments was the SNP (on 45 per cent of votes) which lost no time in hailing its overwhelming victory (in terms of seats, at least) as a mandate for a second Independence referendum. In Wales, in contrast, nationalist support declined a little (to 9.9 per cent) and, while Labour remained the largest party (on 40.9 per cent), the Conservatives were not far behind (36.1 per cent).

Taken together with regional variations in 2017 the two 'Brexit elections' clearly involved a weakening of the North–South electoral divide illustrated and discussed in Chapter 4; we return to this topic in the final chapter. We will also reassess the other electoral divide previously discussed—that between urban and rural areas—which remained striking in 2019. Labour won more than half of the votes (and the Conservatives made least progress) in the very urban constituencies (mainly in cities) but less than 20 per cent in rural seats, while the respective Conservative scores were 30 and almost 60 per cent.

Turning to the smaller parties, the Liberal Democrats clearly had more appeal in the South than in the North and Midlands, and the same is true of the Green Party. In the case of the Brexit Party the reverse is the case—the further south one travels in England, the poorer was the Brexit performance. In part this reflects the pattern of Brexit candidatures but in seats which it contested the party scored 7.5 per cent in the North, 4.3 per cent in the Midlands, and just 2.6 per cent in the South.

As ever, constituency-level changes in party support varied much more than regional trends. Although most media coverage gives the impression that modern general elections are essentially national contests between competing party leaders, the fact remains that they involve 650 separate elections in the constituencies. Consequently, local issues, events, and traditions, as well as demographic changes, campaigning at the grass roots, and the qualities of individual candidates, all have a part to play in affecting results. In 2019, in particular, as we have seen, a number of MPs who had resigned from their parties, or had the whip withdrawn, attempted to retain their seats by standing again under a variety of labels. In England and Wales, twenty-nine seats produced a swing to Labour while the size of the swing to the Conservatives varied from 0.1 per cent (Sefton Central) to a massive 18.4 per cent in Bassetlaw (a Nottinghamshire seat whose voters had sided very heavily with 'Leave' in 2016 and whose outgoing MP, John Mann (a vehement critic of Jeremy Corbyn) subsequently accepted a peerage from the Johnson government).

Although the party increased its support by just over four points across Britain between 2017 and 2019, the Liberal Democrat vote share fell in thirty-eight constituencies where they stood on both occasions (and by more than ten points in five) but shot up by more than twenty points in seven. In Scotland, while the SNP improved its position in all but one constituency, the upturn ranged from just over 1 percentage point to more than 14. In Wales, in the thirty-six seats contested in both 2017 and 2019, Plaid Cymru fell back in fifteen, moved forward in twenty-one, and was unchanged in one. Clearly, then, the changing distribution of party support was far from uniform across the constituencies.

Table 7.8 shows how constituency-level changes in party support were inter-related. It is worth noting, first, that Conservative and Labour changes were even more weakly related than in 2017 (coefficient = −0.22) emphasizing yet

Table 7.8 Correlations between changes in vote shares 2017–19 (England and Wales)

	Change % Con	Change % Lab	Change % Lib Dem	Change % Brexit
Change % Lab	−0.22	–	–	–
Change % Lib Dem	−0.50	−0.18	–	–
Change % Brexit	−0.06*	−0.55	−0.25	–
Change % Green	−0.02*	0.03*	−0.25	−0.03*

Notes: The coefficients that are not statistically significant are asterisked. N=571 in all cases. The Speakers' seats in 2017 and 2019 are excluded.

again that electoral competition is much more complicated than in the days of two-party dominance (even excluding Scotland). More interesting are the effects of the other parties. Conservative vote changes were much more strongly related to Liberal Democrat performance (coefficient = −0.51). This is not surprising in the context of the 2019 election: the Conservatives campaigned for a swift exit from the EU while the Liberal Democrats argued that the UK should remain a member. The relationship is consistent with the interpretation that a segment of voters with a strong preference for 'Remain' were willing to follow Lord Heseltine's advice, switching their vote from the Conservatives to the Liberal Democrats. It is also unsurprising that changes involving the latter and the Greens are negatively related, as these parties tend to appeal to the same sorts of voters. More puzzling is the fact that stronger Brexit Party performances were associated with smaller improvements by the Liberal Democrats, given that the two parties espoused diametrically opposite policies on Britain's relationship with the EU. It is also the case that Jo Swinson's party clearly performed less well where the Brexit Party took to the field (+2.6 points overall) compared with constituencies where Farage's forces were absent (+5.7 points). This probably reflects the fact that the (Conservative-held) seats uncontested by Brexit are more fertile ground for the Liberal Democrats although it may also be that, elsewhere, Brexit simply provided an alternative choice for voters unwilling to support either of the two main parties.

The strongest correlation of all, however, relates to the Brexit Party and Labour (−0.55). Clearly, the better the new party's performance the more Labour suffered. In contrast, there was no significant relationship between changes in support for the Conservatives and the 'Brexiteers'. This gives considerable support to the argument of Nigel Farage during and after the election that his party's presence helped the Conservatives and hurt Labour. Indeed, Farage suggested that the Conservatives won or came close in a number of seats which they would have had no chance of winning had not a Brexit candidate siphoned votes from Labour. There is some substance to this as there were twenty seats won by the Conservatives in which their majority was smaller than the number of votes cast for the Brexit Party. It is even possible that the 'Brexit Party effect' was more helpful to the Tories than would have been the case if there had been a formal pact, which some voters might have regarded as a cynical manoeuvre.

On this occasion a full table of correlations between changes in major party support and the social and demographic characteristics of constituencies would be superfluous, since the 2017–19 patterns are very similar to those for 2015–17. As in the latter case, in 2019 the Conservatives clearly did better and Labour worse the more manual workers and people without educational qualifications there were in a constituency. In contrast, the more professional and managerial workers and people with a degree there were, the weaker the improvement for the Conservatives and the better (or 'less worse') the change in Labour support. In short, working-class areas moved more strongly from Labour to the Conservatives than did middle-class areas. Again, as in 2017, there is a strong positive correlation (0.67) between the estimated percentage 'Leave' vote in 2016 and the change in Conservative vote share and negative relationships for Labour (−0.40) and the Liberal Democrats (−0.27). One partial change from the comparable analysis of 2017 results concerns young people and students. In 2019, Labour offered the same policy on tuition fees; but the changes in the party's vote share were not as strongly related to the presence of the intended beneficiaries (coefficients of 0.17 and 0.24, respectively).

As far as the Liberal Democrats are concerned, their advance was clearly strongest in more middle-class constituencies and weakest in those that are more working-class. Repeating this analysis for Scotland reveals that there was no significant relationship between any of the social and demographic variables and changes in support for Labour and the SNP. Here, it was more a case of the nationalists gaining (and Labour losing) ground across the board.

Finally in this section, we consider how the correlates of variations in Conservative and Labour support across constituencies changed in the three elections from 2015. Table 7.9 presents the relevant data. Some very clear trends emerge from the mass of detail. Thus, over these three elections the occupational class composition of constituencies became a much weaker predictor of the level of major party support, to the extent that in 2019 the proportion of manual workers was unrelated to Conservative vote share, which in turn was barely affected by the proportion in professional and managerial occupations. It is salutary to note that, in comparison, back in 1966 the relevant coefficients were −0.68 and 0.71 for the Conservatives and 0.74 and −0.83 for Labour. The educational variables associated with the 'middle-classness' of an area (per cent with degrees and of those with no qualifications) also weakened markedly over these years. On the other hand, the proportion of students in a constituency became a negative factor for the Conservatives and a positive one for Labour. As noted above, it was apparent in the 2017 election results that Labour polled particularly well in university towns and constituencies. Labour's policy on tuition fees, apparently, produced a significant electoral dividend and in 2019 the level of support for the party (if not

Table 7.9 Correlations between party shares of vote and constituency characteristics, 2015–19 (England and Wales)

	Conservative			Labour		
	2015	2017	2019	2015	2017	2019
% Prof./managerial	0.53	0.30	0.09	−0.43	−0.40	−0.34
% Manual workers	−0.27	−0.27	−0.07*	0.41	0.36	0.28
% Owner occupiers	0.58	0.70	0.70	−0.62	−0.65	−0.68
% Social renters	−0.65	−0.67	−0.63	0.69	0.68	0.66
% Private renters	−0.29	−0.48	−0.52	0.31	0.38	0.46
% Aged 18–24	−0.46	−0.54	−0.53	0.40	0.46	0.51
% Aged 65+	0.45	0.60	0.63	−0.60	−0.63	−0.66
% In agriculture	0.31	0.37	0.39	−0.47	−0.47	−0.45
Persons per hectare	−0.42	−0.58	−0.62	0.53	0.56	0.61
% With degrees	0.30	0.03*	0.16	−0.22	−0.18	−0.10
% No qualifications	−0.48	−0.23	−0.04*	0.40	0.34	0.25
% Students	−0.40	−0.53	−0.56	0.36	0.42	0.50
% With no car	−0.70	−0.79	−0.76	0.75	0.76	0.77
% Ethnic minority	−0.35	−0.52	−0.54	0.52	0.54	0.59
% Leave 2016	0.07	0.37	0.53	−0.12	−0.18	−0.28

Notes: N=572. All coefficients are statistically significant except those asterisked.

the *change* in that level) continued to be boosted by the presence of large numbers of students in a constituency. Population density and the associated characteristics of the percentages of young voters, of people in private rented accommodation, and of BAME residents, all followed the same trajectory—becoming more strongly positive for Labour and negative for the Conservatives. On the other hand, increasing proportions of older people and owner occupiers in a constituency became more strongly associated with better Conservative and worse Labour results over the three elections. Unsurprisingly, given these trends, the constituency 'Leave' vote in 2016 was an even stronger predictor of the performance of the two parties in 2019 than it had been in 2017.

Voting in 2019

At the time of writing, the results of the 2019 BES face-to-face post-election survey have not been released. However, we can use data from a large post-election poll undertaken by YouGov and estimates made by Ipsos MORI to indicate how different social groups voted (Table 7.10). Lord Ashcroft also undertook an on-the-day poll and the results are very similar to those shown here.

If a psephologist were magically transported from 1964 to 2019 then he or she would be flabbergasted by the figures for occupational class in the latter election. The Conservatives led in every group but their biggest advantage—by far—was

Table 7.10 Social characteristics and party choice, 2019

	Con	Lab	Lib Dem		Con	Lab	Lib Dem
Occupational class				*Housing tenure*			
Prof. & managerial	42	32	16	Owners	57	22	12
Other non-manual	43	34	12	Mortgage payers	43	33	14
Skilled manual	49	31	9	Private renters	31	46	11
Other manual	47	34	8	Social renters	33	45	7
Age				*Highest education qualification*			
18–24	19	62	9	None/GCE	58	25	8
25–34	27	51	11	Other	48	31	11
35–44	36	39	13	Degree	29	43	17
45–54	46	28	14	*Ethnicity*			
55–64	49	27	11	White	48	29	12
65+	64	17	11	Ethnic minority	20	64	12
Sex				*Vote in EU referendum*			
Men	46	31	12	Leave	74	14	3
Women	44	35	11	Remain	19	49	21

Notes: Figures shown are percentages. Rows do not total 100 per cent because votes for 'others' are not shown.

Sources: Data for class, sex, education, and referendum vote are from YouGov. Those for age, housing, and ethnicity are from Ipsos MORI.

among skilled manual workers, while their smallest lead was registered by those in professional and managerial positions. Paralleling these differences, the Conservatives easily outscored their rivals among those with no or relatively few educational qualifications, while voters with degrees gave Labour a comfortable lead. The fact that there were clear age differences in party support and that the Conservatives steadily improved with each step up the age groups is less surprising but the scale of the differences is remarkable. Labour held a huge lead among the youngest voters (+43) but the Conservatives had an even larger advantage (+47) among the (much more numerous) over 65s. These data (as well as the pattern of votes across constituencies) suggest that in 2017 and 2019 a generational divide became more marked than the class divide which had long been regarded as the crucial determinant of British voting behaviour. Ironically, the evident desire of many older voters for a return to the more stable and predictable days of their youth was now itself an important contributor to an overall picture of enduring electoral volatility.

As had now become normal—although, again, this was a marked change from the 1960s—women were slightly more inclined to Labour and men to the Conservatives. Predictably, Labour retained an advantage among those renting their homes and BAME voters. The emphatic stance taken by Boris Johnson on Brexit helped his party to secure the votes of about three-quarters of the 2016 'Leavers' (up from 59 per cent in 2017) but its share among 'Remain' voters fell to about a fifth (from a third). As for the Liberal Democrats, they clearly found most support among professionals and managers with a degree who had voted 'Remain' in 2016.

On the face of it, as previously noted in relation to the 2017 election, the 2016 referendum had effected something of a realignment in British (or at least English) electoral politics, with the division between the parties now involving younger, well-educated, metropolitan voters versus those who are older, less well-educated and living in smaller towns and rural areas. Some commentators have seen this as a sign of the emergence of a new 'identity politics', presenting new challenges for political parties, psephologists, and long-suffering teachers of UK politics (Goodhart, 2017; Richards, 2017).

Explaining the Result

As soon as the results of the 2019 exit poll were announced, contributors to the live television coverage attempted to analyse and explain what had happened. Their attention—and that of commentators in the immediate aftermath of the election—focused on Labour's dismal performance and three topics dominated the discussion—Brexit, 'Corbynism', and Jeremy Corbyn himself.

As far as Brexit is concerned, there was a widespread belief—certainly among 'Leave' supporters—that Labour had helped to stymie the process by voting against withdrawal bills in the Commons, supporting extensions to the dates set for departing from the EU and shilly- shallying about whether a second referendum was necessary. From any perspective, it was clear that the party had been damaged by its policy on the issue, which, compared with those of its rivals, seemed to reflect electoral calculation rather than conviction. Labour clearly lost votes to the Brexit Party and suffered in 'Leave'-supporting areas. As just noted, the Conservatives obtained the lion's share of votes from 'Leavers', but Labour won less than half of the 'Remain' vote which was more evenly split among the major parties. It is worth noting also—although it is largely irrelevant to Labour's performance—that none of the 'Remain'-supporting ex-Conservative MPs who sought re-election came anywhere near success. Dominic Grieve, for example, who was perhaps the most prominent, lost by more than 15,000 votes in his constituency. In this respect, while the 2017 election result could be characterized as 'the revenge of the Remainers', 'Leavers' got some of their own back in 2019. For their part, 'Remainers' could argue that, in terms of vote share, parties opposed to Brexit had 'won' the election (by a margin similar to the 52–48 split in the 2016 referendum), suggesting that the real 'winner' in 2019 was the electoral system.

As in 2017, some of Labour's domestic policy ideas (especially re-nationalization of the railways and greater expenditure on the NHS) commanded widespread support. It seems likely, however, that voters were sceptical about the sheer scale of the spending commitments promised by the party. Having fended off claims that its ambitious manifesto pledges were unaffordable, during the campaign

Labour abruptly promised an additional £58 billion to compensate women affected by changes in the retirement age. Even when the Conservatives were promising to turn on the taps of public expenditure to some extent, this was a jaw-dropping addition to the likely cost of a Labour government. *The Guardian* (13.12.2019) reported worries about 'policy incontinence' even among some Labour headquarters staff.

There is less room for doubt about the electoral impact of the Labour leader. As described above, Corbyn lagged well behind Theresa May as the electorate's preferred Prime Minister for most of the inter-election period and his situation worsened when Boris Johnson took over the top job. On another long-standing measure of leader popularity—Ipsos MORI's satisfaction ratings—the news for Corbyn supporters was equally bleak. From February to June 2019 his average net score (% satisfied minus % dissatisfied with his performance) was −57 (compared with −37 for Mrs May) while in September and October, during Johnson's brief 'honeymoon' period Corbyn plumbed new depths for an Opposition leader, recording scores of −60 in both months.

Corbyn's ratings improved somewhat during the election campaign—in Ipsos MORI's December figures he stood at −44 compared with −20 for Johnson—but there was no miraculous comeback such as had occurred in 2017. Just a week before the election Opinium asked respondents whether they could imagine Jeremy Corbyn as Prime Minister. Only 29 per cent said 'Yes' while 59 per cent gave a negative response. Even among intending Labour voters, 24 per cent found it impossible to picture the indefatigable agitator waving from the doorstep of Number 10. Some senior members of the party were repelled by that vision. In what was surely an unprecedented development, fifteen former Labour MPs placed advertisements in local newspapers on the eve of the election arguing that Corbyn was unfit to be Prime Minister. While the Tory-supporting press ploughed on with their usual campaign of personal vilification, what had seemed ineffectual in 2017 now appeared to be unnecessary.

After 2019: Pandemic

All governments encounter unexpected difficulties—often of their own making, sometimes not. However, the problems experienced by the Johnson government just weeks after taking office and the measures taken to deal with them (involving also the devolved administrations in Scotland, Wales, and Northern Ireland) were unprecedented in peacetime. These difficulties arose not from Brexit—which, for the first time since 2016, was rarely at the forefront of political debate during 2020—but from the arrival in Britain of the global Covid-19 pandemic.

The first Covid cases in the UK were confirmed on 31 January—coinciding with the UK's official departure from the EU—and the first death was reported on 5 March. Rates of infection and fatalities increased slowly at first but escalated rapidly thereafter, with the Prime Minister himself receiving emergency hospital treatment in early April. The government response also escalated rapidly with the whole country being forced into 'lockdown' at the end of March. Everyone was advised to stay at home; schools, hospitality venues, 'non-essential' shops, churches and much else were closed; sporting activities were forbidden even when (as in the case of golf) the chances of transmission were minuscule. Millions of workers were 'furloughed' with 80 per cent of their wages being paid from public funds. The NHS was said to be on the verge of collapse. The situation improved significantly over the summer but a 'second spike' in the disease had always been feared by virologists and its arrival in November prompted a new national 'lockdown'. Thereafter, the government (and also its devolved counterparts) introduced a system of 'tiers' under which different areas of the country were placed under slightly different restrictions. Less than a week before Christmas, however, with new cases again rising quickly, London and much of the South East of England were suddenly placed in a new 'Tier 4' with the tightest restrictions, while previously-agreed relaxations over the Christmas period were drastically revised, effectively scuppering the plans of many. Shortly afterwards, most of the country was moved into the top tier, imposing, in effect, a third national 'lockdown', which was established formally after a televised address by the Prime Minister on 3 January 2021. The crucial difference, on this occasion, was that the existence of more than one vaccine made it possible for Johnson to present the draconian provisions as one last national effort, after which there was a realistic prospect of a return to something akin to the old 'normality'.

Quite apart from a minority of unhinged conspiracy theorists and more plausible 'lockdown sceptics'—who suggested that politicians were being bamboozled by various academic advisors and public officials on the basis of contestable interpretations of the relevant data—there was certainly plenty to criticize in the government's handling of the crisis. Promised 'world-beating' test and trace systems failed to materialize; lack of preparation meant that vast sums were wasted on purchasing personal protective equipment for NHS staff and others. Meanwhile, public expenditure—and hence borrowing—ballooned to levels which made Gordon Brown and New Labour look like Ebenezer Scrooge. At a more mundane level, the Prime Minister's controversial chief advisor, Dominic Cummings, became an easy target for media 'scapegoating' and widespread condemnation when he was caught out in an apparently flagrant breach of the initial 'lockdown' rules at the end of March 2020. He nonetheless retained his position until departing abruptly in November 2020, amid well-attested rumours of faction-fighting among Johnson's unelected entourage.

In times of national crisis it is common for the public to rally behind the government of the day, as happened, for example, in the early weeks of the Iraq War in 2003. There was indeed something of a rally when Covid-19 struck (see below) but the government's difficulties were enhanced by the fact that, while Johnson and his colleagues owed their positions to their pro-Brexit stance, in many cases opponents of 'lockdown' were also people who had sought to 'take back control' by leaving the EU. Nonetheless, polls suggested that there was considerable public sympathy for, and appreciation of, the difficulties that ministers faced. Clear—and sometimes large—majorities consistently approved of the various measures introduced in response to the virus. In addition, the swift authorization of a vaccine and the start of a programme to immunize vulnerable groups in December 2020 were positively received.

Figure 7.6 shows how party support developed over the year. In the initial stages of the Covid outbreak, the governing party benefitted to some extent from the natural desire for national unity behind recently elected leaders, a mood which was reinforced during Boris Johnson's illness. In April, however, Sir Keir Starmer succeeded Jeremy Corbyn as Labour leader and immediately set about 'de-toxifying' the party. Indeed, later in the year, Corbyn's reaction to the report on anti-Semitism in the party published by the Equalties and Human Rights Commission resulted in his being suspended from the party and having the Labour whip removed, so that he was no longer even a Labour MP—the first time that a former party leader had ever incurred this penalty. Quite apart from his attempt to offer 'responsible opposition' to the government in its time of trouble, the simple fact that Starmer was not Corbyn was enough to improve Labour's standing with the electorate. With the Conservatives drifting downwards, the two major parties were neck and neck in the polls by the end of the year. The importance of Starmer in this respect is confirmed by the fact that whereas Corbyn had lagged well behind Johnson in polls asking which of them would be the best Prime Minister, according to YouGov Starmer had drawn almost level with his

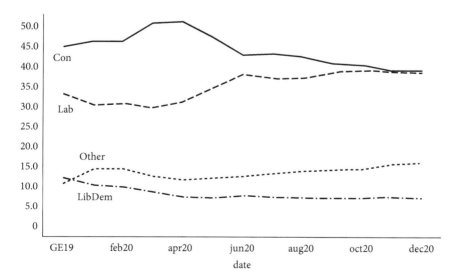

Figure 7.6 Monthly voting intentions, 2020

Note: The data shown are the monthly means for all published polls.

rival by June and led him fairly comfortably from August to the year's end (by 34 per cent to 29 per cent in December with the rest being unsure). Similarly, the satisfaction ratings recorded by Ipsos MORI were strongly negative for Corbyn but consistently positive for Starmer (peaking at +37 in June before declining to +3 in December when Johnson scored −8).

Despite electing a new leader (Ed Davey) in August 2020, the Liberal Democrats made no headway. On the other hand, there was a perceptible rise in support for 'others' from April onwards. This was mainly due to the increasing popularity of the SNP in Scotland where the high-profile handling of the pandemic by the First Minister, Nicola Sturgeon, earned plaudits.

As for Brexit, on Christmas Eve 2020 it was announced that a trade deal had been agreed between the UK and the EU. This was ratified overwhelmingly by Parliament on 30 December, thus (hopefully) bringing at least a temporary lull in a saga that had cost two Prime Ministers their job, brought Parliament into disrepute, and disfigured British politics for more than four years. It remained to be seen whether any of the tangible benefits promised by the 'Leave' campaign back in 2016 would be realized before the next general election—or whether, when the time came, the Conservatives would be able to claim 'getting Brexit done' as one of many examples of 'governing competence'.

Appendix: Campaign Polls

Figures 7.A1 and 7.A2 relate to Great Britain, as Northern Ireland is not included in national opinion polls (data from https://www.markpack.org.uk/opinion-polls/).

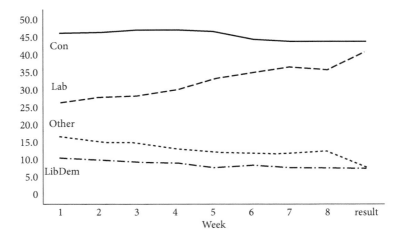

Figure 7.A1 Campaign polls, 2017

Note: Polls included are those conducted after the Commons vote on 19 April authorizing an election on 8 June.

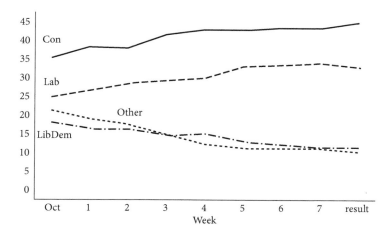

Figure 7.A2 Campaign Polls, 2019

Note: Campaign polls included are those conducted after the Commons vote on 29 October authorizing an election.

8

Conclusion

Diversity, Dealignment, and Disillusion

As the incumbent Conservatives prepared to fight the 1964 general election, they were defending an overall majority in the House of Commons of ninety seats (reduced from one hundred in the 1959 election by subsequent by-elections). In the 2019 contest the Conservatives secured a very similar lead over their combined rivals—eighty seats.

On the surface, it might look as if the electoral wheel had turned full circle in the period covered in this book, despite erratic oscillations in the intervening years. After the 2019 election the Conservatives held exactly the same number of seats (365) that they had won sixty years earlier (admittedly in a House of Commons comprising 650 MPs, compared to 630 in 1964). The Prime Ministers in 1964 and 2019 (Sir Alec Douglas-Home and Boris Johnson) had both been educated at Eton and Oxford, and neither could claim to be a master of policy detail across the full range of government activities. However, in almost every other respect they were very different as were the Labour leaders in 1964 and 2019—the wily, pragmatic Harold Wilson and the apparently unrelenting radical, Jeremy Corbyn.

Lurking behind the headline figures of sizeable Conservative majorities before 1964 and after 2019, however, were contrasts which went far beyond the personalities at the top of the two main parties. In the 1964 general election, the main Opposition party (Labour) won 262 seats; in 2019, the number was 202. The disparity between the parliamentary strength of the official Opposition in 1964 and 2019 is explained by the rise of 'minor' parties, which in the former year were easy to dismiss as 'others'. Ulster Unionist Party (UUP) MPs were then counted as Conservatives and on that basis there were only eight MPs who were not either Conservative or Labour. In the 1964 election the two nationalist parties—the SNP and Plaid Cymru—accumulated a little over 133,000 votes between them; in 2019, their combined vote was almost 1.4 million. The 'others' (including the Liberal Democrats) won a total of eighty-two seats.

Some time-honoured rituals remain in British general elections—the overnight (in most cases) counting of ballots by hand; the announcement of the result in each constituency by the returning officer or (more commonly) his or her deputy; the successful candidate's speech, thanking the staff responsible for running the election as well as the police, and also promising to serve all of his or her

British General Elections Since 1964: Diversity, Dealignment, and Disillusion. Second Edition. David Denver and Mark Garnett, Oxford University Press. © David Denver and Mark Garnett 2021. DOI: 10.1093/oso/9780198844952.003.0008

constituents, irrespective of party. Underlying these tokens of continuity, however, British elections have been transformed. Even (to most people) arcane matters relating to the administration of elections have been altered. The right to vote has been extended to 18–20-year-olds; electors can vote by post if they so choose; the time available for voting on election day has been extended by an hour; candidates can attach a party label and symbol to their names on the ballot paper; citizens can put their names on the electoral register at any time rather than just once a year; rules about campaign spending by the parties have undergone major revisions. Finally, in the first year in office of the Conservative–Liberal Democrat coalition after 2010, legislation provided that general elections should be held at fixed intervals of five years. Although this could be circumvented under certain conditions, the right of the Prime Minister to dissolve Parliament and call an election at a time of his or her choosing was taken away. In a move characteristic of British constitutional change, a major innovation was introduced to serve the short-term tactical needs of the government of the day. Subjected to vehement and well-founded criticism from the outset, the Fixed-Term Parliaments Act was scheduled for repeal in the Johnson government's first legislative programme.

In terms of voting behaviour, a rather smaller proportion of the electorate takes the trouble to vote, and, for most voters, the considerations which influenced their choice of party in 1964 had been superseded by the twenty-first century. The major parties themselves are now barely recognizable as those which contested the 1964 election, and their duopoly has been seriously undermined as the former Liberal Party has strengthened (and then weakened again) and various minor parties have entered the electoral lists with some success. Campaigning used to be confined to a few weeks before polling and—at both national and local levels—was mostly a matter of politicians and volunteers engaging in activities that in many respects would have been familiar to previous generations. Now it is continuous and managed in meticulous detail by public relations experts, campaign consultants from across the world, and party professionals. In addition to an 'air war' and a 'ground war' there is now also a 'cyber war' in the new age of internet electioneering.

In this chapter we attempt to summarize the main changes that have occurred in British elections during our period. First, however, we draw attention to some important ways in which British society itself has evolved, since parties and voters are inevitably shaped by, and respond to, the social context in which they find themselves.

The Changed Social Context

An observer in 1964 looking back over the previous fifty-odd years would have been comparing Edwardian Britain with the 'swinging sixties'. It is no surprise, then, to note that British society—the social context within which politics and elections are played out—has been transformed during the subsequent fifty years. Given that the Labour Party was expressly founded to represent the working class and that in the 1960s Britain was held to be the clearest example of a class-based, two-party system across Western democracies, changes in the industrial and occupational structure are probably most important of all in terms of their impact on parties and elections.

The last census for which data are available was undertaken in 2011 and regular revisions of the industrial and occupational classifications used in official publications complicate comparisons. Nonetheless, it is clear (and well known) that over our period there has been a major shift in the relative importance of manufacturing and service industries. In 1961, about 30 per cent of those in employment worked in manufacturing; even by 2011 this had plummeted to 9 per cent. Employment in agriculture, forestry, and fishing also fell from 4.8 per cent of the workforce to less than 1 per cent. The coalmining industry all but disappeared. In 1961, there were almost three-quarters of a million men working in the industry in England and Wales; in 2011, the figure was close to 40,000, and only three deep coalmines remained. A similar, if less dramatic, story applies to shipbuilding and steelmaking. In 2011, the three largest 'industries' in Britain were wholesale and retail trade, health and social work, and education. Together, these employed 38 per cent of the workforce. In terms of occupations, the years after the 1960s saw the working class, as traditionally defined, dwindle to a relatively small minority. In 1961, 50.5 per cent of those in work (and 59 per cent of men) were manual workers; by 2011, about 30 per cent of the workforce (and 36 per cent of men) were in broadly the same category. Doubtless, these trends have continued in the ensuing years.

Although these industrial and occupational developments began before the advent of Mrs Thatcher, another—a move towards wider home ownership—was greatly accelerated by government legislation after 1979. Between 1961 and 2011 owner occupiers rose from 42 to 64 per cent of households while council tenants fell from 28 per cent to just 9 per cent (although a further 8 per cent lived in what is now known as social housing, in other words renting from housing associations).

To all intents and purposes, then, Britain has become a predominantly middle-class society over the decades since the 1960s. While a substantial group has emerged which is dependent on state benefits (the so-called 'underclass'), the manual working class constitutes a diminishing minority. In the 1960s, it was possible to argue that Labour could achieve electoral success simply by improving its appeal among the party's 'natural' supporters; by 2010, it had felt compelled to become—as the Conservatives had always portrayed themselves in the democratic era—a 'catch all' party, seeking votes across the board from people in all classes. Indeed, under Tony Blair Labour became so concerned with appealing to 'middle England' that it was accused of taking its 'natural' supporters for granted.

The decline in the overall proportion of manual workers has coincided with an increase in women in the workforce. In 1961, in England and Wales women constituted less than a third of the 'economically active' population (32.5 per cent); by 2011, the figure was 46.8 per cent. Put another way, while 38 per cent of women in the relevant age group were part of the workforce in 1961, the proportion had risen to 57 per cent by 2011. The greater prevalence of working women helps to explain the decline of the 'gender' gap in party choice. In the 1960s, Peter Pulzer had observed that 'there is overwhelming evidence that women are more Conservatively inclined than men…sex is the one factor which indubitably counter-balances class trends' (1967: 10). Apart from the fact that women then were more home-centred than men (and thus less involved directly in industrial conflicts), it was also suggested that women were more strongly attached to traditional values relating to the family and religion, and this explained their greater propensity to support the Conservatives. By 2010, however, analysis of the effects of various social characteristics found that there was no significant difference between men and women in relation to party choice (Denver et al., 2012: 222). In later elections, indeed, the gender gap went into reverse with younger women especially being less inclined to vote Conservative than their male counterparts. This may be a consequence of the varying efforts of the parties to appear sensitive to the perceived needs of modern women.

Another politically important area of demographic change concerns the age structure of the population. In 1961, just under 11 per cent of people across Britain were aged 65 or older; in 2011, the figure was over 16 per cent. This modest-sounding percentage point increase represents more than four million extra older folk to be provided with pensions, health care, and other forms of support—and the numbers continued to rise quickly as the post-war 'baby boomer' generation reached retirement. The problems raised by the ageing of the population are illustrated by the fact that, while successive governments have sought to cut spending on welfare, by far the largest element of that expenditure goes on the over 65s. However, given their numbers and their strong record of turning out to vote, the over 65s are very important electorally. The parties—understandably—usually bend over backwards to avoid alienating them. To use an American term, pensioners' benefits—such as pensions themselves, free bus passes and the winter fuel allowance—are like 'the third rail' in an electric railway system. Any party that touches them runs the risk of a fatal electoral shock.

A very visible change in British society since the 1960s is in the ethnic make-up of the population. In one of the earliest textbooks on voting behaviour in Britain, for example, Jean Blondel described the country in the early 1960s as 'probably the most homogeneous of all industrial countries' (1963: 21), and did not even include ethnicity in his outline of the social structure. This is understandable. The 1966 sample census reported that about 2 per cent of the population in England and Wales were born in the 'New' Commonwealth—a rough indicator of belonging to an ethnic minority. By 2011, however, ethnic minorities accounted for 14 per cent of residents, and only 81 per cent of the population were classed as 'White British'. In specific locations with large ethnic minority concentrations, the latter proportion fell to well under half of the population—as in London (44 per cent), Leicester (45 per cent), Luton (45 per cent), and Slough (35 per cent). Again, these trends have continued with immigration from the EU in particular increasing sharply. The growth of minorities has had important implications for politics, parties, and elections. In the 1960s, although the party leaderships closed ranks on the issue, immigration was controversial. Subsequently, all parties have sought to appeal to BAME voters, with varying degrees of success. Nonetheless, immigration and the place of ethnic minorities in British society has remained a highly contentious issue over the whole of our period. The visibly changed ethnic composition of many neighbourhoods, towns, and parts of cities has created resentment in some quarters, and favourable conditions for anti-immigration parties such as the National Front in the 1970s and, later, the BNP. More recently, Britain's apparent inability to limit migration from within the EU also enhanced the appeal of UKIP.

Two other changes in British society with significant electoral consequences are the decline in marriage and an explosion in the numbers of students in higher education. In 1961, two-thirds of people aged 16 and over were married; by 2011, the figure was less than half. Living with unmarried partners (cohabitation) had become much more prevalent, as had single-parent families. Apart from the numerous social problems which some commentators have ascribed to marriage decline, we noted in Chapter 5 that it may also have contributed to lower turnouts in general elections in recent years. As far as students are concerned, in the early 1960s there were just over 200,000 in higher education and 4.1 per cent of 18-year-olds entered university (Robbins, 1963). By 2018, there were close to two million UK students in higher education and close to 50 per cent of the relevant age group embarked on degree-level courses (House of Commons Library, 2020a). Again this development presented policy problems for governments—in particular, how to finance the expansion of the higher education system which was thought to be desirable (especially by New Labour). The approach originally taken after 1945, whereby students received maintenance grants and free tuition, was gradually abandoned and replaced with loans and expensive fees. As we have seen, this issue did much to undermine the reputation of Nick Clegg's Liberal Democrats after 2010. In a number of 'university' constituencies students constitute a significant bloc of potential voters, accounting for 15 per cent or more of the electorate in forty-six seats and reaching 36 per cent in Sheffield Central (on 2011 census figures). As compared with older people, however, students are much less likely to vote, so that politicians are rather less wary of treading on youthful toes, unabashed by the fact that most of the decision-makers were themselves beneficiaries of a much more generous system of student support.

Even this brief sketch is enough to show that the social context of British elections at the start of the 2020s is very different from that which obtained in the 1960s. One does not need to be a social determinist to accept that changes in society, such as those illustrated, have profoundly affected voters, parties, and elections.

Changed Media

The impact of mass media on the values, attitudes, beliefs, and behaviour of those exposed to them—in politics as in other spheres of life—has been the subject of much deliberation and debate. Despite the notorious methodological problems raised by attempts to measure media influence, however, it cannot be doubted that mass media form a crucial element of the context in which general election campaigns are fought and day-to-day politics carried on. Very few people ever meet any politicians—never mind party leaders—in person; and, although no one can evade the effects of government policies, not many can claim even arm-chair expertise across the range of domestic and foreign issues that arise in an election. For the most part, our impressions both of the politicians and policies are gained via media—mostly television but also newspapers, radio (to a lesser extent), and, increasingly, the Internet.

By 1964, television was already established as the dominant source of political information for voters. Partly, of course, this reflected the potency of moving images and the fact that viewing was fast becoming almost universal. But it was also the case that strict regulation forced broadcasters to eschew open partisan-ship, and this made television's coverage of politics seem more authoritative than that of the press. Even so, sustaining public interest in campaigns extending over some weeks was always going to be very demanding for a medium with the immediacy of television. It is not really surprising that voters have increasingly complained of being bored by campaign coverage in elections since 1964—even during contests which were likely to be closely fought. Broadcasting in elections has tended to be designed to cater for the presumed needs of political obsessives, and it is no surprise that the average voter has found this less than enthralling. On the other hand, hardly anyone would welcome coverage which is 'dumbed down' in a bid to attract viewers uninterested in politics. The advent of multi-channel TV in the digital age has at least provided avenues of escape for those who prefer to watch something else. In the meantime, broadcasters have attempted to inject their own excitement, not least by encouraging aggressive interviewing of politi-cians which could be regarded as excessively inquisitorial even in a courtroom.

Although televised leaders' debates had a major impact during the 2010 campaign (if less so on the results) they appear to have declined in significance since then. While they are now established elements of campaigns, the interest of the voters has subsided. Major party leaders (chastened, perhaps, by the 'Cleggmania' stimulated in 2010) have become less inclined to provide their minor party equivalents with previously undreamt of levels of publicity by appearing with them on an equal basis. Nonetheless, the debates (along with lengthy interviews and 'meet the public' programmes such as *Question Time*) are now more important than traditional party election broadcasts. The latter used to be fairly serious and commanded large audiences but are now more like commercial advertisements produced at short notice and often with internet browsers rather than mainstream television viewers in mind.

In the 1960s, there were two pioneering British studies of the impact of television on political opinion during elections (Trenaman and McQuail, 1961; Blumler and McQuail, 1967). Both found that while watching television increased the level of political information among voters, it did not affect their views about party leaders or their choice of party. The impact of television was best interpreted in terms of the so-called 'filter' model of communication. That is, viewers interpreted media messages to fit with their pre-existing predispositions by 'filtering out' uncongenial information and 'filtering in' material that was supportive. If anything, exposure to political television reinforced, rather than challenged, voters' political preferences.

The relevance of these studies to political television today is doubtful, however. For one thing, the authors concentrated on party election broadcasts (finding that people tended to watch those by the party that they already supported), and paid little attention to the coverage of, for example, news and current affairs broadcasts. Today, by comparison with the 1960s, the quantity of political coverage is vastly greater and the quality (in general) much improved. More importantly, however, it was party identification that largely created the communications 'filter' attributed to voters in the 1960s. It was because most voters had strong pre-existing party loyalties that they tended to perceive and remember messages selectively. Thus, Labour supporters would get the impression from broadcasts that Harold Wilson was a very clever man; Conservative supporters would see him as 'too clever by half'. Now that party identification is less pervasive and much less strong, conditions for media influence are more favourable. Moreover, a more 'robust' style of interviewing and reporting (even if 'impartial' in partisan terms) means that the electronic media are more likely to broadcast controversial material which might catch the attention (and influence the opinions) of a less committed electorate.

Nonetheless, there has been no full-scale survey study of the political effects of television since the 1960s, although there has been some suggestive experimental work (see Norris et al., 1999). The reason for this is that demonstrating the existence of such effects is enormously difficult. It may be, for example, that television shapes attitudes over a prolonged period; but that would be almost impossible to monitor. The same problem arises from the diffuse nature of political coverage—from specialized regular features to satirical shows and endlessly updated news bulletins. It is also the case that, as well as receiving information via television, voters are constantly exposed to a variety of other sources of political news and views. Separating out the specific influence of the former would be well-nigh impossible. Nonetheless, there is circumstantial evidence that television can alter people's opinions (and hence, possibly, their votes) in the dealigned age. The increase in opinion poll support for Labour immediately following the 'Kinnock' broadcast in 1987 and the upsurge of the Liberal Democrats following the first leaders' debate in 2010 are two obvious examples. In both of these instances, however, the impact of the broadcasts had declined by election day.

The debates ensured that the 2010 election was dominated by television rather than the Internet, which many had expected to play a more prominent role. Since then, however, political blogging, the use of the Internet as a source of news and, as we have seen in previous chapters, online campaigning have all become vastly more important. Nonetheless, the extent to which voters are persuaded through social media is not at all clear. After all, although left-wing sentiments appear to have predominated in social media, Labour has not won an election since 2005.

Despite uncertainty about the extent to which the Internet is an autonomous source of influence on voters, its growth has undoubtedly played an important part in reducing the number of newspaper purchasers and readers (see Chapter 1). Even when the Internet was in its infancy, the look of newspapers was being transformed by technological changes—with colour pictures rather than black and white, for example, and a marked reduction in the size of many 'broadsheets'. However, the press still plays a major role in politics and elections. Unlike television, most newspapers are avowedly partisan. It has been argued, however, that since the 1990s there has been a perceptible partisan dealignment in the national press (Deacon and Wring, 2002). Most papers now do give space to opposing views, and mixed or unclear messages are sometimes put across, so that, rather than categorizing them simply as either Conservative or Labour, it is better to think of papers' stances in a more nuanced way. Table 8.1 shows, for example, the partisan slant of the coverage in national dailies in 2017 together with the party choices of their readers in that election.

There is clearly an association between the position of the paper that people read and the party they supported in that election. Interestingly, however, the relationship is particularly strong for the (presumably well-educated) readers of *The Guardian* and *Daily Telegraph* among whom only very small minorities voted for the 'opposite' party. An overall correspondence of this kind between newspaper partisanship and vote has been reported consistently at general elections.

Table 8.1 Party choice by newspaper read, 2017

	Paper's party preference	Readers' votes: Conservative	Readers' votes: Labour	Readers' votes: Lib Dem
None		35	47	11
Mirror	Strong Labour	17	73	5
Guardian	Moderate Labour	5	71	16
i	None	15	62	16
Star	None	42	44	2
Times	Moderate Conservative	51	23	20
Telegraph	Strong Conservative	76	11	7
Sun	Very strong Conservative	60	27	4
Express	Very strong Conservative	71	15	4
Mail	Very strong Conservative	71	16	5

Notes: Figures shown are percentages. Rows do not total 100 per cent because votes for 'others' are not shown.

Sources: Party preferences of papers from Wring and Deacon (2018: 349–50). Voting data from BES 2017 internet panel.

This does not mean, however, that there is a simple causal flow from reading a particular paper and voting for its preferred party. Those who choose to read *The Guardian* or the *Daily Telegraph* are likely to have distinctive political outlooks in the first place (and, it might be thought, to be among the minority who still feel a strong allegiance, or at least a definite antipathy, to one of the parties). The papers, therefore, have not necessarily converted their readers but may have reinforced existing predispositions. This was the explanation presented by Butler and Stokes in the 1960s. They conceded, however, that newspapers played 'some role in changing the relative strength of the parties in the short run as well as in forming and conserving more enduring party allegiances' (1969: 244).

As with television, the growth of a more free-floating and less partisan electorate has made it more likely that the press could influence attitudes towards parties and leaders. Some later studies have shown significant—if not sensational—effects when a relatively lengthy period of time is examined (Miller, 1991; Curtice and Semetko, 1994). Nonetheless, the famous claim of *The Sun*, two days after the 1992 election ('It's the Sun Wot Won It') following its campaign of vilification against Neil Kinnock was surely hyperbole. In 2017 a similar campaign against Jeremy Corbyn appeared to have no effect although some Labour-leaning commentators returned to the theme of bias in the 'Tory press' to explain the party's defeat and

Corbyn's abysmal ratings in 2019. Whatever the truth of such claims, it seems likely that, even with a much reduced readership and despite being widely mistrusted, newspapers have more influence on the public's political perceptions and preferences today than they did when the voters were strongly aligned with their traditional parties and (paradoxically) when the papers themselves had more clearly defined allegiances. That helps to explain, no doubt, the enormous efforts that the parties make to influence the media in general and to establish or maintain a cosy relationship with the press—especially the tabloids with larger readerships. After the 2010 general election, the Leveson Inquiry into the practices of the press revealed something of the depths to which politicians were prepared to descend in order to maintain a positive media profile. Lord Leveson (2012: 26) concluded:

> Taken as a whole, the evidence clearly demonstrates that, over the last 30–35 years and probably much longer, the political parties of UK national Government and of UK official Opposition, have had or developed too close a relationship with the press in a way which has not been in the public interest. In part, this has simply been a matter of spending a disproportionate amount of time, attention and resource on this relationship in comparison to, and at the expense of, other legitimate claims in relation to the conduct of public affairs. In part, it has been a matter of going too far in trying to control the supply of news and information to the public in return for the hope of favourable treatment by sections of the press, to a degree and by means beyond what might be considered to be the fair and reasonable (albeit partisan) conduct of public debate.

The influence of the press on elections, then, clearly extends far beyond newspapers' expressed support for a party during an election campaign. Newspapers can influence (or even dictate) the agenda of day-to-day politics between elections (as illustrated by the *Telegraph*'s revelations about MPs expenses in 2009), build up flattering (or negative) images of individual politicians, provide valuable support for governments, or undermine them with a daily diet of critical coverage. Even if the impact on individual attitudes is uncertain, voters—and also the candidates among whom they have to choose—come to elections in a political context which the press has played a large part in shaping. In 1931, Stanley Baldwin accused newspaper proprietors of aiming to wield 'power without responsibility'; despite falling circulations at the time of the Leveson Inquiry, many observers had come to think that to a considerable extent this goal had been achieved.

Changed Electoral Geography

In Chapter 4 we illustrated and discussed the so-called 'North–South divide' and the divergence in party support between urban and rural areas over the period from 1964 to 1992. These aspects of Britain's electoral geography are updated in this section and Figure 8.1 shows regional (and Welsh) deviations from the national picture in elections to 2019. On this occasion Scotland is excluded as the prominence of the SNP in the later elections makes comparing relative support for the Conservatives and Labour less meaningful.

The divergence between the North and South of England (outside London) moderated somewhat after 1992 but subsequently revived to reach a new peak in 2015. In the two succeeding elections, however, the two moved closer together again in respect of their relative support for the two major parties. Even so the 'divide' remains an important feature of English electoral geography. The Midlands, meanwhile, having been close to the national average until 2005 has clearly deviated towards the Conservatives since then, while Wales has become gradually less pro-Labour over the period as a whole. The most striking change in the graph, however, concerns London. The gap between the Conservatives and Labour there closely resembled that in Britain as a whole until 1992. Thereafter, however, the capital became more strongly Labour with the trend becoming particularly marked in the elections of the 2010s. By 2019, London was by far the most deviantly pro-Labour 'region' in Britain. For some commentators this was further evidence that the city is home to a 'metropolitan liberal elite' which is out of touch with the rest of the country. An alternative view is that London is the only part of Britain

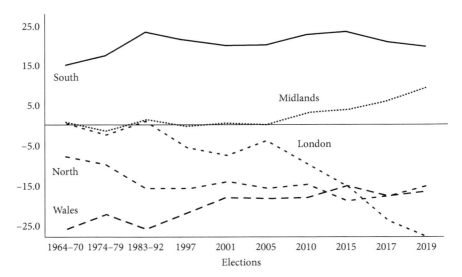

Figure 8.1 Regional deviations from national (GB) Conservative lead over Labour, 1964–2019

Note: The names and boundaries of English regions were revised in 1994. From 1997, 'North' here includes the North East, North West, and Yorkshire and Humber regions; 'Midlands' comprises East and West Midlands; and 'South' covers Eastern England, South East, and South West. The fact that we have combined regions means that the data from the periods before and after the changes are comparable.

which has remained 'in touch' with 'globalized' modernity. From either perspective, it is difficult to deny that London is 'different'.

Although it is not illustrated in Figure 8.1, it is worth noting that there is also a North–South divide in terms of support for Britain's third party—the Liberals and then the Liberal Democrats. Taking account of the national level of support, in the 1960s the former were much less popular in the north of England than in the south. The gap had narrowed significantly by 1983, however, before increasing again in the next three elections. It then declined from 1997 to 2010 but after that the divide widened sharply and by the last two elections of the period was greater than it had been even in the 1960s.

The other geographical divide considered in Chapter 4 is that between big cities and other heavily urban areas, on the one hand, and smaller towns and rural areas, on the other. The long-term trends in this case are shown in Figure 8.2 and the picture could hardly be clearer. Compared with the 1960s, the partisan polarization between more urban and more mixed or rural areas of the country had increased by the 1980s and this trend continued thereafter. In the 2010s, as the very urban areas rapidly moved away from the Conservatives and the mixed and rural areas became even more inclined towards them, the gap became truly enormous. To an extent, of course, the trend in very urban areas is affected by the trend in London but it is also evident elsewhere. For example, in 1997, in the five largest English cities outside London taken together (Birmingham, Liverpool, Sheffield, Bristol and Leeds), Labour's vote share exceeded the Britain-wide figure

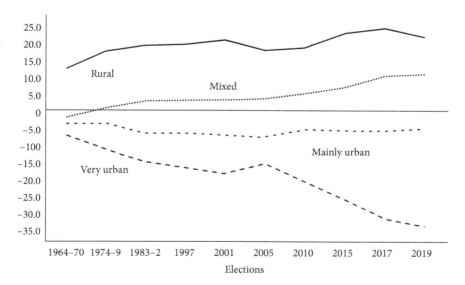

Figure 8.2 Urban–rural deviations from national (GB) Conservative lead over Labour, 1964–2019

Note: See also Figure 4.5.

by 13 points; in 2019 the difference was over 26 points. This growing gap has led some analysts to suggest that the main geographical electoral divide in England is not so much between the North and the South as between the cosmopolitan and liberal-minded residents of cities (and university towns) and a more 'provincial' electorate in smaller towns and the countryside (see Jennings and Stoker, 2017). This contrast was evident, of course, in voting in the 2016 EU referendum. Nonetheless, it is clear that the North–South and urban–rural divisions overlie one another. In 2019, for example, although the expected urban–rural pattern was apparent within both the North and the South, in every category Labour performed better and the Conservatives worse in the former than in the latter.

Change in Electoral Behaviour

Throughout the book we have referred to major changes in the processes by which citizens decide whether to vote and which party to support. As far as turning out on election day (or, nowadays, voting by post) is concerned, the kinds of people more likely to make the effort—strong party supporters, older people, well-educated professionals, those who are married or widowed, those living in rural areas and small towns, and those with strong ties to their community—have not changed a great deal over the years. Some of these turn out to affirm their support for a party (*expressively*); some because they believe it is a duty to do so (*normatively*). Only a small minority are *instrumental*, in the sense of going to the polls in order to get a specific set of policy goals implemented by government. Although some social changes would lead to an expectation of higher turnouts (more older people, a larger middle class, more people with degrees), these factors have been outweighed by declines in the strength of party identification and sense of civic duty, as well as a weakening of community involvement on the part of many people. While Americans are increasingly *Bowling Alone* (Putnam, 2000), rather than participating in organized groups, many people in Britain also seem to be content to live a more privatized existence. It is not at all clear what (if anything) could be done to reverse these trends that have underlain the decline in electoral turnout. Certainly, fiddling with the process of voting in order to make it easier will make little difference; as things stand, lowering the voting age would only serve to make matters worse.

As far as explanations of party choice are concerned, throughout the book we have traced the change on the part of electoral analysts from acceptance of the Butler–Stokes model to recognition of the importance of political issues and of 'valence politics'. For the 2010 election, although the statistics involved would bemuse most non-specialists, the BES authors provided a summary of the relative explanatory value of the various approaches (Clarke et al., 2011), which is presented in graph form in Figure 8.3. 'Demographics' (which refers to a variety of social characteristics, including class) were very poor at discriminating between Labour

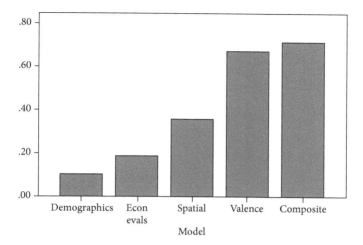

Figure 8.3 The relative explanatory value of explanations of party choice (Labour vs. other parties), 2010.

Note: The scores are McKelvey's r^2. 'Demographics' includes a variety of social characteristics; 'econ evals' relates to evaluations of economic prospects (the 'feelgood factor'); 'spatial' is the issue voting model involving position issues; 'valence' is valence politics; and 'composite' shows the explanatory power of combining all the models shown.

Source: Clarke et al., 2011.

voters and others. Using survey respondents' economic evaluations and applying the issue voting model (on the basis of 'position' issues) was somewhat more successful, but valence politics was easily the best explanatory framework. Even the addition of all the other variables (the 'composite' model) made little improvement to the ability of valence considerations to explain party choice. In later elections, although age became a stronger influence on party choice, other social characteristics—class and education, for example—became less important so that the overall impact of 'demographics' remained at a relatively low level. Labour's clear move to the left and the Brexit issue introduced more ideological and 'position' elements in the elections from 2015 to 2019 but, as we have seen, evaluations of the party leaders remained highly important determinants of party choice. As Brexit becomes an established fact and the Labour party moves back towards the political centre it seems likely that the major components of the valence politics approach—evaluations of party performances and of the party leaders—will continue to be the most important influences on party choice in elections.

Change in Who Gets Elected

From time to time we have commented on the numbers of candidates contesting general elections—almost invariably to notice that a new record high had been set. Figure 8.4 charts the number of candidates at each election from 1964 to

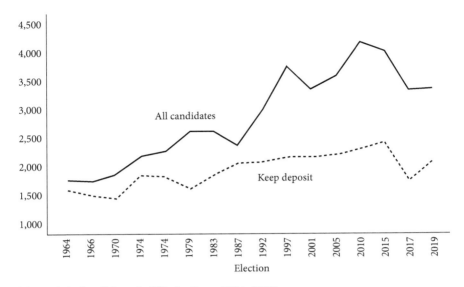

Figure 8.4 Candidates in UK elections, 1964–2019

Note: From 1964 to 1983 a candidate required 12.5 per cent of votes to retain the deposit. From 1987 this was reduced to 5 per cent.

Sources: Rallings and Thrasher (2012); House of Commons Library (2020c).

2019. With only the occasional dip, the trend was steadily upwards to 2015. The 2,000 barrier was breached in February 1974; more than 3,000 stood in 1997; in 2010, the number exceeded 4,000. As we have already indicated the unexpected calling of the 2017 election caught small parties and interested (or eccentric) individuals on the hop and there was a fairly sharp reduction in candidate numbers which then stayed at about the same level two years later. To check whether the long-term increase is simply down to larger numbers of 'no hopers' entering the lists, the chart also shows the trend in the numbers of candidates who retained their election deposit (by winning one-eighth (12.5 per cent) of the votes cast until 1983 and 5 per cent thereafter). In this case, the increase after 1987 is less spectacular. Overall, however, deposit-saving candidates also show a clear upward trend to 2015 and this is another indicator of the increased fragmentation of electoral choices over the period. In 2017 and 2019, however, when the two major parties dominated, fewer of the 'others' managed to claim back their deposit. The number of parliamentary constituencies has crept upwards since 1964, and this alone would be expected to cause a rise in candidatures. If we calculate the numbers of candidates per constituency, however, the steady upward trends are confirmed. Whereas in 1964 the average constituency had fewer than three candidates (2.8), the figure peaked at 6.4 in 2010 and was 5.1 in 2019. The days when 'straight fights' between the Conservatives and Labour were the norm in constituencies now seem as distant as the time when many seats were uncontested.

Table 8.2 Age, sex, and ethnicity of MPs,
1964 and 2019

	1964	2019
Age		
Less than 40	20.6	20.6
40–59	61.3	59.4
60+	18.1	19.9
Women	4.6	33.8
Ethnic minority	0.0	10.0

Notes: Figures shown are percentages.
Sources: Butler and King (1965); House of Commons
Library (2020b).

Turning to the characteristics of those elected, Table 8.2 shows how things have changed in respect of age, sex, and ethnicity. The age distribution of MPs has changed only marginally at successive elections and it is hard to discern any long-term trend. In 2019, as in 1964, most (59 per cent) were in their forties or fifties, with 21 per cent aged below 40 and 20 per cent at 60 and over.

The Nuffield study candidate analysis of the 1964 election blithely commented that 'an election is a choice of men and measures' (Butler and King, 1965: 240), and it is indeed the case that women candidates were then relatively rare (5.1 per cent of the total) and successful ones even more scarce (4.6 per cent). Things have changed markedly, however. By 2019 women comprised a third of MPs. To a considerable extent, the increase was a consequence of Labour's (1993) decision to foster an increase in female representation by requiring some constituencies to select candidates from a short-list which excluded men. This policy originally fell foul of anti-discrimination legislation (and disappointed some men who had expectations of being selected for their local constituency), but the law was later amended to exempt political parties. As we have seen, however, under David Cameron the Conservatives also made strenuous attempts to increase the number of women candidates and MPs. After the 2019 election, the Conservatives, Labour, SNP and the Liberal Democrats had, respectively, 87, 104, 16, and 7 women MPs.

Ethnicity was not a serious issue in 1964. Although immigration and race were beginning to arouse strong feelings, the various ethnic minorities comprised only a small proportion of the population. Unsurprisingly, there were no ethnic minority MPs. By 2019, however, the minorities were playing a much more significant role in public affairs and were represented by 65 MPs (41 Labour, 22 Conservative, and 2 Liberal Democrat), although this still represented a slightly smaller proportion of MPs than of the population as a whole.

Data relating to the occupation and education of MPs elected in 2019 were not available at the time of writing so the comparisons in Table 8.3 are for 1964 and

Table 8.3 Occupation and education of MPs, 1964 and 2017

	1964	2017
Occupation		
Professions	44.4	18.5
Business	18.4	24.8
Miscellaneous/other	20.5	55.7
Manual workers	16.7	1.1
Education		
Public schools/fee paying	45.7	28.1
Grammar schools	–	17.7
All universities	52.9	82.0
Oxford/Cambridge	35.4	24.0

Notes: Figures shown are percentages. The 1964 figures refer to Conservative, Labour, and Liberal MPs only.

Sources: Butler and King (1965); Cowley and Kavanagh (2018).

2017. Assigning a 'formative' occupation to MPs is fraught with difficulty—many of them have complicated career paths—but in broad terms there has been a decline in the proportion of those who worked in the 'professions'. The largest group of these are barristers or solicitors, who formed over 20.5 per cent of the total in 1964 and 10.5 per cent in 2017. Over the same period, teachers of various kinds fell from 9.4 per cent to 5.4 per cent; they are now almost all found on the Labour or Liberal Democrat benches. In comparison, MPs with a business background have become more common, and almost all of the increase has been on the Conservative side.

Perhaps the most striking change in the occupational make-up of the House, however, is that those who started their careers as manual workers have almost disappeared. Back in 1964, thirty-one ex-coalminers sat as Labour MPs (more than the total number of women—twenty-eight), and there were more than one hundred ex-manual workers in total. By 2010, former 'horny-handed sons of toil' had fallen to twenty-five—fewer than the number of Labour MPs who had attended a fee-paying school (thirty-six)—and by 2017 there were only seven. Largely, this is a consequence of social mobility and the overall decline in the size of the working class. Many middle-class professionals in the Labour Party originally came from working-class backgrounds (although Ed Miliband had an academic father who championed the proletariat in print, while both Tony Blair and Jeremy Corbyn attended private schools).

Despite the prominence of old Etonians (as well as other 'posh boys') in recent Conservative Cabinets, there has been a decrease since 1964 in the proportion of MPs who were educated at public schools, and also in those who attended either Oxford or Cambridge universities. The products of these institutions remain notably (and notoriously) over-represented compared with their numbers in the population at large. The same is true of graduates as a whole—more than 80 per cent of MPs after the 2017 election had been at university, and politics was already well on the way to becoming a graduate-only profession when John Major (who was painfully discomfited by his patchy academic record) became Prime Minister in 1990.

While there are those who argue that the House of Commons should be more 'representative' of the population, the electorate as a whole seems rather less exercised about its make-up in socio-economic or gender terms. For the most part, people simply want articulate and able MPs—preferably with roots in the area—who can represent them and their locality effectively, although there is evidence that ethnic minority voters want to see more people from their communities coming forward in elections (Cowley, 2013). However, the increases in the numbers of women and BAME MPs has not coincided with a notable upturn in electoral participation (or, indeed, in a notably more effective House of Commons). These considerations are overshadowed, however, by another criticism of successful parliamentary candidates (regardless of sex or ethnicity). The 'miscellaneous' occupational category, which has grown so markedly in recent years, contains a sizeable proportion of individuals who have never worked outside politics—or, at most, have earned their living in other ways for a brief interlude before securing nomination to a winnable seat. Although no comparative figures are available for the 1960s, in 2017 almost 15 per cent of MPs were classified as having been employed in 'political/social/policy research' or were full-time party officials. To party managers, the attractions of such people are obvious; among other things, they are likely to be 'media savvy', and to appreciate tactical considerations (notably the need to stay 'on message') more than recruits with broader life-experiences. This is not to say that what Peter Oborne (2008) has called 'the political class' is a uniform group—despite the pessimism of some commentators, along with the conformists there are some interesting characters in the House, including outspoken rebels against the party whips (e.g. Jeremy Corbyn, a 'career politician' par excellence). Nevertheless, there are many standard examples of the species on the backbenches, along with more prominent past figures such as Gordon Brown, Ed Miliband, David Cameron, and George Osborne. While complaints about the House of Commons are nothing new, the specific allegation that MPs are 'out of touch' is now a ubiquitous feature of criticism; and it would take a considerable effort from the average 'career politician', isolated within the Westminster bubble, to comprehend the outlook of the average British voter.

Change in the Operation of the Electoral System

By the 2010s, voters in the UK were getting used to casting their ballots under a variety of electoral systems. European Parliament elections on the mainland had involved a regional party list system since 1999, while in Northern Ireland the single transferable vote (STV) system was employed (as it was in elections to the Northern Ireland Assembly). The Scottish Parliament and Welsh and London Assemblies—all established after 1997—are elected via the additional member system (AMS) (also known to purists as a mixed-member proportional (MMP) system). In London and other English cities which have elected mayors, the so-called supplementary vote (SV) is used, while in Scotland STV was introduced for council elections in 2007. Although these changes—and the proliferation of acronyms—might have confused the voters, they have made the UK a sort of petri dish for researchers interested in electoral systems and their various effects.

As far as general elections are concerned, however, first-past-the-post (FPTP)— or, more formally, the single-member simple plurality (SMSP) system—remains in place. An attempt to replace it with the Alternative Vote (AV) system was roundly defeated in a national referendum in 2011 (see Chapter 6) and, in consequence, it seems unlikely that there will be another attempt to change the system for the foreseeable future.

It almost goes without saying that FPTP has always produced disproportional outcomes when seats won are compared with votes gained: it is, after all, designed to have that effect. Minor parties are usually under-represented (unless, like the SNP and Plaid Cymru, their support is geographically concentrated) and the leading party in terms of votes usually secures a 'winner's bonus' of additional seats. Using the simplest (Rae's) index of disproportionality, Figure 8.5 shows how this aspect of the electoral system has changed over our period. From the 1960s, outcomes became distinctly more disproportional. The upward trend is largely explained by increased voting support for the Liberals and their successors (as well as, more recently, for 'others', like UKIP in 2015), which was not reflected in seats won. In 2017, however, with the Conservatives and Labour dominating, the election outcome was more proportional than any in the series and, with the Liberal Democrats still in the doldrums in 2019—and the SNP boosting the number of 'other' seats—disproportionality remained well below average.

Far from being a problem for democracy, disproportionality is reckoned by proponents of FPTP to be one of the strengths of the system. Small parties (including those that might be considered 'extreme') are generally denied representation and, while it is difficult nowadays to conceive of a single party winning more than 50 per cent of the votes, the system usually ensures that the most popular party secures more than 50 per cent of seats in the House of Commons, thus allowing the government to govern. Moreover, the system does allow independent individuals who are popular within a locality a chance of securing a place in Parliament. For some time, however, analysts suggested that the ability of the system to manufacture single-party majorities in the legislature has been weakening—partly because of the increased ability of the Liberal Democrats to win seats but also as a result of the declining numbers of marginal seats, for reasons

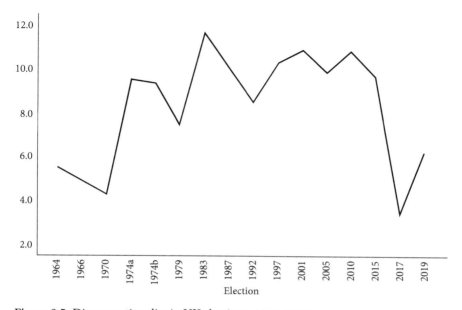

Figure 8.5 Disproportionality in UK elections, 1964–2019

Note: The measure used is the sum of the differences between the percentage of votes and of seats won by the Conservatives, Labour, Liberal Democrats (or predecessors) and others, divided by four. More complicated measures show a similar pattern.

noted in Chapter 4. Eventually, of course, the system failed to produce a clear winner in 2010 (see Curtice, 2010) and again in 2017 (Curtice, 2018). Arguably, an important theoretical justification for FPTP has now been undermined by practical experience.

Up to the 1990s, the operation of the electoral system did not appear to advantage or disadvantage one or the other of the major parties to a significant extent (Johnston et al., 2001: 12–13). Bias in this sense can be measured by calculating the number of seats that the Conservatives and Labour would have won at each election if they had received equal shares of the vote (with all other parties staying constant). In 1964, the Conservatives would have taken about twenty seats more than Labour, but from then until 1987 there was very little bias, except in February 1974 and in 1979, when Labour benefitted by about twenty seats. From 1992 to 2010, however, there was a more pronounced and consistent bias against the Conservatives. Given equal shares of the votes, Labour would have beaten the Conservatives by 38 seats in 1992, 82 in 1997, 141 in 2001, 111 in 2005, and 51 in 2010 (Johnston et al., 2009). Another indication of bias is that after the 2010 election, it was estimated that the Conservatives required a lead of more than 11 points over Labour in order to win an overall majority of seats next time round, whereas for Labour to be in the same position a lead of less than three points over its main rival was all that it required (Curtice et al., 2010).

This bias in the system arose from five features (Johnston et al., 2009). First, given their electorates, Wales and Scotland were over-represented in the House of Commons (despite the reduction in Scottish seats from seventy-two to fifty-nine before the 2005 election) and both were very inhospitable areas for the Conservatives. In 2010, the Conservatives won only one of the fifty-nine Scottish constituencies, while in Wales they took eight of the forty seats. Second, Conservative seats tended to have larger electorates than those won by Labour. In 2010, the former averaged over 72,000 electors while the latter had less than 70,000. Third, Conservative seats had higher turnouts (a mean of 68.8 per cent in 2010 compared with 62.3 per cent in Labour seats). As a consequence of these two factors, the Conservatives amassed many more votes than Labour for every seat won. Fourth, the Conservatives suffered more from the advances made in elections over the period by the Liberal Democrats. Of the fifty-seven seats won by the latter in 2010, the Conservatives came second in thirty-eight and Labour in seventeen (with the SNP as runners up in the other two). Finally, the geographical distribution of the Conservative vote was simply less 'efficient' (in terms of converting votes into seats) than that of Labour. Across constituencies, the Conservatives tended to 'win big and lose small'. Under FPTP, that kind of vote distribution does not yield seats as efficiently as 'winning small and losing big'—which was more characteristic of how Labour's votes were spread across constituencies.

It is not difficult to understand why the Conservatives in government after 2010 moved quickly to establish a review of parliamentary constituency boundaries under new rules, which gave much more emphasis than before to equalizing the sizes of constituency electorates and involved a reduction in the total number of MPs to 600. Obviously, this would not have removed all the sources of bias, but—since Conservative-held seats had larger electorates—it would have reduced the apparent unfairness somewhat by making it likely that the Conservatives would win about twenty seats more than under the old boundaries without improving their vote share. In the event, however, in retaliation for the Conservatives' failure to support his proposed reforms of the House of Lords, the Liberal Democrat leader Nick Clegg decided (in advance of the final proposals) that his party would block the changes and the review was aborted. This appeared to be a serious blow to the electoral prospects of the Conservatives at the next general election.

In fact, when that arrived in 2015, it showed—yet again—that making predictions about election outcomes in modern Britain is a risky business. As noted above, analysts had suggested after 2010 that the Conservatives required a lead of 11 points over Labour to win a majority of seats; in 2015 they achieved that with a lead of just 6.5 points. On this occasion, the pro-Labour bias of the electoral system was corrected and, instead, it benefitted the Conservatives. On a 50:50 division of votes between the two major parties the Conservatives would have won forty-six more seats than Labour. Although Conservative seats still had larger electorates and higher turnouts, other factors now worked in their favour. Labour was obliterated in Scotland (retaining just one seat with almost a quarter of the votes) and the collapse of the Liberal Democrats meant that the Conservatives were no longer heavily punished by buoyant third-party support in England. In addition, the latter's votes were much more efficiently distributed with especially good results being recorded in marginal seats being defended for the first time by incumbents (see Curtice et al., 2016). The same pattern prevailed in 2017 when, once again, the system gave an edge to the Conservatives, although the extent of bias was small, amounting to about twelve seats (Curtice et al., 2018). In 2019, the Conservatives were returned with a large majority and once again the system worked in their favour—to the tune of about twenty-three seats. A detailed analysis showed that they remained disadvantaged by the over-representation of Scotland and Wales and the fact that both electorates and turnout were larger in the seats that they won than in those taken by Labour. Third-party support had little impact, and the disadvantages were outweighed by the efficient distribution of Conservative votes (Smith, 2020).

Even so, the newly elected Johnson government quickly turned to the question of what to do about the resurrected Boundary Review that had finally been submitted in 2018. Thanks to the political and parliamentary turmoil surrounding Brexit at this time, the fact that the government had no majority, and the opposition of a number of MPs fearful of losing their seats, the proposals had made no progress. In early 2020, however, the government announced that a new review would be undertaken but that the requirement to reduce the number of MPs to 600 would be abandoned. The (rather lame) excuse for this change was that Parliament would have more work to do post-Brexit. One can imagine that the members and staff of the Boundary Commissions, having seen years of hard work come to nothing, must have received this news with gritted teeth.

Change in the Parties

Party Membership

Commentators and academics have generally believed that political parties (like voluntary groups of all sorts) depend for their continuing vitality on a high level of personal commitment at grass roots level (Seyd and Whiteley, 1992; Whiteley et al., 1994). Party members raise funds, provide a pool of candidates for local and national elections, maintain a presence for the party in the localities, act as opinion leaders, and undertake the work of campaigning in elections at all levels. Throughout our period, however, the membership of the major British parties has declined steeply. Thanks partly to legislation relating to party finance, but also to innovations such as leadership elections in which members can participate, figures for the membership of the main UK parties are now much more reliable and precise than was the case in 1964. In that year, the Conservative party claimed to have more than two million members; Labour's individual membership (those not affiliated through trade unions) was said to be just short of one million; and there were supposed to be about a quarter of a million Liberals. By 2011, in contrast, Conservative membership was about 160,000; the corresponding figure for Labour was 193,000; and there were 49,000 Liberal Democrats. According to data collected by the House of Commons Library (2019), however, there was a surge in Labour membership under Jeremy Corbyn which peaked at 550,000 in 2017 before falling back to 485,000 in 2019. The Conservative figure stabilized and then crept up to 180,000 by the same date while the Liberal Democrats reached 115,000. Despite this impressive improvement, the latter were outnumbered by members of the SNP (125,000) which had seen a large influx following the 2014 independence referendum. Nonetheless, overall party membership remained much lower than it had been in the 1960s.

It could be argued, of course, that such a sharp decline in this form of political participation reflects the fact that it is simply not very rewarding. Rational choice theorists would point out that, even in the early 1960s, the overwhelming majority of party members were highly unlikely to reap any tangible reward from their membership. The costs involved in being active were considerable and the benefits few. From the 'rational' perspective, many people have simply reacted, albeit belatedly, to reality, and found more rewarding things to do. Nonetheless, there remain plenty of strongly committed people with a passion for politics who ensure that the grass roots of parties have not entirely withered away.

By the time of the 2010 general election, the main parties had made gestures which, on the face of it, provided incentives for 'rational actors' either to renew their subscriptions or join up for the first time. Not least, all main parties now offered the rank and file the chance to vote for the leader. There were also innovations such as policy forums, where ordinary members were given a theoretical chance of winning a serious hearing for their ideas. However, the downward trend in membership continued in defiance of such initiatives. It would seem that parties are among the groups worst affected by a more general decline in active participation in voluntary organizations, which is not confined to the UK.

For the parties at national level, the haemorrhage of members was perhaps a manageable problem so long as adequate funding could be obtained from other sources. Indeed, some in the party hierarchies seemed to view the membership as a potentially embarrassing nuisance. In 2013, for example, it was reported that one of the co-chairmen of the Conservative Party (Lord Feldman) referred to his party activists as 'swivel-eyed loons' (Oborne, 2013). Even if the report was true, the main parties were happy to recruit 'loons' so long as they kept their lunacy within limits. Like the fall in turnout, diminishing membership was not something

to be welcomed; but it was sustainable so long as it affected all the main contenders roughly equally. However, there was at least one potentially awkward result.
Individual constituency members might be mollified by the thought that their
individual votes could help to elect the party leader; but they were rational
enough to know that a more meaningful role for them lay in their traditional
influence over the choice of local constituency candidates. Throughout our
period, however, media interest in by-election campaigns—and in potential stories about off-message general election candidates—made the parties increasingly
anxious to exert greater influence on (if not to dictate) candidate selection.
Interference in the local process was also prompted by the desire to promote the
selection of women or members of ethnic minorities in safe and winnable seats.
Oddly enough, therefore, there has been a tendency for parties to give members
more of a voice over the selection of leaders, while trying to reduce their influence in selecting the local candidates for whom they would have to campaign in a
parliamentary election. Before the 2010 general election, the Conservatives
resorted to the device of holding US-style 'primaries' in 116 seats (fifteen of them
Conservative-held). In these cases, any interested local voter could attend and
participate in the selection meeting, but the choice was restricted to carefully vet-
ted shortlists. This had the effect of diluting the input of party members who had
paid their dues for decades in the expectation that the periodic choice of local
candidate would provide some compensation for long hours of thankless campaigning on behalf of the party.

Election Campaigning

In one of his famous 'Letters from America', broadcast weekly on BBC radio for
many years, Alistair Cooke commented on the 1979 general election in Britain.
Noting that the parties were employing advertising professionals to help their
campaigns he said, 'The British adoption of advertising wizards as political advisers would do well, I humbly suggest, to stop where it started' (Cooke, 1980: 285).

Despite being an acute observer of the American scene, Cooke had clearly lost
touch with British electoral trends. As we have seen, the parties had been using
professionals in media, advertising, polling, and public relations since the 1960s.
Moreover, not only did this not stop after 1979, but rather, as seen in earlier chapters, campaigns became more and more professionalized. The hours of practice
that the party leaders put in to preparing for the leaders' debates in 2010, under
the tutelage of imported experts, is only one example. The role of Lynton Crosby
and his successors in later Conservative campaigns is another. Although the new
professionalism is obvious in the conduct of national campaigns, arguably it has
had an even greater impact at constituency level. Party headquarters are now
involved in planning and managing local efforts to an extent that would have

been unthinkable in the 1960s. Initially, key constituencies were targeted more effectively, then groups of key voters, and finally individuals. Whereas in the 1960s local campaigns were run and staffed by local people with time-honoured routines—canvassing and preparing lists of supporters in advance; taking numbers at polling stations, and 'knocking up' on polling day—by the twenty-first century local campaigns were more like sophisticated marketing operations, masterminded from London by well-remunerated electoral gurus. By the 2010s, indeed, journalists and others were bemoaning the highly instrumental approach to campaigning adopted by the parties. Thus, Fraser Nelson, editor of the *Spectator* magazine, commented on the intense focus on target voters:

> Nowadays our parties believe their computers know the names, addresses, concerns, assumptions and hairdressers of these people—and our politics is shaped accordingly. So elections are not so much a battle for Britain but for a tiny slice of its voters. You don't mean a thing if your seat's not a swing.
>
> (*Daily Telegraph*, 12.04.2013)

The much increased importance assigned to local campaigning by the parties from the 1990s onwards was paralleled among academic electoral analysts. As we have previously described, the academic orthodoxy in the 1960s—established by the Nuffield studies—was that local campaigns made little difference to election outcomes. This widely accepted conclusion was actually based on rather casual research. Before each election, the Nuffield authors would ask regional party officials to nominate seats that were particularly well organized. Afterwards they would compare the swings in these seats with the national average. Since there was rarely a significant difference, the inevitable conclusion was that constituency organization had no impact on specific outcomes. In the later 1980s and 1990s, however, various researchers developed ways of measuring campaign intensity more systematically across constituencies—using surveys of party members and of election agents as well as campaign spending data (Johnston, 1987; Seyd and Whiteley, 1992; Denver and Hands, 1997). These studies all demonstrated that local campaigning could have a significant electoral payoff—and research in subsequent elections reached the same conclusion—although its extent varied from party to party and from election to election. Within a relatively short time, this view became established as the new orthodoxy, and this, at least partly, helps to explain why the local efforts—far from being a ritual or a sideshow—are now integral to the parties' approach to election campaigning.

Changes in Party Finance

Although dwarfed by the cost of campaigning in many Congressional contests in the United States—not to mention by the gargantuan sums lavished on

Presidential races—UK elections still involve the parties in raising and spending considerable amounts of money. With membership in decline, the major parties became increasingly dependent on donations from wealthy individuals or organizations. By the 1990s, journalists interested in the financial dealings of individual politicians found party funding an equally fruitful source for stories about 'sleaze'.

As a result, moves were made to regulate party finance much more tightly. In 2000, the Blair government passed the Political Parties, Elections and Referendums Act, which established an Electoral Commission to ensure more transparency in party funding, outlawed donations from overseas or anonymous sources, and placed limits on campaign expenditure by party headquarters. However, the Act contained loopholes which all the parties were ready to exploit. Labour was accused of using the Honours system as a bait for potential donors; the Liberal Democrats received more than £2 million from a company run by a resident of Majorca who was subsequently convicted of fraud; and there was a general tendency for parties to encourage their benefactors to give money in the form of loans (which were not covered by the terms of the legislation) rather than outright donations, clearly hoping that in due course the 'debt' would be written off. The 2006 Electoral Administration Act included hastily drafted amendments designed to curb these abuses. No doubt calculating that the public would soon tire of stable doors being slammed after the occupants had departed, in the same year the Blair government set up a far-reaching review of party finance under the distinguished former civil servant Sir Hayden Phillips.

When Phillips reported in 2007, his main recommendation was that there should be a major increase in the level of state support for political parties. It could be argued that this would be the best way to prevent the kind of scandals which had blighted electoral politics since the 1990s. However, the problems of implementation—not to mention the likely scale of opposition from taxpayers—were formidable: for example, if state funds were allocated in proportion to performance at the previous election, a party which had gone from hero to zero almost overnight (as the Conservatives did shortly after the 1992 election) would still be able to rely on generous subsidies. The real difficulty was a catch-22: if the major parties were popular, the principle of state funding might win widespread acceptance; but if they needed help because they were low in public esteem there was little chance that taxpayers would approve the reform. Although Phillips reported before the expenses scandal of 2009, UK parties were already unpopular enough to ensure a mixed reception for his proposals. The ensuing Political Parties and Elections Act (2009) predictably side-stepped the issue of state funding, and failed to satisfy critics who were hoping for tighter regulation of the existing arrangements.

It would be tempting to conclude that the legislative efforts of 2000–9 were a fuss about nothing, on grounds which are similar to the debate about media influence: for various good reasons, donors (like newspapers) want to be on the winning side, so it is no surprise that the richest party at the time of a particular election usually emerges as the winner. However, the various Acts have at least ensured much more transparency concerning party finance (especially during the 'short' campaigns and the pre-campaign period) than previously. The evidence since 2000 shows that, after several years in which Labour matched and even bettered the fund-raising efforts of the Conservatives, something like 'normal service' was restored (Fisher, 2010). In other words, in 2010, David Cameron's coffers were much better supplied than those of Gordon Brown. In the last quarter of 2019, the Conservatives reported receiving £37.7 million in donations, Labour £10.7 million, and the Liberal Democrats £13.6 million (while the Brexit party received £7.2 million, chiefly from previous Conservative benefactors) (Electoral Commission, 2020b). The Conservatives have clearly recovered their sources of finance from the business community, while Labour has become more dependent than ever on its link with the trade unions. The stance taken by the Liberal Democrats on Brexit may have brought them considerable financial support in this period even if it did not purchase electoral success.

Voter, Elections, and Parties

In this book we have provided an account of political developments in the periods between the various elections covered, focusing on events which are most likely to have affected subsequent voting. In summarizing the leading themes, we should recollect that the relationship between party decision-makers and the voters cuts both ways: while voters can be influenced by the records of government and opposition parties, in a liberal democracy senior politicians need to take account of changes within the electorate. Since the basic assumptions about electoral behaviour which prevailed in 1964—in particular, the element of stability provided by class and partisan alignment—had been overturned by the start of the twenty-first century, one could reasonably expect a corresponding degree of instability in 'high' politics, with dramatic twists of fortune and regular reconfigurations of the party system.

All students of recent British political history are familiar with the fact that the strong partisanship of voters in the early post-war period co-existed with a marked continuity in the general policy approach of successive governments. It is widely agreed that there was a 'consensus' at the higher reaches of politics. Although some argue that the consensus was more apparent than real and confined to senior party figures (Pimlott, 1988), in terms of the programmes offered to the voters in 1964 there was much common ground between Labour and the Conservatives. For example, both parties were committed to economic growth on the basis of an interventionist strategy thrashed out between government, employers, and unions. The Conservatives had no radical plans to denationalize state-owned industries, and the Labour leadership had no intention of pushing state ownership far beyond the limits established by Clement Attlee's government (1945–51). Neither party was as yet ready to contemplate major reforms in the legal status of trade unions. Similarly, the broad framework of Attlee's welfare state was accepted on all sides and the party leaders were broadly in agreement on key foreign policy issues.

Whether or not this represented a 'consensus', it certainly indicated a state of affairs in which the parties were trying to impress voters with their 'managerial competence' rather than their ideological zeal. While their shared policy object-ives undoubtedly reflected the personal preferences of senior policymakers in the parties, the approach also made good electoral sense. Neither party could be sure of winning office on the basis of their core supporters alone, so they had to appeal to the less committed 'middle ground'. By the end of the decade, however, there were signs that this was changing—not least because it was becoming increas-ingly difficult to conceal Britain's relative decline from a more inquisitive and better-informed electorate. In 1970, the Conservatives returned to office with a programme which suggested a partial reversal of the earlier post-war trend towards greater state intervention. While the Heath government soon abandoned its more innovative intentions, Labour's unexpected defeat in 1970 had seriously weakened its centrist leaders. In 1973, the party conference endorsed a radical programme, including proposals to push nationalization much further. After Labour regained office in 1974, Harold Wilson (and then James Callaghan) tried to act as if it was still the party of the 1960s; but they could not disguise the fact that the radicals, led by Tony Benn, had greatly increased their influence over policy-making.

While Labour had become a radical party still led by moderates, after Heath's defeat in the 1975 leadership election, the Conservatives became a moderate party with a radical at the helm. Thus, when Margaret Thatcher led the Conservatives to victory in 1979, a polarization of British politics was guaranteed: the new government claimed a 'mandate' for change, while those who argued that Labour should cleave to the centre were even less successful than they had been back in 1970. The fact that both major parties had now deserted the 'middle ground' left an obvious opportunity for a new political alignment. The SDP, founded by centrists who thought that Labour had become both damnable and doomed, formed an alliance with the Liberals which came very close to breaking the mould of two-party politics in the 1983 general election.

What part did voters, as opposed to elite politicians, play in this process? To some extent, the polarization of parties could be seen as a consequence of dealign-ment among voters. Since support could no longer be taken for granted, as it largely had been until the 1960s, radicals within both main parties could argue that they needed distinctive policies to win elections. However, while enthusiasts such as Benn and Thatcher interpreted dealignment as a signal that the 'middle ground' should be abandoned, it was just as plausible to argue that politicians should hug it closer than ever. The 1979 election, often regarded as the point at which the British electorate lost faith in the dominant consensus, was certainly not a clear victory for radicalism of either left or right. 'Uncle Jim' Callaghan's unthreatening approach was an undoubted asset for Labour, while Conservative strategists were anxious to soften Mrs Thatcher's image. Residual suspicions of Thatcher's real intentions presumably helped to ensure that she persistently trailed Callaghan as the best choice for Prime Minister in the polls.

When the Conservative victory gave Mrs Thatcher the chance to show her true colours, her ideological supporters were cheered by her apparent refusal to change course in the face of serious economic difficulties; but less partisan voters signalled their disapproval by making her the most unpopular Prime Minister on record and by offering their support to the Liberal–SDP alliance in opinion polls and by-elections. Symptoms of economic recovery in 1982, capped by the Falklands War, convinced many wavering Conservative supporters to end their flirtation with the Alliance. On the other flank, the practical impact of Conservative policies (and a reaction against Mrs Thatcher's abrasive qualities) had ensured that most hard-core Labour voters would stay loyal rather than jumping ship along with the SDP leaders. Thus, in 1983, the non-Conservative majority among the British electorate found itself almost equally divided. By 1987, Labour had begun its journey back towards the middle ground but had not progressed far enough to satisfy many of the voters who had defected to the SDP; in 1992, it had restored itself to something no more threatening than it had been in 1964, but many voters distrusted the leader (Neil Kinnock), who had changed his own views along with his party's policy stance. Meanwhile, by 1992 the Conservatives had deposed the divisive Thatcher and chosen a leader (John Major) who would not have been out of place in the old days of consensus.

For both major parties, it was (or should have been) obvious by 1992 that a decade of polarization had merely underscored the necessity of presenting the public with a centrist programme; only in unusual circumstances would radicalism be rewarded. Labour had gradually come round to this view after its 1983 disaster. In 1992 it chose a suitably moderate leader in John Smith, whose only serious critics (such as Tony Blair and Gordon Brown) thought he was not centrist enough. The Conservatives, by contrast, decided to ignore the lessons; and, having made life impossible for the moderate John Major, they suffered a defeat of epic proportions in the 1997 general election. Like Labour in 1979, the Conservatives chose to regard this as a cue for more rather than less radicalism: to varying degrees, the party's next three leaders (William Hague, Iain Duncan Smith, and Michael Howard) sought to appease their grass-roots party members rather than trying to appeal to the electorate at large. Only with the election of

David Cameron, who had not been a prominent figure under either Thatcher or Major, did the party choose a leader who could launch a credible appeal to the crucial centrist voters who were more likely to be swayed by apparent competence rather than inflexible vision in an age of valence voting.

Thus, between 1964 and 2010, Britain's major parties had turned a full circle; they had started by focusing on the middle ground, then forgot the importance of this terrain and duly received harsh reminders from the voters. After what turned out to be a brief (albeit dramatic) hiatus in the 1980s, a kind of consensus had been re-established among the political elite, this time one in which the presiding spirit was that of Margaret Thatcher rather than Clement Attlee. Thanks to the relative weakness of the British economy and a 'globalized' context, the boundaries of the 'politically possible' were also much more circumscribed for British policymakers than they had been even in 1945. A general feeling that globalization made the choice of government less important was reflected to some extent in electoral turnouts which were significantly lower than in the early post-war period. This trend, however, also reflected social changes; voters had become more choosy (and more difficult to motivate) at a time when it seemed less important for them to decide between increasingly similar party programmes.

In the 2010 general election, thanks to the decline in support for the two main parties, voter choice was by no means as restricted as it had been in 1964. The Liberal Democrats offered a programme which seemed no less radical than the manifestos produced by the Liberals in the 1970s but were now a more significant force—particularly in Parliament. However, the Liberal Democrats had not escaped the new sense of political 'realism' and, in ideological terms, it was not particularly surprising that their leader Nick Clegg was happy to join a coalition with Cameron's Conservatives. The Greens were certainly not part of any new consensus and in 2010 they won their first seat in the Commons. However, like the Liberals of old they were vulnerable to allegations of woolly-minded idealism from their more successful rivals. By contrast, although UKIP continued to make headway after 2010, the other parties could always fall back on the accusation that it was a refuge for unsavoury right-wing elements.

In short, the major British parties had seemingly returned to a 'consensus' after a decade in which they presented clear and contrasting ideological perspectives. This state of affairs was soon to change, however. The rise of UKIP encouraged many in the Conservative party—members and backbenchers for the most part— to regard Britain's membership of the EU as a 'live' issue rather than a disagreeable reality which had been fixed forever by the 1975 referendum. The party steadily became more identified with a Eurosceptic position as the issue created new divisions among the electorate. Labour, meanwhile, responded to post-2010 economic 'austerity' by veering sharply to the left under Corbyn: the whole Blairite 'New Labour', consensus-seeking approach was not just abandoned but vilified.

Thus, in their different ways, the two main parties represented and reinforced divisions in a UK whose continuation was now under serious threat thanks to the rise of nationalism, especially in Scotland. It is particularly telling that both Labour and the Conservatives repeatedly used the consensual language of 'One Nation' in an attempt to conceal the contrasting reality. The issue of 'Brexit' brought these new divisions to a head: it did not create them. However, the failure of British politicians to rally behind a compromise position which might begin to unite the country made it more difficult to conduct constructive negotiations with the EU; it also meant that, when the dangers of the Covid-19 outbreak began to be registered in March 2020, the government's attempted response would be flavoured by its stance on Brexit and thus would itself become an additional source of division at a time when a feeling of national unity was urgently required.

Despite renewed political polarization and the apparent rise of 'identity politics', the evidence of the past sixty years suggests that while voters may have become more fickle in terms of their choice of party, as a body they have remained remarkably consistent in their political outlook. According to taste, one might say that through all the social upheavals since the early 1960s, the British people as a whole have remained unimaginative and risk-averse in political terms—or that their record bears out the truth of Edmund Burke's remark that 'the individual is foolish...but the species is wise' (1906: 355). Whether or not British voters have been 'wise' in their various choices, it seems that they continue to associate moderation with competence; and that in an era of valence voting this gives centrist politicians a decided advantage over their more zealous counterparts. Nonetheless, judgements about competence are themselves volatile and it would certainly be premature to conclude on the basis of the last two elections that we have entered a new period of two-party dominance and electoral stability.

Conclusion

By allowing citizens to pass judgement on their rulers and, if they so desire, remove them from office in an orderly and peaceful way, free and fair elections remain central to democracy. For that reason, they are patently major events in a nation's history and merit careful study.

Over the years since 1964, the British electorate has become much more diverse, and people vote for a much wider range of parties than they did in the 1960s. Class and partisan dealignment has resulted in loosened ties between people and parties. Politicians of all parties command far less respect than they did in 1964, for a variety of reasons which we have explored in this book.

Despite the evidence of diversity, dealignment, and disillusion, elections are still highly enjoyable as well as being important in themselves. Apart from those of us with a professional interest in studying these contests, there are numerous 'election buffs' around the country who do so as a hobby. The attraction is partly the wealth of numbers generated by an election which can be aggregated, averaged, correlated, graphed, and used to construct maps. For the benefit of less eccentric individuals, the mass media compete to find stories which will keep their audiences entertained throughout the campaigns. Elaborate election night results programmes on television attract very large audiences—in 2019, as the coverage started, the BBC had 6.1 million viewers, ITV had 2.6 million and Sky News around 2 million. Four hours later, almost six million were still tuned into the two main channels (*Press Gazette*, 2019). A more volatile electorate makes the outcome less predictable, adding to the drama of an occasion which will have considerable bearing on the lives of spectators as well as participants. Even if some elections since 1964 have been described as 'dull' at the time, the overall and ongoing story of change remains compelling.

References

Abrams, M. and Rose, R. (1960). *Must Labour Lose?* Harmondsworth: Penguin Books.

Adley, R. (1992). 'Railway privatization'. *Public Money and Management*, 12/2: 6–7.

Alford, R. (1964). *Party and Society*. London: John Murray.

Allen, N. and Bartle, J. (eds) (2011). *Britain at the Polls 2010*. London: Sage.

Allen, N. and Bartle, J. (eds) (2018). *None Past the Post: Britain at The Polls 2017*. Manchester: Manchester University Press.

Almond, G. and Verba, S. (1963). *The Civic Culture: Political Attitudes and Democracy in Five Nations*. Princeton, NJ: Princeton University Press.

Alt, J., Crewe, I., and Sarlvik, B. (1977). 'Angels in plastic: the Liberal surge in 1974'. *Political Studies*, 25/3: 343–68.

Ashcroft, M. (2005). *Smell the Coffee: A Wake-Up Call for the Conservative Party*. London: Politico.

Ashdown, P. (2000). *The Ashdown Diaries, vol. 1: 1988–1997*. London: Allen Lane.

Atkinson, S. and Mortimore, R. (2011). 'Were the polls wrong about the Lib Dems all along?', in D. Wring, R. Mortimore, and S. Atkinson (eds), *Political Communication in Britain: The Leader Debates, the Campaign and the Media in the 2010 General Election*. Basingstoke: Palgrave Macmillan, 77–93.

Bale, T. (2010). *The Conservative Party: From Thatcher to Cameron*. Cambridge: Polity Press.

Bartle, J. and King, A. (eds) (2006). *Britain at the Polls 2005*. Washington, DC: CQ Press.

Bartle, J., Mortimore, R., and Atkinson, S. (eds) (2002). *Political Communications: The General Election of 2001*. London: Frank Cass.

Barwell, G. (2007). 'Conservative Party strategy', in D. Wring, J. Green, R. Mortimore, and S. Atkinson (eds), *Political Communications; The General Election Campaign of 2005*. Basingstoke: Palgrave Macmillan, 25–32.

Baston, L. (2000). *Sleaze: The State of the Nation*. London: Channel Four.

Benn, T. (1989). *Office without Power: Diaries 1968–72*. London: Arrow.

Benney, M., Gray, A. P., and Pear, R. H. (1956). *How People Vote*. London: Routledge & Kegan Paul.

Blair, T. (2010). *A Journey*. London: Hutchinson.

Blondel, J. (1963). *Voters, Parties and Leaders*. Harmondsworth: Penguin.

Blumler, J. G. and McQuail, D. (1967). *Television in Politics*. London: Faber.

Burke, E. (1906). 'Speech on the Representation of the Commons in Parliament, May 7th, 1782', in *The Works of the Right Honourable Edmund Burke.*, vol. 3 Oxford: Oxford University Press.

Butler, D. (1989). *British General Elections since 1945*.Oxford: Oxford University Press.

Butler, D. and Kavanagh, D. (1975). *The British General Election of October 1974*. London: Macmillan.

Butler, D. and Kavanagh, D. (1980). *The British General Election of 1979*. London: Macmillan.

Butler, D. and Kavanagh, D. (1984). *The British General Election of 1983*. London: Macmillan.

Butler, D. and Kavanagh, D. (1988). *The British General Election of 1987*. London: Macmillan.

Butler, D. and Kavanagh, D. (1992). *The British General Election of 1992*. London: Macmillan.

Butler, D. and King, A. (1965). *The British General Election of 1964*. London: Macmillan.

Butler, D. and King, A. (1966). *The British General Election of 1966*. London: Macmillan.

Butler, D. and Kitzinger, U. (1976). *The 1975 Referendum*. London: Macmillan.

Butler, D. and Pinto-Duschinsky, M. (1971). *The British General Election of 1970*. London: Macmillan.

Butler, D. and Stokes, D. (1969). *Political Change in Britain*, 1st edn. London: Macmillan.

Butler, D. and Stokes, D. (1974). *Political Change in Britain*, 2nd edn. London: Macmillan.

Butler, D., Adonis, A., and Travers, T. (1994). *Failure in British Government: The Politics of the Poll Tax*. Oxford: Oxford University Press.

Campbell, A. (2010). *The Alastair Campbell Diaries. Vol. 2: Power and the People*. London: Jonathan Cape.

Campbell, J. (1993*). Edward Heath: A Biography*. London: Jonathan Cape.

Channon, Sir H. (1993). *'Chips': The Diaries of Sir Henry Channon*. London: Weidenfeld.

Clark, A. (1999). *The Tories: Conservatives and the Nation State 1922–1997*. London: Phoenix.

Clarke, H., Sanders, D., Stewart, M., and Whiteley, P. (2004). *Political Choice in Britain*. Oxford: Oxford University Press.

Clarke, H., Sanders, D., Stewart, M., and Whiteley, P. (2009). *Performance Politics and the British Voter*. Cambridge: Cambridge University Press.

Clarke, H., Sanders, D., Stewart, M., and Whiteley, P. (2011). 'Valence politics and electoral choice in Britain, 2010'. *Journal of Elections, Public Opinion and Parties*, 21/2: 237–53.

Cooke, A. (1980). *The Americans: Letters from America 1969–1979*. Harmondsworth: Penguin.

Cowley, P. (2013). 'Why not ask the audience? Understanding the public's representation priorities'. *British Politics*, 8/2: 138–63.

Cowley, P. and Kavanagh, D. (2016). *The British General Election of 2015*. Basingstoke: Palgrave Macmillan.

Cowley, P. and Kavanagh, D. (2018). *The British General Election of 2017*. Cham: Springer.

Crewe, I. (1985). 'How to win a landslide without really trying', in A. Ranney (ed.), *Britain at the Polls 1983*. Washington, DC: American Enterprise Institute, 155–96.

Crewe, I. (1986). 'On the death and resurrection of class voting: some comments on *How Britain Votes*'. *Political Studies*, 34: 620–38.

Crewe, I. (1988). 'Has the electorate become Thatcherite?', in R. Skidelsky (ed.), *Thatcherism*. Oxford: Basil Blackwell, 25–49.

Crewe, I. and Gosschalk, B. (1995). *Political Communications: The General Election Campaign of 1992*. Cambridge: Cambridge University Press.

Crewe, I. and Harrop, M. (1986). *Political Communications: The General Election Campaign of 1983*. Cambridge: Cambridge University Press.

Crewe, I. and Harrop, M. (1989). *Political Communications: The General Election Campaign of 1987*. Cambridge: Cambridge University Press.

Crewe, I. and King, A. (1995). *SDP: The Birth, Life and Death of the Social Democratic Party*. Oxford: Oxford University Press.

Crewe, I., Fox, T., and Alt, J. (1977). 'Non-voting in British general elections 1966–October 1974', in C. Crouch (ed.), *British Political Sociology Yearbook*, vol. 3. London: Croom Helm, 38–109.

Crewe, I., Gosschalk, B., and Bartle, J. (1998). *Political Communications: Why Labour Won the General Election of 1997*. London: Frank Cass.

Crewe, I., Sarlvik, B., and Alt, J. (1977). 'Partisan dealignment in Britain 1964–1974'. *British Journal of Political Science*, 7/2: 129–90.

Crick, B. (1964). *The Reform of Parliament*. London: Weidenfeld and Nicolson.

Crossman, R. (1963). Introduction to W. Bagehot, *The English Constitution*. London: Fontana.

Crossman, R. (1977). *The Diaries of a Cabinet Minister, vol. 3: Secretary of State for Social Services 1968–70*. London: Hamish Hamilton and Jonathan Cape.

Currie, E. (2002). *Diaries, 1987–1992*. London: Little, Brown.

Curtice, J. (2010). 'So what went wrong with the electoral system?' in A. Geddes and J. Tonge (eds), *Britain Votes 2010*. Oxford: Oxford University Press, 41–56.

Curtice, J. (2018). 'How the electoral system failed to deliver – again', in J. Tonge, C. Leston-Bandeira, and S. Wilks-Heeg (eds), *Britain Votes 2017*. Oxford: Oxford University Press, 29–45.

Curtice, J. and Semetko, H. (1994). 'Does it matter what the papers say?' in A. Heath, R. Jowell, and J. Curtice (eds), *Labour's Last Chance: The 1992 Election and Beyond*. Aldershot: Dartmouth, 43–63.

Curtice, J. and Steed, M. (1982). 'Electoral choice and the production of governments: the changing operation of the electoral system in the UK since 1955'. *British Journal of Political Science*, 12: 249–98.

Curtice, J. and Steed, M. (1986). 'Proportionality and exaggeration in the British electoral system'. *Electoral Studies*, 5: 209–28.

Curtice, J. and Steed, M. (1988). 'Analysis', in D. Butler and D. Kavanagh, *The British General Election of 1987*. Basingstoke: Macmillan, 316–62.

Curtice, J., Fisher, S., and Ford, R. (2010). 'An Analysis of the Results', in D. Kavanagh and P. Cowley, *The British General Election of 2010*. Basingstoke: Palgrave Macmillan, 385–426.

Curtice, J., Fisher, S. and Ford, R. (2016). 'The Results Analysed', in P. Cowley and D. Kavanagh, *The British General Election of 2015*. Basingstoke: Palgrave Macmillan, 387–431.

Curtice, J. Fisher, S., Ford, R., and English, P. (2018). 'The Results Analysed', in P. Cowley and D. Kavanagh, *The British General Election of 2017*. Cham: Springer, 449–95.

Deacon, D. and Wring, D. (2002). 'Partisan dealignment and the British press', in J. Bartle, R. Mortimore, and S. Atkinson (eds), *Political Communications: The General Election of 2001*. London: Frank Cass, 197–211.

Denham, A. and Garnett, M. (2001). *Keith Joseph*. London: Acumen.

Denver, D. (1993). 'The Centre', in A. King (ed.), *Britain at the Polls 1992*. Chatham, NJ: Chatham House, 101–28.

Denver, D. (1998). 'The government that could do no right', in A. King (ed.), *New Labour Triumphs: Britain at the Polls*. Chatham, NJ: Chatham House, 15–48.

Denver, D. (2007). *Elections and Voters in Britain*, 2nd edn. Basingstoke: Palgrave Macmillan.

Denver, D. (2008). 'Another reason to support marriage? Turnout and the decline of marriage in Britain'. *British Journal of Politics and International Relations'*, 10/4: 666–80.

Denver, D. (2011). 'Shooting yourself in the foot: Labour and "on demand" postal voting'. *Political Insight*, 2/2: 29–31.

Denver, D. and Fisher, J. (2009). 'Blair's electoral record', in T. Casey (ed.), *The Blair Legacy*. Basingstoke: Palgrave Macmilan, 23–38.

Denver, D. and Garnett, M. (2012). 'The popularity of British prime ministers'. *British Journal of Politics and International Relations*, 14/1: 57–73.

Denver, D. and Hands, G. (1974). 'Marginality and turnout in British general elections'. *British Journal of Political Science*, 4/1: 17–35.

Denver, D. and Hands, G. (1985). 'Marginality and turnout in British general elections in the 1970s'. *British Journal of Political Science*, 15/1: 381–8.

Denver, D. and Hands, G. (1997). *Modern Constituency Electioneering*. London: Frank Cass.

Denver, D. and Hands, G. (1998). 'Party campaigning in the 1997 General Election: party effort and electoral effect', in I. Crewe, B. Gosschalk, and J. Bartle (eds), *Political Communications: Why Labour Won the General Election of 1997*. London: Frank Cass, 75–92.

Denver, D., Carman, C., and Johns, R. (2012). *Elections and Voters in Britain*, 3rd edn. Basingstoke: Palgrave Macmillan.

Denver, D., Hands, G., and Henig, S. (1998). 'Triumph of targeting? Constituency campaigning in the 1997 election'. *British Elections and Parties Review*, 8/1: 171–90.

Dommett, K. and Temple, L. (2018). 'Digital camapaigning: the rise of Facebook and satellite campaigning', in J. Tonge, C. Leston-Bandeira, and S. Wilks-Heeg (eds), *Britain Votes 2017*. Oxford: Oxford University Press, 189–202.

Donoughue, B. (2005). *Downing Street Diary: With Harold Wilson in No. 10*. London: Jonathan Cape.

Donoughue, B. (2008). *Downing Street Diary, vol. 2: With James Callaghan in No. 10*. London: Pimlico.

Dorey, P. and Garnett, M. (2016). *The British Coalition Government, 2010–2015: A Marriage of Inconvenience*. London: Palgrave Macmillan.

Dunleavy, P. (1980). 'The political implications of sectoral cleavages and the growth of state employment'. *Political Studies*, 28/3: 364–83 and 28/4: 527–49.

Dunleavy, P. (1987). 'Class dealignment in Britain revisited'. *West European Politics*, 10/3: 400–19.

Electoral Commission (2018). General Election Spending Returns for Larger Parties, posted19March.https://www.electoralcommission.org.uk/general-election-spending-returns-larger-parties-published.

Electoral Commission (2020a). UK Parliamentary Election Candidate Spending, posted 8 August, https://www.electoralcommission.org.uk/2019-candidate-spending.

Electoral Commission (2020b). Record year and quarter for political party donations and loans in Great Britain, posted 27 February, https://www.electoralcommission.org.uk/media-centre/record-year-and-quarter-political-party-donations-and-loans-great-britain.

Evans, G. and Menon, A. (2017). *Brexit and British Politics*. Cambridge: Polity Press.

Evans, G. and Norris, P. (eds) (1999). *Critical Elections: British Parties and Voters in Long-Term Perspective*. London: Sage.

Evans, G., Heath, A., and Payne, C. (1999). 'Class: Labour as a catch-all party?' in G. Evans and P. Norris (eds), *Critical Elections: British Parties and Voters in Long-Term Perspective*. London: Sage, 87–101.

Field, W. (1997). *Regional Dynamics: The Basis of Electoral Support in Britain*. London: Frank Cass.

Fieldhouse, E. and Cutts, D. (2009). 'The effectiveness of local party campaigns in 2005: combining evidence from campaign spending and agent survey data'. *British Journal of Political Science*, 39/2: 367–88.

Fisher, J. (2001). 'Campaign finance', in P. Norris (ed.), *Britain Votes 2001*. Oxford: Oxford University Press, 125–36.

Fisher, J. (2010). 'Party finance: normal service resumed', in A. Geddes and J. Tonge (eds), *Britain Votes 2010*. Oxford: Oxford University Press, 193–216.

Fisher, J., Cutts, D., and Fieldhouse, E. (2011). 'The electoral effectiveness of constituency campaigning in the 2010 British general election'. *Electoral Studies*, 30/4: 816–28.

Fisher, J., Denver, D., Fieldhouse, E., Russell, A., and Cutts, D. (2007). 'Constituency campaigning in 2005: ever more centralisation?', in D. Wring, J. Green, R. Mortimore, and S. Atrkinson (eds), *Political Communications: The British General Election of 2005*. Basingstoke: Palgrave Macmillan, 79–92.

Fox, R. (2010). 'Five days in May: a new political order emerges', in A. Geddes and J. Tonge (eds), *Britain Votes 2010*. Oxford: Oxford University Press, 25–40.

Franklin, M. (1985). *The Decline of Class Voting in Britain*. Oxford: Oxford University Press.

Freeman, S. and Penrose, B. (1996). *Rinkagate: The Rise and Fall of Jeremy Thorpe*. London: Bloomsbury.

Garnett, M. (2005). 'Planning for power: 1964–1970', in A. Ball and A. Seldon (eds), *Recovering Power: The Conservatives in Opposition since 1867*. Basingstoke: Palgrave Macmillan, 192–218.

Geddes, A. and Tonge, J. (eds) (1997). *Labour's Landslide*. Manchester: Manchester University Press.

Geddes, A. and Tonge, J. (eds) (2002). *Labour's Second Landslide*. Manchester: Manchester University Press.

Geddes, A. and Tonge, J. (eds) (2010). *Britain Votes 2010*. Oxford: Oxford University Press.

Geddes, A. and Tonge, J. (eds) (2015). *Britain Votes 2015*. Oxford: Oxford University Press.

Gilmour, I and Garnett, M. (1997). *Whatever Happened to the Tories? The Conservatives since 1945*. London: Fourth Estate.

Goodhart, C. and Bhansali, R. (1970). 'Political economy'. *Political Studies*, 18/1: 43–106.

Goodhart, D. (2017). *The Road to Somewhere*. London: Penguin.

Gould, P. (1998). *The Unfinished Revolution: How the Modernisers Saved the Labour Party*. London: Little, Brown.

Harrison, M. (1965). 'Television and radio', in D. Butler and A. King (eds), *The British General Election of 1964*. London: Macmillan, 156–84.

Harrison, M. (1971). 'Broadcasting', in D. Butler and M. Pinto-Duschinsky (eds), *The British General Election of 1970*. London: Macmillan, 199–230.

Harrison, M. (1974). 'Television and radio', in D. Butler and D. Kavanagh (eds), *The British General Election of February 1974*. London: Macmillan, 146–69.

Harrison, M. (1975). 'On the air', in D. Butler and D. Kavanagh (eds), *The British General Election of October 1974*. London: Macmillan, 140–63.

Harrison, M. (1988). 'Broadcasting', in D. Butler and D. Kavanagh (eds), *The British General Election of 1987*. Basingstoke: Palgrave Macmillan, 139–62.

Harrison, M. (2002). 'Politics on the air', in D. Butler and D. Kavanagh (eds), *The British General Election of 2001*. Basingstoke: Palgrave Macmillan, 132–55.

Harrison, M. (2005). 'On air', in D. Kavanagh and D. Butler (eds), *The British General Election of 2005*. Basingstoke: Palgrave Macmillan, 94–118.

Heath, A., Jowell, R., and Curtice, J. (1985). *How Britain Votes*. Oxford: Pergamon Press.

Heath, A., Jowell, R., and Curtice, J. (2001). *The Rise of New Labour: Party Policies and Voter Choices*. Oxford: Oxford University Press.

Heath, A., Jowell, R., Curtice, J., Evans, G., Field, J., and Witherspoon, S. (1991). *Understanding Political Change*. Oxford: Pergamon Press.

Heath, A., Jowell, R., Curtice, J., with Taylor, B. (eds) (1994). *Labour's Last Chance? The 1992 Election and Beyond*. Aldershot: Dartmouth Publishing.

House of Commons Library (2017). https://commonslibrary.parliament.uk/brexit-votes-by-constituency/.

House of Commons Library (2019). Membership of UK political parties, https://commonslibrary.parliament.uk/research-briefings/sn05125/.

House of Commons Library (2020a). Higher education student numbers, Briefing paper 7857, https://commonslibrary.parliament.uk/research-briefings/cbp-7857/.

House of Commons Library (2020b). Social background of members of Parliament, 1979–2019, Briefing paper 7483, https://commonslibrary.parliament.uk/research-briefings/cbp-7483/.

House of Commons Library (2020c). UK election statistics; 1918–2019. A century of elections. Briefing paper CBP 7529.

Howard, A. and West, R. (1965). *The Making of the Prime Minister*. London: Jonathan Cape.

Hurd, D. (1979). *An End to Promises: Sketch of a Government 1979–74*. London: Collins.

Jennings, W. and Stoker, G. (2017). 'Tilting towards the cosmopolitan? Political change in England and the 2017 general election'. *Political Quarterly*, 88/3: 359–69.

Johnston, R. J. (1987). *Money and Votes*. London: Croom Helm.

Johnston, R. McLean, I., Pattie, C., and Rossiter, D. (2009). 'Can the Boundary Commissions help the Conservative party? Constituency size and electoral bias in the United Kingdom'. *Political Quarterly*, 80/4: 479–94.

Johnston, R., Pattie, C., and Allsop, J. (1988). *A Nation Dividing*. London: Longman.

Johnston, R., Pattie, C., Dorling, D., and Rossiter, D. (2001). *From Votes to Seats: The Operation of the UK Electoral System since 1945*. Manchester: Manchester University Press.

Jones, N. (1997). *Campaign 1997: How the General Election was Won and Lost*. London: Indigo.

Kavanagh, D. and Butler, D. (2005). *The British General Election of 2005*. Basingstoke: Palgrave Macmillan.

Kavanagh, D. and Cowley, P. (2010). *The British General Election of 2010*. Basingstoke: Palgrave Macmillan.

King, A. (1975). 'Overload: problems of governing in the 1970s'. *Political Studies*, 23/2–3, 285–96.

King, A. (1993a). 'The implications of one-party government', in A. King (ed.), *Britain at the Polls 1992*. Chatham, NJ: Chatham House, 223–48.

King, A. (ed.) (1993b). *Britain at the Polls 1992*. Chatham, NJ: Chatham House.

King, A. (ed.) (1998). *New Labour Triumphs: Britain at the Polls 1997*. Chatham, NJ: Chatham House.

King, A. (ed.) (2002). *Britain at the Polls 2001*. New York: Chatham House.

Laws, D. (2010). *22 Days in May: The Birth of the Lib Dem–Conservative Coalition*. London: Biteback.

Laws, D. (2016). *Coalition: The Inside Story of the Conservative-Liberal Democrat Coalition Government*. London: Biteback.

Lawson, N. (1992). *The View from No. 11: Memoirs of a Tory Radical*. London: Bantam.

Leveson, Lord (2012). *An Inquiry into the Culture, Practices and Ethics of the Press: Executive Summary and Recommendations* (HCC 779). London: The Stationery Office.

Major, J. (1999). *The Autobiography*. London: HarperCollins.

McCallum, R. B. and Readman, A. (1947). *The British General Election of 1945*. Oxford: Oxford University Press.

McKenzie R. and Silver, A. (1968). *Angels in Marble: Working-Class Conservatives in Urban England*. London: Heinemann.

McManus, M. (2001). *Jo Grimond: Towards the Sound of Gunfire*. Edinburgh: Birlinn.

Miller, W. (1991). *Media and Voters*. Oxford: Clarendon Press.

Miller, W. and Mackie, M. (1973). 'The electoral cycle and the asymmetry of government and opposition popularity'. *Political Studies*, 21/3: 263–79.

Milne, R. S. and MacKenzie, H. C. (1958). *Marginal Seat*. London: Hansard Society.

Mitchell, A. (1983). *Four Years in the Death of the Labour Party*. London: Methuen.

Morgan, K. (1992). *Labour People: Leaders and Lieutenants, Hardie to Kinnock*. Oxford: Oxford University Press.

Morgan, K. (1997). *Callaghan: A Life*. Oxford: Oxford University Press.

Nicholas, H. G. (1951). *The British General Election of 1950*. London: Macmillan.

Nordlinger, E. (1967). *The Working-Class Tories: Authority, Deference and Stable Democracy*. London: MacGibbon and Kee.

Norris, P. (1990). *British By-Elections: The Volatile Electorate*. Oxford: Clarendon Press.

Norris, P. (1997). *Electoral Change in Britain since 1945*. Oxford: Basil Blackwell.

Norris, P. (ed.) (2001). *Britain Votes 2001*. Oxford: Oxford University Press.

Norris, P. and Gavin, N. (eds) (1997). *Britain Votes 1997*. Oxford: Oxford University Press.

Norris, P. and Wlezien, C. (eds) (2005). *Britain Votes 2005*. Oxford: Oxford University Press.

Norris, P., Curtice, J., Sanders, D., Scammell, M., and Semetko, H. (1999). *On Message: Communicating the Campaign*. London: Sage.

O'Farrell, J. (1998). *Things Can Only Get Better*. London: Black Swan.

Oborne, P. (2008). *The Triumph of the Political Class*, revised edn. London: Simon & Schuster.

Oborne, P. (2013). 'The Tories will never triumph with five chairmen at the helm'. *Daily Telegraph*, 20 June.

Parkinson, C. (1992). *Right at the Centre: An Autobiography*. London: Weidenfeld & Nicolson.

Pattie, C., Hartman, T., and Johnson, R. (2017). 'Incumbent parties, incumbent MPs and the effectiveness of constituency campaigns: evidence from the 2015 UK General Election'. *SSRN Electronic Journal*, 10.2139/ssm 2899931.

Pattie, C., Johnston, R., and Fieldhouse, E. (1995). 'Winning the local vote: the effectiveness of constituency spending in Great Britain, 1983–92', *American Political Science Review*, 89/4: 969–83.

Penniman, H. (ed.) (1975). *Britain at The Polls: The Parliamentary Elections of 1974*. Washington, DC: American Enterprise Institute.

Penniman, H. (ed.) (1981). *Britain at The Polls 1979*. Washington, DC: American Enterprise Institute.

Pimlott, B. (1988). 'The myth of consensus', in L. M. Smith (ed.), *The Making of Modern Britain*. Basingstoke: Macmillan, 129–42.

Pimlott, B. (1992). *Harold Wilson*. London: HarperCollins.

Press Gazette (2019). '4.7 million watch BBC election coverage', https://pressgazette.co.uk/4-7m-watch-bbc-election-coverage-led-by-huw-edwards-as-channel-4-audience-halves/.

Prosser, C., Fieldhouse, E., Green, J., Mellon, J., and Evans, G. (2018). 'The myth of the 2017 youthquake election', https://www.britishelectionstudy.com/bes-impact/the-myth-of-the-2017-youthquake-election/#.X14Zj9FYbIU.

Pugh, M. (2010). *Speak for Britain! A New History of the Labour Party*. London: The Bodley Head.

Pulzer, P. G. (1967). *Political Representation and Elections in Britain*. London: George Allen & Unwin.

Putnam, R. (2000). *Bowling Alone: The Collapse and Revival of American Community*. New York: Simon & Schuster.

Radice, G. (2004). *Diaries, 1980–2001: From Political Disaster to Election Triumph*. London: Weidenfeld & Nicolson.

Rallings, C. and Thrasher, M. (2009). *Local Elections Handbook 2009*. Local Government Chronicle Elections Centre, University of Plymouth.

Rallings, C. and Thrasher, M. (2012). *British Electoral Facts 1832–2012*. London: Biteback.

Ramsden, J. (1996). *The Winds of Change: Macmillan to Heath, 1957–1975*. Harlow: Longman.

Ranney, A. (ed.) (1985). *Britain at the Polls 1983*. Washington, DC: American Enterprise Institute.

Rawnsley, A. (2001). *Servants of the People: The Inside Story of New Labour*, new edn. London: Penguin.

Richards, S. (2017). *The Rise of the Outsiders: How Mainstream Politics Lost its Way*. London: Atlantic Books.

Robbins, Lord (1963). *Higher Education: Report of the Committee Appointed by the Prime Minister under the Chairmanship of Lord Robbins 1961–63*, Cmnd. 2154. London: HMSO.

Rose, R. and McAllister, I. (1986). *Voters Begin to Choose*. London: Sage.

Ross, T. and McTague, T. (2017). *Betting the House: The Inside Story of the 2017 General Election*. London: Biteback.

Sampson, A. (1962). *The Anatomy of Britain*. London: Hodder and Stoughton.

Sampson, A. (1965). *Anatomy of Britain Today*. London: Hodder and Stoughton.

Sanders, D., Ward, H., and Marsh, D. (1987). 'Government popularity and the Falklands war: a reassessment', *British Journal of Political Science*, 17/3: 281–313.

Sarlvik, B. and Crewe, I. (1983). *Decade of Dealignment*. Cambridge: Cambridge University Press.

Scammell, M. and Harrop, M. (1997). 'The Press', in D. Butler and D. Kavanagh, *The British General Election of 1997*. Basingstoke: Macmillan, 156–85.

Seldon, A. (2004). *Blair*. London: Free Press.

Seldon, A. (2007). *Blair Unbound*. London: Simon and Schuster.

Seyd, P. and Whiteley, P. (1992). *Labour's Grass Roots: The Politics of Party Membership*. Oxford: Clarendon Press.

Seymour-Ure, C. (1966). 'The Press', in D. Butler and A. King (eds), *The British General Election of 1966*. London: Macmillan, 149–69.

Shaw, E. (1994). *The Labour Party since 1979: Crisis and Transformation*. London: Routledge.

Shipman, T. (2017). *Fall Out: A Year of Political Mayhem*. London: Collins.

Simpson, J. (1999). *Strange Places, Questionable People*. London: Pan.

Smith, D. (2005). 'The Treasury and economic policy', in A. Seldon and D. Kavanagh, *The Blair Effect 2001–5*. Cambridge: Cambridge University Press, 159–83.

Smith, T. (2020). 'Why did the Conservatives' large lead in vote shares produce only an 80-seat majority?' https://www.democraticaudit.com/2020/01/22/why-did-the-conservatives-large-lead-in-vote-shares-produce-only-an-80-seat-majority/.

Stacey, T. and St Oswald, R. (eds) (1970). *Here Come the Tories*. London: Tom Stacey.

Thatcher, M. (1993). *The Downing Street Years*. London: HarperCollins.

Thatcher, M. (1995). *The Path to Power*. London: HarperCollins.

Tonge, J. and Evans, J. (2018). 'Northern Ireland', in J. Tonge, C. Leston-Bandeira, and S. Wilks-Heeg (eds), *Britain Votes 2017*. Oxford: Oxford University Press, 139–54.

Tonge, J., Leston-Bandeira, C., and Wilks-Heeg, S. (2018). *Britain Votes 2017*. Oxford: Oxford University Press.

Tonge, J., Wilks-Heeg, S. and Thompson, L. (2020). *Britain Votes: The 2019 General Election*. Oxford: Oxford University Press.

Trenaman, J. and McQuail, D. (1961). *Television and the Political Image*. London: Methuen.

Wallas, G. (1910). *Human Nature in Politics*. London: Constable.

Ward, S. and Wring, D. (2018). 'Out with the old, in with the new? The media campaign' in J. Tonge, C. Leston-Bandeira, and S. Wilks-Heeg (eds), *Britain Votes 2017*. Oxford: Oxford University Press, 203–21.

Whiteley, P. and Clarke, H. (2017). 'Understanding Labour's "youthquake"', *The Conversation*, https://theconversation.com/understanding-labours-youthquake-80333.

Whiteley, P., Seyd, P., and Richardson, J. (1994). *True Blues: The Politics of Conservative Party Membership*. Oxford: Clarendon Press.

Worcester, R. (1991). *British Public Opinion*. Oxford: Basil Blackwell.

Worcester, R. and Harrop, M. (1982). *Political Communications: The General Election of 1983*. London: George Allen and Unwin.

Worcester, R. and Mortimore, R. (1999). *Explaining Labour's Landslide*. London: Politico.

Worcester, R. and Mortimore, R. (2001). *Explaining Labour's Second Landslide*. London: Politico.

Worcester, R., Mortimore, R., and Baines, P. (2005). *Explaining Labour's Landslip: The 2005 General Election*. London: Methuen.

Worcester, R., Mortimore, R., and Baines, P. (2011). *Explaining Cameron's Coalition: How It Came About: An Analysis of the 2010 British General Election*. London: Biteback.

Worcester, R., Mortimore, R., Baines, P. and Gill, M. (2016). *Explaining Cameron's Comeback: How It Came About: An Analysis of the 2015 British General Election*. London: Indiebooks.

Wring, D. and Deacon, R. (2018). 'A bad press: newspapers', in P. Cowley and D. Kavanagh, *The British General election of 2017*. Cham: Palgrave Macmillan, 347–84.

Wring, D. and Ward, S. (2015). 'Exit velocity: the media election', in A. Geddes and J. Tonge (eds), *Britain Votes 2015*. Oxford: Oxford University Press, 224–40.

Wring, D., Green, J., Mortimore, R., and Atkinson, S. (eds) (2007). *Political Communications: The General Election Campaign of 2005*. Basingstoke: Palgrave Macmillan.

Wring, D., Mortimore, R., and Atkinson, S. (eds) (2011). *Political Communication in Britain: The Leader Debates, the Campaign and the Media in the 2010 General Election*. Basingstoke: Palgrave Macmillan.

Wring, D., Mortimore, R., and Atkinson, S. (eds) (2017). *Political Communication in Britain: Polling, Campaigning and Media in the 2015 General Election*. Basingstoke: Palgrave Macmillan.

Wring, D., Mortimore, R., and Atkinson, S. (eds) (2019). *Political Communication in Britain: Campaigning, Media and Pollingin the 2015 General Election*. Cham: Springer.

Wyndham Goldie, G. (1977). *Facing the Nation: Television & Politics 1936–76*. London: The Bodley Head.

Young, H. (2008). *The Hugo Young Papers*. London: Allen Lane.

Young, Lord (1990). *The Enterprise Years: A Businessman in the Cabinet*. London: Headline.

Index